Mr James Arnold

The Couple
Who Became
Each Other

The Couple Who Became Each Other

And Other Tales of Healing
from a Hypnotherapist's Casebook

David L. Calof
with
Robin Simons

BANTAM BOOKS
NEW YORK   TORONTO   LONDON   SYDNEY   AUCKLAND

THE COUPLE WHO BECAME EACH OTHER
A Bantam Book / November 1996

All rights reserved.
Copyright © 1996 by David L. Calof and Robin Simons.
Cover design copyright © 1996 by Tom Tafuri Graphic Design.
Book design by Mierre.

Library of Congress Cataloging-in-Publication Data

Calof, David L.
    The couple who became each other : and other tales of healing
from a master hypnotherapist / David L. Calof with Robin Simons.
      p. cm.
    ISBN 0-553-09668-0
    1. Hypnotism—Therapeutic use—Case studies.   I. Simons, Robin.
II. Title.
RC498.C27   1996
616.89′162—dc20   96-5056
                                                  CIP

Published simultaneously in the United States and Canada

PRINTED IN THE UNITED STATES OF AMERICA

BVG   10 9 8 7 6 5 4 3 2 1

Acknowledgments

I wish to acknowledge my parents, Jacob and Thea, who taught me to value service and to seek the humanity in every person; my clients, who have been among my most important teachers; and my sweet wife Anna, who stood by me with loving encouragement, support and useful advice during the creation of this book. I also wish to thank Steve Feldman, Shannon Conway, Victor Bremson, James Levine and Jake Calof, for their valuable comments on the manuscript. I owe a debt of gratitude to my agent, Jim Levine, of James Levine Communications, Inc., and his wife, Joan Levine, for the concept of this book. I was blessed with a darned good agent who was also a superb coach, mentor, and midwife. Finally, I want to thank my extraordinary and gifted co-writer, and now good friend, Robin Simons, and my marvelous editor, Toni Burbank, for making this project so professional, painless and fun.

—D.L.C.

And I offer my heartfelt thanks to Bob for encouraging me to become a writer, and to Jim Levine for making it possible.

—R.S.

Contents

Prologue—The Wisdom of the Unconscious   1

Part I—The Family Trance

1. The Fifteen Pound Chaperone   17
2. The Oracle   39
3. In Praise of Failure   59
4. The Couple Who Became Each Other   94

Part II—The Future as History

5. The Boy Who Was Saved by the Future   131
6. What She Saw in the Crystal Ball   153

Part III—When Mind and Body Talk

7. The Place Where There Is No Pain   193
8. Washing Away Disease   212

Part IV—Voices Within

9. The Woman Whose Eyes Refused to See   237
10. Called From the Grave   283

Epilogue—The Workshop of the Self   332
Selected Bibliography   351
About the Authors   355

"We begin life with the world presenting itself to us as it is. Someone—our parents, teachers, analysts—hypnotizes us to 'see' the world and construe it in the 'right' way. These others label the world, attach names and give voices to the beings and events in it, so that thereafter, we cannot read the world in any other language or hear it saying other things to us. The task is to break the hypnotic spell so that we become undeaf, unblind, and multilingual, thereby letting the world speak to us in new voices and write all its possible meanings in the book of our existence. Be careful in your choice of hypnotists."

—Sidney Jourard, psychotherapist

"David, you have a very intelligent conscious mind. But next to your unconscious mind, it's stupid."

—Milton Erickson, M.D., to David Calof

Prologue

The Wisdom of the Unconscious

I HAD WORKED WITH DOUGLAS FOR OVER A YEAR. AT FOURTEEN, HE WAS BRIGHT and likable, with a quick wit, a charming smile, and a penchant for pushing the limits just a little farther than they wanted to bend. His father had died when Douglas was six, and ever since, his mother had found him "hard to manage." With his engaging gestures and artful rhetoric, he often talked his way around her. And that's what made his case so perplexing. Despite his obvious intelligence and verbal acuity, Douglas couldn't read.

His mother had brought him to me after numerous specialists and programs had failed to bring his reading above a second-grade level, and our work together had included nearly every approach I could think of. We'd gone hypnotically back to childhood to redecide early decisions about reading; we'd worked hypnotically to strengthen his study skills and habits; we'd gone hypnotically into the "future" to help him build a strong self-image as a reader; we'd worked hypnotically to help him relax, smooth his eye movements across the page, and curtail his subvocalizations. He had been a tremendous hypnotic subject, skilled at every deep trance phenomenon I'd taught him. And to both my gratification and vexation, everything had worked—for a little while. Shortly after each session his reading level would rise—then gradually decline again to about the second grade. Douglas had been as frustrated as his mother and I, and finally, feeling he'd done everything he could, he had decided to quit.

Now suddenly he was back. It had been six months since I'd

seen him, and of his own volition he'd decided to try again. Surely I had something else to offer! But I was stumped. And more than that, I was shaken. My hypnotherapy practice was founded on the conviction that we all carry our own solutions inside, that our unconscious mind is our creative resource for problem solving if only we can get out of our way to hear it. But now my belief in that inner wisdom was flickering. Douglas was one of my most accomplished subjects, and still he retained his problem. What did that say about the unconscious? Was it less of a creative resource than I'd imagined? Faced with the evidence, I found myself questioning the most basic assumption of my work.

But no, I argued, this tremendous wisdom *must* reside within—Douglas and I just haven't tapped it fully. Somehow we're stuck in a *set,* a way of perceiving the problem, that's too narrow. If we can get out of our mindset, see the problem differently, we'll be more able to see the solution. Suddenly I had a brainstorm. What if I created a situation in which we literally could see the situation differently? *What if I had us switch roles?* If I played Douglas—if I worked hard and narrowed my concentration so that I really *felt* like Douglas—perhaps I could tap unconscious knowledge about him that my conscious mindset was obscuring. And if Douglas hypnotically played me, if he believed himself to be a "professional"—capable, wise, successful, all the things he felt he wasn't—then perhaps from that position of self-confidence he could tap inner knowledge that *his* conscious mindset was obscuring.

I felt a flush of excitement: this might work! At the very least, it couldn't be less effective than what we'd already tried. So after Douglas had sauntered into the office and we'd had our opening banter, I helped him into a deep trance, telling him we'd be trying something very different. Then I gave him the suggestions. When next he opened his eyes, I told him, *I would be Douglas, and he would be me. We would each have the other's knowledge, and he would tell me what I needed to do.*

Douglas sat quietly, preparing the assignment. Then, after several minutes, I asked him to open his eyes. He stared at me blankly.

"Hi," I greeted him.

He didn't answer.

I waited for a moment, watching for a response. But he just eyed me patiently as if waiting for a cue. I began to worry that the suggestions hadn't taken. "How are you feeling?" I tried.

For several seconds he continued to watch me, his eyes and

posture giving no indication of what was happening inside. Then slowly he leaned forward in his chair, rested one elbow on his knee, and began stroking an imaginary beard. "How are *you* feeling?" he returned. His voice had the perfect therapeutic inflection.

I resisted the urge to grin.

Instead I launched into a litany of complaints, enumerating every intervention we'd tried and its disappointing result. Finally I said, "Look! I've been coming here for a long time and I still can't read! We've tried all these things and nothing's really worked. You gotta help me!"

Douglas eyed me calmly, then coolly waved his arm. "Now, wait a minute. Wait a minute. Give me some time to think." Then, in a gesture that I immediately recognized as mine, he cradled his chin in his hand. A moment later, he leaned forward in his chair. "Isn't it true . . ." he began. His voice was several notes deeper than normal. "Isn't it true that you've been in a bunch of special programs for this problem?"

"Yes," I said.

"And isn't it true that you've gone to a lot of different schools for this?"

"Uh-huh."

"And isn't it true that you've had a lot of special treatment?"

"Yeah."

"And isn't it true that ever since your dad died your mother hasn't really pushed you? If you don't want to practice reading any more you don't even have to! She even lets you stay out late and doesn't even make you do your homework if you don't want to. Isn't that true? You know what I think? I think you're *vested* in this behavior!"

Vested? From an "illiterate" fourteen-year-old? Clearly we'd tapped some unconscious knowledge. And what was this about his relationship with his mother? Was it true that she'd stopped pushing him to read, that she was letting him stay out late instead of making him study? I'd never considered his mother in our therapy; I'd assumed the problem resided in Doug. But he was suggesting a whole new paradigm, an interpersonal dimension to the problem! I decided to follow the clue. "Would it be okay if I brought my mom in here so you can tell her what you told me?"

"Of course!" He waved his arm again. "By all means, bring her in."

So I went to retrieve Douglas's mother from the waiting room. In my tiny quarters there was no way I could do it without Douglas seeing and hearing, so I had to stay in role. "Mom," I said awkwardly, "could you come talk to David?"

His mother looked at me quizzically. Reflexively, her gaze shot down to her wallet, which was lying on the floor, and I saw the thought pass through her mind: I'm paying this guy and he's crazy!

"Please," I pleaded, hoping the look in my eye would assuage her doubt. I knew she liked and trusted me; I hoped she'd realize we were up to something wacky but potentially beneficial.

To my relief, without asking any questions she stood up and followed me into the office. There, she sat down and looked at me expectantly. But still I had to stay in role, so I just smiled and turned toward Douglas.

"Douglas?" she asked, seeing she would get no help from me.

"Madam, if you want to talk to your son, talk to your *son*," said Douglas, and pointed stiffly at me.

"Madam" was not a word Douglas would hear from me. It was his child's attempt to play the role of the grown-up. But I couldn't explain that to his mother. So I merely looked at her and shrugged.

With a sigh of curious good humor she shook her head, then settled back in her chair.

"Would you tell my mother what you just told me?" I asked.

"Of course," replied Douglas. Then he began a polite but pointed tirade, lambasting his mother for her "permissive" behavior. He ended by saying, "Madam, you think you're helping him but you aren't helping him at all, and you should stop treating him as if he were fragile, which is what you've been doing ever since his father died." Then he folded his arms across his chest and sat back professorially in his chair.

So that was the problem! Douglas was demanding limits! He was telling his mother he needed her to treat him like a child rather than let him grow up too soon. Now I saw the reason for not reading: it was a way of hanging on to childhood, on to a time, perhaps, when his father was still alive, on to a time that felt safer than the limitless years since his father's death.

Stepping back into my own role, I glanced over at his mother. She seemed stunned by his accusations, but also relieved, as if in them she recognized the truth. "Do you have anything you'd like to say?" I asked.

Speechless, she shook her head.

So I reoriented Douglas to his identity, while keeping him in a trance. "Now Douglas," I said, "do you want to remember this when you wake up?"

His face tightened as he weighed the question. It was a difficult decision. He'd been expressing these needs to his mother for the past eight years, but in a highly coded form. How would it feel to know he'd shared his feelings directly? Twenty seconds passed, then with one fist he smacked his other palm. "Yeah."

I smiled to myself, impressed that he'd chosen the tougher path. "Okay," I said, "when you awake you will remember what has happened here today and profit from it." Then I awakened him.

Douglas sat up, rubbed his eyes for a moment, then looked dazedly around the room. His glance landed on his mother. For a second he stared at her blankly, then suddenly, visibly, the memory hit. His eyes widened perceptibly, took on a faint look of alarm, caught her eyes, then immediately fell away. But a second later he found her eyes again and held them, and this time his mouth broke into a slow, shy smile.

Immediately his mother began smiling too, her eyes glistening with tears. And as they held each other's gaze, a palpable sense of warmth and closeness grew between them. Fifteen minutes later they left my office arm-in-arm.

Following that session, Douglas and his mother came for therapy *together* two more times. We talked about their family and the loss of Douglas's father, and his mother acknowledged that in an effort to protect him she'd been reluctant to make demands. In the wake of his unconscious revelation she saw the need to change. So gradually she began to set limits, and as she did so Douglas's reading began to improve. Three months later, he was reading near grade level—and his improvement was sustained.

So, how had Douglas *known*? How had he known to steer me toward the relationship with his mother? How had he pinpointed a dynamic that I, the therapist, had been unable to see? The answer lies in the realm of the unconscious, the astounding creative resource that we all have inside. It is the source of our dreams and daydreams, of our hunches and inspirations, of the high-performance "flow" that sometimes guides our thoughts and actions. It is the repository of all our lived experience, even that which we don't remember. It is the foundry of our anxieties, of the defenses we erect to counteract them, and, ultimately, of the solutions we craft to resolve them. It is said that on average we use 3–5 percent of our brain's potential in normal daily activity. The remainder is unconscious potential: the vast, deep ocean on which the tiny island of consciousness floats. We *can* find our own solutions *if* we can clear away the chatter and limitations of our habitual ways of being. The job of a hypnotherapist is to help clients do that: to help them circumvent their mindsets and recruit unconscious resources in the service of solving their problems.

Contrary to the old-fashioned image of hypnosis, we don't do this by exerting power over the client. We don't do something *to* the client to produce a "cure." Instead, we work *with* him, in a relationship of trust and rapport, to call up his own creative healing and problem-solving power. This state—in which the client has moved beyond purely conscious perceptions, thought patterns, and beliefs, and is more in touch with his "inner mind"—is *trance*. It is a state in which he can bypass the part of his mind that is bound by waking logic and the limits of the physical world, and can instead call on a realm of inner resources: physical as well as mental abilities; past learnings and associations; ways of seeing, feeling, synthesizing, and understanding that are less linear than normal conscious thought. In this state, the client is open and receptive to therapeutic suggestions and is able to invoke his own ability to problem solve and heal.

But trance is not limited to the hypnotist's office. It is a natural state with which we're all familiar. If you've ever sat across the table from someone and realized that for the last several seconds you haven't heard a word they said, you've been in a trance. If you've ever gazed out the bus window only to "wake up" suddenly at your stop, you've been in a trance. Daydreaming, "spacing out," "highway hypnosis," getting lost in a book: any time your concentration turns inward, your attention is pulled from the outside world, and your thinking becomes more free-form and intuitive, you are in a trance.

We also go into natural trances to problem solve without realizing we are doing so. Have you ever mulled a problem deliberately and failed to move it forward, then found that the solution came to you as you were staring out the window? Have you ever found yourself performing—whether at a sport, or in a meeting, on a musical instrument, or at a piece of writing—and realized that your mind and body seem to be on auto-pilot, choreographing the performance better than you could deliberately? These experiences, too, are trance: moments when you screen out extraneous input and are more in touch with unconscious process. They differ from what happens in my office only in that they have not been formally induced, and that they are generally momentary rather than sustained.

Most of my clients are surprised when I tell them they've been in trance before, although they quickly see that they've experienced these momentary, natural trances many times. What surprises them more is when I tell them that they've already been hypnotized, that the problem that brought them to my office is itself a result of suggestion, and that my job as their hypnotherapist is to dehypnotize them!

Here's why this is so. A client in trance develops selective awareness: she suspends her awareness of her surroundings and focuses instead on a narrow field. A person with a problem has a similarly limited perspective: she sees her problem from a single point of view *as if* I'd suggested to her in trance, "This is the only way to see your situation; there is no other way." In addition, she *self-suggests:* she interprets her inner dialogues, body sensations, feelings, and images in ways that confirm her perception of her problem.

So hypnotherapy is a meeting ground: my clients come to me in trance and I join them there, using their own hypnotic patterns to help them. Rather than the infamous "one up/one down" relationship we see in old movies, modern hypnosis (as practiced by hypnotherapists) is a collaboration—a reciprocal relationship between therapist and client.

Of course, this wasn't always so. The earliest "hypnotists," beginning in the late 1700s with Franz Anton Mesmer (to whom we owe the word *mesmerize*), didn't endow their patients with the wisdom or capability that we do today. They credited their cures to either external forces (Mesmer believed that a force in the universe he called *animal magnetism* was responsible), or to physiological phenomena (James Braid, in the mid-1800s, claimed trance was induced by the tiring of the optic nerve, which led him to name the practice hypnosis, after the Greek god of sleep). It wasn't until Braid, Hippolyte Bernheim, and others in the late 1800s recognized the importance of *suggestion* that practitioners understood that hypnosis was the product of the interaction between people.

Hypnosis gained great favor in the late 1800s when it was used extensively by Jean Martin Charcot, France's leading neurologist. Realizing that hypnotic phenomena were similar to the symptoms of his hysterical patients (including sudden amnesia, paralysis, blindness, and hallucinations), Charcot concluded that hypnosis was merely a doctor-induced form of hysteria. His theory was eventually discredited, but because of his prominence and his endorsement of trance, he legitimized hypnosis in the medical field.

Among Charcot's students was the young Sigmund Freud, who began using hypnosis with *his* hysterical patients. He used it to suggest his patients' symptoms away (which worked only temporarily since he wasn't addressing the symptoms' underlying causes), and also to help patients remember traumatic incidents in childhood that had led to their adult symptoms. Once the incidents were remembered, the symptoms often disappeared.

But despite his success, Freud rejected hypnosis, believing it was his relationship with his patients, rather than hypnosis, that caused their recoveries. And as Freud turned from hypnosis, so did his followers in the budding fields of psychoanalysis and dynamic psychiatry. Hypnosis was left behind, relegated to parlor antics, traveling shows, and lay practitioners.

Professional interest revived again, however, during the two world wars. Faced with rampant *war neuroses* (insomnia, anxiety, flashbacks, phobias, and other symptoms of what we now call *posttraumatic stress disorder*), doctors found hypnosis a highly effective treatment. In the mid-1950s both the British and American Medical Associations recognized the use of hypnosis as an adjunct to other forms of treatment for pain and habit control, psychological disorders, and other complaints.

But it wasn't until the work of Dr. Milton Erickson in the 1970s that clinicians fully appreciated the resources brought by the subject to the hypnotic encounter. Unlike Freud, who viewed the unconscious as a dark, uncontrollable force, Erickson saw it as a source of tremendous creativity and wisdom. He championed the belief that "trance belongs to the subject," not to the clinician, and that when strategically approached, clients will forge solutions to their problems from within. Erickson's work—and particularly his ability to elicit remarkably ingenious solutions from his patients—brought him a worldwide following, and profoundly influenced the generation of hypnotherapists and family therapists who followed him.

I was introduced to Dr. Erickson's work while studying hypnosis and found an immediate kinship with his ideas—I think because they paralleled notions of my own. Even as a child I'd had the sense that my mind was "bigger" than my self, that it held realms more powerful and distant than any I'd explored. At night, while waiting for sleep, I would invent mental games—taking myself to imaginary locales, or imagining the biggest number I could. I thought of my mind as an inexhaustible toy.

My parents, who were active liberals in the days of union organizing and civil rights, taught me that each person has intrinsic value, regardless of race, occupation, or social class; a person's value, they preached, resides *inside*. Their philosophy was reinforced by our Judaism, which encouraged a belief in one's inner strength, and a spirituality that looked inside as well as out. In my teens and early twenties, I read Eastern philosophy, which gave me a sense of the "wholeness" of things and the belief that we each possess a wisdom that transcends the individual. And my growing interest in matters holistic was encouraged by the popular culture of the time: in the early 1970s, books, television, and magazines were full of stories of transcendental meditation and mind/body control—all suggesting that the human mind was far more powerful than traditional Western medicine believed.

Until I studied hypnosis, all these ideas had percolated in me, but without a focus. Once I learned that hypnosis was a collaborative process—not the authoritarian maneuver I'd seen on TV—I knew that my beliefs had found an outlet: *Hypnosis could be a way to help people tap their inner wisdom.* In trance, I could help them bypass their conscious mindsets to reveal the knowledge within. When I was introduced to Milton Erickson's work, his remarkable cures confirmed my excitement. It was as if through his casebook he was saying, "Yes, we do have our healers within."

I was so moved by Erickson's case reports that I felt I had to work with him. I was too naive at the time to know that acolytes came from around the world to study with him at his home in Phoenix. I had no idea that his teaching seminars were highly restricted, open only to people with advanced degrees. (I had not so much as a B.A. at the time.) But ignorance is often propitious—not knowing any better, I called him up and asked to become a student.

"What are you?" Erickson's voice barked at me over the phone. It was a peculiar question, and I had no idea how to respond.

"Well . . ." I hemmed, "I'm a hypnotherapist!" I thought *those* words, at least, would be welcome.

"What is your degree and where did you get it?"

"I . . . I don't have one."

"You don't have a college degree?" Erickson thundered. Then, for minutes that felt like hours, he berated me royally for calling him without the proper credentials. "Even my daughter waited to learn hypnosis until she was in medical school," he finally fumed. "Call me back when you're a doctor!" Then he slammed down the phone and I was left redfaced and deflated.

But undeterred. A year later I tried again. I sent him a description of a case I'd recently concluded that had been directly inspired by one of his, and thanked him for the inspiration. Erickson didn't respond. So I sent a second. This time I got a reply: "Dear Mr. Calof, I received your case report. Sincerely, Milton Erickson, M.D." Buoyed, I sent a third. "Thank you for your case report," he wrote back, "Sincerely, Milton Erickson, M.D." He'd thanked me! Encouraged, I sent a fourth. This time he wrote back, "Dear Mr. Calof, Received your interesting case reports." I felt like the gates had opened.

Still I dared not call him back.

Two years went by. I was working with John Grinder and Richard Bandler, who had popularized Erickson's work (along with that of therapists Virginia Satir and Fritz Perls) in a form of therapy called Neuro-Linguistic Programming. *Go see Erickson,* they urged me. I told them of my earlier attempt. *Try again,* they pressed, *use our names.* So I did. This time I rehearsed my lines exactly.

"Dr. Erickson, this is David Calof from Seattle. Do you know who I am?"

"Yes."

"John Grinder and Richard Bandler told me that if I wanted to learn more about hypnotherapy I should come study with you, sir. So I was wondering *when you could make time to see me.*" I was using a hypnotic pattern—an *interspersal suggestion*—that Erickson himself had perfected. Embedded in my comment was the presupposition that he could—and would—make time to see me. I didn't expect to slip it in unnoticed. Rather, I *wanted* Erickson to notice—and to see that I was a worthy student.

There was a pause that seemed interminable, during which I braced for another tirade. But instead I heard him say, "Yes. Mr. Calof. When would you like to come?"

Thus began an almost five-year mentorship that lasted until Erickson's death in 1980. What I had appreciated in his papers—his emphasis on the uniqueness of every client and his willingness to work with each client in an individual way—was reinforced in person. From him I learned the *utilization principle*, the belief that everything the client brings to therapy—even his staunchest resistance to being helped—can be used to solve his problem. I learned to read my clients' behaviors for even tiny bits of information that could help me help them: frequent turns of phrase, the ways they sit, the values they hold dear—all can be used to help them craft inner solutions to their problems.

But perhaps the most important thing I learned from Erickson was that hypnosis is a form of communication. The client makes himself available to the therapist's suggestions, and the therapist in turn influences the client, using both verbal and nonverbal language. This redefinition of hypnosis was profound, and it opened the door to a whole new dimension in my practice. If hypnosis is a form of communication, I hypothesized, couldn't it also occur *outside* the therapist's office? Couldn't it occur, for instance, between members of a family—who, by virtue of their very closeness, are particularly receptive to each other's messages?

I began to look for evidence of hypnosis within the family, as families were becoming the bulk of my practice. And as a result of that investigation, I developed the therapeutic orientation I use today—the belief that the properties of family interaction are essentially hypnotic, that families pass along thoughts, behaviors, values, and attitudes, up and down the generations, through a process that differs little from what happens between hypnotherapist and client. Many of the stories in this book will show how this is so.

Ironically, while I owe the basic tenet of my practice to Milton Erickson, I gradually moved away from his techniques. Erickson pioneered strategic therapy, in which the therapist takes the initiative for solving a client's problems and creates the structure for the intervention. (This is a far more proactive form of therapy than, say, traditional talk therapy, in which the therapist primarily listens to the client and follows the client's lead.) Erickson was brilliant at effecting client change. His creativity and intuition enabled him to craft highly successful, innovative interventions. Sometimes these interventions were shocking or abrasive—such as his prescription to a painfully shy young woman that she squirt water at a suitor through a gap in her front teeth. But even these shocking interventions were carefully calculated: designed to work within the client's values, cognitive style, environment, and personality.

For the first five or six years of my practice, I revered Erickson and emulated his style of working. But as both I and my practice matured, two things happened. First I began to feel a tension between what I was doing and what my clients needed. I was seeing more and more victims of childhood sexual abuse, for whom strategic therapy seemed unsuited. Men and women who had endured great trauma didn't need to be *changed:* their pasts were scarred with people trying to change them. Instead they needed to be accepted; they needed to learn that it was possible to relate to another human being in an intimate and trusting way.

So little by little I developed what I feel is a more "transparent" way of working. I listen more; I work more slowly; most often I let the client set the pace and the direction. Erickson sensed my move away from his directive techniques and supported it: in subtle ways he began to discourage me from coming back, suggesting that it was time for me to establish my independence. At the time he died, although I was still visiting and participating in his seminars, my working style had become much more my own.

When I look back now on those "Erickson years," I see that their hallmark was experimentation. Erickson was a maverick, one who refused to practice by the book, and in that sense we were colleagues of the heart. He encouraged me in my drive to innovate, and it was thanks to that encouragement that I was able to create many of the interventions described in this book.

The stories you are about to read come primarily from those years. I chose them, in part, because I know through long-term follow-up that these clients have retained their gains. Some of these gains may seem surprising to you. A client's vision improves markedly after seventeen years of "irreversible" blindness; another "washes" precancerous cells from her cervix with mental imagery; another recovers from bulimia in essentially a single session. These are not the recoveries of traditional talk therapy. If you have been schooled exclusively in Western thought and Western medical notions, you may read these tales with skepticism. I can't blame you! Even I, after a quarter of a century of practice, am still awed by what I see in my office. I can still sit with someone who's in a trance, knowing he believes he's in another time and place, and marvel: if I talk with him this way he can stop the flow of blood to a wound, yet if I speak with him differently he'll be unable to tie his shoe! How is this possible?

We can hazard guesses, but I'm not sure we'll ever fully know. Western science can measure the results of these phenomena, but it cannot yet explain them. The eye specialists who declared my client's eye condition "irreversible" acknowledged afterward that her blindness had reversed; the gynecologist who diagnosed my client's precancerous cells later tested and found them gone. But these doctors and others have no way of explaining why these "miraculous" cures occurred.

Unfortunately, our Western notions of healing are rather narrow compared to those held in other parts of the world. Ever since Descartes and the Rationalists elevated humans above nature by emphasizing our ability to *think* rather than merely to act and *feel*, Western ideology has valued almost exclusively the ability to solve problems through rational, linear, conscious thought. This kind of problem solving is vital—but it has blinded us to a realm of problem solving that lies outside our rational understanding. Traditional Eastern medicines have long tapped that realm to bring about healing. Hypnosis is a way that we can do the same.

Some of the clients in this book were capable of such feats of healing because chronic, brutal childhood abuse made them particularly adept at deep trance. But many were "ordinary" people who, like Douglas, came to me for help with "ordinary" problems. They, too, were able to search inside for answers that eluded their conscious minds. In telling their stories, I have altered identifying characteristics to protect their identities while remaining true to the stories of their treatment. Because most of their sessions were not tape recorded, I have had to reconstruct dialogue from memory, but I've tried to do so in a way that will accurately convey the essence of each intervention. I have also shortened the language of trance induction and suggestion: To highlight the operative phrases and make them less repetitive for the reader, I have reduced sequences that might have lasted forty-five minutes to a single paragraph.

In three cases I've extracted short stories from much longer cases. Helene Townsend ("Called from the Grave") and Terry Yeakel ("The Place Where There Is No Pain") were both long-term clients who worked with me on a variety of issues. Jane ("The Woman Whose Eyes Refused to See") was in long-term therapy with another therapist before coming to me for a consultation. For the sake of brevity I've written about a single aspect of each case, because those aspects give particularly fascinating perspectives on the human mind. But singling out one aspect creates two problems. First, it gives the impression that the work described is independent of what came before, which is never so; the clients' successes could not have happened were it not for the therapeutic relationship they'd already established and had they not already made significant gains. The second problem is that in chronicling a long process of treatment it is impossible to describe every therapy session; by force, I've had to write about the highlights. This may create the impression that the therapy was a continuous chain of highly dramatic moments, when in fact these cases had periods of great momentum and dramatic breakthroughs, and many more periods of slow, painstaking work. Professionals often liken therapy to a snail climbing out of a well: the snail crawls two feet upward during the day, then slips one foot back at night. So it was with Helene and Terry and Jane.

Writing a book about one's clients presents a quandary for a therapist. My clients share their secrets with me because they know those secrets are safe, and I in no way want to invalidate their trust. But at the same time I have witnessed remarkable demonstrations of human nature and behavior: in the course of a day I see things that most people never see, and it's hard not to want to share my experiences with others. Ultimately, for two reasons, I decided in favor of telling. The first was that I realized I could disguise the individuals to the point where no one would recognize them, thus preserving their confidentiality. The second was that I believed that the stories are larger than the individuals themselves. In what they reveal about the workings of the human mind and body, they teach us a bit more about what it means to be human.

The processes that enabled these phenomena in my clients are present in us all. We *all* can use the unity of mind and body to minimize pain and promote physical healing. We *all* can "ask inside" for wisdom that will help resolve our toughest problems. We may not all be capable of doing it to the extent these clients did. But unconscious wisdom is a gift we've all been given.

Part I

The Family Trance

Chapter I

The Fifteen Pound Chaperone

WHEN JENNY ELLIS ARRIVED IN MY OFFICE ON A COOL SPRING MORNING IN 1978, nothing suggested that she would usher in a radical change in my thinking. Her appearance was unremarkable: tall and a little stocky, with straight brown hair pulled neatly back in a barrette. Her flowered slacks and round-collared blouse seemed conservative for a nineteen-year-old. She had told me on the phone that she wanted my help in losing fifteen pounds, and I had registered surprise. Usually people request hypnotherapy to drop fifty, sixty, or even over one hundred pounds, so it struck me as odd that she'd want help with only fifteen. Perhaps, I'd thought, her request was signaling a different issue, and, somewhat curious, I had scheduled an appointment.

New clients typically reveal their "stories" in the first few minutes of a session, and if I tune in, I can glean a tremendous amount of information. Jenny was no exception. She entered my office quickly and eyed the set-up: a large couch filled the center of the tiny room, facing a recliner and an upright chair. Almost immediately, she chose the recliner and settled in. She's ready to go to work, I thought, for the recliner is deep—harder to get out of than an upright chair—and farther from the door. Clients who are ambivalent about therapy, afraid of the expected probing, or simply more cautious in their approach, may take seats that are easier to exit and closer to the door. While all therapists encounter this resistance, I think it's even stronger in hypnotherapy, where clients often harbor the misconception that trance is a form of truth serum that will force them against their will to reveal their darkest secrets. I spend part of virtually every new client session addressing this myth.

"So tell me what's going on for you," I prompted after we'd small-talked a little and she'd reiterated her desire to lose the fifteen pounds. "Knowing a bit about you can help me plan treatment that speaks to your needs."

Jenny spoke eagerly. She came from a "tight-knit" family, she told me, and although she'd graduated from high school the previous spring, she'd postponed college because she hadn't felt ready to go. She'd spent the year working in a burger joint—to which she attributed her weight gain—and although she was still a little "iffy" on going to school, she had decided to go in the fall.

"And now you're ready to live healthily without that extra weight?" My question sounded simple, but was in fact a trio of suggestions. By asking if she was *ready* to live without the weight, I was suggesting that losing the weight was possible; the only question was whether she was ready. By asking if she was ready to *live healthily* without it, I was suggesting that she *would* live without it; the only question was how. And by framing the weight as *extra,* I was suggesting that, whatever its function, the weight was unnecessary; she could live without it. I had no idea which, if any, of these suggestions would have an impact. I was simply seeding the possibility of change.

"Uh-huh," Jenny nodded earnestly. Indeed, sitting brightly in her chair, she looked ready.

"Well, good, then I think you'll find hypnotherapy helpful. You'll probably be able to take control of your eating, and you may even be able to do some things that will make it easier to think about going off to school. Perhaps a boost to your self-confidence—would you like that?"

Jenny opened her eyes wide and her head bobbed eagerly up and down.

"Do you know much about hypnosis?"

"I know you go into a trance, but I guess that's about all."

"Well, let me tell you about it."

With every new client I spend fifteen or twenty minutes giving what hypnotherapists call a preinduction talk. This talk corrects the client's misconceptions about hypnotherapy, addresses her specific concerns, and builds her sense of positive expectation. So as Jenny listened and asked me questions, I gave her a sense of what to expect. She would feel very relaxed, I told her, although her mind would feel alert. We would build the trance together, for all hypnosis is essentially

self-hypnosis: the client puts herself into trance with the hypnotherapist's help. And we would work together to achieve change: I couldn't
magically "cure" her; she'd have to continue our work at home and
take responsibility for her own behavior.

I also told her that while she was in a trance, she would do
only things she found acceptable. I would give her positive suggestions
based on what we had discussed, and if they sounded helpful and appropriate, she would just need to imagine them as vividly as possible.
I would not ask her to do something that was not in her best interest,
nor would her unconscious mind let her. In response to her question,
I assured her there was no chance she could get "stuck" in a trance, for
if anything should happen to me, she would wake up naturally as if
from a nap.

As I spoke she nodded impatiently, obviously eager to get on
with the work.

"How does that sound?" I asked when I had finished.

"Good," she said. "Let's do it."

"Okay," I grinned. "Then in a moment I'm going to ask you to
do something that will be impossible for you to do consciously. But
that's okay, because your unconscious will know how to do it and is
perfectly capable of doing it. So in a moment when I ask you to do it,
all I'd like you to do is try to make the best response you know how.
That's all you'll need to do. And it won't matter what your response is
or how quickly it develops. What's important is that you be comfortable while you await your unconscious response."

Jenny nodded, more slowly now. Already her eyes looked a little glazed. As her conscious mind tried to follow along and make sense
of my rambling introduction she had begun to move toward trance.

"Good . . . Now just look down at that hand which you think
might be the hand that your unconscious mind will allow to *go numb
first . . .*"

Jenny lowered her gaze to her right hand and stared immo-
bilely. As she did so her eyelids began to flutter.

"That's right. . . . Now, it doesn't matter if you are right or if it
is the left one that becomes numb first . . . either hand can be the right
one to respond before the one that is left will follow . . . or it may be
that both hands will go numb together . . . or neither might become
numb . . . or they might just feel heavy as if they were wearing thick
leather gloves. . . ."

There are many ways to induce a trance, each one tailored to
the client. Jenny seemed so eager; I was concerned that with a direct

induction (such as "your eyelids are growing heavy . . .") she would anticipate my words and try too hard to follow them. She might analyze her own behavior, wonder if she was doing it right, keep her conscious mind too actively involved—thus diverting attention from my suggestions. So to circumvent her conscious thinking, I spoke in this rather convoluted way, using a long run-on sentence filled with puns and choices. The choices covered every possible response her hands might make, so that no matter what happened she could feel she was responding "correctly." Meanwhile the confusing nature of the sentence would occupy her conscious mind: as she labored consciously to decipher my meaning, her unconscious would take in the suggestion. The suggestion itself—the presupposition that one of her hands would go numb—had been dropped so unexpectedly that, in her surprise, she would have little time to dispute it.

Numbing a hand is what hypnotherapists call a *conviction phenomenon:* the client finds herself doing or feeling something quite out of the ordinary, which helps convince her that other out-of-the-ordinary things can happen too: why, she can even go into a trance! Secondarily, it suggests that something equally out of the ordinary can happen to her problem: it can go away! There are numerous conviction phenomena: we may suggest to a client that she can't say her own name, we may tell her that her hand is stuck to her leg, we may suggest that her eyes are unable to open. Rather than seeming alarming, these sensations are pleasing to the client, for they connote the possibility of positive change.

"Now as you sit there watching that hand, let us discover whether you were right or whether your unconscious mind has a mind of its own," I continued. "Did you choose the right one or did your unconscious mind choose to surprise you?" By calling it "that" hand rather than "your" hand, and by asking her if her own mind had surprised her, I encouraged a process of disconnection: first from her body, second from her mind, third from the external world. Bit by bit, I wanted to draw her attention inward.

"I chose the right one," she said softly, staring at her right hand.

Did she mean she'd chosen the right one as opposed to the *left* one? Or the right one rather than the *wrong* one?

"Is that the one that's going numb?"

"Uh-huh. It's tingling."

"Good."

Jenny had responded. That moment—when the client begins

to move toward trance—is always moving for a hypnotherapist, for it is never taken for granted. Ten percent of the people who walk through my door can be hypnotized easily, but the other 90 percent are a challenge: I never know how long it will take or what it will take to get there. In pre-Ericksonian hypnotherapy, the hypnotist used one or two standard inductions, and if the subject didn't immediately respond she was considered unhypnotizable. Today we believe that virtually every person is hypnotizable; the challenge is to work with each person to find her or his own trance.

Often this means changing courses midstream. If I tell a client that her hand is growing lighter and after several minutes it's still planted in her lap, I will switch to saying that her hand is growing heavier . . . heavier . . . assuring her that whatever she is doing is absolutely right. The key is to find the route to trance that is comfortable for *her*, to use what she brings to the encounter to help her into trance.

Jenny had turned out to be a ready subject.

"Is it tingling in the fingers, yet?" I asked.

"Uh-huh."

"And do you think you can let that tingling spread to the rest of the hand?"

Jenny's head slipped forward slightly.

"Let me know when it's to the wrist." Implied in my question was that the tingling *would* spread to the wrist.

A few seconds later she nodded again.

"Good . . . and do you think it will move to the forearm before or after the other hand has had a chance to start to go numb?"

"After," she said dully, accepting the *embedded suggestion* that her other hand would go numb.

"Okay . . ."

Gradually, through a series of similar questions and forced choices, I encouraged her to let the tingling spread through her body and then to her head. "Now," I asked, finally, "do you think your eyes will close before or after the tingling reaches them?"

Her eyelids fluttered as if the sensation had just arrived.

"That's right . . . you can close them now."

Immediately her eyes closed, her breathing grew deeper, and she developed a noticeable slackness around her mouth: she was in a moderate trance.

"Very good . . . Now . . . I'm speaking with your unconscious mind so you don't need to pay a lot of attention. . . . Your unconscious mind can listen independently without you even needing to know it's listening and it can sort through these suggestions to help you find the ones that will have the greatest value for you and for the goal you're here to achieve. . . ." By calling on her unconscious mind, I helped foster *dissociation*—a split between Jenny's conscious and unconscious minds. This is the goal of trance induction: it frees the unconscious from the constraints of the conscious so that it can take suggestions and call up its own resources for problem-solving and healing.

"And in the future, whenever you, or you and I together, count from one to five, you will go right back into this relaxed state. This will happen only at times and in places that are appropriate, and only when it is in your best interest. Should anyone else count from one to five it will have no effect on you whatsoever." This *reinduction signal* would make it possible for Jenny to go into future therapeutic trances quickly, freeing for therapy the twenty minutes an induction normally takes.

I then began the *trance utilization,* or therapeutic, phase of the intervention. I had gleaned from Jenny that snacking was a problem and that she had a tendency to "lose her mind" around food. She also said that she couldn't imagine herself losing weight; she simply saw herself getting fatter and fatter. So I offered suggestions designed to counteract those attitudes. I told her that she would become more *mindful* of her tendency to eat between meals, and more mindful of the taste, texture, and aroma of food, so that she would derive more satisfaction from each bite. As a result, she would be sated with fewer bites. I told her that when she felt the urge to eat between meals she would realize that she wasn't hungry, it wasn't food she craved, but rather a tall, cool glass of water, and that she might drink as many as twenty such glasses a day.

I also helped her work toward a new self-image by asking her to envision her ideal self in a reflecting pond. "Step into that image," I suggested. "Try it on; imagine it at home, at school, with friends." I suggested a reflecting pond rather than a mirror because we all have bad associations with mirrors; I didn't want her to associate to those. I asked her to "step into" the image in order to represent it to herself in as many sensory ways as possible. Just seeing the image wouldn't do it: I wanted total immersion.

"Make any changes you want to in the image until it is exactly the way you want it to be. Then, because you seek more self-confidence, and because you desire to shed that extra weight, you will find that with every day that passes, you will do what you need to do, both consciously and unconsciously, to become more and more like that ideal self, until one day you will be unable to distinguish the actual Jenny from the ideal one."

Jenny had also suggested in our earlier talk that she didn't date very much, and I knew that weight gain is sometimes a teenager's way of disguising her growing sexuality. So I also told her that as she adopted her new self-image, she would retain all the options she'd formerly had, including the option to say no.

Jenny sat quietly in the chair, eyes closed, a faint smile curling the corners of her lips as she absorbed the suggestions. After a few moments I continued.

"And in the future you will be able to return to this state to mentally reinforce the things you've done here today, or to achieve other personal development. All you'll need to do is close your eyes, remember these feelings, and then count from one to five. And as you do you will return one-fifth of the way into this state, deeper with every count. . . . And in this state you can take some time simply to reflect on things, or to relax, or to ask your unconscious mind to sort through a problem and come to a solution. . . . And when it is time for you to return to the ordinary waking state, it will be as easy as counting from five back up to one. . . . and each time you do you will return refreshed and relaxed with a positive outlook." I was suggesting to Jenny that she would be able to self-hypnotize in the future.

"Now in a moment I will count from five to one, and when I do you will return to your ordinary waking state. When you do, you will be fully alert and energized, in a positive frame of mind, and you will bring back with you all the positive feelings you are experiencing right now. . . . And there will be no need to have to strain to remember exactly what has happened here today. Your unconscious mind has been making mental notes and should you need to refer to them at any time you will be able to do so. But for now it's best just to let them go deeply into your unconscious, where they will do the most good."

This was a veiled suggestion for posthypnotic amnesia, an effort to keep the experience encapsulated in the unconscious, where it could be mulled and absorbed without conscious interference. I didn't want Jenny's conscious mind arguing with what she'd done, counteracting her acceptance of the ideal image or the weight-loss suggestions. Suggesting amnesia also gave me a way to measure Jenny's trance. Since amnesia is primarily a deep-trance phenomenon, her acceptance of that suggestion would tell me she had been quite deep.

Jenny awoke buoyant and refreshed. Like many clients coming

out of trance with an amnesia suggestion, she called the experience dreamlike, and as she tried to pin it down, it fizzled into mist.

"Now I want you to test your self-hypnosis," I said. "I'm going to ask you to self-hypnotize, and once you've done that, to give yourself a *posthypnotic suggestion*. That means I'll ask you to suggest something to yourself that will affect your behavior or perceptions after you wake up. Are you willing to do that?"

Curious, she nodded.

"When you're ready, then, I want you to close your eyes and count slowly from one to five, and go back into a state of trance. When you're there, I want you to tell yourself that when you wake up I will give you some sugar, but that when you taste it, it will taste very bitter. Tell yourself that the longer you hold it in your mouth the more bitter it will become until I tell you to stop. Imagine this very vividly. Can you?"

"Uh-huh."

"Then after you've given yourself this suggestion, you can count from five to one and bring yourself back into the room, fully alert."

Immediately Jenny closed her eyes and began a silent count. Sixty seconds later she opened her eyes.

"Are you ready to taste this?" I offered her sugar from a bowl I keep on my desk.

Cautiously she dipped a finger in and put it to her tongue. Within two seconds her face relayed a comical chain of reactions: first quiet consideration, then disbelief, then mild aversion. Finally she blurted, "Ugh! What is that? That's not sugar!"

I waited. A moment later her face wrinkled even more. "Yuck!" she cried, looking around the room for a place to spit it out. "It's getting worse!"

"Okay," I said. "Stop. Now let yourself know how it actually tastes."

Jenny took the bowl from my hand and looked in, her face reflecting first wariness and then surprise. "It's really sugar?" Her disbelief was palpable.

I nodded.

"But . . . ?"

"You gave yourself a posthypnotic suggestion. You told yourself it would be bitter and it was."

Her eyes opened wide as she fully understood what she had done.

"And if you can do that, just think what else you'll be able to do." I didn't need to draw the obvious parallels—that having altered her perception of sugar, Jenny could now alter her perception of other things; that she could transform a desire for a snack into a desire for a glass of water; that what used to be pleasant could now be undesirable. In effect, the experience had empowered her to handle her situation on her own.

With that I ended the session, scheduling a follow-up appointment for two weeks later.

Jenny came to see me five more times over the next three months. On these visits we talked about a number of things in addition to weight loss: her feelings about going to college, about dating, about leaving home. I hypnotized her each time and reinforced her developing self-image and behaviors. Because one of the best ways to help a client become proficient at self-hypnosis is to tape a session and have her use the tape at home, we did that, and she used the tape for daily reinforcement.

Her weight came off steadily and accompanied a variety of other changes. Jenny confided that she'd never dated much, and now, for the first time, was finding herself quite popular. She was also spending more time with friends, and was increasingly eager to leave for college. In every way, her self-esteem and confidence seemed to have blossomed. She called me just before she left to thank me for my help and to tell me she'd just lost the fifteenth pound. I was delighted and wished her well at school. Then I hung up the phone and entered a final record in my case notes.

Because at that time most of my clients came via word of mouth, I was not terribly surprised a month and half later to answer the phone and find Jenny's seventeen-year-old sister on the line.

"I wonder if I can come see you," she began. "I've gained some weight in the last few months and I want to take it off. My mother says she'll give her permission if it's needed."

"Sure," I answered. "How much have you gained?"

"Oh, about fifteen pounds."

So, anticipating another successful intervention, I scheduled an appointment.

Now, Katie was quite different from her older sister: smaller, more controlled, a little more self-conscious. Whereas Jenny had worn slacks and flats to every appointment and had immediately chosen the recliner, Katie arrived in a tidy skirt and blouse and sat primly in the upright chair. I suspected in the first few minutes that she'd be more wary than her sister, fearful that to go into a trance she'd have to give up control. More than I had with Jenny, I'd have to probe her values, perceptions, self-image, to find a way of working that would appeal to her.

"I wonder if you can tell me three words that describe you?" I asked. This kind of question is called a *projective*. In answering it, the client unconsciously projects her feelings, attitudes, and perceptions. By listening closely—to her choice of words, her inflection, her use of puns, symbols or metaphors—I can glean a great deal of information.

Katie pondered the question seriously. "Work hard, I guess; people always tell me I'm a hard worker." She thought some more. "Serious. I guess I'm pretty serious . . . and . . . ," she giggled, "over-weight."

I smiled. "And how do you think hypnotherapy can help you?"

She answered quickly. "It's like I just can't control myself all of a sudden. When I want something to eat I just let myself have it. I can't say no. I thought maybe you could help me get it back under control."

"Did you ever watch your sister practice self-hypnosis?"

"Yeah, a couple of times. It looked kind of weird."

"But not too weird to try?"

She shrugged awkwardly. It seemed obvious that only Jenny's success had brought her in.

"Well, let me tell you a little bit about it and answer any questions or concerns." I then began a preinduction talk similar to her sister's. Katie had numerous questions and I took a great deal of time to answer them; I don't proceed until I've exhausted a client's concerns. "So do you think you're ready to take the next step?" I asked finally, when it seemed we'd covered them all. My wording suggested she'd already taken one successful step toward change.

She nodded uncertainly.

"Are you sure? You know, if you're not sure, we don't have to do this right now." Katie seemed so cautious about the intervention; suggesting we *not* do it could be a way to strengthen her resolve. If *I* adopted the voice of caution, it might free *her* to argue the opposite.

"I'm sure." Her voice didn't ring with confidence.

"You know, there are lots of other ways you can lose weight. Just because your sister used hypnosis and was successful at controlling her eating . . ."

"I want to do it," she cut me off a little sharply. Apparently my strategic comparison with her sister had struck a nerve.

"Okay," I smiled, "I just wanted to make sure. Then tell you what. There are some things we can do before we start. . . ." In fact, we were already starting, but had I announced that, Katie might have panicked. This way I could ease her gently into relaxation. "As we begin to get ready, all you need to do is sit there and pay attention, and look down at either of those hands resting comfortably in your lap . . . just sit there and listen and know that you can relax at whatever rate you want . . . it can be as slow or as fast as you find comfortable. . . . And the more you seek a sense of self-control, the easier it will be for you to simply let go of tension . . . the more relaxed you become, the more in charge you will feel. . . . You are completely in charge of this state. . . . It belongs to you . . . you have created it and you can lighten it or deepen it at will. . . ." I emphasized all the ways Katie could control her experience. "And as you sit there you may discover that you'll be able to concentrate better with your eyes closed, so you don't need to strain to keep them open any longer."

Katie's eyes remained open, her body firmly upright.

"And isn't it nice to know that you can be in charge of when and if they close?" Since she wasn't responding to my suggestions, I needed to change direction, to fit my words to her response. I needed to make her feel that whatever she was doing was right, that she could control the path to trance. Ultimately, I suspected, her eyes *would* close—but even if they didn't, we could proceed. It's possible to work in an open-eyed state, though the resulting trance may be more shallow.

Because of Katie's resistance, I decided to use an arm-levitation induction rather than a numbing. Numbing relies on the phenomenon of *paresthesia*—an abnormal sensation. (Other paresthesias include tingling, prickling, burning, lightness, tightness, and so on.) Paresthesias developed as part of an induction can happen quickly and, while they are nonthreatening to an eager client, they can seem overwhelming to one who is cautious. An arm levitation, on the other hand, occurs more slowly. The client's arm rises incrementally, in tiny jerks and twitches, toward her face. Meanwhile, she feels fully awake and normal, and realizes only gradually that her arm is out of her conscious control, responding independently to the therapist's suggestions.

"Now, just keep looking down at that right hand," I said. Since Katie was already looking at her hand, I wanted to incorporate that into my suggestion. "That's it, just watch it. . . . There's really nothing else you need to do. Just stare at it and begin to wonder, really wonder, just how anyone can keep her hands perfectly still without one or the other just naturally twitching a little. . . ."

Sure enough, as we watched, Katie's left hand twitched slightly. Almost instantly it seemed to stiffen a little as if it were separate from the rest of her. Katie's eyes widened and her pupils dilated as she watched it.

"There, that's right, it did twitch, and you didn't even need to make it happen. It happened quite automatically, as if it had a mind of its own. . . ." By suggesting that her hand had a mind of its own, I was fostering Katie's dissociation—reinforcing the "split" between her self and her body, between her self and her sensations, ultimately between her conscious and unconscious minds.

"And I wonder whether it will be that hand or the other one that will twitch again and begin to inch its way slowly upward toward your face. . . ."

Each time Katie inhaled, her arm lifted slightly, a natural movement caused by the expansion of her chest. I made use of that movement by speaking in sync with her breathing. "And as that arm gets lighter and lighter, with every breath, perhaps you can begin to imagine that there's a helium balloon tied to the wrist, tugging it upward. . . ."

Katie's hand jerked noticeably.

"Is it a red balloon?"

"Yes."

"And can you enjoy feeling it in the wind, tugging at your arm?"

"Yes."

"That's very good. And for now, as your inner mind thinks over the concerns that brought you here today, you can just be comfortable watching for those tiny twitches, the sign that your inner mind is listening and responding."

As I spoke her palm raised slightly from her leg.

"Now all heaviness is leaving that hand and arm. It's so nice to be able to enjoy just floating and relaxing as that arm responds in its own way and at its own rate, lifting now."

Her palm jerked higher, so that only her fingertips touched her leg.

"Up it goes, higher and higher, closer and closer to your face."

Katie continued to stare, virtually unblinking, as her fingertips lifted from her leg.

"And you can become fascinated watching that hand as it seems to develop a mind of its own. And it moves upward in small steps, but only as fast as you truly wish to call upon the wisdom of your inner mind to help you feel *lighter* and more in control of your behaviors and emotions."

I talked on for several minutes as Katie's hand gradually jerked upward. By the time it reached her shoulder all the wariness had slipped from her face and her jaw had slackened as if she'd relinquished even the need to verbalize objections.

As her middle fingertip grazed her cheek I suggested, "and now, as that hand touches your face, you will be able to let your eyes close and finally rest, and you will drift even deeper as that hand begins to inch its way back down toward your lap."

Immediately her eyes closed.

"And as that hand inches its way back down, just drift deeper and deeper with every breath and with every movement down . . . and now, one, deeper with every count . . . two, the more you seek a sense of personal control the easier it is for you to let go . . . three, further and further . . . four . . . five. . . ." By the count of seventeen the arm was almost in her lap. "That's right, twenty . . . now just take a deep breath and hold it . . . and as you let it go, just go loose and limp all over, that arm collapsing into your lap, free of any remaining stress or tension."

Katie's arm sank into her lap as if suddenly released and her head slumped forward. She was in a deep trance.

"Now there is nothing you need to do except let these ideas sink deeply into your mind where they will do the most good. And in this state of deep inner focus we are going to call upon your unconscious mind to help you plan a future in which you can achieve your goals, becoming more and more the you that you wish to be."

I then gave Katie weight-loss suggestions similar to her sister's, emphasizing themes of self-control, achievement, and mastery to resonate with her self-description. I taught her self-hypnosis and, as I had with Jenny, had her prove to herself that she could transform her perception of sugar into something bitter. Then, after making an appointment for two weeks later, we said good-by.

Over the next several months Katie came to see me every other week. By the third month she, too, had dropped nearly fifteen pounds and, as her sister had, reported feeling better about herself and more confident with peers. I was delighted. Two sisters; thirty pounds: I felt doubly successful in one family! So I was almost not surprised when two months later I got a phone call from Mrs. Ellis, Jenny and Katie's mother. "I wonder if you'd see my third daughter, Tina," she said, sounding just a little sheepish. "She's gained a little weight recently, and you were so helpful with my other two . . ." She laughed self-consciously. "I guess it's like a family epidemic."

"Of course, Mrs. Ellis," I replied. "How much weight has Tina gained?"

"Oh, I don't know exactly," she replied. "I guess about fifteen pounds."

Fifteen pounds? Wait a minute, I thought, what's going on here? I closed my eyes, and as I did an image flashed in my mind: the three girls standing in line, handing the weight from one to the next, like a bucket in a fire brigade.

It's the same weight! I realized. They've just passed it on, from oldest to middle to youngest. Then suddenly it came to me. These aren't individual weight-loss issues; this is a *family* problem. These girls are carrying a burden for their family. I had been right to suspect Jenny's request to lose fifteen pounds; it *had* expressed another problem. But I'd been seduced by her easy weight loss into overlooking the family dynamic. Now my job was to figure out what was really going on.

I mentally inventoried what I knew about the Ellises. They were a "tight-knit" family whose oldest daughter had just left home. The younger two would be gone within three years. The emptying of the nest is a difficult transition for any family; it's even harder for a family as enmeshed as I sensed the Ellises were. All families are bound by invisible ties—loyalties, traditions, values, history, unacknowledged experience—into a complex web I call the *family unconscious,* and this system guides the feelings and behaviors of individual members in ways we often cannot see or understand. For family members are like the five fingers of a hand wrapped with a rubber band: a pull on one finger causes all the others to shift: conflict in one part of a family can produce symptoms elsewhere, and those symptoms in turn stabilize the conflict that produced them. A mother, for example, may become withdrawn when her oldest child leaves home; her husband's sporadi-cally high blood pressure may spike—and these changes may inspire the child to return. Or the child herself may develop headaches—and the headaches may serve the family by delaying the child's departure.

That's what I suspected was happening with the Ellises: Jenny's departure was triggering the weight gains. But why were the girls handing off the symptoms to each other? And what was happening with the parents? I had a hunch. Parents' anxiety when their children leave home is often less about missing the children and more about becoming a couple again. Without the buffer of children between them, couples sometimes fear this abrupt increase in closeness. Was that the situation with the Ellises? Was playing "buffer" the burden the girls were passing down the line? That was my hypothesis. To test it, I'd have to get the whole family into my office.

"Mrs. Ellis," I began cautiously—I wanted to avoid putting her on the defensive or seeming to pass blame—"I'd be happy to see your daughter. But, you know, sometimes, in cases like this where a problem seems to run in a family, it's useful to see the whole family together. I wonder if you'd be willing to bring the whole family in?" I half expected her to refuse, but she didn't. She agreed quite readily, and we scheduled an appointment.

When I opened the door to my waiting room to greet them I wasn't surprised by what I saw. Mr. and Mrs. Ellis sat at opposite ends of the long couch, their two younger daughters sandwiched in between. They all sat primly upright, coats folded neatly in their laps. They might as well have been in church. None of the family was overweight. Tina hid her fifteen pounds as well as her sisters had, and if the parents were carrying weight as a symptom of Jenny's departure, it was equally disguised. They filed neatly into my office and took up similar positions there: the two girls on the couch, their parents flanking them in chairs they'd pulled over to either side.

We engaged in some opening banter, then I turned to Mr. Ellis. (Since mothers are usually the hub of communication in a family and most likely to confer a "family line," I generally start with the father and address the mother last.) "Mr. Ellis, it seems like there's a lot of change happening for all of you right now. I wonder if you can tell me how your family is working around that." I purposely made the question vague to see where he would take it. Had I come right out and said, "I believe your daughters are gaining weight because they're upset about Jenny's leaving, and I believe that you, Mr. and Mrs. Ellis, are concerned about your emptying nest," the family would have left my office and never returned. If, as I suspected, they hadn't faced their anxiety about the girls' departures, that's the last thing they would want to talk about. We'd have to work toward that realization slowly.

"How my family is working around that?" repeated Mr. Ellis,

obviously baffled by the question. "Well, it's a wonderful family. We love each other. We're tight-knit." There was that word again, one more clue that the Ellises were as enmeshed as I'd suspected— inappropriately sharing emotions because the boundaries between them were not well defined. I waited a moment, but he seemed to have said his piece so I turned to the daughters.

"How about you two?" I asked. "What can you tell me about the family?"

The girls shrugged and glanced at each other. They seemed embarrassed.

When it was clear that neither one would speak I tried again. "Do you think each of your folks has a good sense of how the other one is dealing with the change in your family?" Like other family therapists I often use this kind of *circular questioning* when I work with families: I ask one member to speculate on how a second family member believes a third member thinks or feels. This enables me to learn about the "target" members without engendering resistance.

After a pause, Katie volunteered, "I think they're doing OK. I mean, I think they miss Jenny and all. But, you know, we still do things as a family. I'm not around so much now because I work after school, but Tina's home a lot."

Katie had walked right into the major issue. I decided to follow her lead. She opened the door for us to talk about her parents' feelings.

"Do you think your parents are sad about Jenny leaving?"

"I guess so."

"Of course we're sad about Jenny's leaving," Mrs. Ellis interjected defensively. "We miss her terribly. But we're happy she's in college. It's so good for her." She spoke as if that were the final word. It didn't surprise me that she would express happiness about Jenny's being in college. No doubt parts of her were genuinely pleased, while other parts felt conflicted. If, as I suspected, she had transferred her focus to the other girls, her fear and grief could be well below the surface.

"Tell me about life before Jenny," I suggested. I wanted to ease her back to the periphery for a while to give her a chance to build rapport with me before we tackled the "heavy" issue. I also wanted to introduce the notion that families have predictable developmental stages, and that the Ellises were now embarking on a new one.

"Oh," she laughed, "there *was* no life before Jenny. No married life, I mean. I got pregnant right after we married. Then we had the other two. We've just always been a family."

We've just always been a family. What telling words. When a couple has children right away, they deny themselves time to be alone together. They often become *parents* before they've learned to be *spouses,* and as a result never develop a strong spousal relationship. If that was the case with the Ellises, no wonder they were scared. They were afraid of what they now would face. The intimacy, or the conflicts, or whatever they'd been protecting themselves from, would now confront them.

"What do you do for fun?" I asked, including both Mr. and Mrs. Ellis in my glance.

"Oh, we have lots of fun," Mrs. Ellis said, brightening. "We go to the movies, we garden, we play games. We all love playing games."

I realized she had misinterpreted my question and answered it for the whole family.

"Sounds like you do a lot of things together." All four heads bobbed up and down in unison.

"Do you two go out much together? Alone?" I looked pointedly at Mr. and Mrs. Ellis, who glanced at each other briefly. Mr. Ellis said nothing; Mrs. Ellis looked vaguely guilt-ridden and embarrassed. The silence went on a moment too long, then Katie burst out. "Well, Daddy's busy a lot. He works late. And mom has her garden and her sewing. And she's always driving Tina places 'cause Tina can't drive yet. So they don't have a lot of time to go out together. They're *busy.*"

I smiled. There was something sweet about the way Katie had jumped to her parents' defense. But it was more than just sweet. It struck me as an attempt to rescue them. I turned deliberately toward the girls. "What about you guys?" My question was intentionally open-ended. I wanted to see where they would take it.

They looked at each other and shrugged.

"Anything changed recently?"

Long pause. Finally Tina piped up. "Well, now Dad and I play chess on Friday night."

"Yeah? Tell me about that."

"We're just learning.

"Why Friday night?"

"It's family night," she said as if the answer were obvious, as if every family had family night on Friday. "It used to be that Jenny played the guitar and we all sang, 'cause we all like to sing, but now since Jenny went to college we don't do that anymore. For a while we did it anyway, without the guitar, but then Katie started going out a lot on Fridays so . . ." She raised her arms as if to offer the only logical solution. "So Dad and I started playing chess."

It was such a wholesome image—a family of five singing in the living room every Friday night; a father and daughter playing chess. But something inside me balked. Why would three teenage girls give up every Friday night? And why was Tina the only one still involved?

"Katie, tell me more about family night."

Katie shrugged. "We've just always done it. Ever since we were little."

"But it sounds like you're not always home for them now."

She looked down for a moment as if embarrassed, then recovered. "Well, Tina's still home."

It was the second time she'd offered her sister as the one who was "still home," as if Tina's presence somehow got Katie off the hook. I pictured the family in the living room, a compact semicircle, girls in the center, just as they were in my office. In my picture, first Jenny then Katie left—and each time Tina's voice grew louder, until it filled the spaces left on the couch by her sisters. Mr. and Mrs. Ellis smiled at each other over the sound of their daughter's singing. And then I got it. The girls had been *literally* buffering their parents: they'd been singing with them, playing games with them, giving up their social lives for them—doing anything it took to keep their parents from being alone together. But now Jenny and Katie had relinquished that role—and Tina was left carrying the burden.

Suddenly I recognized the clues I'd gotten from Jenny but had overlooked. That's why she hadn't dated: she was tied to her parents. That's why she'd postponed college: she was needed at home. She was the key player in her parents' game, signed up even before she was born to keep them together by keeping them apart. This was all unconscious, of course. She didn't know she'd been drafted, any more than her parents knew they had recruited her. They never told her they needed her, never asked her to chaperone their activities. They just gave subtle, unconscious messages that, nonetheless, made their meaning clear. "How could we manage without you?" they might have exclaimed, adding a hug that in its very tightness told her they couldn't. "Of course you'll go away to school," they might have urged, "but no need to rush; if you're not ready wait a year"—offering her freedom while ever so gently pulling her back.

With this tangle of mixed messages, the Ellises had gradually constructed a double reality. On the surface they were a tight-knit, loving family, a family that played—and stayed—together. But underneath, in a place nobody acknowledged, a well-defended system kept them bound together in a frightened pact of mutual dependence.

For nineteen years that pact had been unchallenged. Then Jenny got serious about going to college. Suddenly her needs conflicted. She wanted her freedom—but something kept her from taking it. She wanted to go away—but who would take care of her parents? Gradually, the unconscious chaperoning began to seem like a burden, and the more she fought it, the heavier it became—until fifteen extra pounds anchored her to home. Finally, when she could bear the weight no longer she made a choice to lose it—in the process forging a stronger self that desired a life outside the home. *That's why she began to date! That's why she grew eager to go away to school!* But the family couldn't leave the parents unprotected, so when Jenny quit the job, Katie unconsciously stepped in. But she quickly dropped the burden too, so it passed again, to Tina. And now here was Tina, unwitting carrier of fifteen extra pounds, unwilling recipient of the family's unconscious chore.

It was a perfect example of a family system. An issue existed between the spouses, but the symptoms had sprouted in the daughters. Now I knew what I had to do, and it wasn't help Tina lose weight; that we could tackle down the road. The first priority was helping Mr. and Mrs. Ellis learn to relate as spouses. But first I needed them to come back.

I turned to Katie and Tina. "How do you think Jenny felt about going off to college?"

"She was excited," offered Tina.

"I think she was a little nervous," countered Katie.

"Nervous?" I asked.

"Yeah. She'd never been away before. She was nervous about going away."

"Do you think she was also nervous about leaving you guys behind?"

"Yeah, she probably wonders how we'll all survive without her!" Katie laughed.

"You know, that's not an unrealistic statement," I said. "Very often, children do worry about their families when they leave home. Especially in tight-knit families." I looked deliberately at Mr. and Mrs. Ellis, then back at Katie. "Do you think Jenny worried about your folks?"

Katie pondered for a moment, then she nodded slowly. "Maybe."

"Jenny worried about us?" Mrs. Ellis asked incredulously.

"It's not unusual," I reassured her. "It's natural for children to worry about their parents when a family is close. They love you."

Mrs. Ellis wasn't reassured. "Katie, do you worry about us?"

Katie looked down at the floor. "I guess so. A little," she stated quietly.

A look of pain crossed Mrs. Ellis's face. She glanced quickly at her husband, then at me. There was something pleading in her eyes. Suddenly I remembered her quick agreement to come to therapy. She *wanted* to come, I thought. *Consciously* she called me about Tina's weight, but *unconsciously* she called because she knew she needed help.

I smiled inside as I recognized the pattern. Families often send their symptom carriers into therapy, ostensibly to treat the individual's problem. But if the therapist has a family systems orientation, the entire family may soon be in therapy working on the larger conflict. In effect, the symptom carrier acts as a "scout," testing therapy before the rest of the family joins. This is an unconscious maneuver of the family system, the family's way of asking for help without realizing they're doing so.

"Mrs. Ellis," I said. "You've raised three wonderful daughters. One of them has just left home, and that's not easy for any family, especially one that's as close and loving as yours. It might reassure your daughters if you and your husband came back a few more times to talk about this transition. Do you think that might be helpful?"

Mrs. Ellis nodded. Without meeting my eyes she managed to look grateful.

"Do you think you can get your husband to come with you?"

She looked at Mr. Ellis who nodded once, unenthusiastically.

"Good," I said warmly, and taking out our calendars, we scheduled another appointment.

The Ellises came to see me seven times over the next four months. We talked about their marriage, about learning to be a couple, about developing a life apart from their daughters. Each week I gave them assignments: go for a walk together after dinner; go out together once a week; accompany your husband on a business trip. These people had never been on a vacation without the girls!   .

After four months they seemed noticeably more comfortable as a twosome, so I called the family together for a final interview. I also planned to schedule a hypnosis session with Tina to help her lose her fifteen pounds. As the foursome settled into my office, I sensed something different about them, but I couldn't put my finger on it. So storing it in the back of my mind, I began the session.

Tina had tucked a black rectangular box beneath her seat. "Is that a musical instrument?" I asked.

"Yeah," she grinned. "I'm in the orchestra at school."

"She loves it," said Mrs. Ellis. "Between lessons and rehearsals and practicing, it feels like we hardly see her anymore." Mrs. Ellis smiled. I smiled, too. Earlier she would have said that last line sadly. It seemed that both mother and daughter had appropriately loosened their bonds.

We continued to talk. Katie told me about her after-school job, Mr. Ellis commented briefly on his work, and while they were talking, I realized what was different. Tina had lost weight. She'd worn the weight so gracefully at our first meeting that I'd barely noticed it. But now she had an angularity about her that she hadn't had before.

"Looks like you've lost some weight," I commented.

Her family members looked at her as if seeing her for the first time. Apparently the previous concern with weight had slipped their minds.

Tina just shrugged. "I guess so," she replied self-consciously.

"How'd you do it?"

"I don't know," she answered impatiently, as if I'd posed an irrelevant question. There was silence for a moment, and then, since no one seemed to have anything else to say about the matter, the conversation turned to other topics. Mrs. Ellis announced that she and her husband had decided to take a trip to Europe. They gave me the latest news from Jenny, who seemed to be enjoying college, and then the Ellises left.

Afterward, I sat in my office, staring in wonder at their empty chairs. Tina had lost the fifteen pounds. In seven years of practice I'd helped many people lose weight through hypnosis, but this was the first time I'd seen someone lose weight without direct intervention. All I'd done was talk with her parents! It showed the remarkable power of a family's unconscious process.

All family members distance themselves from difficult feelings or project them onto others; all unconsciously tailor their behavior to unspoken loyalties and rules. So it was with the Ellises. Mr. and Mrs. Ellis had denied that they feared their daughters' eventual departure; instead, through the years, they had projected their fear onto the girls. "Do you think you're ready to sleep over at a friend's?" they might have asked when the girls were little. "Or would you be more comfortable waiting 'til you're older?" "Dating can be a little scary, can't it?" they might have empathized as the girls moved into their teens. "That's okay, you can wait a little longer." In these and countless other ways they had projected their own unreadiness for the girls to venture out, and the girls had come to accept that timidity as their own. They wanted to stay home, wanted to be with their parents, as if the desire had originated with them.

Once Mr. and Mrs. Ellis felt comfortable as spouses, however, that need for filial protection vanished. Their messages to the girls became ones of independence rather than need, and the chaperoning burden ceased to exist. Tina's extra weight could disappear.

The Ellis case marked a turning point in my practice. I had begun my practice as a conventional *intrapsychic* therapist; that is, I'd believed the solution to a client's problems lay inside her own head. But gradually I had been moving toward a family systems approach: I'd begun to believe that many problems reside not within the individual but within the client's family, and that resolving a client's symptoms often requires intervening in the family dynamic. The Ellises were my first graphic demonstration that this was so.

The family, I realized, is like an archipelago, each member a separate island in the chain. Above the surface, the members appear separate and distinct; below, a single land mass—the family unconscious—binds them. Above the surface, connections are apparent: just as mountains on one island cause another's weather, the storms of one family member echo through the chain. But the connections below the surface are far more influential, for they are invisible and therefore harder to resist. When pressure builds below the surface, any island can feel an earthquake; likewise any family member can erupt with symptoms. And just as any island can be a vantage point for studying the land below, any family member can be an entry point for accessing the family unconscious.

Chapter 2

The Oracle

JULIA CURRAN WAS NINE YEARS OLD, PLUMP, AND SULLEN, WITH AN ADULT'S boredom in her eyes and a teenager's sarcasm in her voice. My heart went out to her the minute I saw her.

Her parents had brought her to me because of her tenacious depression. She had always been "a little difficult," they admitted: there was a long history of battles over cleaning her room, doing homework, and setting the table. Her schoolwork was uneven, at best. And she had never been particularly adept at making friends, preferring from a young age to spend time by herself, often just staring into space.

But in the last year, Julia's lassitude and obstinacy had dramatically increased. Now she refused to do her chores or her homework altogether and refused to even eat with her parents. Instead, she spent long hours parked with a bag of Cheetos in front of the TV and pretended not to hear her parents when they called. About two months before, she had begun having recurring nightmares. These disturbed her sleep, which left her tired, and seemed to make her other symptoms worse. Not surprisingly, her schoolwork had fallen precariously behind, and she had become a behavior problem in class. Her guidance counselor had finally recommended that her parents seek therapy, and, through the recommendation of a friend, Mrs. Curran had selected me.

I always pay a lot of attention to the source of my clients' referrals, because the experience of the person making the referral usually colors the new client's expectations. In this case, the referrer was also a woman with a "problem daughter." This daughter, at age thirteen, had suddenly developed bothersome "allergies." When restrictions and treatments failed to ameliorate them, the girl's doctors attributed her symptoms to stress and recommended family counseling. In our third session I hypnotized the daughter, and in the most clear and self-assured voice she explained that she, her two siblings, and her mother felt anxiety about the mother's impending remarriage, and that her symptoms were caused by her own apprehensions about that event. In effect, they were an autoimmune response, a reaction to the presence of a foreign substance in the *family body*, just as an allergic reaction signals an individual's sensitivity to an invader. Following that session, the mother asked her fiancé and his son to join herself and her children in counseling, and over the next three months, as they talked through their feelings about the merging of the families, the girl's allergies disappeared.

It was interesting to me that Mrs. Curran had followed this woman's recommendation—for that woman had brought in a symptomatic daughter only to find that the cause of the problem was more closely tied to herself. Was Mrs. Curran, unconsciously, expecting something similar? I am always suspicious of childhood depression, for I believe it is invariably a product of family interaction. I didn't want to jump to conclusions before meeting the family, but so far the data suggested that Julia's depression would have less to do with her and more to do with her family system.

Whatever Mrs. Curran's subconscious motives, she was not prepared consciously to participate in the therapy. When I explained to her on the phone that she and her husband would need to come in, she balked.

"My husband works long hours," she hedged. "It would be very difficult for him to come. Do we really need to be there? It's Julia you need to see."

"We're all part of Julia's team," I explained. "I need to know the team if I'm going to coach it effectively."

She tried a few more arguments but I was intractable, and eventually she agreed.

*   *   *

The reason for her reluctance became clear shortly into the first session. Within minutes of entering my office, she and her husband erupted in a vicious fight.

"You sit there, Julia," Mr. Curran directed as the family entered my office. His voice, I thought, matched his body: thick and muscular, with a militaristic edge.

"Don't tell her where to sit, John," Mrs. Curran jabbed. She glared at him with her heavily made-up eyes and tucked a wisp of platinum blonde hair back into the beehive on her head. Her voice was thin but firm. It reminded me of spider's silk—fragile looking, with the strength of steel.

"That's the doctor's seat, that big one." He pointed to the recliner toward which Julia was headed. "She can't sit there."

I reminded Mr. Curran that I wasn't a doctor and told Julia she was welcome to the recliner. A picture of the family dynamic was already forming in my head.

Julia settled her large body into the recliner, cast a bored eye around the office, then pinned her gaze in her lap as if daring us to make contact.

"Julia," I asked lightly, "do you know why you're here?"

"No." It was a grunt more than a word.

"I thought you told her . . ."

"I did."

Her parents' words knifed the air.

I'd instructed Mrs. Curran on the phone that she and her husband would need to talk with Julia before they came about what they hoped to accomplish in hypnotherapy. I couldn't tell from Julia's answer if they really hadn't spoken, if whatever they had told her hadn't been enough, or if she was merely being petulant.

I put my hand up to stop the parents, then turned back toward Julia. "I understand from your parents that you've been feeling down in the dumps lately. You know, sometimes I can help kids feel better by teaching them a special way to listen to their inner mind and use their imagination. I know from what your parents told me that you're smart enough to be good at that, and I thought that was why you came here today. Is that something you might be interested in?"

"I don't know." The three words collapsed together into one.

"Julia, honey, speak up." Mrs. Curran's voice was gentle.

"And try telling the truth."

"Don't accuse her of lying, John."

"Who said anything about lying? I just said she should try telling the truth for once. I thought you said you told her."

"I did tell her. She's shy. You know how she is in front of strangers. It takes her a while to warm up."

"Strangers! This is no stranger, it's a doctor."

Again I put my hand up to stop them, but they didn't seem to notice.

"Stop yelling, John. It's your fault she's depressed. Look at her. You know what happens when you yell at her. She falls apart. Yelling only makes it worse."

"If she'd be a little more cooperative—you know, act like a member of the family—I wouldn't need to yell at her. Maybe if you'd yell at her once in a while she'd be more helpful."

"I won't yell at her. She's sensitive. She's just like me. She can't take it when you yell at her." Mrs. Curran sniffed and looked away.

"You see what you do?" Mr. Curran glowered now at Julia. "You upset your mother." He turned toward me. "And then she takes it out on me."

"Don't blame her John. It's not her fault. If you want to yell then yell at me, but don't bring her into this."

"Don't bring her into this? Who's bringing her into this? She *is* this! If it weren't for Julia we wouldn't be here."

"You see," whined Mrs. Curran, looking at me, "he always does that. He blames Julia for her problem. But he just makes it worse—the way he pushes himself on her."

Throughout this scene, Julia sank lower and lower in her chair as if trying to disappear. I sensed she'd heard this argument a hundred times before, that it was a well-worn family pattern.

In fact, everything I was seeing confirmed my suspicion that Julia's depression was not endogenous to her but was her reaction to living in her family. Her parents were so intrusive! They pounced on her the minute she uttered a syllable; they turned each of my attempted dialogues with her into their personal battleground. No wonder she could hardly hold up her head: she was constantly under fire! Her refusal to participate with them was her way of establishing some control, some sense of self, in whatever childish way she could. And since her parents blamed her for their marital problems, it was no wonder she was depressed: she must have felt evil, inadequate, and angry.

But what was causing her parents' fighting? On the surface it was about Julia, but underneath I suspected a different cause—some deeper issue between them. Parents often mask their arguments with each other as arguments about their child, because doing so stabilizes the marriage. It distracts the couple from their actual conflict: by focusing on the child's problems, they avoid having to deal with their own. And it provides a lightning rod for their powerful emotions: instead of having to feel or express them toward one another, they can direct them toward the child. Thanks to this charade, the family was now locked in a vicious cycle: the more the parents projected their conflict onto Julia, the more depressed she grew; and the more depressed she grew, the better they could believe that she was the cause of the problem.

Precisely what was causing their battle—and why Julia's depression had escalated now—I didn't know. But I did have an idea about how to proceed. I would work nonhypnotically with Mr. and Mrs. Curran to change the structural dynamic of the family. I'd try to strengthen them as a parenting team; I'd try to remove Julia from their conflict; I'd try to reestablish them as a couple. And as for Julia's depression, that would take care of itself. Once her parents stopped channeling their conflict through her, her symptoms would disappear. But how long would that take? We all wanted to see improvement in Julia quickly. So I decided I'd also do adjunctive hypnotherapy with her. In separate sessions I'd give her suggestions that would mitigate her lethargy and nightmares and that would bolster her depressed and damaged self-esteem.

Having determined my plan of treatment, I turned to Mr. Curran. "We've talked quite a bit about Julia so far," I noted. "I wonder if now you could help me understand your family a little better. What can you tell me about yourselves?"

Mr. Curran didn't bat an eye before he launched his answer. "I don't know what more you need to know than what you're seeing here. We've got a kid who's depressed, she's ruining our lives, and we want to get back to normal."

"John! Watch what you say!" Mrs. Curran turned apologetically toward Julia. "He didn't mean that, sweetheart, about your ruining our lives. He's just angry. He loves you, you know that."

"Don't tell me what I mean. At this moment she is ruining my life. You may want to spend the rest of your life putting up with her bullshit, begging her to join us at the table as if she were some kind of princess, but I don't. I want to go back to normal."

I saw another opening. "I wonder if you can tell me a little bit about 'normal.' What would 'going back to normal' mean?"

But Mrs. Curran stole the floor. "You know I don't want to spend the rest of my life like this! That's an unfair accusation. You blame me for Julia's behavior as if it were all my fault. As if she weren't your daughter, too."

"Mrs. Curran, I wonder if we can just let your husband answer the question. . . ."

"Sometimes I wonder if she *is* my daughter!"

"Don't talk to me that way, John."

"Mr. Curran, Mrs. Curran, I know you both have strong feelings about this, but I wonder if we can . . ."

"The way you protect her from me . . ."

"She needs protecting . . ."

"You both seem to be getting caught in a loop that is spiraling and spinning out of control. . . ."

As the salvos richocheted between them I launched effort after effort to interrupt the battle and shift the conversation to therapeutic ground. But all of my efforts failed. Their bickering continued right to the end of the hour, and after we'd scheduled a session for the following week, it followed them out the door.

To my dismay, at the second session a virtually identical argument broke out.

"Why don't you tell him what happened this morning when we asked you to get dressed for school?" Mr. Curran snapped. I'd started again with Julia, hoping to lure her into a relationship before talking with her parents.

"Let's let Julia speak," I suggested. But even before the words were out of my mouth, Mrs. Curran entered the fray.

"She wasn't feeling well. She needed a few more minutes in bed. John always rushes her."

"Thank God someone does! If I left it to you she'd stay in bed all day."

"She was tired. I don't think that's such a crime. She's growing and that takes a lot of energy."

"Yeah? I'd like to see some of that energy. I'd like to see a little energy for taking out the garbage, for instance. Or a little energy for cleaning up so her parents don't have to do all her dirty work for her."

Once again I held up my hands and tried to raise my voice above theirs. But as before, they had turned my question into fodder for their argument. By the time half the session had gone by, I'd run out of strategies to interrupt them.

I was getting anxious, even angry. We'd already had one session in which nothing had been accomplished; I didn't want a second. But I had no idea of what to do.

I glanced at Julia. As in the first session, she'd sunk deep into the recliner and now sat immobile, eyes vacant, staring straight ahead. A stranger walking into the room would have thought she was in a formal trance.

I remembered her parents' description of her time alone staring into space, and of her long periods in front of the TV. Julia, it occurred to me, was adept at trance. She used it all the time—by escaping into fantasy, or watching television, or mindlessly tuning out—as a way of dissociating from life at home. It was the way she coped with her parents' intrusions and battles.

Well, if she used trance to escape at home, she'd probably like to do the same thing here, I thought. In fact, she might enjoy learning formal self-hypnosis. So, out of frustration, out of irritation, out of simply not knowing what else to do, I decided to hypnotize her. At the least, I thought, I could give her some helpful suggestions. At the best, putting her in trance might interrupt her parents' fighting: presumably they'd stop arguing long enough to watch.

But that wasn't all, I realized. Once she was hypnotized, I could influence their fighting in other ways. I could talk to them indirectly: under the guise of talking to Julia, I could say things that were intended for them. And perhaps even more important, we might set a precedent for a new family dynamic. By going into trance, Julia could be in the room with her parents' argument yet feel removed from it. And her parents, with their foil removed, would have to deal more directly with each other.

Newly encouraged, I turned to Julia. "All this arguing must be hard on you, Julia," I said.

She turned toward me and I saw, to my surprise, that her eyes were blue; it was the first time we'd actually made eye contact. "Do you sometimes have daydreams just to get away from it?"

She looked at me with a mixture of surprise and embarrassment, as if I'd caught her out at something. "Sometimes," she said gruffly.

"I bet sometimes you wish you could just go away."

Very faintly, as if she hoped her parents wouldn't see, she nodded.

"Well, if it's okay with your parents, maybe I can teach you a way to do that, so when things get really tense at home you can just go away for a little while and take a break. Would you like that?"

She gave a cautious glance toward her parents. "I guess so."

I, too, turned toward her parents. "Would that be okay with you—if I hypnotize Julia?"

Eagerly, they both nodded, as if to say, *Finally, you're doing what we came for!*

I turned back to Julia. "Okay. But before we begin, I have a question for you. What's your favorite movie?"

"Mary Poppins!" The answer flew out of her mouth, startling me with its speed.

I smiled. How understandable that a child mired in a painful family would love a movie in which a woman with magical power elevates children from their ordinary lives.

"Would you like to see that movie again? Here?"

Her face lifted eagerly toward mine. "Yeah."

"Do you think you can?"

She looked at me confused. "I don't know."

"Well, did you know you have a movie arm?"

Her face clouded and her eyes searched mine as she tried to make sense of my words. It was a moment of suggestibility, a moment when, as she struggled to understand my question, she would go inside to find an answer; a moment when she would be extremely open to me in hopes that I would end her confusion. "No," she said uncertainly.

"Well, let me show you."

I got out of my chair and stood in front of her, then very gently wrapped my thumb and index finger around her wrist. "See," I said, and slowly, suggesting the movement more than leading it, I lifted her arm in the air. As I did I looked up, emphasizing the upward movement. When her arm was at the level of her eyes, I delicately let go. The arm remained suspended, rigid, a foot or two in front of her face.

"Now why don't you just close your eyes and watch that movie . . . and just forget about that arm because it will come back down just as fast as you can see that movie. . . . It will reach your lap when you've seen the whole movie from beginning to end."

Within seconds, Julia's eyes began to move rapidly behind their lids and her arm began to descend. Her mental movie—images and impressions stored in her brain from actual viewings—had begun.

"That's right. . . . And as you see that movie you can just let your body relax and go deeply asleep. . . ."

Asking Julia to see the movie was a way of helping her to become internally absorbed, split off from exterior reality. Levitating her arm was a conviction phenomenon: it met her expectation that something unusual would happen in my office and helped persuade her to follow my next suggestion, that she relax and go deeply asleep. (Equally important, it served as a conviction phenomenon for her *parents*, assuring them that they were right to have brought her to my office where remarkable things could happen.) In this two-part induction, the two parts reinforced each other. Both fostered dissociation (she dissociated from her conscious mind as well as from her arm), which is tantamount to trance.

Slowly, centimeter by centimeter, the arm descended. Forty-five seconds later her hand was in her lap. Now her head leaned heavily against her shoulder; her breathing, through her open mouth, was deep and regular. She was in a deep trance.

"And now as you just sit there, relaxing, knowing everything here is being taken care of, there are some things I want to talk to you about. . . . But it's really the innermost part of your mind I'm talking to, because you can look forward to using that part of your mind and these comfortable feelings every day to help you feel better and better. . . . Whenever you're home, and things are pushing at you from outside, you can remember how you're feeling here right now and come right back to these feelings. . . . You can do that any time you want. . . . You can just take some time for yourself, away from those things that bother you. . . ." In this indirect way I was giving Julia a suggestion for self-hypnosis.

"And there is something else I want you to think about in the deepest part of your mind, without even needing to know that you're thinking about it. . . . Sometimes when people say things that hurt our feelings it's not because we deserve it . . . sometimes it's just because those people have their own problems. They may even have chores to do that are left over from when they were children and somehow we may be getting mixed up with those old chores. . . . It can be very *depressing* to get mixed up in other people's old chores, but it doesn't have to be. . . . At times like that we can remember it is *their* work, not ours, and that those people still love us, and we can stay connected to the deepest part of us where we know that we're really okay. . . ."

My suggestion that Julia's parents might have chores left over from childhood was just a suspicion. Spouses often act out with each other their unresolved issues from childhood, and it seemed possible that that was the source of the Currans' endless fight. If it was, I hoped that my words would have two effects: I hoped they would loosen the tie between Julia's depression and her parents' arguments, and I hoped they might prompt her parents to consider a relationship between their present-day arguments and their pasts.

"Now in a minute I'll wake you up, and when I do you'll feel better than you've felt in a while. . . . And with each day that passes you'll feel better and better. . . . You'll have more energy, things will seem more interesting and fun to you, you'll want to do more things . . . and you'll find that you sleep really soundly and peacefully at night. And you won't need to think about any of those old problems you used to have. . . . Now I want you to see yourself with all these things coming true." After giving her a few seconds to visualize her better self, I counted her up, from five to one, and as I reached the count of one she awoke.

Throughout the hypnosis, Mr. and Mrs. Curran had watched attentively. They seemed to be fascinated by what they were seeing, though Mrs. Curran also evidenced some concern. As her daughter's arm hovered in the air, she looked worriedly from the girl to me, and when Julia's head slumped to the side her mother's face grew tight. At one point Mr. Curran reached out and touched his wife's hand with his own. What they made of my comment about other people's "chores from childhood" was impossible to tell.

Julia woke up far cheerier than she had been. She opened her eyes, glanced around the room to get her bearings, then allowed herself a shy smile.

"Ready to get on with the rest of your day?" I asked.

She turned toward me. "Yeah!"

"Well good. Maybe you can talk your parents into bringing you back here next week so you can see another movie."

We both looked over at her parents.

Mr. and Mrs. Curran had been sitting silently, as if waiting for a cue. Now they looked uncertainly from Julia, to me, to each other.

"Well, yes, dear, I'm sure we can," ventured Mrs. Curran, tentatively. Her voice wavered a bit as if she were addressing a stranger, as if the child I had returned to them was somehow fundamentally different. "How was . . ." She fished for a word. "How was that?"

"It was neat."

"What was it like?"

Julia's face clouded as she tried to put words to the experience.

"Was it a little like a dream?" I suggested. I wanted to get her off the hook—away from her mother's probing, and also away from the need to consciously explain what she'd done.

"Yeah," she agreed, pleased with my choice of descriptor.

"So, what time would work for you next week?" I asked, turning back to the parents. I wanted to get their commitment to return while they were still "entranced" by what they'd seen. And without a word of protest, they scheduled another appointment.

To my disappointment the Currans returned for their third session with all the acrimony they'd brought to the first two. They held their argument in check long enough to get settled in my office, but within minutes the familiar battle broke out.

"Julia was much better this week," commented Mrs. Curran, looking me fiercely in the eye as if through the steadiness of her stare she could exclude her husband. "She was much perkier and happier."

"If you call two days a week," growled Mr. Curran. "Look at her now."

Indeed, as we all glanced over at Julia, she seemed to melt into the recliner as if hoping we'd lose sight of her among its padded cushions. With her head bowed and her dark hair masking her eyes, she suddenly seemed frail to me, like a frightened immigrant stranded at Ellis Island.

Apparently, I gleaned from her parents' quibbling, her demeanor had been much improved after the hypnosis, but within two days she'd become as depressed as ever.

"I'm getting sick to death of this," Mr. Curran ranted. "I don't know how much longer I can take it. And I don't know how much longer I can take the way you coddle her. For Chrissake, I don't know a kid who doesn't help with chores around the house. The girl's getting away with murder."

Mr. Curran had made the same comment last week. It had struck me then as surprisingly harsh, and now he was saying it again.

"She's fragile, John. She can't be expected to do things like other girls."

"She's not fragile, she's just depressed. And I say the best cure for depression is to get up and do something."

As they talked I realized what had happened. The hypnosis *had* interrupted the family pattern. Julia had left the session noticeably less depressed—and her lack of depression had robbed the parents of a focus for their battle. As a result, the entire family system was awry. For years now, perhaps since Julia's birth, Mr. and Mrs. Curran had argued over Julia. Of course the subject had changed—perhaps from feeding schedules when she was an infant to clothes, or homework, or bedtime as she grew older; for the last year they'd argued over her depression. But regardless of the topic, the battle itself was the organizing force in their marriage—the primary means through which the parents related. Now suddenly, posthypnosis, that organizing vehicle was gone. How were they to relate? The discomfort must have been extreme—so extreme that, out of fear, out of habit, out of sheer confusion, the parents had resumed their argument, more tenaciously, more vociferously than before—and Julia's symptoms had returned.

Now I had to find another way to break the pattern.

I thought of the Titus family who had referred the Currans to me. In that case I had hypnotized the "problem daughter" and by doing so enabled her to take a meta-position to the family from which she could see the family dynamic more clearly. What if I did the same thing now? What if I hypnotized Julia and programmed a hypnotic dream?

Hypnotic dreams are much like real dreams: messages from the unconscious that are symbolic, free-form, impressionistic. But unlike naturalistic dreams, they can be programmed: I can tell a client to have a dream about a certain subject or to repeat a dream but with a different ending. They are a predictable way to move past a client's conscious mindset on an issue and to tap a broader, deeper perspective.

I turned back to the parents, who were still debating the cure for Julia's depression.

"I have to apologize to you," I interjected suddenly.

My words were so unexpected that the Currans halted their argument to look at me.

"I really have to apologize to you for not realizing sooner what a gift you've given us in Julia. Her dreams and daydreams may be the key to solving the problem."

They stared at me in confusion. What was I talking about? Julia *was* the problem.

"If it's all right with Julia, I'd like to hypnotize her again, and see if maybe that will help us out." The Currans had been unwilling to hear *my* comments on their fight cycle, but they might be less able to overlook their daughter's. As a third party to the fight, Julia was intimately acquainted with it. Much of her knowledge was unconscious, just as her parents' was; none of them knew consciously why the fighting was so entrenched. But her hypnotic dream could offer us a key: if she commented on how her parents' behavior made her feel, or on how they sometimes reminded her of other people, or on what she observed in them while they were fighting, she might help bring some of that unconscious knowledge to light. And perhaps her parents, sparked by her revelations, would be moved to examine their behavior.

I turned toward Julia, who had sat up in her seat and was looking eagerly at me. "Would you like to see another movie?"

"Yeah!"

"What movie do you want to see today?"

She thought for a second. "I want to see *Mary Poppins* again."

"OK, then, why don't you just close your eyes and get comfortable . . . that's right . . . and then whenever you're ready, you can just begin to see that movie." I didn't need to do the arm *catalepsy* this time. Julia already knew she could go into trance, and her familiarity with the feeling would enable her to find the state quickly by herself.

"Now, as that movie plays, you can go deeper and deeper . . ."

Within two minutes, Julia's head slipped to the side and her breathing grew deep and even. She had finished *Mary Poppins* and was now in a deep trance.

"Very good . . . and now you can listen to me as you let yourself go into a deeper state of sleep in which you can dream. . . . Your body is like Raggedy Ann's and it's so heavy that you can just let it sleep, can't you? . . . And even as you are going deeper to sleep you are listening just to me and not paying attention to anything but this voice and your own pleasant drifting. . . . Now, in a moment you will have a dream and it will be a dream about *what has happened here in this room, time and time again, and what has happened so many times before* when tempers flared and voices got louder and louder and feelings got hurt both here and there. . . . Dream about what it means here today that might be important to all of us in this room, and dream about what it has meant any time it has meant something that might be important to us all. . . . You won't even have to understand this dream, but you will be able to have this dream right now."

My suggestion was purposely vague. I hoped merely to suggest that past and present were connected, that the parental fights were part of a pattern, that all the things to which we had alluded in this room—Julia's symptoms, the family's anxiety, the baggage from childhood, the fights—were somehow related. I wanted Julia to search inside for whatever she could find that might be a connecting thread. And I knew that as her parents watched, they, too, would search inside, for on some level they would understand the implications in my words.

For several seconds the girl sat absolutely still. Then suddenly her eyelids began to flutter as if recording an active dream. Fifteen seconds later they grew quiet. When it was clear that her dream was over I told her that she would be able to tell us about it comfortably, without fear or concern of any kind. Then I awakened her.

She woke up looking vacant, perched between trance and the waking state.

"Can you tell us your dream?" I asked her gently.

She looked in my direction but she seemed not to see me, seemed to be looking through me at some distant point. "I see mommy yelling at daddy," she said slowly, her voice a hollow monotone. "And he's yelling back at her." She paused and looked confused. "But it's not really *my* dad because it's *her* dad too." Then there was a long pause before she added darkly and ominously, "And my daddy's jealous!"

Her father was jealous? I glanced quickly at Mr. and Mrs. Curran to see what they made of her remark. Each sat in waxy silence, staring at Julia as if transfixed. I realized that they had gone into spontaneous trances themselves: their eyes were glazed, their attention wholly inward. Apparently the words had triggered a raft of thoughts and feelings that they were now trying to manage. When it was clear that Julia had no more to say they looked at each other, visibly unnerved, and remained—for only the second time in my presence—silent.

What did Julia's remark mean? I had no idea, but it had clearly set off a powerful reaction in her parents. Perhaps in the conscious state Julia could provide a useful interpretation. So, wanting her to hear it again in the waking state, I asked her to repeat it.

No sooner had I done so than her eyelids began to flutter and she began to slip back into trance.

"That's okay . . . you can tell me. . . ." I prompted.

But despite the prompt, her eyes closed. A moment later they reopened, then half closed again, then her eyelids fluttered. She was trying to keep herself awake.

"That's right . . . you can be here with us now . . . you can tell us what you said."

She tried once more to open her eyes, but they seemed barely under her control. And as we watched they closed entirely, her chin sagged toward her chest, and she went back into trance.

"Julia . . ." She breathed deeply several times, then slowly began to shake her head. A moment later, her head lifted and her eyes flew open. She looked vacantly toward me.

"Julia, you can be here with us now, wide awake. . . ."

She blinked several times.

"Can you remember where you were just now? Can you re-member what you said?"

She looked at me as if I'd spoken a foreign language.

"You can just take your time . . . and think back to what you said just a moment ago. . . ."

Again she looked at me in confusion, her eyes cloudy. Then slowly her head began to droop and I could see that she was going back into trance.

I realized I needed to stop prodding. Julia didn't need to know what she had said; her unconscious was telling me as much by foreclosing the knowledge from her conscious mind. To push for more would be an error. So instead I turned my attention to bringing her fully out of trance. "Okay, I'll begin to count now, from five to one, and as I do you will come back into this room, fully awake, alert and calm, and feeling good about yourself and about the experience you have just had. . . ."

As I counted Julia's head lifted, her eyelids opened, her eyes regained their focus. When I reached the count of one she sat up in her chair and looked around the room.

"Let's just give her a moment to reorient." I spoke before either of her parents could. I wanted to prevent them from hammering her with questions. And I wanted them to think quietly about what they had just heard.

What had Julia's dream meant? I didn't know for certain, although it had implicated Mrs. Curran's father, which suggested that an important source of the conflict might indeed be something from childhood. I was curious to hear their thoughts but resisted the urge to ask. I wanted them to mull the session unconsciously, interpreting it from their own experience. Conscious comments now might interfere with that process. So I merely said, "Well, it didn't have a lot to do with her, did it?" and then, after scheduling another appointment, quickly ended the session.

After they left I thought about what had happened. Clients develop spontaneous amnesia for a trance when the material revealed is too "hot" to handle consciously, and obviously that had happened here. But it struck me that Julia's amnesia served two other purposes as well. It took her out of the firing line: her parents couldn't ask her questions, couldn't target her with their concerns, because she literally couldn't remember. Nor could she elaborate on what she'd said. Now her four simple sentences had to stand alone, like a Zen *koan,* inviting her parents' interpretation.

*   *   *

The following week the Currans were noticeably chastened. They entered my office quietly and arrayed themselves in their usual chairs, but instead of breaking into a formulaic fight, they looked at me in silence. Mrs. Curran fiddled with her handbag in her lap. Mr. Curran stared at my bookcase as if he'd just noticed it. Only Julia seemed at ease, flashing me a conspiratorial look.

"You look like you're feeling pretty good," I tossed out to her.

"Yeah."

"What's going on?"

She shrugged. "I dunno. I just feel happier."

"More energy?"

"Yeah."

"How are the nightmares?"

She wrinkled her brow and cocked her head to the side. "I don't remember dreaming this week."

"Well, that sounds like good news."

Her confusion transformed into a grin. "Yeah."

It was obvious that something had changed dramatically in the Curran household. I turned to the parents. "And how are things going with you?"

They looked at each other nervously. For several moments neither spoke. Finally Mrs. Curran cleared her throat. "We've been doing a lot of talking since we were here, and . . ." She looked at her husband for help but he continued to stare at the bookcase. "And we've decided there are some things we need to talk to you about."

She stopped awkwardly and I beckoned her to continue.

"We think . . ." She stopped again and this time looked toward Julia, who was watching avidly from the recliner.

Apparently whatever the parents had to say they didn't want to say in front of their daughter. I considered for a moment. Generally in family therapy I like all members to be in the room. Each person has an impact on the family system, and it helps for every member to hear and react to what is expressed. But I remembered Julia's slipping back into trance after her revelatory dream. Apparently whatever lay behind her parents' conflict was something she didn't need to know.

"Well, kiddo," I smiled at Julia, "it sounds like things are going better for you, and now it's my chance to talk a little with your parents. So how about if you sit in the waiting room for a little while? There are some magazines out there you might like. And as soon as we're done in here we'll come and get you."

Julia looked at me in disappointment. I suspect she was equally sorry that she wouldn't get to be hypnotized again, and that she wouldn't get to hear her parents' revelations.

"Maybe we'll get to do some more hypnosis in the future," I offered. "And anyway, you don't need me to do that. You can do it by yourself."

At this she brightened.

"Remember how to do that stuff I showed you? How to just remember those feelings and go right back to them?"

"Yeah . . ."

"Well, maybe you could go out to the waiting room and try that right now."

"Okay," she agreed, and she climbed down from the recliner and disappeared out the door.

Once she was gone Mrs. Curran sighed and placed her pocketbook on the floor. Then, after observing it for several seconds, she moved it several inches to the left. The maneuver bought her thirty seconds of delay.

"You were saying?" I prompted her.

"Yes, well, we talked a lot this week, and . . . and we decided that there are some things we need to talk to you about. About our marriage . . ." She glanced at Mr. Curran, who offered a pained smile. "As you know we fight a lot . . . and we decided it doesn't all have to do with Julia. Some of it does, of course . . . but not all of it. Some of it just has to do with us." She spoke rapidly as if eager to get the words out before she lost her courage. When she finished she looked helplessly at her lap.

"Can you tell me any more?" I asked.

"We realized it last week when she had that . . . that dream . . ."

Apparently the Currans had endowed their daughter's dream with great authority. They had discussed it at length and had come to regard it as a kind of truth serum designed to prod them into candor. As a result, they had finally acknowledged that they carried hidden feelings of frustration and anger toward each other and toward their families, and that their daughter's behavior was likely a mirror of their own unresolved emotions. We ended that session by agreeing that at our future sessions, their marriage, rather than their daughter, would be the subject of our therapy, and that they would return weekly without Julia.

*   *   *

Over the next several sessions the Currans' openness continued. Gradually, in a halting voice, Mrs. Curran revealed that her father was a raging, abusive man of whom she'd always been afraid. He had molested her once, she said, when she was nine, and she had never recovered from the experience. It lived like a viper inside her, condemning her to shame and secrecy. Years later, she met her future husband, fell in love, and decided to marry. On the first night of their honeymoon, burdened by her secret, fearful it would jeopardize their marriage, she steeled herself and told her mate. Unfortunately, Mr. Curran was unsettled by the news. Instead of providing the loving support his new wife needed, he turned away, withdrawing from her both sexually and emotionally. Thus the couple began a muted, desperate decade, avoiding with surgical precision any discussion of sex, their honeymoon, or their families of origin. This pact of secrecy placed a tremendous strain on the marriage as each partner felt guarded against and angry at the other. But rather than face their conflicts directly, they projected them onto their daughter. And as so often happens in a family system, her symptoms of lassitude and immobility reflected her parents' impasse.

Now I understood why Julia's depression had escalated so dramatically this year. Julia had reached the age of nine, the age at which Mrs. Curran had been molested. With her own feelings from that time unresolved and a propensity to identify with her daughter, Mrs. Curran began to fear unconsciously that history would repeat itself. Without knowing why, she became more intrusive and protective toward her daughter and more hostile and reproachful toward her husband. Mr. Curran retaliated in kind, escalating his attacks on both his wife and child. And in the crosshairs of their heightened combat, Julia's symptoms worsened.

Seen against her parents' background, Julia's dream seemed nothing short of oracular. Somehow, she had pinpointed the very seat of their conflict. "It's not really my dad because it's her dad too," she had said. "And my daddy's jealous!" To her parents, who read between her words, it was as if she'd known about her mother's incest and known her father's feelings on his wedding night. Events and feelings they themselves had disowned had seemed to surface in her mouth.

How had Julia known these things? I believe she didn't really "know" them—that is, she couldn't divine events that had happened before her birth. But she did know unconsciously that uncomfortable feelings were smouldering below the surface of her parents' lives. She sensed their presence in her parents' words and actions. Perhaps Mrs. Curran behaved ambivalently toward her father, sometimes acting childlike and afraid, at other times aloof. Or perhaps Mr. Curran hovered jealously when his father-in-law was present. Perhaps Mrs. Curran castigated her husband with the damning words, "You're just like my father!" Perhaps their arguments mushroomed whenever Grandpa came to visit. It's likely Julia saw those behaviors without knowing what they meant; likely she recognized her parents' feelings without knowing their source. Children often intuit parental feelings that the parents themselves are unwilling to admit.

It's entirely possible that her parents' language also played a part in clueing her in to the family secret. I remembered her father's assertion that she was "getting away with murder" by shirking her chores. At the time I was surprised by his analogy; it seemed extreme. But the Currans' conversation wasn't really about Julia. They were using her as a cover to talk about themselves. Seeing the whole picture, it now seemed Mr. Curran was referring to his father-in-law, who did, in a sense, get away with murder: he'd committed a terrible act and gotten off scot-free. When he said "the best cure for depression is to get up and do something," was he really saying to his wife: "I know you were abused, but let go of it; move on"? When Mrs. Curran complained that her husband "pushes himself on" Julia, was she really describing what her father did to her? And when she asserted repeatedly that Julia was "fragile" and "sensitive," was she really telling her husband how *she* felt, broken by her father's rageful behavior? Julia had heard these and similar fights for most of her life. While she certainly didn't understand their veiled, unconscious references, I'm sure she sensed the underworld of feelings that they masked.

The Currans had buried those issues because they were too painful to confront. But burial merely increased their power. Left to fester below the surface, they still influenced the parents' actions and, through the parents', Julia's. Thus the conflict became part of the family unconscious, part of that undifferentiated mass of fact and fiction, event and feeling, that binds family members together and shapes their attitudes, behavior, and emotions. There, smouldering in the unconscious realm, it was accessible through hypnosis, and Julia, one island in her family archipelago, revealed it.

Why Julia? Any member of the family might have revealed the same information. But Julia was convenient—partly because she was a child, and children, with their tendency toward naturalistic trance in the form of daydreaming and fantasy, easily access unconscious material. And partly because Julia was the symptom carrier. Just like the daughters in the Ellis family, she bore the symptoms of the family problem; and like them, she was the "scout," unconsciously appointed to lead the family into therapy. Like most families with unconscious conflicts, the Currans had ambivalent feelings about therapy. They wanted to tackle their problems, but they were terrified to do so. Hence their reluctance to come to my office; hence their awe of Julia's hypnosis. But by sending Julia in as the problem, they could have their cake and eat it too. They could avoid resurrecting the painful material themselves; Julia would do it for them.

And indeed, that's exactly what had happened. Through Julia, the Curran family's underlying conflicts became visible just long enough to bring important issues to the therapeutic table. Then the curtain closed and Julia awoke with total amnesia. Her parents were right to regard her as an oracle. For like the ancient soothsayer, Sibyl, she spoke from a trance of things she could not know, and, like the Sibyl, she abandoned the information when her job was done.

Mr. and Mrs. Curran continued to see me on and off for eighteen months. Mrs. Curran made considerable progress on her issues concerning her father, and the couple worked on their sexual relationship and on questions of power and communication. After those first four sessions, Julia never came back, but her parents reported that shortly after the dream her depressive behavior began to disappear. Within two months she'd become cooperative and energetic. Apparently as her parents began to resolve their problems with each other and ceased routing them through her, she no longer needed to behave symptomatically in response.

That was seventeen years ago, and since then I've worked with most of my clients to study the invisible geology of their families. We've examined the layers of sediment that were laid down over generations: the family's experiences and knowledge, their beliefs and behaviors, all calcified by the weight of time into bedrock that connects each of the islands in the family chain. And time and again I've seen how conflicts, buried beneath the layers, destabilize the strata above them, causing fractures in each of the islands. The Currans are not alone. We are all islands in our family archipelagos. We are all captives of our family unconscious.

Chapter 3

In Praise of Failure

THE FIRST THING I NOTICED ABOUT THE HILDTS WAS THEIR SHEER ATH-leticism. At thirty-eight and thirty-seven, Jim and Margery had the wiry bodies and healthy, weathered look that come to people who spend a lot of time outdoors. As they strode into my office with their ruddy complexions and determined gaits, they looked more like wholesome hikers in an L. L. Bean catalog than like parents who had been "hypnotized" by *their* parents and who were, in turn, hypnotizing their child. But as our first session soon revealed, that was exactly what was happening, and Kathy, their twelve-year-old daughter, was now struggling to free herself from their suggestions.

I knew from Margery's phone call that Kathy was a competitive swimmer on her way to a major regional competition, but that recently fierce daily headaches had been interfering with her practice. Medical and neurological exams had found nothing wrong, so the family physician had referred the Hildts to me.

"We need to see you right away," Margery had said on the phone, her voice businesslike and urgent. "The regionals are in just ten days."

Immediately my antennae had gone up: Margery seemed more concerned about the race than about her daughter's headaches. Was she telling me something about the family? Headaches and other physical symptoms are often a reaction to pressure, and in children often an indication of family problems. So I'd said that I would be happy to

see Kathy, but that the family would need to accompany her to participate in her treatment. Margery had readily agreed.

My sense of pressure intensified as I glanced at the family's
intake form. Next to "Reason for Seeking Hypnosis" in Margery's neat,
unembellished handwriting were the words: "To beat everyone else at
swimming, especially Jill." "Headaches" followed on the line below,
almost like an afterthought. This family isn't here to cure Kathy's headaches, I thought. *They want me to help her win.*

I looked around the room at them. Jim and Margery, exuding
energy and purpose, had claimed the seats in front of me. Kathy, quiet
and cautious, had taken a seat to the side. The contrast in body language could not have been greater. Was this family really unified, I
wondered? Was the emphasis on winning shared? Or did it belong
solely to the parents? Kathy's headaches were effectively keeping her
out of the pool: was that her unconscious way of telling her parents to
back off? I needed to hear from the family.

"So, Jim," I said, turning to Mr. Hildt. He sat squarely in his
chair, massaging its arms with his sinewy fingers. "Tell me about your
family." I deliberately said nothing about the headaches. I wanted
them to wonder: was I implying a connection between her headaches
and the family? If my question made them anxious, so much the better,
for seeing them under pressure would give me a more realistic look at
how they interacted.

Jim ran his fingers across his short-cropped hair. "The family,"
he repeated. He seemed to be weighing my question like a challenge.
"We're a tight family. Spend a lot of time together."

"What kinds of things do you do together?"

"Mountain bike, racquetball, skate. Swim, of course." His
speech was clipped, as if not to waste any words.

"You sound pretty active," I noted, thinking he couldn't have
named more demanding sports.

"Oh yeah," he chuckled. "We like to stay on the move."

"On your intake form it says you're a civil engineer?"

He nodded. "I work for a small outfit now doing bridge design.
Actually hoping to find something bigger."

"Jim won an award last year," said Margery.

"They put his picture in the paper," chimed in Kathy.

I bowed my congratulations. "Anything else? What else can
you tell me about your family?" So far he'd given me surface details,
but no information about how they interacted.

He placed his fingertips together and pushed them hard

against each other isometrically. "We spend a lot of time at the pool. Of course. For Kathy." He nodded toward his daughter. "And we insist on having dinner together every night. Some families don't go in for that these days, but we think it's important."

"Sounds like close family time is important to you."

"I'd say it's a value. As much as our schedules will allow."

"How else do you express your closeness?"

He peered through the bridge formed by his fingers as if the question didn't entirely make sense. "We read together. We play games. Sometimes we build models. How does any family express its closeness? We do things together."

I nodded. Jim seemed to equate closeness with activities rather than with emotions, and I could see that it would be hard to get any sort of emotional information from him, so I turned my gaze toward Margery.

"And you, Margery," I prodded. "Can you tell me a bit about the family?"

Margery tightened. "Oh," she laughed. "What do you want to know?"

"Whatever you want to tell me. How do you all get along? What goes on in the Hildt family?" I was after information about the family's interactions, but Margery misinterpreted my question.

"Well," she smiled as if on stage, "I'm a lawyer by training, but I decided to stay home with Kathy." She smiled at her daughter. "And now I manage Kathy's career."

Career? I thought. That seems a bit strong for a twelve year old. "What does that involve?"

"Monitoring her practice, scheduling her competitions, making sure she gets her homework done so she has time to swim, getting her to the pool on time so she gets her hours in. There's a lot involved when you take swimming as seriously as we do." She paused. "We've all had to adjust our schedules to Kathy's." I thought I heard a note of resignation in her voice.

"Sounds like it's demanding of all of you."

She smiled. "We enjoy it." And she rested her hands deliberately in her lap.

What had happened to her resignation? It was as if in the folding of her hands she'd pushed it down and out of sight. Was Kathy, too, learning to hide her feelings? Were her headaches an outlet for what she couldn't express? I turned to the girl.

"Sounds like you and your mom spend quite a bit of time together."

She nodded. "My mom's taught me a lot."

I noted the word "taught." Its connotation of learning and achievement reinforced everything I'd heard so far: father in an exacting profession in which he wins awards; mom a lawyer, now focused on her child's "career." I was getting a sense of the kind of pressure Kathy must be under.

"It sounds like swimming's quite important to you," I ventured, including the whole family in my glance.

Both parents sat forward slightly in their chairs.

"Of course." Jim turned and smiled warmly at his daughter. "Kathy is our star. We do everything we can to help her."

"Kath, tell Mr. Calof about your times," urged Margery.

Kathy rattled off a list of times she'd achieved in various classes of competition. Her voice was proud, but lacking animation.

"Kathy's been competing since she was eight," said Jim, drawing his wallet from his pocket. He pulled out five or six well-worn snapshots and handed them to me. All showed younger-looking Kathys grinning at the camera, holding up a stopwatch. The last one showed Kathy, no more than three, poised to dive at the edge of a pool, her father waiting for her in the swim lane.

"You've been swimming a long time," I noted.

She nodded. "I've been swimming since I was born, practically. My dad used to take me to the pool with him when he practiced, and sometimes he put me on his back and we pretended I was swimming. I don't really remember that, but they tell me about it and I've seen the pictures."

"So your dad swims too?"

"Oh yeah, he's really good. He's fast."

Jim smiled a little half-smile that couldn't disguise his pride. "I broke a few records," he affirmed, then looked at Kathy. "Kathy will too."

"We don't *know* that, Dad," said Kathy.

"Honey, I know that, and you have to know it too. A lot of winning is in the head."

Kathy nodded mechanically as if she'd heard those words a thousand times. I had the sense that I was watching not father and daughter but coach and athlete.

"You're a competitive swimmer?" I asked Jim.

"He was really good," Kathy jumped in before her father could answer. "He was almost in the Olympics."

"Wow. That *is* really good." I turned toward Jim who crossed his arms against his chest and smiled.

"I was in the Olympic Trials." He turned his head toward Kathy. "But Kathy's gonna go all the way. She's gonna make the Team."

Kathy looked pained.

Jim turned back toward me. "She's got the stuff, but she's not sure enough of herself. That's her only problem."

"What do you think, Kathy? You think you've got the stuff?" I inquired.

She just shrugged.

"You seem less certain than your dad."

"He says I can do it if I put my mind to it." She spoke so quietly I could hardly hear her. "But I don't know."

"It seems like you've done very well so far."

She sat quietly, looking at the floor, her hands fidgeting in her lap. We all waited for her answer. "I just don't think I have what it takes. I mean you have to really want . . ." She stopped quickly. "I'm just afraid I'm not good enough."

"Kathy," said Jim sharply, irritation palpable in his voice. "We've talked about this a thousand times. Success is in your head. If you can't . . ." He stopped, looking at me. "This is what I mean She's got the talent but her mental attitude . . ."

"Kathy, sweetie," soothed Margery, "Daddy's right. You have to think positively. Even Coach Soloman says that." She smiled at her daughter, but Kathy looked glumly at the floor.

What had Kathy started to say? That she didn't *want* to swim enough to compete at the national level? I had worked with two other Olympic-bound athletes on performance issues. Both had met grueling schedules, with hours of practice before and after school and hours more on weekends, their freedom and social lives sacrificed to their sports. But those young women had had few misgivings. They loved what they did and could imagine their lives no other way. I didn't sense this passion in Kathy. "Kathy," I prodded gently, "what *if* you're not 'good enough'?"

She looked at me quickly and opened her mouth as if to say something, then closed it again.

"What does 'good enough' mean?"

"Making the Olympics."

"Is that important to you?"

She looked quickly at her parents. "Yes," she said flatly. I tried to catch her eye, but she resisted my gaze.

"That's why we need your help," urged Margery. "The regionals are in ten days. We've been working very hard but now her headaches . . ."

"Are getting in the way?"

"Yes. Kathy is missing a lot of practice and we can't afford to lose . . ." She halted and peered for a second at Kathy as if searching for the word. "We can't afford to lose the practice time."

"Even Coach Soloman is disturbed," added Jim.

This was the second time that "even Coach Soloman" had been invoked.

"Tell me about Coach Soloman," I prompted.

"He's one of the best in the country," stated Jim. "That's why we moved here. To work with him."

"Wow," I said, looking at Kathy. "You moved here to work with a coach, that's pretty serious." I was curious to see her reaction. If she was as invested in swimming as her parents were, I'd expect a display of pride. If she were less committed, moving across the country to work with a professional could be a heavy burden.

"Uh-huh," she murmured noncommittally, lowering her eyes. I thought I had my answer.

"How does it feel to be working with a pro?"

"He's very good for me."

"What does that mean, 'good for you'?"

"He doesn't let me get sloppy."

"Do you tend to get sloppy?"

Kathy nodded as if impatient with herself.

"Kathy has tremendous *potential*," said Margery. Her emphasis on the last word turned her compliment into chiding. "She's at the point where we thought a professional coach could help her."

"How long have you been working with him?"

"About two months."

Two months? I remembered something else from the intake form. "Isn't that about when your headaches started?"

Kathy looked down as if ashamed, but suddenly looked back up. "But I think they're just when I haven't practiced enough," she said quickly, as if apologizing.

"Kathy's had headaches before," Margery interjected. "Smaller ones."

"Any idea what those were about?"

"Oh . . . girls get headaches, I guess." She laughed. "I used to get headaches from time to time when I was her age. I think it's growing pains."

"Is that what it was for you?"

She looked at me sharply, then looked away. "That's what my mother said," she said drily.

"What do you think is causing them?" I asked Kathy.

"I don't know," she murmured.

"You've just gone through a big move. That can be pretty difficult—leaving your school, your friends . . . Do you get a little sad about that?"

"No."

"No?" I had difficulty concealing my incredulity.

"I never get sad."

She never gets sad? I muzzled my disbelief. "I'm surprised. Most people get a little sad when they make a major move."

"I think Kathy's been too busy to get sad," laughed Margery. "She's been on a pretty grueling schedule getting ready for the regionals." I thought there was a note of pride in her voice, as if a grueling schedule were a badge of honor.

"How about you, Margery? Have you been sad about leaving your old home?"

"I probably should be," she chuckled again, "but, honestly, we've been so busy practicing. We just haven't had time."

I didn't point out to her that most people don't need *time* to feel sad. Apparently Margery was uncomfortable with sadness, just as she'd been with her feelings of resentment. And she seemed to be transmitting that discomfort to Kathy.

"Kathy, you've been here such a short time. I wonder if you've had a chance to make any new friends. Do you see other kids outside of school?"

Kathy looked at me quickly. "I wanted to go to the movies with some girls. . . ." She looked at her mother. "But I knew I had to practice."

"Sweetie, you know how important practice is right now. You'll have time after the regionals to go to the movies."

Kathy clamped her jaw shut and looked away.

"I know you wanted to go to the movies with those girls." There was the faintest trace of derision in Margery's voice. "And I'm proud of you. This is a time when we all have to make sacrifices. It's a big race and . . ." She smiled at Kathy flirtatiously. "Just think how happy it makes you to win."

Kathy looked glumly at the floor. "Uh-huh." The dissonance between her verbal and nonverbal language couldn't have been greater.

"Listen, kid," Jim leaned forward in his chair, literally thrusting himself between his wife and daughter. "Of course there are times when we don't want to practice. When we want to go out and do things with friends. But you can't give in to that. You're a winner." He dipped his head to punctuate the thought, then turned back toward me. "Heck," he proclaimed, "this is a tough time for all of us. The move, the schedule. We'd been in Houston all our lives. Our families are there. We had a nice house. I had a good job. But you don't get a chance to work with a coach like Soloman every day. When the opportunity came we had to take it."

With his words I felt the pressure vise close around Kathy. In every area she was being squeezed! Her family had given up a home, a job, friends, and family to further her "career." Her dad had said the move was tough on all of them, then laid responsibility for the move on *her*. She wanted to be a kid—to make friends, to build a life—but her parents weren't giving her a chance. She was facing her toughest race with a brand new coach, so the swimming pressure was intense. And she had no room to express her feelings. No wonder she was having headaches! It was as if she were saying, "Ouch! I'm in emotional pain!"—expressing in her body the conflicts she couldn't express in words.

Jim and Margery seemed to have no sense of how painful the pressure was. Perhaps it was because they put equal pressure on themselves. Jim's swimming history and engineering award suggested that he pushed himself very hard. And Margery tackled Kathy's "career" with a lawyer's determination. Both seemed driven to maximum performance. Why did they drive themselves so hard? Had they learned that from *their* parents? And, if so, what did that mean for Kathy?

"You know," I submitted, "you've looked and found there's nothing physically wrong with her, and we're glad about that. Sometimes these symptoms can be a way of trying to communicate something. I wonder what her headaches might be saying?"

From the corner of my eye I could see Kathy watch me as I talked. I was prepared to say more but Margery interrupted.

"Well, I'm sure she's nervous. This is her biggest race and she'll be facing the stiffest competition of her career."

"Do you think the headaches are telling us something about pressure?"

"You mean you think we're pressuring her?" Margery was immediately defensive.

"Well, it sounds like she's been feeling pressure in a number of areas."

"Kathy's been under pressure many times before. After all, she's been competing since she was eight. She thrives on pressure."

"It sounds like that runs in your family." I tried to sound jovial to defuse the tension that was building in the room.

"Oh yeah," said Jim, smiling with an intensity that virtually radiated heat. "We're all sons of bitches when it comes to competing. None of us likes to lose." Then he looked at Margery and Kathy and both smiled back. I had the sense that a three-way visual handshake was passing between them.

I watched the Hildts' collusion and felt for Kathy, for I knew that she had little ability to disagree. Her parents had written a code of behavior for the family, and Kathy was tied to that code with a million invisible strings. The code's content—the conviction that self-worth is tied to hard work and high performance—was easy to see. How it had come to entrap her I could both see and intuit.

Kathy, like all children, depended on her parents. She looked to them for help and guidance, and absorbed their responses like gospel. How could she not? A child needs to trust her parents and to believe that they're acting in her best interest. To do otherwise would be untenably scary, for the child knows she can't take care of herself. So Kathy was wide open to her parents' messages, and like all parents, Jim and Margery communicated constantly through the myriad words and gestures that comprise family interaction. As Kathy listened to her parents' conversations—with each other, with friends, with her—how often did she hear the words "Kathy is a swimmer," or "Kathy thrives on competition," or "Kathy's gonna go all the way"? How often did she note the intensity in their voices as they talked about her "career," or the way they sat forward in their seats, or lifted their heads, or raised their voices slightly when they talked about competing? How often did she sense their anxiety when she failed to meet their expectations, and then feel the sting of their words as they communicated their disappointment? All those subtle messages imprinted on her unconscious. They shaped her thoughts, her feelings, and her behavior just as if they'd been delivered by a hypnotist.

I thought about some of the messages I'd seen transmitted in just the twenty minutes I'd known them:

- I remembered the look her father had given her when he called her "our star." That proud and penetrating look, accompanied by such a loaded word, would have been an arrow to Kathy's unconscious mind.

- I remembered the irritation with which he'd reprimanded her when she'd said she wasn't "good enough" for the Olympics. The urgency of his response had belied a sense of threat, as if *he* were being judged by Kathy's self-assessment; as if he, too, would not be good enough. That message, so emotionally delivered, would be communicated directly to Kathy's unconscious mind.

- I remembered Margery's words, "we can't afford to lose . . . ," and her pregnant pause before adding "practice time." Her real meaning, I realized now, was the first one, communicated silently to Kathy with her glance. And there was a second message implicit in those words—in her mother's pronoun "we"—as if the parents were racing, too; as if *their* well-being required a win. Both messages, hidden beneath the conscious words, would have penetrated Kathy's unconscious.

- I remembered Jim's pride as he handed me the photos. Kathy's accomplishments were not stashed in the family album, but carried—well-fingered—in her father's wallet. How often in her presence did he pass those photos out to others—his *need* for her to swim transparent to her unconscious?

I knew that what I was seeing here had gone on for years, each message driving home the code: *work hard, Kathy; our well-being depends on your success, Kathy; don't fail!*

Until recently, apparently, the "family trance" had seemed successful. Kathy had gone along, swimming, competing, performing as if she fully embraced her parents' commitment and values. But recently things had changed. With the move, the signing of the coach, the pressure of preparing for a higher class of competition, she had developed headaches that were keeping her out of the pool. Why the sudden change? I suspected it wasn't really so sudden. I suspected that Kathy had *never* subscribed fully to her parents' program, but that in order to safeguard her position in the family she had split off her dissenting sentiments from her conscious mind. Her adaptive self had struggled to accommodate her parents' needs, while a deeper self fought to be heard.

She'd had to distance from that deeper self because her parents gave her no room to "own" her conflicted feelings. Each time she hinted at sentiments different from theirs they grew anxious, discounted them, or framed her differences as undesirable. Each time her behavior or sentiments paralleled theirs, they rewarded her with attention and approval. I'd seen this unconscious process in action. When Kathy had doubted her ability to make the Olympics—"I don't have what it takes"—Jim had ignored her admission of doubt and conflict, then reframed it as a liability. When Kathy had chosen practice over going to the movies, Margery had acknowledged her conflicted feelings, then reframed them as something to be overcome.

In numerous subtle ways, Jim and Margery were selectively reinforcing their daughter's thoughts and emotions, encouraging those that made them comfortable, subtly squelching those that made them anxious. And Kathy responded as any child would—by trying to conform. Parental anxiety is frightening to a child, for it threatens her sense of safety. By matching herself to her parents' model, Kathy preserved the family's sense of harmony, reducing her anxiety and theirs.

I realized as I thought about it that I had seen Jim and Margery model this behavior for their daughter. I remembered Margery suppressing her resentment over Kathy's schedule as well as her sadness about the move. I remembered Jim minimizing the "toughness" of the move in deference to working with the coach. In both situations they'd put aside their own dissenting feelings in order to maintain the family code. How many other times had they done the same thing—unconsciously teaching Kathy to override her own dissenting voice?

In essence, through all these subtle messages, they'd framed a hypnotic suggestion: "Don't hear the voice that disagrees." And like a hypnotic subject who splits off particular sensations or information on demand, Kathy dissociated the messages that were coming from inside. I thought about a research demonstration I'd recently seen in which a hypnotized woman's arm had been placed in a pan of ice water. The woman had been instructed not to feel the freezing chill, and, indeed, as the audience watched, her arm turned red—yet she remained impervious, chatting gaily with the researchers on stage. Like that woman, Kathy was dissociating information from within. But disregarding such messages commands a price. Long-term exposure to icy water could damage that woman's arm. Long-term denial of her inner voices was damaging Kathy's sense of self.

But the suggestions weren't coming only from the parents. They were coming from Kathy, too, for she had internalized her parents' voices—their values, their feelings—and the parts of her that genuinely agreed with them were now using their words in a form of *self-hypnosis.* "He's good for me," she'd said about her coach—describing him, I was sure, in her parents' words. "I get them when I haven't practiced enough," she'd apologized for her headaches—reiterating, I was certain, the family interpretation. By repeating those "mantras" to herself, she could overpower the dissenting voices inside and reinduce herself into the family trance.

How had Jim and Margery come to "hypnotize" their daughter? I had no evidence to prove it, but I suspected the answer. These kinds of suggestions don't originate with parents: they are passed through the generations as a family legacy. Just as Kathy had learned the code from her parents, Jim and Margery had learned it from theirs, who, in the same subtle ways, had equated self-worth with high performance. The Hildts were now so bound by the code that they had no choice but to pass it on to their daughter.

Until now the hypnosis had seemed successful: Kathy had been able to silence her dissenting voices each time they had spoken. But now she had headaches, and even her best self-suggestions couldn't make the headaches go away, for the headaches were both a symbol and an attempt at a solution. As a symbol they said, "My parents and these pressures are a headache to me!" As a solution, they temporarily got her out of the pool. Until Kathy had room to explore her conflicts and express her deeper self, the headaches would remain.

How could I give her that room? The intervention, I knew, would need several parts. I'd need to work with Kathy hypnotically to build her sense of self: ego-strengthening suggestions could help her crystallize a self that was separate from her parents. I'd also need to talk with her privately, to give her the safety and support she'd need to vent her dissonant voice. And I'd need to make it safe for her to voice her dissonance to her parents, for just the act of doing so would differentiate her within the family. All these things would mitigate Kathy's conflicts and hopefully give her the sense of self she needed to resist her parents' suggestions. But if I wanted to really free Kathy from the family code, I'd need to do something else as well. I'd have to tackle the source of the suggestions themselves—by encouraging Jim and Margery to examine their own family hypnosis.

"Tell you what," I said, looking Jim and Margery in the eyes. "I'd like to chat with Kathy for a while while you have a seat in the waiting room. Is that okay with you, Kathy?" I turned to face her to make a point of asking her permission.

"I guess so," she said cautiously, looking at her parents.

"Good." I turned to Jim and Margery who were looking at me with some concern. After the way I'd implicated the family in Kathy's headaches, the last thing they wanted was for me to speak to her alone. "Of course you understand this will be private," I said firmly. And then before either of them could protest I stood up, tacitly bidding them leave.

When they had closed the door behind them, I looked at Kathy conspiratorially. "Well, we got them out of the way," I joked, hoping to confirm that I was her ally.

She looked at me warily, but for the first time with a sense of life behind her eyes.

"Would you like to come a little closer?" She was seated as far from me as she could get, in the corner of the room.

"Kathy," I started, after she'd taken her mother's seat, "I have a hunch we're going to talk about some things that you may want to listen to again, or maybe even share with your parents. So with your permission, I'd like to tape this conversation. Would that be okay? The tape would be yours to use in whatever way you want." I knew Kathy couldn't tell her parents directly how she felt, but if we had her sentiments on tape, perhaps we'd find a nonthreatening way to play the tape for them later.

She agreed. Apparently the knowledge that our conversation would be private and that *she* could control the use of the tape was enough to reassure her. Perhaps she also sensed unconsciously that this might be a chance to share her "secret" with her parents.

I put a tape into the machine. "I think the best way to help you, Kathy, is to be very direct. If I'm wrong, tell me. But I don't think you care as passionately about swimming as your parents do. Is that true?"

Kathy's eyes and mouth opened wide as if she were stunned by my question, then she quickly closed them and shook her head.

"I love swimming," she protested. "It's the most important thing in the world. I work at it really hard."

"Kathy," I said gently. "Was I right back there? Have you been feeling a lot of pressure recently?"

Kathy looked down, and I could see tears seep from under her eyelids. She wiped them away with her hand. After a few moments of silence I asked what was making her cry.

"Nothing."

"Must be something." I handed her a box of tissues.

She dabbed her nose forlornly. "I like swimming, but it's like . . . I get up at five o'clock every morning so I can swim for two hours before school, and then after school I swim for two hours again and then we have dinner and then I do my homework and then it's time for bed. . . ." Her eyes filled up again and her voice wavered. "It's just that sometimes I just want to be *normal.*"

"It must be very hard to have it run you that way. Do your parents know how you feel?"

Kathy shook her head morosely.

"What would happen if you told them?"

"My dad would . . . I don't know, it would be awful."

"What would he do?"

"We'd be . . . I mean he'd be really *disappointed.*"

"Disappointed?"

In a very soft voice, "Because I let him down."

"How would you have let him down?"

Kathy's eyes again flooded with tears and her voice cracked as she spoke. "By not being what he wants me to be."

"What does he want you to be?"

"A champion swimmer. To make it to the Olympics."

"Do you want that too?"

Kathy sighed. "I don't know," she said wearily. "I used to think so. I used to watch the videos of my dad and think 'I want to be like that.' But now . . . I don't know, in Houston my friends were going out and having fun . . . and I was always *swimming.*" She stopped and looked out the window. Her eyes filled again with tears. "Sometimes I just wish I could blow it and have it be okay."

I used to watch the videos and think 'I want to be like that.' I wish I could blow it and have it be okay. Kathy's voice was so plaintive my heart went out to her. She'd just admitted the two things she'd been given no permission to feel.

"You're really sad about that aren't you?" I asked gently.

She nodded.

"And scared, too?"

Her eyes blinked rapidly and tears seeped down her cheeks.

"What happens when you blow it?"

"I hate myself."

"That's pretty strong."

She shrugged as if to say, "How could I think otherwise?"

"Kathy, we all blow things all the time, but it's not usually a reason to hate yourself."

"I think it is," she said miserably.

"Do your parents think it is?"

She looked at me quizzically but said nothing.

"I'm curious about something, Kathy. What do your parents do when *they* screw up?"

I expected her to hesitate over this question, but she immediately shot back, "They get real angry. My dad? When I was little and we used to go to meets with him, when he screwed up he used to hit the wall really hard with his fist."

I wasn't surprised. "And your mom?"

"She gets like this . . ." Kathy puckered her lips and furrowed her brow. "Then she gets real quiet and you know you need to stay away from her for a while."

I smiled. "It sounds like your parents are hard on themselves, too. In fact, it sounds like you and they are a lot alike."

Kathy pondered that for a moment. "I guess so," she ventured slowly, as if checking my words against her memory before fully agreeing.

"You know, Kathy, sometimes it's okay to fail."

She looked at me blankly.

"Failure is good. It's useful. We learn from mistakes."

She wrinkled her nose. "My parents don't think that."

"I know," I said. "But think about it for yourself. Have you ever learned to do anything *without* failing? It's impossible. Think about how you get better at swimming. Don't you feel your body doing it wrong, and then learn to do it differently next time? The only way to learn something is to make mistakes—and then do it differently in the future."

Kathy looked interested, but skeptical. "I don't think my parents think that," she said again.

"I think you're right." I paused. "I think your whole family is working on that lesson."

Kathy didn't respond. She sat quietly with her hands in her lap and looked impassively out the window. Her long silence was broken by the click of the tape recorder as it shut itself off.

"Well," I said, congenially. "The tape recorder thinks it's time to stop. Do you?"

She nodded.

I popped the tape out of the machine and handed it to her.

"This is yours to take home. I bet you'll rush home and play it for your folks."

"No way," she said. "You can keep it here."

I grinned. "Okay. Let's call them in."

Jim and Margery came back for a few minutes—just long enough for me to say that I thought we'd made some progress and that I'd like to see Kathy alone in a few days. As they rose to leave, I reminded them that my session with Kathy was confidential. I wanted to stop them from questioning her about our conversation, and to remind them that Kathy was a separate person, in some ways beyond their reach.

When they left I silently cheered Kathy for her bravery in admitting her feelings. Although it wasn't only bravery: it was also self-protection, or even opportunism. She had finally found an ally, someone who would understand her plaint, support her to her parents, and, hopefully, persuade her parents to listen. I knew she'd feel a reduction in tension as a result of our conversation.

But what about Jim and Margery? I'd challenged fundamental ways they'd lived their lives, going back to their own childhoods. And I'd hinted at a family subtext that was less harmonious than they believed. How would they respond? Often after a session like this, clients feel uneasy, although they don't know why. They may have uncharacteristic arguments or unusually vivid dreams as their unconscious minds mull the material covered. This kind of disequilibration is painful, but crucial. It is the crumbling of the familiar that must precede important change.

Three days later, Kathy and Margery returned. I was immediately delighted to see a bounce in Kathy's step and eagerness in her face. Margery, on the other hand, looked taut.

After a few pleasantries in the waiting room, I invited Kathy into the office. Margery immediately moved to join us.

"Kathy and I need to do some work alone," I reminded her politely.

She began to say something but realized she had no choice. Reluctantly she took her seat, and Kathy and I stepped away.

"So tell me," I invited when we were sitting in my office, "how are you doing?"

"I only had one little one!" she grinned.

"Wow. Big improvement. You'd been having them every day."

"Yeah. And twice on some days."

"Well, that's great."

Kathy looked down a little sheepishly. "But I have a little one now."

"Well, that's good news. You know why?"

She shook her head.

"Because we can use hypnosis to get rid of it. And then I can show you how to do hypnosis at home so you can get rid of them yourself."

Kathy looked intrigued.

"Would you like to do that?"

"Yes."

The reduction in headaches was an excellent sign. It meant the pressure was lightening. She had safely expressed her forbidden feelings; she'd had a taste of separateness from her parents. Her world was opening up.

"Are you comfortable now?"

"Yes."

"Well, why don't you get really comfortable. . . ."

Kathy wriggled back in her chair and let her shoulders droop.

"That's good . . . and now you can just let your hands rest in your lap . . . and as you sit there watching your hands I want you to feel a sense of calmness and relaxation coming over you . . . that's right . . . very relaxed . . . you may even want to close your eyes. . . ."

Kathy's eyes closed and her head slipped slightly to the side.

"And as you think about your hands in your lap you may find that one of those hands begins to go numb . . . and now as I count it is getting number, just a little number with every count . . . one . . . two . . . you can feel it happening . . . three . . . it's getting even number . . . four . . . five . . . very good. And now the hand begins to move on its own . . . slowly . . . slowly . . . you can discover it inching its way toward your head. . . ."

Ever so slowly, Kathy's left arm began to rise, moving in short, jerky motions upward from her lap.

"That's right . . . a little higher now . . . and as it moves toward your head you can think about how pleasant it will feel when that hand touches your head . . . how all the pleasing numbness and coolness will move into your head . . . and as the fingers touch the forehead you can feel the forehead relaxing . . . then the whole head relaxing, giving you relief. . . . When you feel that happening give a little nod."

Slowly Kathy's fingers touched her temple. For several seconds she sat motionless, then her head inclined slightly.

"Good . . . and now as the hand sinks down toward your lap you will go even deeper . . . and in a moment when it touches your lap you will be very deep . . . deep and relaxed and free of discomfort of any kind."

Kathy's hand crept back toward her lap and came to a rest. She leaned back heavily against the chair, looking quite serene. The entire sequence had taken less than ten minutes.

"And now, when I count from five back to one you will feel yourself coming back into the room, a little more with every count . . . five . . . still feeling very relaxed . . . four . . . feeling very good . . . three . . . halfway back now . . . two . . . feeling wide awake and very refreshed . . . one!"

She opened her eyes and looked around.

"How are you feeling?"

Kathy squinted, looking for signs of her headache. "It's gone!"

I smiled. "Want to learn how to do that at home?"

"Yeah!"

So I taught her to do self-hypnosis, and when she had demonstrated that she could put herself in a trance I told her that she would be able to recreate the feeling of numbness in her hand by simply remembering how it felt. She could then transfer the numbness to her head just as she had done today. I knew that with practice Kathy would get to the point where merely *imagining* numbness seeping into her head in trance would be enough to relieve a headache. Because her headache was caused by tension, I also told her to imagine, in trance, the muscles in her head, neck, and shoulders growing looser and more relaxed. Such imagery wasn't necessary for one-time relief in my office, but it would further help Kathy manage her headaches on her own.

Kathy put herself back in trance and practiced those two phenomena. When it was clear she had mastered them, I gave her additional suggestions that would strengthen her sense of self. For her whole life Kathy had been living her parents' dreams; now it was time to develop some of her own. "Picture yourself the way you'd like to be," I instructed. "See yourself acting, thinking, feeling, and believing exactly as you would like to be, exactly as you *can* be, exactly as you are becoming even as we speak. See yourself at school and with friends. See yourself studying and with your family. Now, with every day that passes the actual you will become more and more like this ideal image."

Kathy awoke jubilant. She was positively beaming when we called Margery into the room.

"Well, you look happy," Margery commented to her.

Kathy grinned. "My headache's gone."

Margery looked at me with wonder—which enabled me to get away with what I told her next.

"I've taught Kathy how to use self-hypnosis to manage her headaches, and she needs to do it for a half-hour every day. Given her schedule, I think she'll probably need to do a half-hour less swimming in order to fit it in."

Margery started to protest but realized she was in a bind. If she wanted Kathy to lose her headaches, she had no choice.

"And I'd like to schedule another appointment with your whole family."

"Why?"

"Kathy's going to be able to eliminate her headaches if they come, but I think it would be helpful to get the whole family involved in her efforts."

I knew Margery would find that reassuring. She'd believe that I once again planned to include her and Jim in the session, and that we'd work directly on Kathy's headaches. My actual intent, however, was quite different. I hoped to talk with Jim and Margery about their families of origin in the hope that by probing their own feelings about performance and failure we'd find some relief for Kathy. Margery readily agreed to bring Jim to the next session, and we scheduled an appointment for three days later.

It was now three days before the regionals. Kathy had had no headaches since her last visit, and Jim and Margery were clearly delighted. From their eager handshakes I could see that I had achieved "miracle worker" status in their eyes. Perfect, I thought, for asking some difficult questions.

"You know," I stated casually after some opening small talk, "headaches are often a reaction to stress. And we all know Kathy's been feeling stress about the upcoming race. Kathy," I said, turning to her, "how do you think your folks would feel if you didn't do well?"

Kathy looked quickly at her parents, then down at the floor. "I think they'd be upset," she answered quietly.

"You think they'd be disappointed in you?"

She nodded.

"Kathy, it's not that we'd be disappointed, it's just that we know you *can* do well," Margery jumped in.

"How *do* you think you'd feel if Kathy didn't do well?"

"I really don't think about it," she averred, smiling. "We believe in positive thinking."

"Positive thinking is important. But sometimes failing is important, too."

Margery looked at me as if I'd spoken Greek.

"Much as we all like to succeed, we also learn a lot from failure."

"I don't know why you're saying this," she replied stiffly. "We work very hard to build Kathy's positive attitude and we don't like to encourage failure."

"I'm not talking about encouraging failure. I'm just pointing out that it isn't always a bad thing."

Margery shuddered visibly and looked at me as if she were sorry she had consented to this appointment.

"It sounds like you disagree. What are *your* feelings about failure?"

Margery raised her palms in the air as if the answer were patently obvious.

"Are you hard on yourself when you fail?"

"I . . ." she shook her head. "I don't see what this . . ."

But Jim cut her off. "I guess you can call it being hard on yourself," he said, shifting his weight stiffly in his chair. "Or you can say you hold yourself to a high standard. I choose to believe I hold myself to a high standard."

"How did you learn that? Do you remember?"

"Sure. My dad was a drill sargeant. I slipped up, he laid into me."

"How'd that make you feel?"

"Hated it. But he was right. He taught me good habits."

"And we've tried to pass those habits on to our daughter," said Margery.

"I think you've done an excellent job." I tried to sound complimentary. "And now she's trying to learn some valuable lessons about failure."

"What do you mean?" Margery's tone was pointed.

"Well, it sounds like she's struggling with something that you didn't have a chance to learn as kids—that sometimes mistakes are okay. That we can learn from them. That sometimes they even help us succeed."

Jim's eyes grew narrow and his broad, square jaw grew tense. Irrationally I wished there were a desk between us. But at the risk of provoking him I went on. "We're all human, and sometimes we can't perform at 100 percent. Sometimes we just have 75 percent days. But we're no less good for being imperfect." I stared into Jim's opaque blue eyes. "I think that's a lesson your daughter is trying to teach you."

"I think Kathy *chooses* to push herself hard," interjected Margery. "She's very competitive. She likes to do well, and she knows what it takes."

"How would you feel if she pushed herself less hard?"

Confusion spread across Margery's face. "Why would she want to do that?"

Faced with her confusion, my own tone softened. "You know, I think Kathy wants very much to live the way you do, and when she feels she isn't, she gets very critical of herself. Maybe she needs to hear from you that she should try her best, but that when she can't it's still okay."

"Kathy tries her best all the time. She's a superb athlete, an excellent student. . . . I don't think Kathy has anything to worry about. She knows we adore her and would do anything for her."

"I wonder how Kathy knows that? How does she know you would adore her even if she weren't a superb athlete?"

"How does she know? Of course she knows," Margery snapped.

"How do you show her? Could you show her *now?*"

Margery's face twisted in confusion. "Show her now? What do you mean?

"Can you show her with words, with gestures? Can you find a way to let her know that you would love her just as much, even if she weren't a superb athlete?"

Margery looked at Jim then back at me. I returned her gaze. Finally she sighed in resignation and turned toward Kathy. "Kathy, you know Daddy and I would love you no matter how you do in the races, don't you?"

Kathy looked at her mother. Her eyebrows raised slightly and her lip quivered. Then she averted her gaze to the floor.

"Kathy, you know that, don't you?" Margery's voice was impatient, frightened.

Kathy nodded numbly, her head still bowed.

"Kathy, do you think that your parents know that *their* parents would love *them* no matter how *they* performed?"

She looked up at me startled, then with a slight shrug of her shoulder gazed back down at the floor. Jim and Margery exchanged a glance.

I realized the moment had come to play the tape. It gave voice not just to Kathy's dissenting feelings, but to the feelings her parents had split off as well, and in their anxious glance I sensed a possible openness to its message. "Kathy," I said gently, "do you think this might be the time to play the tape?" I hadn't meant to put her on the spot like this. When we'd made the tape, I'd imagined that *she* would choose the moment to play it. But inadvertently I'd created a situation in which the opportunity was ripe.

Kathy looked at me, clearly frightened.

"Tell you what," I said. "I know this is hard for you. Why don't you put your finger on the stop button and stop the tape the minute you feel you want to."

Kathy kept looking at me. I had the sensation that she was sinking, and that my face was both her anchor and her lifeline. In what felt like slow motion she reached out and took the tape player from my hand.

What was going through her mind? I'm sure she was afraid of revealing her feelings to her parents. But at the same time she must have sensed a powerful opportunity, a chance, in the safety of my office, to make a break with her parents and finally speak for her *self*.

Jim and Margery watched, looking ashen themselves, their thoughts telegraphed in the worried glances they exchanged. *What are we going to hear? That our daughter doesn't know we love her? That we've failed her as parents? That we've failed our own high standards of performance?*

Kathy pressed the button and the tape began. Jim and Margery sat quietly in their chairs, listening intently. Both seemed transfixed by the conversation. Jim shifted his weight from time to time; Margery crossed and recrossed her legs. But gradually even those movements stopped. Slowly their eyes grew glazed, their expressions fixed and trancelike. At one point Jim blinked several times and I noticed with surprise that his eyes were moist: I hadn't expected him to be able to cry. But that, too, was momentary. When the tape stopped and the recorder shut itself off both sat silent, gazing into space and also, I suspected, back in time. Finally Margery broke the spell.

"Kathy, we thought . . . Why didn't you tell us . . . ?"

Kathy looked stricken as she faced her mom. Her eyes were wet and her lip quivered.

"We thought you loved swimming or we never would have . . ."

"Mom, I do love swimming! I just . . . I just want to do other things too." Her voice was barely audible.

Margery shook her head. "We had no idea."

They were silent for a few moments.

"You feel we've pushed you? How have we pushed you?" There was genuine confusion in her voice.

Kathy didn't answer.

"We just want you to be the best."

"Sometimes I don't want to be the best." Kathy spoke so softly we could hardly hear her.

Margery peered at her intensely, as if by looking harder she could somehow see and understand this statement. Finally she sighed deeply and looked at me. "I've always wanted to be the best. I've never understood how anyone could feel differently."

Jim cleared his throat. When he talked his voice was scratchy. "I guess I understand."

Margery looked at him, surprised.

Jim breathed in deeply, then talked from a place that seemed far away. "When I was, I don't know, eleven or twelve, I placed second in a meet. The guy who won was a lot older than me, and I thought I'd done really well. I ran into the house and yelled, 'Mom, Dad, I got second!' After what felt like hours my mother came out of the kitchen. She looked at me— I remember her hands were wet—and all she said was, 'Who got first?'

"At that moment I *hated* swimming." He looked at Margery. "I hated having to be the best."

"But I guess that didn't last long," he said after a minute, "because the next day I was back in the pool." He turned and smiled at Kathy. "I think that was the first time I ever punched the wall."

Kathy smiled weakly back.

"You know where that comes from, don't you? You ever see Grandpa pound the arm of his chair when he's stuck on a crossword puzzle?" He looked at me. "When I was a kid, every Sunday no one could look at the paper 'til my Dad had done the puzzle. He always did it in pen. That was a mark of pride with him, that he never made a mistake. But if he couldn't get the last couple of words, he'd get so angry he'd pummel the arm of the chair." He chuckled. "We always loved that moment because it meant we could race for the comics."

I smiled. His words were lighthearted, but in Jim's recollections I could see the intricate weaving of the hypnotic family code—the unconscious transfer of suggestions from Jim's parents to him, just as he had transmitted them to Kathy.

I thought about his mother's deflating question, "Who got first?" In one deft swipe she had robbed him of the pride and excitement he had carried home. What had happened to those feelings? How had he handled the painful dissonance between his own pleasure and his mother's disapproval? He'd buried it; he'd had no choice. It was far safer as a child to adopt his mother's viewpoint—to believe as she did, that second wasn't good enough—than to risk losing her by feeling proud. And what about his fleeting feeling that he didn't *want* to swim or be the best? Again disowned, to mute the contradiction between his sentiments and hers. The next day he was "back in the pool," swimming as if he believed that winning were all that mattered.

I thought about Jim's father and the crossword puzzle. The repetition of the Sunday morning ritual, the solemn expectation of a perfect performance, the dramatic pummeling of the chair when the standard wasn't met: it was easy to see how all those things could imprint themselves on a boy's unconscious, reinforcing the message: *perfection is what counts.* How many other incidents had reinforced that message by persuading the boy to abandon his feelings and adopt, instead, those of his parents?

I knew the answer was "many," for even as an adult, Jim was frightened of being less than perfect. He still feared his father's wrath, his mother's disdain, each time he came in second. That's why he, too, pressured Kathy. She was his foil: she could redeem him—by becoming the swimmer he'd been groomed to be. If *she* worked hard, if *she* didn't fail, he could disown his own fear of failure.

"Your dad's a lot like mine," said Jim suddenly, as if the thought had just occurred to him. He turned toward Margery.

She seemed far away, to have barely heard his remark.

Jim waved his hand in front of her eyes and she flinched. But immediately she recovered and smiled wanly.

"Your dad's a lot like mine," he repeated. "Perfectionist. Tough."

She nodded. "You could say that."

"Tell me about your dad," I suggested.

Margery sighed. "My dad." Her voice had a flat, childlike quality, as if she were reciting a grade school composition. "My dad is sales manager for an insurance company."

"That sounds like demanding work."

"Demanding? That's a good word. I'll tell you about my dad. He keeps charts on all his salesmen. Every Friday night he *scores* them according to how many policies they've sold. Then on Monday morning he calls them one by one into his office and berates them because their scores are too low. Then he comes home, has a couple of drinks, and brags about how he set them straight, how he really lit a candle under their asses." Margery's eyes narrowed. "He's been doing that for as long as I can remember."

"Was he tough on you growing up?"

She shrugged.

"He hit her when she didn't get A's," said Jim.

Margery shot him a glance.

"It only happened once or twice." Then she smirked. "I got a lot of A's. Anyway, he didn't mean to hurt me, that was just the way he was. He wanted me to do well."

He wanted me to do well. Her father had *hit* her, and she'd excused his action by saying he wanted her to do well. Where were her *feelings*? Where were the rage and humiliation, the hurt and fear a child should feel after her parent hit her? I knew the answer: Margery had buried those feelings, as she had buried so many others, because to feel them would have been too hard. The knowledge that a parent has mistreated a child is so frightening that the child disowns it and accepts instead the parent's rationale. *I do this because I love you, because you deserve it, because I want you to improve,* the child hears her parent say, and the words have the force of hypnotic suggestion. They explain the parent's frightening behavior. They become the "truth" the child continues to believe.

And what of Margery's claim that her father had hit her "only once or twice"? I was skeptical: parental hitting is rarely so circumscribed. More frequently, the child minimizes the trauma to shield herself from pain. *It only happened once or twice and it wasn't all that bad,* she thinks—sparing herself full knowledge of her parent's acts.

"What did your mother do when your father hit you?"

"She put ice on my face and told me he only wanted what was best for me." Margery looked at my face and heard the coldness of her words. "I mean she wasn't brutal or anything. She loved me. But what could she do? Besides, she wanted me to do well, too."

So Margery's mother had reinforced the hypnotic code. She, too, had denied her daughter's feelings. She, too, had acted as if it were reasonable for a father to strike his child, as if Margery deserved to get hit when she didn't get A's. And Margery followed their suggestions. She believed her safety required being perfect.

"Tell me more about your mom," I urged.

She sighed. "My mom is brilliant. She was the first woman in her family to go to college. Her diploma is on the wall in the den. She was going to be a chemist. She did all the coursework and graduated magna cum laude. . . . Then she gave it all up when she married my father." She rolled her eyes. "He didn't want her to work. So she channeled all her brilliance and energy into the PTA."

"You sound angry."

"Angry? I'm not angry. I just think it's a waste. She could have been so much more."

"How does *she* feel about it?"

Margery shrugged. "I don't think she thinks about it. She's busy. She's chair of her alumni association. She's on the board of the local Red Cross. She's raised so much money for those organizations she's got awards all over our house."

I noted that although I had asked about her mother's *feelings*, Margery had recounted her *activities*. I was also struck by her use of the phrase "our house" as if she were still a girl, still living there. But more telling than anything was the proliferation of communications reinforcing the message that perfection was required.

• I thought about the pervasive suggestions for success: the chronicling of her mother's college career, the magna cum laude diploma on the wall, the ubiquitous awards commemorating her volunteer achievements.

• I thought about Margery's mother relinquishing a career to stay at home and then applying her voracious energy to volunteering.

• I thought about Margery's dad tallying his salesmen's scores—the ritual nature of the act, the brutish power wielded, the intoxicating pride displayed.

All these acts would make formidable impressions on a child. How could Margery escape the suggestion that she, too, must strive to perform?

And as she yielded to her parents' pressure, had Margery, too, tried to rebel? I remembered her allusion to her headaches as a girl. Had they been signs of protest, just as Kathy's were? If so, they apparently hadn't been as fierce, or her rebellion hadn't been as strong, for clearly Margery had given up. She now followed her parents' suggestions as closely as a person can—her dissenting feelings buried.

And now her daughter was having headaches, too. Was that

coincidence? I doubted it. The unconscious works in mysterious ways, few of them coincidental. It was more likely, I believed, that Margery's headaches formed a blueprint for Kathy's—that Kathy was living out the rebellion that Margery had not completed. Margery's pressure had never been relieved; now her daughter was struggling to relieve it.

As I considered the evidence of the session, I felt I'd found the evidence linking Kathy's "hypnosis" to her parents'. I saw how Jim and Margery had been conscripted to their family codes; how they'd learned to equate self-worth with never failing; how they'd learned to mute their dissenting voices and listen instead to their parents.

And I saw how Kathy's behavior directly fed or assuaged their anxiety. When Kathy performed well, they felt the same comfort they'd felt as children—when they'd performed well and earned their parents' praise. But when she didn't—when she asked to skip a practice, when she didn't win a race—their own self-worth was threatened, just as it had been when they'd let their parents down. I saw that in a sense Jim and Margery had never grown up: inside they were still small children who felt scared and worthless when they or their daughter failed.

And they had another reason for needing her to obey the family code. Kathy's dissension must have reminded them of their own dissenting voices, voices they'd muted so long ago. And those reminders must have been painful—nagging confirmations that they'd sold out their truer selves.

But now Kathy was rebelling. Under the current pressure her own dissension was spilling out, and Jim and Margery could no longer avoid the anxieties and truths they'd run away from. How would they react? So far their responses had been extremely positive. Instead of closing down again, they'd used the opportunity to reexamine aspects of their childhoods, to think about how some of their own attitudes and behaviors had been formed. Would that continue? Kathy's conformance to the code had served her parents for a dozen years. Would her rebellion also serve them? Would it serve to liberate them from their own hypnosis? I was cautiously optimistic.

It was quiet in the office while both parents wandered in their own thoughts. Finally Margery turned toward me.

"Do you think we're too hard on her?" she asked quietly.

I returned her gaze but didn't answer.

"I'd never hit her," she added quickly. "But maybe . . ." She looked out the window. "We're close in age . . ."

I looked at her puzzled. "Close in age?"

She looked at me and then started, as if surprised. "I mean . . . I don't know what I mean," she laughed, drawing herself up in her chair.

"Do you think you're too hard on her?" I inquired.

"I hope not," she murmured.

Jim took a deep breath and exhaled loudly. "Well, Kathy," he asked sociably, "what do *you* think about all this?" It was an obvious attempt to lighten the mood.

Kathy had been sitting upright in her chair, head inclined toward her parents, clearly fascinated by their revelations. But she was unprepared for her father's question. She looked at him wide-eyed, like a child eavesdropping from the top of the stairs.

He laughed. "Lot to think about, huh?" He looked at his watch then turned back toward me. "Guess our time's about up, no?" In fact, there were about ten minutes left in the session, but I saw no reason to detain them. Jim was right: they did have a lot to think about.

"Thanks for your hard work today," I offered as they headed for the door. Then I remembered that this was the last time I'd see them before Kathy went to the regionals. "By the way," I called, "good luck in the race. What do you think—third place?" I smiled impishly to show that my words were half-joking. I wanted them to know I wished them well—and that in this case that might not mean first.

After the Hildts left my office, I continued to muse on the hypnotic tapestry they'd shown me. I was particularly intrigued by Margery's comment, "We're close in age," for it seemed so telling. It suggested that, at least unconsciously, Margery identified with Kathy, that hearing Kathy's feelings had rekindled her own. Would that be enough to help alleviate the pressure? And what would be the impact on the regionals?

The session had been surprisingly powerful, even more so than I had anticipated. So it was now with great eagerness—and curiosity— that I anticipated the Hildts' next visit.

The Hildts returned ten days later, and if I was looking for an immediate sign of progress it seemed disappointingly absent. The family took their customary chairs. Jim saluted me with his head, Margery gave the briefest of smiles. Only Kathy seemed a little perkier than usual.

"Well," I opened, "how are you doing?"

Jim flashed a big smile. "Went great," he said. "She did well."

I turned to Kathy. She was smiling too.

"I placed sixth," she announced.

Sixth? She'd placed sixth and Jim had said she'd done well?

"It was an excellent performance," he went on. "She was a little nervous on the start, which slowed her down, but she had smooth strokes, good strategy. Overall she did almost everything right."

I positively grinned with pleasure. Kathy had come in sixth and Jim was complimenting her! He'd acknowledged her mistakes without criticizing!

"There were some excellent swimmers there," he continued, as if reading my mind. "Very fast. This was a big step up in competition for Kathy." He looked over at Margery. "We felt she really held her own."

Margery returned his gaze for a moment then looked away. Kathy beamed in the corner.

I thought it was interesting that neither of them had mentioned Coach Soloman. Apparently his thoughts on Kathy's performance had ceased to carry such weight.

"You look pretty proud of yourself, young lady," I said.

She nodded, grinning. It was the first time I'd seen her truly happy.

"Did you have *fun,* too?"

"Oh yeah! There were activities every day." She looked over at her parents. "My parents wanted me to rest. But . . ." She grinned again.

"Sounds like you tasted a little independence."

She looked like the cat that had swallowed a canary.

"And *you* got a taste of adolescence," I observed to Jim and Margery.

Jim rolled his head in mock resignation.

It was remarkable. Whole pieces of the family code were beginning to crumble. Jim and Kathy had both begun to relinquish their unreasonable drive for success. Jim had told me the absolute truth: given the stiff level of competition, a step beyond anything Kathy had previously experienced, her performance, imperfect as it was, was excellent. For perhaps the first time, they could see her swimming honestly, unclouded by the need to win. And Kathy's willingness to defy her parents—at her biggest race, in a way that could presumably impair her performance—suggested that for the first time she was entertaining priorities different from theirs.

"I get to go to Zones," said Kathy, referring to the next higher class of competition.

"Whoa! That's terrific!" I exclaimed, then paused as if I had just remembered something. "Wait a minute. *Is* that terrific?"

She beamed. "Yeah. I want to go."

That Kathy wanted to go to Zones didn't surprise me. She'd been groomed for competition all her life and I'm sure she was genuinely pleased. Plus I knew from working with my other Olympic-bound athletes that these competitions, which draw adolescents from a wide geographic area, are a lot of fun. I was curious to see how her new attitude would hold up in that even more competitive environment.

I turned to Margery. "You seem a little quiet today."

"I'm fine."

"Did you enjoy the trip?"

She nodded, though not enthusiastically.

"What was hard about it?"

"Hard?"

"I get the sense that this race was harder, somehow, than others."

Margery narrowed her eyes. I could tell she felt picked on but also sensed that part of her wanted to talk. When it was clear that I would wait her out, she sighed. "It's hard to describe," she said. "I didn't enjoy it as much. I don't know why."

"You didn't enjoy the swimming?"

"I enjoyed it . . . but I felt uncomfortable."

"What do you think made you uncomfortable?"

"I don't know. I guess I was nervous about Kathy's performance. She'd lost so much time to those headaches and I didn't know how she'd do. And it was such a big race. All those fast girls. I guess I was just nervous for her."

"Nervous for *her*?"

Margery shot a look at me. "Yes."

"A little nervous for you too, maybe?"

Her eyes narrowed again. "Why would I be nervous for me? I wasn't swimming."

I smiled and gestured as if to return the question.

Margery's fingers laced together and she looked pointedly out the window.

I decided not to press her. Although something was bothering Margery that she couldn't identify, I intuitively trusted her to grapple with it alone. Maybe it was that I knew she'd tackle it with the same determination she applied to every challenge in her life. Maybe it was just that I felt I didn't need to press her because her husband and daughter already were. The current of change seemed inexorable in her family. I had already suggested that there might be more to her discomfort than she acknowledged. Now I decided to sit back and let that current carry her along.

So after some casual conversation I dismissed Jim and Margery and worked with Kathy on self-hypnosis. As I had before, I helped her into a trance and then asked her to see herself the way she wanted to be. "And as you see that ideal image, you can know that you are an independent person . . . and that this independent person can be like her parents in some ways, but she can also be different from her parents . . . even in some important ways. . . . And as you continue to listen to your own voice . . . to that deepest voice inside you . . . you will find in your own heart the path that's right for you.

"In the process of doing so you may notice that your parents grow anxious, but understand that they are only being reminded of their own issues with failure and performance . . . In their anxiety they may even seem a little cross or irritated with you, but in your heart of hearts you will know that they are really irritated about their own issues and not about you . . ."

When Kathy and I had finished I called Jim and Margery in to schedule another session. Interestingly, no one asked why we needed to meet again. Technically we'd accomplished their original objectives: Kathy's headaches were gone and her performance had enabled her to go higher in competition. Were they so accustomed to therapy that they didn't question coming back? Or, on an unconscious level, did they endorse my goal of freeing the whole family from its hypnotic bonds?

Our fifth and last session occurred a month later. On arrival, all three seemed genuinely happy to see me.

"It's been a while," I observed. "What's up?"

They reported that Kathy had been practicing regularly, although somewhat less than her coach and parents wanted. She was adamant about protecting her half-hour a day for self-hypnosis, which her parents grudgingly permitted; more problematic were her requests to spend time after school with friends. However, she and her parents had worked out a compromise: she was permitted one afternoon a week to visit until Zones, more thereafter.

"Adolescence," I reminded them, half-jokingly. "It's only going to get tougher. She's going to demand more and more to be herself."

Jim and Margery nodded ruefully. Apparently this truism was already being tested.

"You know," I said, "one of the hardest things parents can do is to let their children be themselves." I paused and looked deeply into their eyes. "Many parents can't. They can't release their children from their own interests . . . and values . . . and ways of being." I spoke slowly, giving weight to my words. "The children often feel sad and angry. They yearn for the freedom to be themselves. But after a while they stop yearning. Do you know why?"

Jim and Margery both looked at me intently, the way children listen to a storyteller.

"Because after a while it's easier to go along. It's easier to be *like* your parents than to fight for the right to grow away." I looked closely at Jim, then at Margery, hoping to touch a nerve that would allow them to recognize themselves in my words. After a lengthy pause I continued. "A lot of parents can't allow their children the space to be different—but I think you two can."

Jim and Margery slowly turned away from my eyes, then each became absorbed in private thoughts. It was quiet in the room for several moments.

"Did you see my name in the paper?" piped up Kathy suddenly, bored with the silence.

I looked down at the bit of newspaper she had handed me. It was a local story about the Zone swimming championships. "Here it is," I said proudly. "Kathleen Hildt."

She grinned.

"Are you all looking forward to the race?"

"I'm actually going to have to sit this one out," said Jim, a little sadly. "I've got a conference that weekend. Can't get out of it."

What? I thought. *Kathy's biggest race and Jim isn't going?* The man who gave up a better job and moved his family cross-country for his daughter's swimming is now forgoing her biggest race because of a conference? I was stunned. Gratified, but stunned.

I started to comment but thought better of it. The unconscious works in mysterious, often surreptitious ways, and I've learned through the years that commenting on a client's changes may be counterproductive. Like Wile E. Coyote in the *Roadrunner* cartoons who runs confidently past the cliff edge until he looks down, clients are often stablest in their change when it's not pointed out. Once back on solid footing they can discover their differences gradually.

I turned instead to Margery. "You had some discomfort with the last race. How are you feeling about this one?"

Margery breathed in deeply. "I'm a little nervous."

I waited for more.

"Same stuff. Bigger competition. Faster swimmers." I waited for more.

She gave a nervous titter. "I'm kind of a fifth wheel these days."

I looked curious.

"Well, now Kathy has Coach Soloman."

I smiled. Language is such a telling thing. In earlier visits Margery would have said "We have Coach Soloman." Now she was granting ownership to Kathy. Was *she* slowly releasing her daughter, too?

"Maybe it's time for a new role?" I suggested.

She smiled sadly into my eyes.

I began to pursue that thought but then decided against it. There was something about the way Margery had looked me in the eye, her own eyes so full of feeling. It was the first time she had not avoided my glance, the first time she'd openly shown emotion. Margery's change was quieter than that of her husband and child, I realized, but it was happening on as many fronts—and with minimal prodding from me. So once again I decided to leave her alone.

We talked casually for a few more minutes, then I did a short tune-up with Kathy on her self-hypnosis.

"Give me a call when you get back from Zones and we'll do one last session," I suggested before they left. Then I wished them luck and said good-bye.

When two months later I hadn't heard from them, I called. Kathy answered. "Mr. Calof!" she shouted, and gleefully filled me in on the news. She had done passably at Zones—placed twenty-fourth in a field of thirty-two. But her swimming had been fine for a first timer, she said. Far more exciting was the fact that she'd stayed in a hotel room with two other girls and had spent much of the time "hanging out" with other swimmers.

"Where was your mom?" I queried.

"Oh, she didn't go," said Kathy nonchalantly.

"She didn't go?"

"Unh-unh. She got a job and couldn't go."

One more jolt from this surprising family.

"Tell me more." I tried to sound as nonchalant as she did.

"I don't know much about it. Here's my dad," Kathy said and waltzed off the phone.

Jim confirmed that a week before they were scheduled to leave Margery had seen an ad in the paper for a paralegal. On the spur of the moment she had applied, interviewed, and been offered the job. That evening she was out at a meeting with her new boss.

Again I felt it best not to comment on the magnitude of the change, so we chatted a bit about other things and then I wrapped it up.

"It sounds like you guys have outgrown me," I remarked jovially. "I don't think you'll be needing my services any more."

Jim chuckled. "Yeah, we're doing all right. And you know, that self-hypnosis . . . I don't know. I might want to come talk to you some time about that. I'll give you a call."

"Fine," I said. "I'd love to see you."

I hung up the phone, sat back in my chair and mused on this latest turnaround. Margery had gotten a job! She'd actually been reading the classifieds! I marveled at the process of the unconscious. Like the earth itself, the unconscious contains layer upon layer of experience, pressed by the weight of time, emotion, and repetition into a seemingly calcified bedrock. Yet the stroking of the finest tool—a well-timed question, a collusion of events—can be enough to disturb the layers and yield change.

As much unconsciously as consciously, I suspected, Margery had probed the layers of her childhood that contained the suggestions to excel and saw again her own ancient desire to grow away, long buried beneath the need to be a loyal daughter. Having excavated those memories she was free to "redecide" them, to examine them from a more rational perspective and free herself from their grasp.

Was it surprising that she and Jim had changed so quickly, had given up decades of suggestion in the space of a few months? Not really. Both were in their thirties, a time when, after the strident self-defining of our teens and twenties, we tend to reflect on our past and on the relationships that have made us who we are. They were prompted as well by Kathy, for in *her* struggle to rebel they dimly recognized their own. Hearing her feelings reminded them that they, too, had once craved freedom from their parents' agendas.

It's an irony of families that what parents disown, their children oftentimes live out. The late Carl Whitaker, a preeminent family therapist, said, "we get the children we deserve," meaning our children give us a chance to confront and resolve the issues we have with our parents. And so it was with the Hildts. Jim and Margery had buried their own rebellious urges but, through their daughter, were forced to deal with those feelings. Kathy's tape, so painful at the moment it was played, became their tool of liberation. Margery was right to call her headaches "growing pains," for that's exactly what they were. They enabled the entire family to grow beyond its hypnotic bonds.

Time and again clients have wondered why, at the age of thirty or forty or sixty, they still hear their parents' voices in their heads; why their parents' words still issue from their mouths; why, in their parents' presence, they act like children once again. Invariably, as we comb their unconscious minds, we tease out scores of messages as potent as those that governed the Hildts: messages transmitted daily through the subtlest of codes; the rebukes and embraces that color a family's interactions.

Secreted in the unconscious, those messages have hypnotic power. But when the feelings that lie beneath them are revealed, when the person's unconscious rules are challenged, when the person's real self has room to flourish, those messages often wither. They may still tug at us from time to time, as if a familiar voice were calling us to think or feel a certain way. But they no longer have the power to blindly shape our behavior, for they no longer bind us in the family trance.

Chapter 4

The Couple Who Became Each Other

FLOYD AND JUDY MASTERSON COULD NOT HAVE BEEN MORE DIFFERENT FROM each other. Floyd, at six foot four, was a bear of a man, burly and muscular, crew-cut and blunt-edged. Judy, his wife, was a vole. She was thin and pale, with flowery gestures and a nervous laugh, and eyes that rarely smiled. Floyd wielded his policeman's body like a billy club; Judy handled hers like antique lace. Floyd barked and expected the world to stop; Judy whispered and hoped someone would notice. I often wonder where the idea for an intervention originates, but not in the case of Floyd and Judy. It took a while to permeate my conscious mind, but the idea for their treatment must have sprouted in my unconscious soon into our first encounter. Why else would I have thought to have them switch identities and become each other?

As usual, our first contact occurred on the phone.

"We're calling it quits," Floyd huffed. He might have been throwing in his hand in a card game. "We've tried everything and nothing's worked. We're filing for divorce. Linda Brenner said you're good so we're giving it one last shot, but I can tell you, I don't think it's gonna work."

"Well," I countered pleasantly, "why don't you tell me what you've already tried so I know what to avoid." I figured I might as well start differentiating myself from their failures.

"Jiminy," he barked, "you name it. We've made thirty-nine visits to three different marriage counselors in the last five years."

I imagined a calendar on their kitchen wall, each visit neatly scratched off and tallied. Suddenly I was nervous. In my five years of practice I'd done a lot of weight loss, a lot of smoking cessation, but not a lot of couples work. If three marriage counselors had failed to help them, what could I accomplish?

"But Linda said you're different," Floyd went on. "You use hypnosis or something, and you're quick. So we decided to give it one last try." His voice was bored as if he already knew the outcome.

"Is Linda a friend of yours?" I asked. Linda Brenner was a former client.

"Yeah. Judy's best friend."

My heart sank. Usually those words are welcome: a referral by a best friend sets a client up for change. But now I felt only pressure. Linda had wanted weight loss, which was relatively easy. These people would be far tougher. Already I could see how entrenched they were.

As if to confirm my fears Floyd continued, "But I got to tell you, Judy told Linda she didn't think it would work."

Their pessimism seemed boundless. My best recourse would be to mirror or *pace* their doubt. By echoing their sentiments I could let them know I was on their side and avoid engendering resistance. By establishing myself as an understanding and empathetic ally, I could begin leading them toward change. "You both sound sure that your marriage, and this therapy, will fail," I said.

"What *else* can we think?" Floyd asked with exasperation. "We're like explosives. Everything we do sets each other off." He sighed deeply and was silent for a moment. "It wasn't always like this."

"No?"

"Heck no. The first few years were terrific. We met in the service ten years ago, and we got along great. Then, I don't know what happened. Judy got pregnant; that's what started it. So we decided to quit the service and move back up here. I wanted us to be closer to our folks." He paused as if hearing the sound of his words. "I mean, it's not Ryan's fault, or anything. God, we love him. And he's a great kid, a decent kid, not like some kids nowadays. But he gets these little episodes where he won't come out of his room. I don't know what that's about and we're both pretty worried about it . . ." Floyd stopped as if he were thinking; I waited for him to continue. "We decided a long time ago not to have any more kids."

"Why is that?"

"Would you, if you were fighting all the time?" His voice was belligerent, but then softened. "You know, it's not like the spark is gone or anything. We still love each other. Just everything turns into a fight.

"Like last night. We had this fight about money. Judy wants to pay the bills. Well, she doesn't need to pay the bills. I pay the bills. You got a system that works, you don't fix it, right? But every few months, up it comes again. 'Floyd, let me pay the bills.' And when I say no she starts carping on me about something. Last night it was how much money I spent on our new TV, as if she doesn't watch it every night too." He sighed in irritation. "I can't win, you know? I try to make things easy for her and then she nitpicks me. Or she starts to cry."

A picture of their marriage was beginning to form in my mind. Floyd was apparently strong-willed and controlling, and probably steamrolled through life without a clue to Judy's feelings. But Judy, instead of asserting herself directly, apparently countered with barbed attacks. The result seemed to be a Mexican standoff: the more Floyd controlled, the more nettlesome Judy became.

My image was formed partly from the information Floyd had given me, both in his words and in his manner, and partly from an intuitive sense of couples. Even without a lot of experience, I knew that certain predictable patterns govern most relationships, and this kind of "one up/one down" power dynamic was one of the most common.

I could imagine Floyd and Judy meeting in the military ten years earlier, young and insecure, away from home for the first time. Judy would have admired Floyd's apparent strength and confidence; Floyd would have relished her dependence. A three-month courtship would have felt nourishing to both. But what pleases in the short term often grates in the long, and it was easy to see how ten years of marriage could turn their paradise into a prison. For the marriage to be saved, I suspected, Floyd would need to become sensitive to Judy's needs, and Judy would need to learn to assert herself directly.

"Look, doc," Floyd continued. His use of the term "doc" seemed to contain so little respect that I didn't bother reminding him that I wasn't a doctor. "We're pretty unhappy and Linda said you're fast. Can't you just zap us or something?"

So that was the secret hope—that in one quick, painless session I could accomplish what the thirty-nine sessions of talking therapy had not. That, too, jibed with what little I knew of them. They had enlisted in, and apparently enjoyed, the military, which meant they were comfortable taking orders. And they were tired of probing and analyzing their marriage. Now they just wanted to sit back and get zapped. Mindlessly. Passively. The way a commander would issue them an order. Well, if that was the style of communication that worked for them, that's what I would use.

"You don't think it will work, Floyd!" I charged as authoritatively as I could. "And what's more, Judy has her *own* ideas about why it won't work! But you don't know a thing about me! And neither one of you can ever hope to understand my methods—or how you will change as a result."

He was silent at the other end. I had chosen my words quickly but carefully. While still pacing his belief that the marriage and the therapy would fail, I wanted to establish myself as an unquestionable authority, one with methods different from any they had experienced in the past. And I wanted to lift myself above the fray so that I couldn't be pulled into, or *triangulated* in, their drama. My last words, "how you will change as a result," were actually an embedded suggestion.

This authoritarian tone was a bit uncomfortable: it was wholly contrary to my nature. But at the same time there was something soothing about it. It covered my insecurity; it cloaked me with the self-assurance I wished I really had.

"Now," I continued since Floyd had remained silent, "I am unwilling to see the two of you until I have a chance to hear from your wife just how pessimistic *she* is."

Floyd muttered something unintelligible but a few moments later Judy's voice came over the phone.

"I'm sorry we bothered you," she said softly, her first words an apology.

"Floyd was saying you're interested in therapy."

"Yes, well, we're having trouble, I mean . . . Oh, I think we're beyond hope, but Linda knows about this kind of thing and she thinks you're good and well, oh . . . what's the use, we're finished." At this she began to cry.

"You see?" demanded Floyd's voice suddenly. "What's the use? She's always getting hysterical like this. Sorry we bothered you. Goodbye."

But before he could hang up I thundered into the mouthpiece, "You get her back on the telephone NOW!"

Without a word he called to Judy and her voice came back on the line.

"What do you want?" she asked, sniffling.

"You're upset," I approached gently, pacing her feelings. "You don't know what to do. You're sure I'll fail like all the rest, although you're not totally sure. . . ." But then my voice hardened. Instead of scheduling the couple for an appointment I had almost caused them to hang up the phone; now I had to reverse that situation. If hope for the marriage wouldn't get them into therapy, perhaps a sense of responsibility toward an authority figure might. "You have taken me away from important work," I barked. "I am at least entitled to fail in person, so you get him here with you tomorrow at 11:00 A.M. sharp and don't be late—or I'll know you can't be helped. And don't either of you call me back!" Then I dropped the receiver firmly onto the cradle.

Rude, Calof! I thought, *you were downright rude. Floyd and Judy will never come in.* But as I analyzed the phone call, I believed I had done the right thing. Judy, when she came on the line, had confirmed my impression of the marriage. Her quick apology and deferential manner made her a perfect target for Floyd's insensitive controlling. For the marriage to work, she would need a strengthened sense of self and power.

It was to that end that I gave her the stern directive. By ordering her to "get him here by 11:00 A.M. sharp" I had placed her in a double bind. To please me (as well as her friend), she'd have to get her husband in my door. But to do that, she'd have to act assertive, behavior that would be uncomfortable. Would she rise to the challenge? I didn't know. How would Floyd react if she did? I didn't know that either. But if the dynamic in their marriage was going to change, it was a step that had to be taken.

My directive to Judy had also contained a second, hidden, challenge. By warning her that lateness would indicate the couple "couldn't be helped," I had given Judy an indirect suggestion. I'd implied the statement's very opposite: that by arriving on time, they would tell me they *could* be helped, that they were ready to make a change.

Driving home that evening, the car radio tuned to the news, I let images of Floyd and Judy drift through my mind. My images, like their backgrounds, were military. I pictured Floyd and Judy at war, with different types of armies, different types of weapons massed at their sides: Floyd commanded tanks and cannons, Judy wiry guerrillas wielding bows and arrows. As their war raged in the back of my mind, I realized that their grossly mismatched forces held each other at bay, for what Judy's soldiers lacked in strength, they more than made up for in speed, deception, and knowledge of the terrain. If war was the image, I decided, it would also be my intervention, and I constructed a parable to tell them the following day.

Parables can be a powerful way to speak to the unconscious, for they evoke the child in us, the part of us that "lost ourselves" in stories when we were young and that can still readily access our inner mind. And by tantalizing the conscious mind with plot twists and details, they enable deeper, more metaphorical messages to penetrate the unconscious. They also disarm our conscious resistance: we can listen to a story, take it in, while believing that it is not about us. Floyd and Judy, with their chosen military careers, would be particularly receptive to stories, for they were used to listening, used to taking orders, used to playing "children" in the military family. I had no assurance that they would actually show up, but if they did, I now had a strategy that I hoped might lead to détente.

Much to my pleasure and surprise, I found Floyd and Judy pacing my waiting room the next morning (a Saturday) at 10:45.

"So you've decided you can be helped." I greeted them without smiling, and because I still needed to pace their belief that the marriage and the therapy were doomed, I added, "Even if the marriage can't." Then, before they had a chance to respond, I executed a crisp military turn on my heel and strode into my office, gesturing for them to follow.

Floyd sat down immediately in the large recliner. Judy, following behind, sat gingerly on the adjacent upright chair. Suddenly I had an impulse.

"Would you mind sitting over there?" I said to Floyd, pointing to a chair several feet away.

He looked confused, but complied.

"And Judy, would you mind sitting here?" I indicated the chair in which Floyd had been sitting.

She glanced at Floyd but did as I asked.

I looked from one to the next, then frowned as if this arrangement, too, were unsatisfactory. "Floyd, would you take that chair, please?" I pointed to a chair in the corner. "And Judy, I'd like you in this one." I indicated *my* chair and then moved to the one Floyd had originally occupied.

"Good," I said, after they'd rearranged themselves. "Now, if you'll take a few minutes to fill out these forms. . ." And while they scratched out their answers I asked them to switch chairs one more time so that each now sat in the chair the other had originally claimed. In this way I began my intervention.

Floyd's commandeering of the largest chair had reminded me how in control he needed to feel. The initial chair switch was a way to defuse that—to replace his control with mine, and to put Judy in his appointed seat of power. But once they had switched I realized I could profitably continue that gambit. By asking them to switch again and then again, I reminded them that I was the authority who issued orders and conditioned them to follow my directives; and I made it clear that I was different from any therapist they had already seen. In fact, the longer the switching went on, the more I built their expectation that something *unusual* would happen. Putting them in each other's seat was also a way of helping them metaphorically to see from the other's perspective—an ability critically lacking in their marriage. This symbolism was no doubt lost on their conscious minds, but might have been transparent to their unconscious.

"Judy, I understand from our phone conversation yesterday that you and Floyd often fight. Do you have any ideas about what causes the tension between you?"

Floyd rolled his eyes. "You name it," he grumbled. "Money, who folds the laundry, I don't call her parents enough . . ." His tone was mincing, mimicking Judy's inflection.

"I addressed my question to Judy," I stated flatly, then turned deliberately toward her.

Judy shifted in her chair, first uncrossing then recrossing her legs. "Well," she responded, leaning forward, her fingers laced tightly in her lap, "it's not just one thing. It's everything. Everything I do irritates him."

"Everything you do doesn't irritate me."

"Well, just about everything."

"Judy's exaggerating."

"I'm not. You criticize me all the time."

"I criticize you? What do you do to me? I can hardly step foot in my own house without you telling me I've done something wrong. From the minute I get home it's: honey, you put the toilet paper in wrong; honey, you left your clothes on the bed. Jesus, Judy, I'm tired when I come home. I just need to sit and drink a beer and be quiet for a while and you expect . . . I don't know what you expect."

Judy looked chastened. "I just . . ."

Floyd cut her off. "This happens every night. I come home. I'm tired. All I want is a little time to unwind at the end of the day. And the minute I walk in the door she's . . ." He stopped himself. "Look, I don't want to get on her. I know she's been alone all day and she's happy to see me. And I'm happy to see her." He looked at Judy. "I am, babe. I just need some time."

Judy brightened at his admission. Now her voice was sweet and placating, like honey. "I know, honey. I'm sorry I get on you. I know you're tired. It's just that I look forward to your coming home."

Floyd smiled wanly.

I sensed they'd had this conversation many times. "Judy, does it make sense to you that Floyd might need some quiet time when he gets home?"

"Of course," she murmured sympathetically. "He's been working hard all day, especially now that he's out on a beat. I forget, I'm home all day. It's so much less stressful." She turned toward Floyd. "I'll try to leave you alone for a while, honey."

"That's what she says," spat Floyd irritably. "But the next night it's the same thing. It's like we never had the conversation."

Judy's face darkened. "I try to remember," she said sullenly. "Maybe if you got home earlier I wouldn't be so lonely."

Floyd flashed her an angry glance. "Judy, you know we're short on manpower and that as soon as we get new police officers my hours will be cut back. I don't like it any more than you do."

"It's been that way for almost a year."

"I can't help it. We're short three men. I don't like it either. But I have no choice."

"You like working late!"

"Of course I don't like working late!"

"You do! It's more fun to stay there with your buddies than to come home to me."

"Judy! I hate when you do this! You distort everything. You take everything personally."

"Well, it is personal. I'm your wife and I want to spend time with you." Her voice quivered.

"When you do this you *make* me want to stay late! Do you realize that? You *make* me want to stay away. You're pushing me away!"

Judy began to sob. "You see?" she blubbered. "This is what happens. This is what always happens."

And I could see why. This latest barrage had given me another clue about their pattern of communication. Not only were Floyd and Judy conducting a war of wills, they were locked in a campaign of deafness and retaliation: each side felt *unheard* by the other. In revenge they launched spiteful retaliatory salvos. Judy had told Floyd that she *needed* his attention, and when he didn't acknowledge her feelings she made barbed accusations. Floyd had told Judy that he *needed* time alone; when she merely paid lip service to his feelings, he grew angry and pushed her away.

Their lack of empathy was striking; they would need far more than a chair switch to help them see things through each other's eyes. In the past I'd used role-play to help partners appreciate each other's point of view. . . . I decided to suggest a role-play for session number two.

Meanwhile, I handed Judy a box of tissues and waited for her to regain her composure. Then, adopting my authoritative manner, I looked each of them sternly in the eye. "I've had a chance to observe your marriage, both here and on the telephone, and I am not at all sure it can succeed. But since you have taken up my time I am willing to work with you at least once.

"You have chosen me because I am unorthodox. You have heard that I use hypnosis. You'd like me to 'zap' you—but you're not sure what that means. And you," I looked at Floyd, "are not sure you have the courage to go first." Floyd immediately lowered his eyes, as if my challenge had raised a similar doubt in him.

"Now what you will do is to sit there silently for five minutes without looking at each other. During those minutes you will consider what you want for yourselves, what you want from me, and just how frightened you are of hypnosis and change." I then folded my arms and waited for them to obey my instructions.

Without a word, they did. Floyd cleared his throat and made a production of settling himself in his chair. Judy uncrossed her legs and folded her hands in her lap. Then both slowly turned themselves over to the process of thinking. As one minute crept toward two their bodies relaxed noticeably. As three minutes became four, and then five, both developed signs of a light trance. Their eyes turned glassy and unfocused, their bodies grew still; they seemed to be looking inward.

I was encouraged by this response. The fact that they had each gone into trance without a formal induction was a sign that they would be good hypnotic subjects.

"OK," I said when the time had expired. "Floyd, what have you decided?"

Floyd and Judy both shook themselves slightly and refocused their eyes on me. Floyd sat up stiffly in his chair.

"I want to know what you did to Judy on the phone last night," he demanded.

"What do you mean?"

"I mean she was a different person when she got off. She told me I had to come here with her today no matter what and I've never seen her like that before." The corners of his mouth eased into a reluctant grin. "It must have been some powerful medicine."

So it worked, I thought, and Floyd was pleased.

"I don't know what came over me after our conversation last night," said Judy. "I suddenly felt hopeful, and I haven't felt that way in months. So I knew Floyd had to come here with me." She eyed him coquettishly. "And he did."

"Do you want to pursue therapy?"

She nodded.

"Have you ever been hypnotized before?"

She shook her head, then giggled. "But I know I'll be good at hypnosis. I think I'll go out like a light."

"Floyd?"

"I got hypnotized once before, in the military, when I had some dental work done. It worked pretty good." He chuckled. "And I'll be damned if I thought it was going to."

"Do you remember anything about it?"

"Nah. Soon as it was over it was like it never happened." He paused as if thinking back. "But I was just a kid then. I don't know if that stuff would work for me now."

I resisted pointing out that Floyd had just put himself in a trance with no effort at all.

"Well good," I declared. "You have both expressed a desire for hypnotic treatment. Now all that remains is for you to decide which of you will go into a trance first and which will go into a trance watching the other." Contained in my apparent choice was the embedded suggestion that both would go into a trance.

Neither responded to my words, but almost immediately both developed eye flutters and sagged slightly in their chairs. I then used a standard relaxation induction with Judy, interspersed with frequent directives to Floyd to recall his earlier hypnotic experience, and after fifteen or twenty minutes both had achieved a moderate trance. At that point I began my parable.

"On an island in the Pacific were two small nations with a long history of war. Now, one of these countries seemed far

more powerful than the other. It was larger, it had access to more natural resources, it had more powerful weapons. Yet it was unable to overpower its neighbor. For despite the neighbor's smallness, it had remarkable power and prowess. Its tiny army was highly trained; it was quicker and more agile than the large army of its opponent; and with fewer weapons it had developed more stealthy ways of fighting. So the two armies, while seeming so ill-matched, were deadlocked year after year.

"Meanwhile, the war was exacting a terrible toll. Both countries were impoverished, weakened, and demoralized. Both yearned for peace, but peace was elusive, for each side refused to capitulate, believing itself correct.

"As conditions worsened, both countries longed for a resolution. Commentators theorized about the benefits of peaceful coexistence: mutual defense, free trade and travel, cultural exchange. Families talked about making a world that would be safe and hospitable to children. As these alternative visions of the future were promoted, pressure grew within each country to seek a negotiated solution. And finally, after years of warfare, officials at the highest level within each government agreed to meet. The meetings were held in secret, lest the other side interpret the effort as a sign of weakness.

"However, news of one government's secret meetings leaked to a member of the press. Realizing what powerful information he held, the reporter didn't relay it to his paper. Instead he went to a colleague on the other side, who reported that in his nation similar meetings were under way. Over the next few days the reporters spoke surreptitiously with friends in government and, as they ferried messages back and forth, an agreement was negotiated.

"The two governments agreed that on the stroke of noon on a given day, a cease-fire would take place and the prime ministers of both nations would step onto a platform that straddled the border and sign their names to a truce. At the moment of the signing, military bands would begin to play and the flags of both countries would be raised over the two national capitols.

"The truce came about as planned. At twelve o'clock precisely the last shots were fired, and a flourish of trumpets from each side announced the cease-fire. The two prime ministers stepped onto their platform. Following the signing, they made gracious speeches, thanking their former enemy for its willing-

ness to negotiate. 'By working together in peace we can draw on each other's strengths and offset each other's weaknesses,' the prime ministers proclaimed. 'We were each strong in war. Together in peace we will be stronger.' After the speeches, the two prime ministers embraced."

Throughout the story, Floyd and Judy had stared at me in rapt attention. Now they remained fixed in their seats as if waiting for a sequel. Their involvement gave me an idea. Since they were such good hypnotic subjects, why not do the role-play next session under hypnosis? I had never done hypnotic role-play, but if it were effective in the waking state, wouldn't it be more so in a trance? Each person would have access to his unconscious knowledge of the other: to shared memories not consciously remembered, to words spoken but long forgotten, to intuitive understandings built on years together. Research has shown that we constantly give each other tiny clues as to how we're feeling—a minute widening of the pupils, a subtle change in breathing, a microscopic flinch. These clues are so involuntary that we don't know we're giving them, and so subtle that conscious perception doesn't pick them up. But they register in another person's unconscious mind. Perhaps that's what accounts for the tendency of long-married people to "read each other's minds." Unconsciously we know each other far better than we realize. Why not tap that reservoir to help this marriage?

I looked deeply into Floyd's and Judy's eyes. "In our next session," I said, "I will ask you to undertake a very important mission. This mission will play a major role in determining your individual futures as well as the future of your son. It will require your full cooperation. Because of the grave importance of this mission I will brief you about it ahead of time, and in the next two weeks you will work diligently to prepare for it but without being consciously aware that you are doing so." Judy and Floyd had already demonstrated that they were able to make progress on their own: their behavior after our initial phone call had told me they were unconsciously ready to "work." So I had reason to believe that they could accomplish a lot in the next two weeks. By keeping the knowledge out of consciousness I gave their unconscious minds room to work unimpeded.

"You will return here in two weeks at the same hour you came today. At that time you will be placed in a deep trance. Your conscious minds will not be curious about what is to happen and will be dismissed. When I give the signal, Judy will become Floyd and Floyd will become Judy. You will think, act, feel, and believe as if you are the other person. The exchange of identities will be so complete that during it you will not remember ever having been yourself. In this altered state you will draw upon a decade's worth of experience with each other to reason out and, if necessary, battle out, the kind of future you will have together. On every point of contention you will arrive at mutual agreement. You will then be restored to your natural selves and awakened from your trances."

Floyd and Judy looked at me intently as if waiting for further instructions.

"Do you understand your mission?"

They nodded.

"Good. Over the next two weeks you will begin to notice changes in each other. You will not be sure what those changes are, but you will have a sense of change and possibility and hope. As the weeks go by you will find yourselves feeling more relaxed and less anxious about your problems.

"Now I am going to wake you up. There is no need for you to have to remember what has happened in this trance. Everything that is important will be stored in your unconscious. You will resume your earlier conversation as if this trance had never occurred." I then counted from five to one, which woke them up. The count also served as an indirect suggestion to them to go back into trance the next time they heard me count from one to five.

The pair awakened slowly, looked around the room, blinked, and shook their heads.

"Now, what were we talking about?" I asked confusedly, as if I had innocently lost track of the conversation.

Immediately Judy started in. "You see?" she whined. "There's no point. Everything we say ends up in a fight and we wind up threatening to leave each other. We might as well just leave."

"If you didn't take everything so personally," Floyd whined back.

"I do take it personally, Floyd. I'm your wife. I want to be with you. I hardly ever get to see you. And now with your late hours . . ."

It was as if the intervening forty-five minutes had never taken place.

"I'm sorry to have to stop you," I interrupted, "but our time is up for today."

They both looked at me as if they had forgotten I was there.

"I'm sorry I wasn't more help this time. But I think we've set a good foundation. Why don't I see you again in, say, two weeks?"

Floyd scowled but nodded and we scheduled an appointment—for the same time two weeks later.

"It's important that between now and our next appointment you not talk about this session," I warned as they headed toward the door. "And don't call me for any reason." I wanted to minimize opportunities for them to think consciously about what had happened or to argue with me about the therapy. I wanted the suggestions from this session to "cook."

Floyd shrugged at my words as if to say, "If you say so," then grabbed the door and held it open for Judy. Her eyes widened in surprise at his gesture.

"He sure didn't do much. Are you sure he's any good?" I heard him say as the door closed behind them.

"Oh," Judy lamented, "you know, they're all alike."

Two weeks later at 10:45 I heard them open the door to my waiting room. At 11:00 when I went out to greet them, they were sitting side by side on the couch. Floyd immediately stood up and offered his hand to Judy. She smiled as he pulled her up.

"Well let's get on with it," I directed. "If I'm going to fail I want to do it quickly, but I might not because you don't know yet what to make of me." I was still pacing their belief that the marriage and therapy would fail, while inserting an element of doubt. I then ushered them into my office, showing each to the chair last occupied by the other.

As they sat down I noticed that both appeared more relaxed and composed than they had the previous session. Judy's eyes, which had been swollen and bloodshot, were clear, and the dark circles under Floyd's eyes were gone. Both seemed more jovial and talkative.

"Judy, tell me about the last two weeks," I prompted. "How have things been between you?"

Judy smiled pertly. "I've been feeling quite cheerful, actually. I don't know why. Everything has just seemed . . . lighter." She looked at me eagerly, as if expecting a grade.

"You feel better but you don't know why?"

"Oh, well, I think there are a lot of things. The weather has been beautiful . . . and Ryan is doing well in school . . ."

"How are things between you?"

"Oh." She chirped as if my question had caught her off guard. "I think things are a little better." She looked at Floyd for confirmation and he agreed.

"I think we're both being a little more cooperative?" She sounded as if she were testing the idea. "Floyd's been a lot more helpful around the house. He's done the dishes every night without my asking, and . . . ," she looked at him coyly, "he even cooked dinner once."

Floyd wagged his head and raised his palms as if to deflect the praise. "Just grilled some steaks was all."

"And Floyd, how have things been for you?"

"I've been feeling pretty good," he acknowledged. "Things at the station are good. I've been sleeping well."

"And things between you?"

He moved his jaw from side to side and drummed his fingers on the chair arms. "I'd say we've been off each other's backs more."

"Less tension between you?"

He nodded.

"What stayed with you from our last session?"

"Hey, how long were we here anyway? We thought it was only about half an hour but when we got out and looked at our watches we saw we'd been here an hour and a half. It was like we lost an hour or something." He frowned as if disturbed by the idea that time had escaped him unnoticed.

"Yes, well, it's better to lose some things unexpectedly," I remarked casually, "but what else? What else do you have to tell me about yourselves?" My allusion to unexpected loss was meant as an unconscious signal: I hoped they would each lose some more things unexpectedly, namely behaviors and attitudes that were counterproductive in their marriage.

Both were quiet for a few moments, then Judy spoke. "You know, we've had these periods before when we get along well for a while. It's like the stars are in the right place or something." She laughed. "But then," she threw up her hands, "it just kind of falls apart."

"Falls apart?"

"Yeah." She looked forlorn. "I mean, we're really pretty different, I guess, and I don't know, we've tried so hard, but I just don't know if we can change. . . . I mean, we've tried so many times before, and every time things get better for a while but then they fall apart again. I just think . . . it's probably too late." Tears welled up in her eyes.

"It sounds like things feel better now, but you're not sure you should trust it."

She nodded and sniffed.

"Well, you feel like you still have your same old problems and neither of you knows if this will work, so let's get it over with once and for all."

Judy nodded again and wiped her eyes. By echoing her words I'd made her feel understood. I'd also dropped in a suggestion. "Let's get it over with once and for all" could be heard as a deathknell—"Let's pull the curtain on this sorry marriage"—or it could be a spur to change: "Let's resolve your differences once and for all." I hoped this ambiguity would pace their doubts about the marriage improving, while also raising their belief that it might succeed.

Floyd and Judy glanced at each other uncomfortably, then turned back to me. I looked each of them in the eye, slowed and lowered my voice to the cadence of trance induction, told them to listen closely to what I was about to say, then counted slowly from one to five. As I began this reinduction signal their eyes fluttered, and by the time I'd uttered five both were in a light trance. I used deepening suggestions to deepen their trances considerably and then told them they would be in hypnotic rapport with me and me alone: although they were sitting next to each other they would be unaware of the other's presence.

"Judy," I began, "last time we met I described the mission you would undertake. You have had two weeks to consider it. If you are ready to proceed as we discussed, then just let your head nod to indicate that."

Judy's head gave a slight nod.

"Good. Now you will discover that you can speak, and even the sound of your own voice will carry you deeper into trance." Clients new to hypnotherapy don't automatically know that they can speak in trance; I often have to tell them they can do so. I gave Judy a moment to deepen her trance, then asked her a question. "Do you wish to repair your marriage?"

"Yes." Her voice was quiet and sober. In a deep trance no energy is wasted on extra words or motions. The client is often virtually immobile, and even voice inflections are restrained.

"Is there any part of you that has any questions it would like to bring to my attention?"

After a long pause, she murmured flatly, "No."

"Okay." I then repeated my questions and statements to Floyd, whose answers were similar until I asked if he had any questions.

"How will I be able to find myself again?" he wondered.

I realized that I had neglected to explain how they would assume their own identities after the exchange.

"Would it be all right for you to find only those qualities you *want* in yourself, and perhaps lose some of the ones you don't want?"

Floyd thought for a moment. "Can I change my mind later?"

"Of course you can. Both you and Judy," I faced her slightly to signal her to listen, "can choose to change your minds about any number of things." Then, turning back to Floyd to remove Judy from hypnotic earshot, I continued. "Floyd, would you feel reassured if I gave you something as a reminder of who you are, something that can guide you should you ever wish for your old self again?"

Slowly he nodded.

"Okay. I'm going to hand you a piece of paper and on that paper I want you to write your full name, your social security number, your telephone number, your driver's license number, your mother's and father's names, and your birth date. You will be able to open your eyes to complete this assignment, and when you close them again you will go even deeper into trance."

Floyd opened his eyes and reached slowly for the paper. With the studiousness of a first grader, he did as I asked. Then I asked him to study the paper while I talked. "This piece of paper will be a powerful reminder to you, Floyd, of your present identity and ways of living in the world. In a moment I will ask you to fold it and tuck it in your shirt pocket behind your cigarettes. If at any time in the future you wish to resume your present identity, or if you need to be reminded of that identity for any reason, or if your unconscious mind thinks it would be desirable, you will be able to merely read that piece of paper."

Dutifully Floyd creased the paper and placed it in his shirt pocket. Then he closed his eyes. Apparently his concern was allayed and he was ready to go on.

"Now Judy, over the next few minutes you will feel yourself becoming Floyd. You will begin to think, act, and feel like Floyd. You will have Floyd's feelings, thoughts, beliefs, and sensations, and while you are being Floyd you will forget your own feelings, thoughts, beliefs, and sensations. You will *believe* yourself to be Floyd, and when you look at yourself you will see Floyd. You will have Floyd's memories, although you will have only those memories that are useful and appropriate to this mission. When you return again to yourself, you will bring back with you the wisdom and deep learnings you have made.

"While you do this, Floyd will be in the process of becoming you. Once you are Floyd and you open your eyes, you will see Judy sitting in the other chair. Do you understand?"

Judy nodded, and I made similar statements to Floyd. When he, too, had nodded I addressed them both. "You will now have five minutes of clock time to prepare for your assignment, but to your inner minds it will seem like all the time in the world. After five minutes I will ask you to stand up and switch chairs, and when you each sit in the other's chair you will go even deeper into trance and will fully become the other. You will discuss and perhaps argue over your disagreements and misunderstandings, and you will find common ground so that you can grow together. You will feel fully awake, and you will be aware of me in the background making sure you are safe and that things go well. And if you need help for any reason you will be able to ask me at any time."

For the next five minutes I watched them closely. As their trances deepened their bodies slumped, heavy with relaxation. Although their eyes darted behind their closed lids, their faces remained expressionless and still. Their outward serenity gave no clue as to what was happening inside. Finally I asked them to open their eyes, switch chairs, and notice each other.

What followed was remarkable. Judy rose heavily from her chair as if she suddenly carried a hundred pounds of additional weight. She lumbered to the neighboring chair and dropped heavily into it. On her normally smooth forehead, faint lines and wrinkles appeared. Floyd meanwhile sat down gracefully in Judy's former chair, crossing his ankles and folding his hands tightly in his lap. His usually tightly pursed lips now parted slightly in a manner that was unmistakably Judy's.

No sooner had they taken their seats and eyed each other when a muted fracas began.

"Everything I do irritates you," stated the new "Judy." The voice was lower in pitch than Judy's and had the monotoned restraint of deep trance, but nevertheless captured Judy's whining intonation.

"Everything you do doesn't irritate me," "Floyd" rebutted. This voice, too, while closer in timbre to Judy's and flattened by trance, managed to contain Floyd's frequent impatience.

"That's how it feels to me. You criticize me all the time."

"I criticize you? What do you think you do to me? I can hardly step foot in my own house without you telling me I've done something wrong. From the minute I get home it's: honey, you put the toilet paper in wrong; honey, you left your clothes on the bed. Jesus, Judy, I'm tired when I come home. I just need to sit and drink a beer and be quiet for a while and you expect . . . I don't know what you expect."

It was virtually verbatim the argument they had had during our first session! It lacked the cadence of their original speech—subdued by trance they seemed to be reading numbly from a script—but the words and the feelings behind them were the same.

This gave me an idea. By joining Floyd and Judy in their pre-trance world, I could strengthen their hypnotic reality; by once again playing the brusque commander I could reinforce their belief that Floyd was Judy and Judy, Floyd. So sloughing off the supportive demeanor I had adopted while inducing their trances, I cut the argument off. "Look folks, you've peddled this stuff to three other therapists. It didn't work there and it won't work here. So get on with it. Do you need my help?"

They stared at me in silence.

"All right, I see you do." I looked at Judy. "Floyd, you were complaining that Judy doesn't leave you alone when you get home. Can you tell her what it is you need?"

Judy, playing Floyd, looked at me glazedly. "Yes," she said. Then with the mechanical movements of trance she turned slowly and stiffly toward her husband. "You're on my back the minute I walk in the door. You don't give me time to unwind."

"I'm home alone all day," rebutted Floyd, playing Judy. He spoke slowly and deliberately without turning toward his wife, but his mouth had the finest traces of a pout. "I miss you. I want to see you when you come home."

"You see me all evening. I just need . . ."

"Hold it," I interrupted. "Do you hear what Judy is saying? Can you hear what she's asking you for?"

Judy turned slowly back toward me. Her voice carried the sting of Floyd's. "She's asking me to pay attention. I just need . . ."

"We'll talk about what you need later. Right now we're talking about what Judy needs."

Judy skipped a breath.

I turned toward Floyd. "Judy, can you try to explain to Floyd how you feel, and what you need from him when he comes home?"

Floyd sat straight in his chair, hands clasped like a woman's, ankles pressed tightly together. His lower lip protruded slightly. "Time with him," he said flatly.

"Is it *time* you want? Or something else?"

He thought for a moment. "Something else."

"Can you tell Floyd what that is?"

Floyd's fingers, laced together, twitched. "I want him to show me he loves me."

"Can you say that to him?"

He hesitated for a second, then slowly, as if pushing against a current, turned his head toward Judy. In Judy's voice he said, "I want you to show me you love me."

Judy's hands lifted slowly in a muted gesture of frustration. "Judy, I tell you every night I love you. First thing when I come home I hug you and kiss you and tell you I love you. What more do you want?"

Tautly, Floyd drew his trousered ankles up and crossed them neatly underneath his chair. "You just say it. It's a routine."

Frustrated, Judy raised her hands again. "You know I love you, Judy. I'm tired when I get home. I can't make speeches."

"I don't want speeches, Floyd. I want . . ." Floyd's fingers briefly fanned the air. "I want you to *see* me. I want to feel *important* to you." His voice wobbled to a halt and the plea hung in the air.

Softer now, wanting to support them rather than challenge, I turned to Judy. "Floyd, Judy just spoke to you from her heart. Can you feel what she said? Can you hear her feelings, not her words?"

Only a slight narrowing of Judy's eyes indicated she had heard me. She stared at a spot on the floor halfway between my desk and her chair, and as her husband so often did, sawed her jaw from side to side. Ten, then twenty seconds passed. I was about to rephrase the question when she spoke. "She's saying she wants me to show her I love her." The words were halting, like a tourist wrestling unfamiliar phrases from a guidebook.

"Can you say more?"

With Floyd's tenacity she worked her jaw, staring at the floor. "She's afraid I'm going to stop loving her. . . . She needs to know I won't. . . ." Because of the monotone it was hard to know if she was finished; any closing inflection was missing. But a moment later she continued. "I won't stop loving her. That's what she needs to know."

I looked at Floyd, playing Judy. "Is that right?"

He nodded.

"Is it time you want when Floyd comes home, or just that reassurance?"

"Just the reassurance." Floyd's voice was softer, more vulnerable than I had ever heard it.

I turned back to Judy. "Floyd, do you think you can give Judy that reassurance when you come home?"

For a second Judy's jaw resumed its sawing. Then carefully she nodded.

I smiled.

"Now, Judy," I looked intently at Floyd, "did you hear what Floyd was saying to *you*? What he was telling you *he* needs?"

Floyd's hands curled tightly in his lap. "He wants time alone," he said.

"That seems hard for you."

In the style of Judy, his lips pursed ever so slightly.

"Is that hard for you?"

"I want him to want to be with me."

"You feel hurt that he wants to be alone?"

He nodded, lower lip thrust out in Judy's pout.

"Floyd, can you look at Judy and explain to her how you feel?"

Judy, playing Floyd, slowly turned her body so it faced her husband's. "I *want* to be with you, Judy. I just need time alone first."

Floyd looked straight ahead.

Judy tried again. "Judy, you know what my work is like. When I get home I'm beat."

Still Floyd gave no indication that he'd heard, so Judy turned back to me. I nodded for her to go on. "Just for a few minutes, babe. It would help if you could understand."

Something in her tone must have touched him, for Floyd turned stiffly toward his wife. His eyes met hers and for twenty seconds they held each other's glance. Gradually Floyd's face, which in that moment almost looked like Judy's, softened.

"Judy," I said, looking directly at him, "can you get a sense of how Floyd feels at the end of the day?"

Almost sheepishly he nodded.

"I'm just tired, Judy," Judy said. "But you gotta know I love you."

Floyd's lips parted in an awkward, involuntary smile.

"How much time do you think you need, Floyd?" I asked.

"Twenty minutes." The speed of Judy's answer suggested that in preparing for the part she'd already thought this through.

"Judy, if Floyd gives you the reassurance you need when he comes home, do you think you can give him twenty minutes to himself?"

Floyd, playing Judy, turned his upper body back toward me and nodded.

"Well, it sounds like you've reached an agreement. Is there anything either of you would like to add?" I looked first at Judy-playing-Floyd, who shook her head, then at Floyd-playing-Judy.

"I thought he didn't want to be with me," Floyd said, a note of wonder in his voice.

"I *want* to be with you," said Judy. "I'm tired, babe, but I love you."

I was touched by this exchange. Despite the restraint imposed by the hypnosis, it was clear that Judy, played by Floyd, had made a heartfelt admission and that Floyd, played by Judy, had heard it in a way the real Floyd never had. But time was short and their list of grievances was long, so after a period of silence I moved them on.

"On the phone you told me you fight over Ryan," I said.

Immediately both swallowed, a sign the subject was painful.

"Kids need to know the rules," said Judy. Her fingers massaged the arms of the chair just as Floyd's had earlier.

"Do you disagree about that?"

"Judy believes in rules. We just have different approaches."

"What's Judy's approach?"

"She says, 'Please stop doing that, Ryan. Mommy wants you to stop.'" As Floyd imitating herself, Judy adopted a high-pitched whine. "Now, what kid's gonna listen to that? You gotta show him who's boss. Wallop his bottom. Make him pay attention."

It was a telltale answer. Subjects in deep trance generally keep their words to a minimum. Judy's long and inflected response suggested she had heard Floyd utter those phrases many times.

"Judy?" I asked, turning now toward Floyd.

"I won't hit him. I don't think it's right."

"Why not?"

"There are better ways to do it." Floyd laced his fingers in Judy's nervous gesture.

"How?"

"You can talk things over. He's bright. He understands."

Suddenly Judy-playing-Floyd cut in. "He understands a spanking, that's what he understands." Her hand twitched as she talked, as if reflecting Floyd's vehemence on the issue.

I looked at Judy, surprised by her interruption, but Floyd's voice, cool and even, drew my attention back to him. "Floyd's afraid his son will be a wimp."

"My son will not be a wimp."

"That's what you're afraid of."

"My father walloped me when I did wrong. That's what I do to my son."

"Why do you think Floyd is worried his son will be a wimp?" I asked. Floyd's pronouncement, made as Judy, warranted probing.

"Because Floyd is soft inside. Outside he's tough but inside there's a little boy, and it makes that little boy feel weak when Ryan isn't strong." Floyd looked me in the eye as he spoke, then lowered his eyes with Judy's characteristic deference.

"That's hogwash." Judy's voice was sharp, her husband's inflection exactly.

"No it's not," Floyd, playing Judy, stated. "That's why I love you."

Judy blinked and ran her hands along her thighs. I recognized Floyd's gesture.

"Remember when Ryan got in a fight," Floyd continued. "He lost and you were so broken up because it reminded you of *your* first fight? That was so hard on you." Floyd sagged a bit, as if the effort of speaking as his wife had tired him. "You want to make sure Ryan's tougher than you were. You're protecting him."

Judy's face tightened.

"I love you for being strong," continued Floyd, as Judy, "but I also love that little boy. Sometimes more than you do."

Judy swallowed. Ten, twenty, thirty seconds passed.

"Floyd?" I asked her.

Her jaw, set squarely like her husband's, twitched from side to side.

"Is there a part of you that agrees with Judy's words?"

Judy looked away, then looked me in the eye. Then very slowly, almost imperceptibly, she nodded.

I felt a flush of validation. In the second that her eyes had captured mine, I'd seen a second set of eyes, the real Judy's eyes, behind the eyes that were playing Floyd. And those eyes had telegraphed a message so clear it was almost startling. *We're getting somewhere!* they'd said, *he's never admitted his fear before.*

"Judy," I said turning now to Floyd, "why do you hate it when Floyd spanks Ryan?"

"I don't believe in spanking," Floyd returned. Despite their trancy slowness, his words had an uncomfortable urgency.

"Why not?"

"I don't think it's right."

"What's wrong about it?"

"I don't want to have to do it." Floyd touched his hair in a nervous woman's gesture.

"Why is that?"

He paused. "It isn't right for a mother to hit her child."

"What would happen if you did?"

His thick fingers slowly laced together.

I watched him, waiting for an answer, but instead Judy's voice, mimicking Floyd's, answered mine.

"It's for the same reason she can't say no to him."

I turned to Judy who was sitting straight-backed in her chair, staring straight ahead.

"And why is that?"

"She just wants things to be good between them."

I looked back at Floyd-playing-Judy. "Is it uncomfortable to have Ryan be angry at you?"

"I don't want to alienate him is all. You know how it is. Kids grow up and rebel and then they move away and you never see them again."

"Ryan is only eight years old," said Judy. Even trance couldn't mask Floyd's impatience in her words.

"But he gets so angry sometimes, Floyd. I don't think he gets that way with you but he does with me. He gives me that look, that evil eye—just like my father does—and it makes me feel so . . . so awful. You don't understand this, Floyd, because you're so big and strong, you never feel this way, but I'm so little. I'm like a mouse. You all can step on me . . . and all I can do is squeak."

Floyd's words, spoken as Judy, must have stirred his wife, because she turned to face him. Her eyes met his and caught, and for the longest time peered fixedly into them. Her face was largely immobilized by trance but the eyes were vivid, and even from six feet away I could see the expression in them. It wasn't impatience, or irritation. It was curiosity, a surprised, uncertain questioning, as if Floyd, played by Judy, had suddenly blinked and found a different woman sitting in the adjacent chair.

Floyd, as Judy, silently received the gaze. His eyes were wide and clear, seeming to both answer and absorb his partner's curiosity.

As they held each other's glance, energy, like an elastic band, stretched taut between them.

But as the moment pressed on, the two figures remained expectantly inert. Glances locked, neither moved to extend or alter the contact. I realized they couldn't: the trance had muted their ability to initiate an action toward each other. So, quietly, I cleared my throat. Both turned reluctantly toward me and as they did I nodded—a small gesture, but just enough to let them know that they were free to act. Judy, playing Floyd, immediately looked back toward Floyd, then slowly, as if reaching out to a frightened child, leaned forward and touched his hand. Floyd, playing Judy, regarded the hand for several seconds, then haltingly brought it to his lips.

For the next few moments it was quiet in the room and I replayed the conversation in my mind. They hadn't reached a compromise on discipline, but they had shown remarkable insight into each other's behavior. Floyd's understanding, stated as Judy, that Floyd was threatened by weakness in Ryan was quite sophisticated, as was Judy's realization, spoken as Floyd, that Judy feared angering her son. How had their unconscious sleuthing produced such insight?

I knew it wasn't because they had developed uncanny intuition: it was because they were talking about *themselves*. When Floyd-as-Judy claimed that Floyd was protecting himself through Ryan, it wasn't really Judy talking—it was Floyd revealing himself. When Judy-as-Floyd charged that Judy was afraid to anger Ryan, it wasn't Floyd interpreting Judy—it was Judy describing herself. Just as they had tapped their unconscious understandings of each other, they had tapped unconscious knowledge of themselves, and for the first time thoughts and feelings they couldn't access consciously were coloring their conversation.

"Well," I said finally, signaling an end to the moment.

They released each other's hands.

If I stuck to the mission's ground rules, I would need to urge Floyd and Judy toward a compromise on discipline. But given the honesty and empathy they had demonstrated—and the large number of issues still to tackle—I decided they could continue to move toward compromise on their own.

"You are still far apart on discipline, but I wonder if, with your new understanding of each other, you could go home and talk about this some more. Perhaps after a few more conversations you might come to some agreement. Do you think that's possible?"

Without looking at each other, Floyd and Judy nodded.

"Good," I smiled. "Let's move to another issue."

Over the next forty-five minutes Floyd and Judy talked through other problem areas in their marriage, including money, in-laws, household chores, and table etiquette. These areas were considerably easier than the discipline issue, and they were able to arrive at compromise positions. Midway through I gave each a pad of paper and asked them to note their agreements as they reached them. When they had finished I asked them to combine their notes into one mutually acceptable list with both having a hand in the actual printing. Remarkably, their notes were quite similar and the redraft took only a matter of minutes.

When they were finished I said, "In a moment you will return to your original chairs. As you do so you will become yourselves again, still deep in trance, and you will bring back with you the wisdom you have found today and in the preceding weeks. The new possibilities that took root here today will grow into a powerful blueprint for your growth both as individuals and as a couple over a lifetime of mutual discovery. And you will begin that process *now*."

Judy and Floyd stood and moved toward their original chairs. Out of hypnotic rapport now that they were returning to their own identities, they passed each other blindly. In the singular logic of trance, one is able to hold two contradictory ideas at the same time without being bothered by the contradiction. Hence, Floyd and Judy were able to avoid colliding in the narrow space yet not acknowledge the other's presence because in their hypnotic reality the other wasn't there.

When they were seated again I deepened their trances and reminded them that they had returned to their true identities. "Now that you have had the opportunity to see the world differently," I continued, "you can never again be blind, deaf, or unfeeling toward the other. In the days and weeks, months, and years to come, you will appreciate the differences as well as the deep similarities between you. You will discover that there is much to learn from each other and from within yourselves. This process of growth will become more powerful each and every day.

"In a moment I will awaken you. Upon awakening, you will experience emotions of many kinds. Then you will review the agreements you have made and, if you desire, change them in mutually acceptable ways. Once you leave here you will abide by them.

"Some time over the next several weeks you will find yourselves together at a bookstore purchasing a book on self-hypnosis. You will probably enjoy learning and practicing self-hypnosis together and may find it useful for helping you solve other problems in your lives.

"Now, if you will hand me your list of agreements, I will wake you up."

Judy handed me the sheet of paper on which they had jointly written their agreements, and I placed it on the floor midway between them. Then I awakened them.

At first, they seemed unaware of each other's presence. Floyd yawned loudly and stretched as if after a nap; Judy peered curiously around the room as if trying to remember where she was. But moments later their eyes met and for nearly ten seconds they simply stared at each other in silence. Finally Floyd broke the spell.

"Aw, hell!" he said and grinned broadly.

Judy instantly began to laugh and cry at once. Then both jumped out of their chairs and gave each other a prolonged hug, literally standing on the document they had created.

After several moments I interrupted. "Hey folks, isn't there some work you need to finish?"

Both looked at me, confused. Then Floyd followed my pointing finger, saw the piece of paper and picked it up. "This?" he asked.

I nodded.

He turned to Judy whose look pleaded, "Do we have to?"

"Tell you what," Floyd suggested. "We're pretty tired right now. We'll make whatever changes we need to at home."

I considered insisting but thought better of it. In a sense, all the work they'd done that day had really been done at home. In the two weeks since our last session they had reflected unconsciously on the mission, preparing their list of problem areas, formulating solutions, probing their own unconscious motives, and using their unconscious knowledge of each other to imagine how the other lived in the world. By the time they appeared in my office the work had already been done. It lacked only a ceremony to cement it. That's why Judy, playing Floyd, was so quick to offer "twenty minutes" as the time Floyd needed when he came home. That's why Floyd, playing Judy, was so ready with an explanation of why he spanked his son.

The conversation I witnessed was merely the recording of their new understandings, the signing of the treaty after the cease-fire. Out of force of habit or perhaps as a way to test their new personas, they had approached the signing warily, edging first into old familiar arguments. But with relatively little prodding from me they had slipped into empathetic negotiation. If they had been able to formulate this "first stage" peace agreement at home, who knew what else they could accomplish? So I nodded my assent.

"Before you go, though," I said, motioning for them to sit down.

Reluctantly they took their seats.

"I have one more question . . ."

As I spoke Floyd reached into his pocket for a cigarette. Along with the pack came the slip of paper he had placed there an hour and a half before.

"What's this?" he muttered, examining it. Then he crumpled it mindlessly into a ball and tossed it in a wastebasket. "Sorry, doc," he apologized, realizing that I had stopped talking to watch him. "I'm always stuffing things into my pockets. Go ahead with what you were saying."

I couldn't help but smile.

"Would both of you agree that if you each honor at least eighty percent of the agreements you've made today you will have failed to make this marriage unsuccessful?" My question was convoluted, but it was a way of honoring their initial belief that the marriage, and the therapy, were bound to fail.

"Why would we want to make this marriage fail?" demanded Judy, galled. "We came here for help."

I held up my hands in a gesture of "I don't know."

"Well, I think you're very wrong to think this marriage might fail. Don't you, Floyd?"

"Of course," Floyd muttered. "I thought we could make it all along, or we wouldn't have put in so much time and money." And he looked at me coolly, as if disturbed that I'd had no faith in him. But behind his look another look was visible, as if his eyes were peering through a mask. *Despite this guff,* the eyes were saying, *I can feel the change, and now I'm having to work hard just to act normal.*

I chuckled inside at the ruse they'd created for themselves. They'd come in committed to the idea that they couldn't change, that the marriage was doomed, that I would be unable to help. But then *unconsciously* they found themselves changing. It would be too uncomfortable to admit *consciously* that they had changed—they'd have to admit that they were wrong, that they'd let someone "in," that they'd been malleable enough to alter—so they'd found an elegant way to accept the change while denying it had occurred: they continued resisting *me!* As long as they were opposing me, as they had when they had arrived, everything felt the same. They could overlook the 180 degree reversal that now had them feeling the marriage would work.

By taking the "failure" position myself, I had used their own oppositional energy to their advantage: I'd made it possible for them to *resist me in the direction of change.* I'd also strengthened their union, for by taking the opposing point of view, I'd given them a chance to band together against me.

I bowed my head as if to apologize. "Well, you've learned some useful skills of negotiation and compromise today," I continued, "and you've reached an agreement about how your relationship will change. But I want you to be realistic. You shouldn't expect these changes to occur all at once, and you should expect to fail from time to time just so you can perfect your practice."

"I don't know why you're so stuck on failure," Judy chided. Beneath her indignation I could sense a smile.

"I'm sorry," I conceded. "Clearly I may be wrong, and I hope you'll prove me wrong in the long haul. But should you ever find yourselves succeeding at failing again, I would be delighted to see you again. But you'll have to wait at least three weeks before calling me."

"No problem there," snorted Floyd and grinned at Judy. "Anything else?"

I shook my head.

"Well, we'll be going then." He stood up even before the words were out of his mouth and offered Judy his hand. As they approached the door he turned back briefly. "Thanks, doc . . . I think," he muttered, then the two of them left my office arm in arm.

Six months later Floyd called.

"Hey, sorry we didn't call sooner," his voice boomed over the telephone. "We meant to call you a while ago, but, you know how it goes." He huffed a little, as if to excuse himself.

"Good to hear from you, Floyd. How are things going?"

"Things are okay. No, things are better than okay, they're good."

"I'm glad to hear that."

"Yeah, in fact, we're both doing . . ." he lowered his voice a notch as if afraid someone would overhear, "we're both doing a little self-hypnosis ourselves. You know, it's pretty good stuff. I've already cut down my smoking to about four or five a day."

"That's great, Floyd! Good for you."

"And, uh, I also wanted to tell you . . ." I had the sense Floyd was reading from a list. "We took a vacation. Just the two of us. Hey, would you believe it was our first vacation in years—since before Ryan. We went to Hawaii. But to tell you the truth . . . ," Floyd chuckled. "We spent a lot of time in the hotel." For the moment his awkwardness had given way to beer-buddy familiarity.

"Well, Floyd, I'm really delighted. How *is* Ryan?"

"Ryan's doing great. You wouldn't believe it. Remember those little episodes we told you about? Well he hasn't had one in months. He's gotten into soccer. I think that's what's done it."

"Really."

"Yeah. In fact," Floyd steamrolled on, ignoring my skeptical response, "we're actually thinking about adopting. You know, we both wanted to have another kid all along, but the marriage just seemed so, so shaky there for a while."

"Floyd, I'm happy for you."

He was silent for a moment as if reviewing his good fortune. "Yeah," he sighed with pleasure, "things are good. You know, we've been wanting to call you for a couple of months, but we both felt—now this is going to sound crazy, don't hold it against me, doc—but we both felt like we left something with you that we didn't want back. And we didn't call because we didn't want to go near it again."

I smiled. Floyd was right. Attitudes, beliefs, behaviors *had* been left behind, but since the process had been unconscious, neither he nor Judy had any conscious idea of what they'd lost. "Floyd," I responded conspiratorially, "I understand exactly what you mean. In fact I understand better than you'll ever know."

Floyd didn't reply, so I made moves to end the call. Suddenly he blurted, "Wait! I haven't actually got to why I called!"

"Oh? What was that?"

"Well," he paused. His awkwardness seemed to have returned. "Judy and I still have a kind of foggy memory of that last session and we were wondering . . ."

"Yes?"

"We were wondering . . ."

He was stuck and I suddenly remembered how to help him

over the hurdle. "Come on, man! Get to the point!" I barked. "There are people who really need my services!"

"Well, what I mean is . . ." he stammered. "Did you work with us sexually? I mean did you do something about our sexual relationship?"

I could feel him sweating at the other end of the phone. "Why do you ask?"

"Well, it's great! I mean, it wasn't that bad before, but now it's fantastic. What did you do?"

I had to chuckle to myself. I had played the commanding hypnotist so thoroughly that they really believed I had "zapped" them. Now, however, it was time to place the credit for their changes where it belonged. "Floyd," I said, "what *I* did is not important. What's important is what *you* did. Now, what is *your* explanation?"

To my surprise Floyd responded immediately. "Well, Judy and I have a theory. It's kind of far out, but they're writing about it lately and, I don't know, I mean we're pretty straight and all but . . ."

"Spit it out, man!"

Immediately, as if to get it over with quickly, he blurted out, "Well, I think I've discovered more of my woman side and Judy thinks she's discovered more of her man side. Do you know what I mean?"

I had to control my urge to chuckle. *If only you knew,* I thought. But I told Floyd what he wanted to hear. "Floyd, by now you and Judy should know that many things are possible for you that were impossible before. If you feel like you need to understand *why* you are experiencing these changes, we can talk about that. But it's really not necessary. All you need to do is enjoy them."

"Yeah?"

"Yeah."

"Well that's good, doc. I like that."

He was silent for a few moments. Only the sound of his breathing came over the phone.

"Anything else?" I invited.

"No, that was it."

Despite his disclaimer Floyd seemed unwilling to hang up.

"Doc?"

"Yes."

"You're okay."

I felt myself flush. "Thank you, Floyd."

There was another pause during which we were both embarrassed.

"Well, anything . . ."

"Nah, that was it. We know where to find you if we need you."

"Yes, you do," I agreed.

Then we both laughed and hung up.

Floyd and Judy never did call again. For a long time I assumed that was because my role-play intervention had helped them empathize more deeply and had helped create a process of dispute resolution. And I assumed that their expectation of failure had been replaced by one of success. But more recently I have come to wonder: did the intervention fundamentally alter the marriage, or was it merely a marital Band-Aid that forestalled divorce? Unquestionably it helped them resolve immediate conflicts, but did it teach them long-term skills of negotiation? Did they learn to relate intimately while still respecting their own boundaries? Did they create a new marital dance in which they engaged as mature and empathetic partners? Or did they merely change some of the steps in the old dance?

I don't really know. I know that if Floyd and Judy came to see me today I would treat them very differently. In those days hypnosis wasn't often used with couples, but since I didn't know what else to do that was what I did, and the authoritarian technique was my perfect foil. It enabled me to hide my insecurity behind the brusque persona. I was like the Wizard of Oz, engaged in bravado while hoping my clients would never see the little man quaking in his boots behind the curtain.

Today I am much less interested in hiding behind technique and have a bigger "doctor's kit" from which to choose an intervention. I don't always use hypnosis with clients and don't feel the need to rush my clients to resolution. I've learned (through my own journey with intimacy and mortality) that the struggle is an important part of the path. Were Floyd and Judy to call me today, I wouldn't work so hard to get them into my office (I'd trust them to come when they were truly ready). And if they did come, I'd spend the first session listening quietly to their perceptions of the problem. Later I might do hypnotic role-play, but only as part of a larger, more comprehensive intervention.

Ironically, I also realize that this newer strategy might fail, for it would be similar to the thirty-nine talk-therapy sessions they'd already had. Floyd and Judy were terrified of the idea of change: they needed to approach that idea in trance. By being so directive I set the stage for a hypnotic morality play that they then wrote and performed themselves. Had we done more work in the waking state, it's possible that the curtain on that play would not have lifted.

A second change also separates me from the therapist who treated Floyd and Judy years ago. In those days, while I was aware of intergenerational influences on my clients, my work was primarily confined to the forces operating in the client's immediate sphere. Today I understand that our problems are multidimensional, but that some of the biggest contributors are the patterns of relating we learned in childhood. I believe that we constantly recreate our family-of-origin-based dramas in our present lives, and that the ultimate goal of therapy is to help clients differentiate themselves from those early family scripts.

Ironically, Floyd and Judy seemed to know that truism better than I. Intuitively they brought intergenerational intimations into the therapy—their hints about Ryan's "episodes," which stopped as soon as the marriage conflict was resolved, and that Judy feared Ryan's anger just as she had feared her father's—but I didn't make use of them in our work or appreciate the role they played in their problems. Fortunately, the unconscious wisdom of the client can exceed the wisdom of the therapist, and I think Floyd and Judy were able to profit from their unconscious connections even without my "therapeutic" attention. But the irony doesn't escape me: while I thought I was directing the intervention in my technique-laden, authoritarian way, my clients were dancing on ahead, more attuned to growth than I.

And just as I missed the importance of their intimations, I also missed the larger, more significant, story: the fact that what I was seeing was not just a spontaneous exchange of unconscious information, but rather a microcosm of the profound transmission network that exists within all families. I was seeing the vast emotional Internet through which we transfer ideas and feelings, expectations and beliefs, values and behaviors—a family's resolved and unresolved issues—across the generations. I knew I was seeing Floyd and Judy's unconscious knowledge of each other. But what I'd also glimpsed, as clearly as if it had popped up on my screen, was the family unconscious at work.

I knew that when Floyd, playing Judy, acknowledged fearing Ryan's anger just as "she" feared her father's, Floyd was tapping information Judy had given him. Perhaps he'd noted her casting anxious glances at her father's eyes; perhaps he'd heard an undertone in comments about her parents; perhaps he'd noted telltale sighs or pauses as she leafed through family albums. In thousands of subtle ways she had laid her story bare, and Floyd, unconsciously, had scanned it. Well, just as he had gleaned those messages from Judy, he had gleaned other messages from *his* family. And Judy had gleaned messages from hers. And Ryan was gleaning messages from *them!* The unconscious transmittal of information was happening all the time, zillions of times a day, a nonstop relay of emotional ones and zeroes across the intimate receptors of the family. And the messages weren't limited to "real time." They traveled back and forth in time, linking Ryan with his grandparents, linking relatives who had died with relatives not yet born, in a continuous stream of unconscious communication, all of it building a family code.

Today I realize that we are all hooked up to an equally vast network of unconscious data. When we anticipate our spouse's response to his parents, when we see the resemblance between our child and our grandparent, when we note that the patterns of relating in our nuclear family are similar to those in our families of origin, we are merely noting the efficacy with which the network operates. We are all connected to a vast unconscious Internet. We all know the members of our families far better than we think.

Part II

The Future As History

Chapter 5

The Boy Who Was Saved by the Future

FOURTEEN-YEAR-OLD PETE HANDLEY WAS HEADED FOR TROUBLE. CHRONIC truancy, refusal to do schoolwork, and inveterate lying had become his signature behaviors. The school guidance counselor had all but given up on him, and his mother, June—a devoted if overly controlling single mother who supported herself and her three children by working as a secretary—was demoralized, frightened, and pained.

Pete had not always been so difficult. Until his father's sudden death two years before, he had been generally obedient, an average student who did what was required. But since his father's death he had grown increasingly difficult to manage. Six months earlier he had begun sneaking out of the house at night and disappearing until early morning, and neither threats nor tearful cajolings could restrain him. The harder June tried, the more Pete resisted, until one night she was awakened by a call from the police. Pete had been detained with five other boys, all several years his senior; they had been arrested for stealing a car.

Since Pete was a juvenile and this his first offense, he was sentenced to five hours of community service and the arrest was wiped from his record. It was understood that a second offense would not be treated so lightly. When Pete was released to his mother he cried pitiably, promised to avoid the older boys, and swore he would mend his ways. Three months later he and his friends were at it again. This time they were caught hot-wiring June's car.

There was no way June would call the police (a fact the boys, no doubt, inferred). But she feared for her only son's future. How could she prevent what now seemed like an inevitable slide into crime? A friend who had taken a self-hypnosis class from me suggested she give me a call, and after listening to her story, which was laced with caustic anger and frustration, I set up a time for them to come in.

As I expected, I found them sitting in the waiting room as far apart as the tiny area would allow. June, who appeared to be in her mid-thirties, with a slight build and a tight, delicately lined face, immediately rose to greet me. Pete, a baseball cap pulled low over his eyes, slouched behind a copy of *Sports Illustrated*. His right hand was sheathed in a dirty white bandage.

"Come in," I invited. June's desperation filled the room like a warm mist.

She immediately moved into the office, where she dropped with a loud sigh onto the couch.

Pete sullenly lugged himself from his chair and followed his mother in. Everything about him radiated contempt—for himself as well as for others. His compact, muscular body seemed tightly wound. His face seemed locked in a permanent scowl. His posture was tough and angry and defiant. For a moment I felt the chill I often feel with new adolescent clients: can I work with this boy? Will he talk to me? Can I possibly establish hypnotic rapport?

But at the same time I felt for him, for it was clear how oppressed he felt. His mother's anxiety had permeated the waiting room just as her anger and frustration had dominated our telephone conversation. I could imagine how this might feel to Pete. Perhaps anger and defiance were the only ways he knew to forge some separation.

Once in the office, Pete looked around expressionlessly, then took the seat that would place him farthest from his mother. In the cramped space his effort put him all of five feet away, facing the other end of the couch on which she sat. I took the single remaining chair, immediately to Pete's right. I was now looking Mrs. Handley in the eye.

"I'm so glad you were able to see us quickly," she blurted out. "I've been . . . well, I told you on the phone what he's been doing so you can imagine. . . . I just don't know what to do any more . . . and I have nowhere to turn. . . . I'm sure this isn't all his fault . . . if his father were here . . . his father used to say . . ." She rambled on for several moments, spilling her concern like rice from an overfull sack. Pete, meanwhile, looked dourly around the office, arms laced tightly across his chest.

"What is it you hope to achieve here?" I interrupted June's monologue, which seemed likely to last for many minutes.

She looked at me in surprise, but before she could respond I continued. "And then when you're done, I'll let *you* tell us the truth." I turned and winked at Pete.

His lips parted in surprise, then he quickly looked away.

June seemed unsure of what to make of my remark, but continued a version of what she'd told me on the phone. She finished with, "I don't know why he's acting this way. It's not like *my* Pete . . . ," then turning to face him, added, "He was always so good. Always helped around the house, did what he was told. His father used to say he was a good boy, never any trouble."

"Tell me about Pete and his father."

"Oh, Petey idolized his father. You know, Jeff was a maintenance engineer down at Boeing, and Petey used to say he wanted to be a maintenance engineer, too. He really loved his dad." She showered a proud maternal smile on Pete, who disregarded her aggressively. Her tone hardened. "So wouldn't you think that now when I ask him to do a few things around the house he would? It's not like I ask him to break his back or anything. Just put up the storm windows. Fix the toaster. Little things like that. You know, he's the man of the house now so you'd think he'd want to help. You'd think he'd take some pride in it. . . ." She turned toward Pete, "like your father used to."

What a tragically mixed message. In the very same breath June was infantalizing her son, talking about him as if he were five, and then making him the man of the house, responsible for filling his father's shoes. I understood why she did it. She was doing the best she could to cope with the loss of her husband, the demands of heading a family by herself, and her son's delinquent behavior. In pain, in fear, in confusion, she was using Pete to assuage her loss, demanding greater ties to the family at a time when developmentally he was preparing to break away. And Pete was understandably rebelling. The loss of his dad, the stress and demands of the new family configuration (in which he was the only male, as well as the oldest child), the biological storm of adolescence: all had colluded to pressure him simultaneously, and he was buckling under the strain. His recent behavior was an act of desperation.

Throughout June's monologue Pete had sunk lower and lower in his chair, his reactions to her words painfully apparent. At times his lip had protruded in a childish pout, his eyes looked close to tears. At other times he'd tightened his arms across his chest and steeled his surly stare. At yet other times, he'd looked away, feigning lack of interest, as if he could dismiss us both by pretending we weren't there.

I felt for both of them, this mother and son, for as mutually irritating and self-defeating as their behavior was, they didn't mean it to be so. They were merely the sad survivors in a family with a traumatic loss.

"I just never expected this of him," June was prating on. "He's so much better than this. You know, his first-grade teacher said he was the kindest, quietest boy in the class. She used that word, kindest. So what I want to know is . . ." she trained her face on Pete and fixed him with an accusatory glare, "how does the kindest boy in the class become like *that*?"

It was clear that Pete had no intention of answering, so she turned back toward me and said resignedly, "He just doesn't care any more. He can't see where this path is going to take him. I don't know what it's going to take to get through. Obviously *I* can't do it. Maybe you'll have more luck with him."

I lifted my eyebrows as if to say "perhaps," then turned to Pete. "So, what's the truth?" I asked him, smiling. My question was serious, but I wanted to remove the sting.

He grunted a little to acknowledge my attempt to side with him, but kept his eyes on the floor.

I waited for his answer.

"Peter, Mr. Calof asked you a question."

"Let's give him a chance to speak."

Pete turned toward me slightly, trying to avoid his mother's glance.

"What do *you* think is going on?" I was more serious now. "Is it true you don't care any more about what happens?" I was sure that inside the kid cared intensely, but had no way to express himself safely and no idea of how to stop his accelerating slide.

He mumbled something unintelligible.

"Speak up, Pete," June ordered. "Mr. Calof can't hear you."

I realized that I'd never be able to develop a relationship with him—much less a hypnotic rapport in which he could be the sole focus of my attention—as long as she was in the room.

"Well, why don't Pete and I talk privately for a little while," I said, smiling at June. "I think if we were alone it might be a little easier to evaluate if he has the powers of concentration of an engineer. That's a gift that some people have that lets them really make use of hypnotherapy. After all, if he's not a good hypnotic subject there's no point in doing this. It would just be a waste of our time, and *your* money." I wanted to ease June out of the room while reassuring her that I was looking after her interests, and at the same time boost Pete's interest in hypnosis. Since his dad had been an engineer, I hoped the concentration challenge might hook him.

June eyed me with a mix of uncertainty and relief. "Well, all right," she relented, "that sounds fine." Then she rose from the couch, smoothed her dress, and left the room.

As soon as she was gone, I felt a familiar terror. In those days, despite some notable successes with teenage boys, every angry adolescent made me want to run the other way: in the heat of their anger, I felt small and subject to annihilation. This was compounded by chronic performance anxiety. I took failure very personally, and who potentiates that prospect more than a defiant, cross-armed teen? Yet at the same time I felt a tremendous sense of exhilaration, for I knew that if I *could* establish rapport, if I *could* induce a trance, then the chance of success was excellent, for in trance the boy's unconscious resources would likely guide me to a solution. The moment must be akin to what a surgeon experiences as he bends his head to the incision, or to what an actor experiences as he steps out on the stage. It is the chess match between success and defeat that occurs in a fraction of a second before the actual performance begins. And, as I turned toward Pete, I knew the opening move was mine.

For starters, I thought, I'd try a gambit. "Why don't you turn your chair toward mine a bit?" I was actually less interested in improving our position than in seeing how he would respond. He'd spent much of the session so far tuning his mother and me out. Turning his chair would be a sign that he was willing to relate, to at least open up a dialogue. It might also indicate a willingness to follow my directive. To my relief, without a word he angled his chair toward mine.

"I don't know if you know this or not," I began, "but everything you say here is confidential." I gestured toward the door to reference his mother. "Do you understand what I mean?"

Glumly, he nodded.

"I wonder if there's anything you'd like to say to me privately." I was hoping to make Pete feel he could speak his mind with me, without the fear of censure that I knew he felt at home.

He stared at the door, unwilling to meet my eyes, and shrugged his shoulders slightly.

"I don't believe that you just don't care. I bet you have a whole lot of feelings about what's going on."

He tossed his head in an expression of disgust. "She doesn't get it. We weren't gonna steal it. We were just gonna borrow it for a while. It was no big deal. She's always making things into a big deal."

"Sounds like you run with a pretty tough crowd."

"Yeah, so? What's wrong with that?"

"You want to be like them?"

"Yeah." His voice was tough and he fingered the bandage on his hand.

I could see that this line of conversation would get me nowhere. Consciously he was committed to his behavior and a discussion wouldn't change that. It made more sense to do whatever I could to get him into a trance.

"Do you understand that you're here for hypnotherapy? Do you know what that means?"

"Yeah. It means you can put me in a trance."

"I can do that. And then what? How do you think I might help you?"

"I dunno. Make me get better grades or something."

"That might be something we could think about. And perhaps there might be some other things, too." I stopped for a moment to let the thought percolate. "I'll tell you about hypnosis, but before I do, do you have any questions?"

He shrugged, still looking at the floor.

"Well, there are a few things I'd like to tell you. You need to know that this is a partnership. It's not something I do *to* you, it's something we do together. And you won't do anything here that you don't want to do or wouldn't normally do. Hypnosis is just a way you can use your inner mind to help you—in ways that you decide for yourself. I don't even have to know what those ways are." I gave him some time to consider. "Does that sound interesting to you?"

He lifted one shoulder noncommitally, but it seemed to me that a bit of the hardness had left his face.

"Do you think there might be something here for you?"

"I dunno."

"Look, let me be clear with you. I think you're a good guy who deserves to feel better about yourself, but you don't have to do this. I'm willing to work with you if you want to, but I'm not going to do something just because your mother wants it. I can't work with you unless *you* hire me. And I don't want you to say 'yes' just because *she* wants you to."

He looked up; our eyes met for a second, then he looked away.

"So what do you think? Do you want to find out what we might be able to do together to help things get better? 'Cause I don't need to waste your time or my time if you're not interested. Your mom's going to pay me either way."

A half laugh, half snort belched from his mouth.

The kid's tough, I mused, but he's interested. I'd worked with teenagers who had told me flatly in no uncertain terms that they wanted no part of me. The fact that Pete had listened and responded with even a flicker of interest suggested that he wanted to proceed. And despite his obstinance, I held out hope for change. On a conscious level he was seemingly committed to a delinquent course. But *inside,* behind the tough facade, he was still the boy he had been before his father died—the "good boy," the "kindest boy in the class." I remembered June's comment that Pete didn't see where his path would take him. But that inside boy could see. *He* knew Pete was misdirected; *he* could see a better path. If I could appeal to *that* boy, if I could bring him to bear on Pete's conscious stance, then I might have a successful intervention. Suddenly I knew what I needed to do.

Now the only question was how to help him into trance. He'd certainly resist a direct induction: he was far too skittish for that. I'd need to approach him indirectly, by appealing to his unique motivations, values, and needs. I studied him for a moment, reviewing what I knew about him, looking for a "hook." As my eyes swept his well-worn Seattle Supersonics sweatshirt, I thought perhaps I'd found one.

"Hey, did you know that basketball teams hire hypnotherapists?" I brightened my voice to change the tenor of the conversation.

"Unh-unh," he grunted, but his eyes reflected interest.

"Some teams use it to harness the power of their inner minds. They use that power to increase their concentration and improve their performance. Do you know what I mean when I say 'inner mind'?"

"Sorta." He pulled his baseball cap low over his eyes and looked at me from under it.

"Yeah, I bet you do. You've had hunches. You've had things just pop into your mind. You know what I'm talking about."

I could see the tango in him: the desire to hear more coupled with the need to maintain his reserve of cool. The Sonics connection had caught his interest; now I needed to build on that. Again, I studied him—the hooded eyes, the tough persona, the arms folded across his chest . . . And there, in his bandaged arm, I saw something I could offer that Pete might want.

"You know, I just got an idea about how your inner mind can help you. But I wonder if you have the kind of intelligence and concentration necessary for it to work. . . . Are you willing to find out?"

Without looking at me, he mumbled, "I guess so."

I gestured toward his bandaged hand. "You hurt yourself there?"

He looked at the hand as if it betrayed him. "Yeah."

"Does it hurt?"

He wasn't sure how much weakness to reveal. "A little."

"Want to make it stop?"

His eyes glimmered. "Yeah."

"Yeah?"

"Yeah."

"Good." I'd arranged the conversation in a way that led him to say "yeah" three times in a row, engendering a *yes set,* a responsive frame of mind in which he'd be more likely to agree to whatever came next. "Well, it's simple enough. All you have to do is sit there and look down at your hands. . . ." I lowered my voice to the cadence of trance induction. "Everybody's trying to get you to do things. . . . Well, right now you don't have to do anything but sit there and notice whether it will be the left one that will go numb first or the right one. . . ." This would be another hook for Pete. He was resisting being made to do things, and I was offering him a respite, a place where he didn't have to do anything at all. "It doesn't much matter the order. What matters is your ability to notice the change as it happens. Maybe both will go numb at the same time . . . or maybe it will start in the thumb, or in the edge of the hand, and then slowly spread to the fingers and finally to the palm . . . or maybe it will all go numb at once . . . or maybe it will just sit there heavy as lead and disconnected, as if it had on a heavy leather glove. . . ."

Pete stared at his hand as if it were a foreign object in his lap. His eyes were fixed, his body immobile, his expression completely glazed. With a child's ease and rapidity he'd gone into a light trance.

"That's right. . . . Now, can you tell me if it has started in the hand you expected, or is the one that is left the right one to begin? Or have you found that it has begun in both hands?" The question was purposely confounding, designed to distract his conscious mind and free his unconscious to accept the suggestion.

"Both." His voice was leaden.

"Very good." I was relieved: the hardest part was over. I'd helped him into a trance and we had established hypnotic rapport.

But I couldn't help him further without his investment in some outcome. So far he had agreed to go into a trance, but he hadn't told me that he wanted to change—and any therapy needs the client's commitment in order to work.

"Okay, Pete," I raised my voice to a normal speaking tone. "Now come back into the room, fully alert, but there's no need to wake up that right arm." It was a posthypnotic suggestion—indirect and permissive, so as not to engender resistance.

Pete sat up and looked at me. His face lost the glazed expression as he came back toward the waking state. A moment later he looked down and flexed his left hand. The right one remained immobile in his lap.

I knew he was incapable of moving it—and I could imagine the drama that was taking place inside. Unconsciously he'd feel relieved: the immobility was a sign that unusual things were possible, and that held out promise for his problems. But consciously he'd feel disturbed: he'd need an explanation for what was happening, and to save face he'd want to hide his immobility from me. (Clients often go to great lengths to mask and rationalize the strange phenomena of trance. One client was so determined to hide her inability to move her arm that she protested mightily that she *could* move it, she just "didn't want to." I thought I'd stump her by asking her to look at her watch and tell me the time, but nonplussed, she picked up the immobile arm with her other hand, held the wrist in front of her face, and proudly announced the time. Her demeanor suggested there was nothing unusual about this contorted maneuver.)

"Feels better, doesn't it?" I said, gesturing toward his hand.

He stared at the hand, then at me, then quickly back at the hand.

"You know, I had a hunch that you had a really fine mind, and I'm glad to find out I was right. I bet you can use hypnosis really well."

He regarded the hand but said nothing. I could see that he was still caught in the tango, both wanting and not wanting to participate. But he was clearly tantalized by what had happened, and was far closer to agreeing than he'd been before.

"You have some pretty amazing potential we can tap," I nodded toward the hand. "Would you like to take another step?"

He ran his left hand along his forehead just below the cap, then mumbled something under his breath.

"What was that?"

He mumbled again, slightly louder.

"Sorry, Pete, I couldn't hear you." I wanted to press him to commit.

"O*kay*," he said, louder this time and annoyed.

"Pete, it won't work unless you put something on the line. I'm not going to do all the work here. This is a partnership. I can't do it alone."

"Look, I said okay. What do you want?"

"I don't want any bullshit. Are you serious about this or are you just trying to get your mother off your back?"

"Look, man, I said okay. You want me to yell it?"

"No. I just want to know you're serious."

"Jeez, I'm serious, okay? I'm serious."

"Well, I'm glad. For a while there I thought you were just going along with this because your mother wanted you to."

He flicked his head dismissively.

"So, you ready to get started?"

"Yeah."

"Okay." I looked him squarely in the eye and for the first time he held my glance. I could see he was ready to begin. "Now do you remember what we did a minute ago?" I indicated his hand. "Well, that hand is still resting there, isn't it? Why don't you just look at it. . . ."

Pete looked down at the hand.

"That's right . . . *just watch it the same way you did before* . . . now why not just let what's happening in that hand begin to spread . . . but only as fast as you're ready to make deeper and deeper discoveries about your inner potential . . . that's right, just let it spread and begin to wonder just how relaxed you'll be when those sensations move up the hands to the arms and down the legs . . . and perhaps you'll want to keep your eyes open for just a little while longer until the sensations reach your eyes and then you'll be able to rest them. . . ."

Pete's eyes fluttered.

"That's right . . . you can just close them now."

His eyes sagged shut.

"That's it . . . just go deeply to sleep *now.*"

Pete's head fell to his chest; his body slumped in the chair.

"Now just rest comfortably, with every breath becoming more and more relaxed. . . . Now in just a moment I will count to three . . . and when I reach the count of three your eyes will open and in front of you will be the image of a twenty-one-year-old man. . . . I want to

tell you some things about that young man. . . . I want you to understand that when he was a boy he was happy, and happy with himself
. . . he did well in school and had lots of friends. . . . But something
happened at about age twelve. . . . He stopped caring about himself
and about his schoolwork, and he started getting in trouble. . . . Part
of him saw what he was doing and very much wanted to stop, but it
didn't see a way. All that part could do was be sad for the boy. So things
continued to get worse. . . . He started to hate himself . . . people looked
at him with disgust . . . all his friends were losers . . . his old friends
left him . . . they went on to college, then they got good jobs, but they
didn't want to have anything to do with him anymore . . . and so on it
went, getting worse and worse and worse. . . . And when you see him
at twenty-one, Pete, things will really have gone downhill for him . . .
and when you see him you will examine him very carefully and you'll
work to understand him. You'll work to understand what happened to
this boy who once had everything going for him."

I could have asked Pete to see his future directly rather than
via this imagined "future Pete," but I was concerned that his defenses
would get in the way; that if he knew he was constructing an image of
himself, he would give the picture a rosier glow. By distancing Pete
from the image slightly I hoped to give him room to imagine unre-
strainedly.

"And now just drift on, and as you're drifting, your unconscious mind is preparing to carry out the suggestions. . . . I will start
to count . . . one . . . getting ready . . . two . . . that's right . . . now three,
eyes open!"

Pete sat up in the chair and opened his eyes. They peered out
emptily for a second then narrowed to a hard focus on the empty
couch. He craned his head slightly as if to get a closer look.

"That's right. Just take a good look. Take it in. See him for what
he has become."

Pete stared at the apparition, fascinated, as if it were a mildly
mutated animal he was viewing with a mix of curiosity and horror.
The corners of his mouth tensed slightly; his head retracted as if putting distance between himself and what he saw. What was he seeing?
Was it a life gone to seed, troubled, derelict, in emotional and perhaps
physical pain? The tensing and backing away suggested that whatever
he was seeing was unattractive, yet he continued to watch with that
curious fascination as if the figure were of no more relevance to him
than a character in a film. For the intervention to work I'd have to
eliminate the screen and pull Pete in.

"And now," I said, my voice as slow and penetrating as oil on wood, "as you watch intently, it will slowly dawn on you that the man you are watching is *you*, the way *you* will be at the age of twenty-one if you choose to continue on the path that you have chosen. . . ."

For three or four seconds Pete sat immobile, apparently unmoved by my words. Then slowly his face began to change. First disbelief, then understanding, then disbelief again, then horror . . . a parade of emotions swept his face until suddenly, with a little muted cry, Pete turned his head sharply to the side, averting his eyes from the sight.

"Look, Pete, look!" I whispered.

He pressed his cheek against the chair.

"No, Pete, look!"

Reluctantly he turned toward the empty couch, then immediately jerked away. A pitiful whimper limped from his mouth.

I got up from my chair, walked around behind him and placed my hands on either side of his head. "You must look, Pete, you must understand!" And with the slightest pressure of my hands, I urged him to face his future.

Had Pete been in the waking state I never would have made that kind of gesture, for he would have felt it as an effort to overcome his will. But by going into a trance, Pete's unconscious had already opened itself to my help. It would feel the gentle pressure of my hands not as an act of force but as a physical suggestion, a nudge that said, *You can handle this; you have the strength to look.*

Pete hesitated for just a second, then easily, like a well-oiled pivot, swung his head and faced the apparition. I felt him tense under my hands, and pull back again in the chair. "No," he moaned, not to resist the act of looking, but in horror at what he saw.

"Yes."

"No . . ." But before the word was even out of his mouth he began to cry. His head began to quiver between my hands and his narrow shoulders heaved. From his almost adult-sized body came the high-pitched sobs of a child.

"Now you've seen it, Pete . . . and now you understand in the very core of your being that the way things are going, you'll end up like that. . . . Unless you make some different choices, that will be you. . . . But you also know that that's just a future possibility. . . . That hasn't happened . . . that doesn't need to happen. . . . The choice is yours. . . . Do you understand?"

Pete's head lowered in acquiescence.

"OK. Now just let that image go . . . it's a relief to let it go . . .

just let it go *now*. Whether that imaginary picture ever becomes real is completely up to you now."

I felt his body loosen beneath my hands.

"Now I'm going to ask you to use your imagination again." I moved out from behind him and returned to my chair. "In just a moment you are going to see pictures of yourself in a *better* future . . . they will be as bright and clear as the ones you just saw. . . . And in this better future you will see yourself as the person you really want to be . . . the person you truly are deep down inside. . . . You will see yourself in great detail exactly as you really want to be and as you will be more and more with every day that passes. . . . When I count to three and your eyes open you will see that vivid image and it will be of yourself at age twenty-one, looking, acting, thinking, feeling, and believing exactly the way you really want to be deep down inside. . . . Okay . . . one . . . getting ready now . . . two . . . going deeper . . . and now three, eyes open!"

Pete opened his eyes and focused toward the empty couch. His face at first was neutral but as I watched, it grew alive: his features softened, his lips parted, his eyelids twitched into a look of wonder. Finally his mouth gave way to a small, closed smile.

"Study it. Watch it very closely as if you are trying to memorize it." I waited several moments while Pete took the image in. "Now close your eyes and in just a moment I'm going to count to three again and when I do you will step into that ideal image and you will *be* that twenty-one-year-old, the way you truly want to be. You will try it on . . . be it, feel it . . . to be sure it's truly what you want. . . . Getting ready now . . . one . . . drifting deeper and deeper . . . two . . . that's right . . . and now three." Earlier I'd asked Pete to hallucinate with his eyes open so that the image of the bad future Pete would appear outside him. But I wanted the new ideal Pete to be *inside* him. For that reason I asked him to close his eyes.

Within seconds his eyelids began to twitch and his smile deepened.

"That's right. . . . Now just take some time to learn about what it's like to be this better version of you. . . . Feel it, sense it, notice how it feels to move and act and think. . . . Notice how you sound and how you look to yourself. . . . Now imagine yourself being with others . . . at home . . . at school . . . with friends, and in all the different places of your life . . . and be very pleased by what you experience. . . . And as you do this, and become more absorbed with it, with every moment and every breath, your deep inner mind will record these new learnings, these new possibilities, and use them to plan a different path into your future."

Pete sat serenely in the chair, his face quiet with pleasure. I gave him some time to absorb the experience.

So far, Pete had visualized a better future and had felt that future as his own, but he had yet to chart a path to get there. Next I'd have to help him do that. "Now, leaving things exactly as they are, I want you to look back to when you were fourteen, to the day seven years ago, when you first came to see me in my office, and you will see a series of snapshots. These will be of all the steps you took from that day forward to get to where you are today . . . the ways you grew . . . the changes in your thinking, in your beliefs, in your behavior . . . and how others around you changed and grew as you did. . . . Okay, now getting ready to do that . . . preparing to do that. . . . Okay, do that now."

I waited for Pete to absorb the images, then continued.

"Good. Now leaving things exactly as they are again . . . In a moment I will count from one to three, and when I reach the count of three you will be back at that day seven years ago, back at the present day . . . and all those snapshots will still hang in the air, forming a bridge between you at fourteen and you at twenty-one . . . and while you watch, those snapshots will fold up on themselves like an accordion and will go right into the back of your mind where they'll be stored until you need them. . . . Do you understand?"

He made a tiny nod. By absorbing the "snapshots," by storing them in his mind, he would absorb the blueprint that would carry him into the future.

"All right now, one . . . beginning to go back . . . two . . . growing younger again . . . and three, fourteen years old again and now let all those pictures of the future fall right into the back of your mind."

Pete sat quietly for a moment, the same beatific expression on his face. Then gradually his breathing speeded up. He seemed almost to glow.

"Good. . . . And now that you've done this you can know that, thanks to the power of your deep inner mind, you will do everything you need to do, in just the right way, at just the right time, for these wonderful changes to occur. . . . It's as if they were already true for you. . . . And with each and every day that passes you'll find yourself becoming more and more like those ideal images. . . . Now let your mind grow clear and rest. . . . You've done a lot of very good work here today. . . . You can be proud of what you've done, pleased with your ability to use your deepest mind to create the kind of future you really want to have. . . . Everything that you started here today will continue to work at a very deep level without your even needing to think about it."

As a result of the intervention, Pete had crafted a new self-image, one that was already unfolding in his mind. Now he needed a tool to reinforce his blueprint whenever it began to fade. That tool would be self-hypnosis.

"And from time to time you will want to *return to this special state*—whenever you want to give yourself positive suggestions or whenever your unconscious mind thinks it would be best. . . . In this state of self-hypnosis you will find the space and time to think and feel about things that you wouldn't normally consider in your waking state . . . things that may have needed your attention for some time. . . ." I had in mind Pete's mourning for his father, his differences with his mother, his developing sexuality: the raft of difficult feelings that would present themselves over the coming months and years. If he could use self-hypnosis to make peace with those feelings, it would mitigate the need for further acting out.

I also wanted him to use self-hypnosis as a tool for developing independence. The more he rehearsed his ideal images, the stronger his new sense of self would grow, and the better he would be at asserting that self with his mother and others. June, I realized, could inadvertently help that process along. If I suggested that Pete practice self-hypnosis every time she nagged intrusively or asked inappropriately for help, I'd turn her otherwise debilitating energy into a trigger for his growth.

"And when your mother leans on you, not as a son but as the man of the house, you may find that the best way to help her is to be an example of calmness and relaxation. In fact, it will remind you to practice this special state, and in that way you may even be able to teach *her* about relaxation." Certainly June could profit from relaxation. My goal, though, was not to have Pete teach her self-hypnosis: that was too unlikely. But by suggesting to Pete that he *could* teach her I hoped to change his self-image in relation to her; to take him from being the boy who needed constant correction to a young man with something to offer.

"And now as these suggestions sink in very deeply, just let your mind go clear and blank. . . . In just a few moments I'm going to count from five to one and as I do you'll find yourself coming back to the waking state. . . . And when I reach the count of one you'll feel alert and refreshed and with all the energy you need to complete the tasks remaining in your day. . . . And when you awaken you will remember as much or as little of this session as your inner mind thinks best. . . . Shortly after you awaken you will notice the clock on the table and you will be both surprised and deeply pleased by what it says you've been able to achieve here today. . . . And tonight when you go to bed, in your dreams you will continue to develop these new thoughts, images, and feelings, and they will become even more powerful in your mind and body. . . . Now getting ready . . . five . . . the heaviness is getting ready to leave now . . . four . . . getting ready to come back . . . three . . . feeling more alert and refreshed with every count . . ."

At the count of one Pete sat up and rubbed his eyes, then looked curiously around the room. He looked drained, as if he had done a hard day's work, but there was a new-found peacefulness about him. His dark eyes were softer and his slouch was one of exhaustion rather than defiance.

"Well, it looks like you've got plenty to mull over." I acknowledged what I knew he felt inside, that something inexplicable and profound had just occurred. "So what do you say you get out of here before your mother decides to cancel the session?" It was a ridiculous question: we both knew the session had already taken place. But given his still heightened suggestibility, it would make him wonder: *Can* it be canceled? Does that mean it didn't really happen? The effect would be to strengthen his amnesia for what had happened. It would also remind him that I was aligned with him, not with his mother.

Pete chuckled a little, then followed my gaze to the clock. He did a double take. "It's five o'clock?"

"Time flies, huh?"

"Whoa. . . ." He raised his eyebrows in disbelief.

I didn't want him tampering consciously with what we'd done so I re-evoked the posthypnotic suggestion that he not work to remember what we'd done. "Oh well, I guess you don't need to think about that, do you? And besides, this way if your mom asks you what happened you can just tell her you don't remember!"

He considered this for a moment, brows knitted together, then shrugged as if dismissing the entire matter.

"Speaking of your mom, should we go get her?"

He seemed to ponder my question carefully, then nodded. So together we walked out to the waiting room.

June was already standing when we got there. I had the impression she'd been listening for my hand on the doorknob.

"I think we're done," I announced. "We may want to schedule another appointment at some point, but let's see how things go for a few weeks."

She opened her mouth to ask a hundred questions but I brushed them away with a smile. "We had a very good session. Now I think it's best if we just let things simmer for a while. I've given him a lot of homework, and . . ." I smiled at Pete, "he knows how to reach me if he needs to." Then I held out my hand, first to Pete and then to June, and then, with June following close on her son's heels, they left.

Three weeks later she called.

"Well, it's a mixed blessing," she reported. "Mostly it's a lot better. He's staying home at night. He's playing with his sisters. And he's seeing some of his old friends again. But he's doing the weirdest things. I just don't know what to make of it. The other night he asked me to look at a model he built. Now he hasn't done that since he was in third grade. And then last night he came into my room in the middle of the night crying. So I put my arms around him and said 'poor Petey, poor Petey,' and he pushed me away and said, 'Don't call me that!' real angrylike. Now, I've called him that all his life, Mr. Calof, I don't know what's come over him now."

"I think . . ."

But June wasn't finished yet. "And he's started making up all these rules. He'll wash the car but he won't wax it. Or he'll help Dina with her homework but he won't put her to bed. I don't know where he got all these rules from suddenly, it used to be he either did the thing or he didn't, but now suddenly he has to make rules about everything." I could hear the confusion in her voice. "I don't want to sound ungrateful, Mr. Calof. I mean I'm glad he seems to have given up that other dumb stuff, but I just don't know what to make of it. One minute it's like having the old Petey back, and the next minute he's just . . . different. Is that normal?" Then she tittered, realizing it was a silly question.

"It sounds like your son is trying to grow up, June," I explained. "He's trying to deal with the loss of his dad, and the fact that his family has changed, and the fact that his body is changing, and his hormones are raging. . . . He's trying to figure out who he is, what belongs to him and what doesn't, what his boundaries are, and that's all very normal. You know, at fourteen a boy is caught in a difficult place. He's partly still a little boy but he also wants to be a man, and he wobbles back and forth between the two. He's trying on both roles and seeing how they fit. It sounds like you're just seeing more of that process than you did before."

I could hear her breathing at the other end of the line.

"You know how you can help him with that process?"

"How?" Her voice clutched at my question, hoping for a reassuring, concrete answer.

"Just by letting him wobble. By knowing it's going to happen and not expecting anything different. By trying to support him in both roles, whichever one he's working on at the time. Of course, you have to establish your own limits. He has to live within your household framework and values. But within that you have to try to make room for him to experiment with who he wants to be. Let him become the Pete he's trying to become. I can assure you that he now has an ideal image powerfully etched in his mind that he feels compelled to try to achieve."

I wasn't convinced that June would be able to give Pete the range he needed to experiment, but I was optimistic nonetheless—because I believed that, regardless of June's changes, Pete would be able to grow. He now had a vision, a road map for how to get there, and a tool for making corrections along the way. All three would help him forge an identity in his newly configured family.

What June was seeing were his first attempts to walk that road. That's what was responsible for his sudden creation of rules; that's what enabled him to say, "Don't call me Petey!" and push her away. It's also what enabled him to release the little boy—the part of him that cried at night, that mourned his father's death, that wanted to be held. For the first time Pete was feeling, hearing, *trusting* the self within; for the first time he wasn't defining himself by the voices of others around him.

What did this mean for their relationship? Given June's need to hang on to Pete in compensation for her husband, I didn't expect her to make room for his new self easily. I foresaw a lot of conflict. But even about that I was optimistic, because as long as Pete was responding to his mother differently, she would be forced to respond differently to him. As he laid down more and more rules about what he would and wouldn't do she would be forced to negotiate with him, and as his positions reflected increasing maturity she would find herself coming to respect them. Bit by bit, they would begin to relate to each other adult to adult.

"Well, it doesn't sound like I need to see Pete again right now.

But I would like it if you would tell him that I expect him to keep practicing self-hypnosis."

"All right," she said quietly, her voice a bit shaky.

"You know, with less worry about him you can spend more time with your own healing. Do you have someone *you're* talking to?"

"Oh, I don't know. . . ." She seemed embarrassed.

"You may want to think about doing that." I let the thought linger for a moment. "Why don't you give me a call in a month and let me know how things are going?"

"All right," she murmured. And I could tell from the waver in her voice that I'd really thrown her off-kilter.

June did call a month later and her report was much the same. Pete was going to school, staying in at night, helping out around the house. Delinquency seemed to be behind him. But the relationship between them was testy. "He just seems to have a will of his own," she lamented. "But at least he's not doing that foolishness anymore."

"So how does it feel to be the mother of a normally developing fourteen-year-old?"

She clucked her tongue. "I guess it beats being the mother of a fourteen-year-old JD. Boy, you really did something to him, huh?"

"I didn't do anything. He's doing it to himself." I had helped, but I wanted to empower Pete in his mother's eyes.

"Well, what did he do to himself, exactly?"

"He did exactly what you suggested. He looked to see where his path would take him. And you know what? It turns out he knew the answer all along. I just helped him be able to use it."

"Oh." There was an uncomfortable pause. "Well, whatever works, I guess."

"And now it sounds like you're on the right path as a family. I don't think I'll need to see you any more, but you know you can call me if you need to."

"Oh yeah," she said. "I'm sure I will."

June never called back. I suspect she would have, had Pete resumed his delinquent behavior, so I assume he is still on the straight and narrow. I know she didn't fully comprehend my final answer, although it was absolutely true. Pete did have the answer all along. He just couldn't see it. All the external pressures—his mother, the change in his family, his friends—interfered with his ability to listen to his inner voice. In response to those pressures he'd mustered the only response he could: delinquency was the only way he knew to carve out a sense of self. In hypnosis, however, I was able to quiet those external voices and package his inner voice in a form that he could hear. Freed from the constraints of conscious thought, from the limitations of the physical world, from the corral of a single place and time, he was able to see his self and his situation differently. He was able to see a future in which a different self matured, a self that he more truly wanted to be.

I suspect that had Pete come to me later—when he was more entrenched with his delinquent friends, further split off from the "good boy" he'd been—the intervention might not have worked so well. But we were fortunate that June had acted when she did: Pete was still of divided mind; he still cherished, with part of himself, the "good Pete" inside. That part was ready for change, ready to work, ready to build a new future.

The fact that his future was merely a mental construct made it in no way less persuasive, for to him that future was completely real: as real as if it had been lived and felt and tasted, as real as if it had been captured in memory and preserved in the pages of an album. Neurologically speaking, Pete had already lived an approximation of that future: the initial neuropathways had been created; the images and sensations had been recorded in the brain and body *as if* they had actually taken place.

This phenomenon, in which imagined activities spark actual neurological and physiological responses, is intrinsic to trance. When a combat veteran, for example, experiences a spontaneous flashback (a naturally occurring trance)—when he drops to the ground to escape imagined mortar fire, when his breathing quickens, when he flushes to the hairline and his body grows wet with sweat—his brain is communicating with his body as if the event were real. When a person at rest in a formally induced trance imagines he is riding an exercycle, the level of fatty acids in his blood will rise, just as they would if he were actually exercising. His brain will communicate to his body as if the imagined activity were real. I once saw a hypnosis demonstration in which the subject was told he was about to be touched with a hot poker, then was actually touched with an ice cube. Within minutes his skin formed a blister—just as it would have had the poker been real—because his brain communicated his *imaginings* to his body.

This phenomenon is hardly restricted to trance. Who hasn't

had a nightmare from which he woke up sweating? Or tensed in a movie during a moment of surprise? Or felt his mouth begin to water at the thought of a favorite food? Activities that originate in our minds often reverberate in our bodies, as electrochemical messages traversing the pathways of the nervous system communicate back and forth.

In fact, we sometimes deliberately use this overlap between the real and imagined. Dancers, actors, and musicians often rehearse performances in their minds before setting foot on stage. Basketball players often mentally rehearse their games before stepping onto the court. A person learning tennis may imagine hitting the perfect forehand over and over while sitting in a chair. And I will sometimes stand in the empty auditorium, imagining the audience before me, as I mentally rehearse a speech I am scheduled to give the following day. Intuitively, and demonstrably, we know that mental rehearsals make for stronger performances—in part because they strengthen the neuropathways that guide our future behavior.

So it was with Pete. He created mental blueprints for thinking, feeling, and acting in the future, and having imagined them he was predisposed to follow them. It's always easier to follow a broken trail than to chart a new one—especially if the trail leads to a desired end. That was certainly the case for Pete, whose future trail offered resolution for a pressing problem.

Plus, he had built-in reinforcement for taking that trail. He had defined the steps he would take along the way—the incremental changes in thinking, feeling, believing, and acting that would make that future possible. As a result, he didn't have to scout the underbrush for the right direction: the turns in the trail were clearly marked. And Pete reinforced his path with the practice of self-hypnosis. Each time he imagined his future in a trance, he drew it into sharper focus: he literally strengthened the neuropathways that made it real.

And there is yet another reason why Pete lived out the future he had imagined. In two decades of doing this work I've come to conclude that human beings have a tropism toward healing. We get confounded by obstacles and often move along seemingly self-destructive paths, but when the obstacles are removed we stretch in the direction of repair. So it was with Pete. Once his problems had been reframed, once his old way of seeing had been amended, he did what human beings do: he reached for health. He did it as naturally as a cut heals itself, as reflexively as a plant reaches for the sun.

So Pete lived the future he imagined—as do we all, for no one can take an action without imagining it first. The smallest as well as the greatest actions of our lives are charted first in our minds. We start our car with motions so familiar that they seem reflexive. Yet inside our brain neurotransmitters are firing—triggered by the familiar context, remembering the ways they fired in the past—essentially *imagining* the actions before our body takes them. We find our lives unrolling in ways similar to our parents'—not because we want that (indeed, we vowed we would be different!)—but because that is the familiar path, the path we have already imagined. We tell ourselves that the day that's dawning will be a disaster—and lo and behold it is, because that is the outcome we've imagined. Our images of the future—whether conscious or not—dictate the paths we follow, for, like Pete, we all prefer the broken trail. Rather than some great unnavigated terrain, the future is a land to which we *all* have traveled. It is no more than the meandering of our bodies along the maps we have created in our minds.

Chapter 6

What She Saw in the Crystal Ball

. . . attempted suicide twice within the last year . . . severe bulimorexia . . . no longer gets her period . . . arrested for shoplifting . . . presently living in a psychiatric group home . . .

IT WAS TEN MINUTES TO TEN AND I REVIEWED WHAT I KNEW ABOUT CAROL Ferguson. At nineteen years old she was clearly in a lot of pain. Three months of treatment at a community mental health center had apparently produced "intellectual insights" about her condition but little change in her behavior, and now the director of the center, Paul Ellicott, was referring her to me. Paul was a family therapist for whom I had the highest respect and whom I was hoping to bring on as my partner. Hence, his referral was both welcome and a challenge. I was nervous—I had never treated a client who was so acutely self-destructive—but at the same time I was excited. At five years into my practice, every client was an object lesson in the wonders of the human mind. So I awaited Carol with nervous anticipation, just as a child, in the shortening days of August, spins a web of hopes and questions about next year's teacher.

At ten o'clock sharp Carol knocked on the door.

"Hi!" she said cheerily. You would have thought she was arriving at a party.

I invited her to take a seat, and she did so quickly, dropping her coat on the adjacent couch. Then she looked expectantly toward me.

"Did you have any trouble getting here?"

"Oh no," she chirped. "Your directions were really great. I just did what you said." When I didn't immediately answer she continued. "I like coming downtown. We live in Bellevue. Well . . . now I don't live at home any more, but when I did I didn't come downtown that much, so it's always fun." As she talked she sat forward in her chair, her hands folded neatly in her lap. Her spidery wrists and legs, extending prominently from her sweater and short skirt, seemed to advertise her eating disorder. Her straight blonde hair was pulled neatly back in two barrettes, and long bangs heightened the gauntness of her face.

"Do you have your own car?" I asked, hoping through a bit of small talk to get a sense of her personality.

"Uh-huh," she replied eagerly. "It's a Chevy Impala. It's a little old," she wrinkled her nose, "well, not real old, just two years old. My dad gave it to me." She bounced a little as she talked. I wondered if she had been a cheerleader.

"A nice present," I commented.

"Yeah. Well, that was a while ago he gave it to me, before . . . well, before I tried to kill myself."

"Can you tell me a little about that?"

"Uh-huh," she said pleasantly. "About three-and-a-half months ago I overdosed on this medicine I take for petit mal seizures. I've had them ever since sixth grade. I was in the hospital for a while. Then they let me out and made me go to mental health counseling. I've been doing that for about three months. But the counseling center said I could choose between staying there or coming here and I decided to come here."

"And why did you do that?" The fact that she had chosen hypnotherapy was a positive sign: presumably she thought hypnotherapy would work; if so, her positive expectations would boost our chances of success.

"Because I thought you could help me stop binging and vomiting."

"Uh-huh." I waited to see if she would add anything else.

"That's all," she said firmly. "I don't want to gain any weight. I just need to stop being so crazy about food—you know, thinking about it all the time. And I need to stop vomiting. That's all."

Paul had mentioned that she believed that her weight of ninety-two pounds was more than adequate for her height of 5'5" and that she was adamant about not gaining weight. Clearly, her self-image was out of touch with reality. This misalliance is common in people with eating disorders—I knew they often viewed themselves as fat—but Carol's disjunction struck me as more profound, for her entire *affect*, the casual, emotionless way she had spoken, seemed to bear little relationship to the events she had described. She had narrated her suicide attempt in the same lighthearted way that she'd described her car! Where were the feelings that underlay those actions? Feelings that would lead one to try to take one's life? To self-starvation? To consignment in a psychiatric group home? Obviously she'd talked about those events at the mental health center, and repeated talking might soften the sting. But still—to describe them so offhandedly, as if the behaviors belonged to someone else, suggested that she had totally intellectualized them, divorced them entirely from her emotions.

I was intrigued by this dichotomy. "Well, what do you think I should know in order to help you?" Asking an open-ended question is often the best way to find out what the client thinks is important.

She pursed her lips and cocked her head to the side. "Well . . . this was the second time I tried to kill myself. The first time was about a year ago. I did it the same way. I was in the hospital that time too. But I didn't have to go to counseling when I got out. I just got an apartment."

"Until then you'd been living with your parents?"

"With my mom and my brother. He's younger, but he and I are pretty close. I have an older sister too, but she's away at college." She ran her fingers through her hair. "My parents are separated. I think this all started with that."

"Really?" An alarm went off inside me. The year was 1977; the diagnosis of eating disorders was becoming more common, and several prominent therapists had begun to advance the theory that they were not a disease of the individual, but rather a disorder of the family, a by-product of family interaction. Although I'd had no clinical experience with eating disorders, that notion made intuitive sense to me—and now here was Carol suggesting perhaps the same thing. I wanted to know more.

"Can you say more about that?"

She tilted her head to the side again. "Well, it started right after they separated, about three years ago. I just started binging a lot and vomiting. I got really weight conscious."

"And you think there's a connection between your eating and their separation?"

She nodded. "When they were separating I didn't want to have anything to do with anyone anymore. Just the family. I was really involved in the separation."

"In what way?"

"Oh, my mom came into my room every night crying and saying mean things about my dad. We stayed up late and talked. I tried to help her. But then it made my dad mad that I was talking to her so much. He wanted me to live with him."

"Did you want to?"

She looked at me as if the answer were self-explanatory. "I couldn't. My mom needed me. She would have been too sad."

"How do you get along with your mom?"

"Sometimes we're pretty good friends, like when they were separating and she was talking to me every night. But most of the time I think she gets along better with my sister. But anyway now she has a boyfriend and I don't see her so much." She shrugged, then added detachedly, "Our relationship is kind of on-again, off-again."

"How is that for you?"

"I'm pretty used to it. And anyway she can't help it. I think she's not so happy. So sometimes she takes it out on me. And on my dad."

"In what ways?"

"Like she won't talk to him for a while. And then he won't talk to her. And I get caught in the middle. They're always trying to get me to take sides."

"What do you do when that happens?"

"Most of the time I side with my mom." Then, as if anticipating my next question, "She needs me more."

"What does your dad do when you side with your mom?"

"He gets angry and stops talking to us."

I found myself getting excited. Everything Carol said seemed to match what I'd heard about families with eating disorders. Their interactions seemed typical of what therapists now call *psychosomatic families* after a book of that title by Salvador Minuchin. Typically, in these families the parents have serious marital and family-of-origin conflicts, but rather than deal with their conflicts directly—by acknowledging them and talking them out—they "detour" their conflicts through the child. That is, they make the child a pawn in the marital game—by asking her to take sides, by asking her to meet needs that are unmet by the spouse, by giving and withholding love as she meets or disregards their needs.

If the child has any kind of physical symptom—headaches, stomachaches, asthma, quirks regarding eating—that symptom may become over time the focal point of family interactions. When that happens, the tense dramas that follow—over getting her to eat, getting her to the doctor, getting her the life style that she needs—displace the underlying marital conflict. On the surface the family appears to be healthy, but the root problem festers, reinforcing the child's symptom.

In this way the child's problem and the family's attempts to resolve it become central to maintaining stability in the family. In fact, it is no longer the child's problem; it is the family's problem, and in myriad ways every family member reinforces it. They collude to keep the child a child, to keep her attached, to keep the family intact. And the child, instead of developing a sense of self with independent needs, becomes an instrument of the family, her needs subsumed in the service of others. This was precisely the scenario Carol had described: meeting her parents' needs, being asked to take sides, withdrawing from her own life to take care of the family.

Of course, in a perverse way, Carol's needs, too, were being met. Her disorder drew attention and worry from the family, and it helped her stake out an independent self. "You can't control me: you can't make me eat!" she was asserting, in her behavior if not in her words.

Paul had told me that Carol had a good "intellectual understanding" of her family's dynamics, and indeed she had just demonstrated it. But once again I was struck by her lack of emotion. It was as if her knowledge were entirely cerebral, as if she had banished the feelings that the knowledge ought to bring.

"You said that when they were separating you didn't want to have anything to do with anyone else, just the family?"

"I was really worried about them so I felt like I had to put everything else on the back burner."

"What did you put on the back burner?"

"Oh, sports, and going out. Stuff like that. I just felt like I needed to be home more."

Carol was describing her junior year in high school, a time when most teenagers are bursting out of their families in fervent attempts at independence. Yet during that year she had clung closer and closer to home. This, too, had been noted in families with eating disorders. Because the child cannot see herself as separate from the family, she meets the challenge of adolescence by drawing inward and intensifying her family focus.

"Is there anything else you think I should know?"

She leaned back in her seat for a moment thinking, then sat up pertly and looked me in the eye. "Right after they separated and I began binging and vomiting, I went from 130 to 88 pounds. But then my electrolytes got weird and I had to go into the hospital. In the hospital they made me gain weight until I weighed 92. That's what I weigh now. At the mental health center they made me promise to stay there."

"And how does that feel to you?"

"Well, I guess it's all right . . . I'd really like to lose a little more weight, but I want to keep my promise."

"That's important to you, keeping your promise?"

"Oh yeah! I always keep my promises!" She was so earnest about this that she reminded me of a Girl Scout. Milton Erickson called bulimic girls "little saints" because they hold themselves—and others—to a rigid moral code. Being honest, being good, treating others well become behavioral imperatives, as if by maintaining "perfect" behavior they can reorder the imperfect world around them. If they meet everybody's needs perfectly, if they achieve the perfect weight, if they get perfect grades and wear perfect clothes, then maybe they can gain the emotional constancy they crave. Of course perfection is impossible, so they are caught in an endless trial, pushing themselves ever harder toward an unachievable goal.

I was fascinated by Carol's report. Each of her statements opened a field of questions, but for the moment we had to move on. This was an intake appointment; we had only fifty minutes together. So I made copious notes on the pad in front of me and then asked her a few last questions.

"How's dating?"

She blushed. "I don't date much."

"Have you had boyfriends?"

She looked down. "A few. But I kind of stopped dating when my parents separated. And my mom . . . well, every time I wanted to go out my mom just got so uptight about it. Like I was going to get raped or something."

"You think she's concerned about your safety?"

"She just doesn't want me to have sex." She giggled. "I mean we never talk about it or anything." She paused. "But that's okay. This wouldn't be such a good time for me to date anyway."

"Why is that?"

"I just need to get some of this stuff sorted out. I mean, stop vomiting probably." She gave me a meaningful look. "I hope you can help me, because this is really my last resort. I'm probably going to have to kill myself if this fails."

Ordinarily I take suicide threats very seriously, especially when the speaker has already attempted suicide twice. But Carol's threat didn't strike me as serious. Her tone was hardly urgent, and I knew from her counselor at the mental health center that her suicidality was, at least for the moment, stabilized. So rather than take it as an ultimatum, I heard in her words a plea: *Please work with me. I've tried "talk therapy" and it hasn't helped. Now I'm turning to you.*

In the time remaining I decided to hypnotize her—in part because she expected to be hypnotized and I wanted to acknowledge her expectation. A short, relaxing trance would let her know that this therapy would be different from what she'd had previously and would boost her motivation to return. It would also build a sense of intimacy between us that might aid our future work. But I decided to hypnotize her for another reason as well. I was curious. Her presentation had been so rational, so spoken by her conscious mind. What was it not revealing? Perhaps thirty minutes would be enough for her unconscious to drop some clues.

Carol had written on her intake form that she was "scared, sort of" of hypnosis. Yet when I asked, she told me that she had actually been hypnotized once before, during a stage hypnosis act at a local club. I was even more surprised when she told me that she recalled almost nothing of that experience. Amnesia is usually a product of deep trance, which meant that Carol was in the minority of the population for whom deep trance is readily achievable. Perhaps I shouldn't have been surprised. People who are capable of deep trance have a marked propensity to dissociate, and what was Carol's presentation if not a masterful act of dissociation? Her ability to reveal her painful history with not a trace of feeling was due to her ability to split those feelings off. For that matter, what was her bulimorexia if not a task of dissociation? In the moment of binging, nothing existed but the food in front of her; at the moment of purging, her world was reduced to the sensations in her body; both those activities served to draw a curtain between Carol and her emotions. Carol's entire experience was dissociative, making trance, in essence, a familiar state.

To help her into a trance, I asked her to sit in the same position she had been sitting in on stage and to report everything she could remember from that session in the nightclub. At this, she sat back fully in her chair, closed her eyes, and laid her hands, palm up, in her lap. She then began to describe in halting sentences what had happened. As she did so, I interjected suggestions for trance development, borrowing liberally from the stage hypnotist whom I had heard on several occasions. As I spoke, Carol's body relaxed visibly in the chair.

"And because you are interested in finding solutions to the problems that have brought you here today, you may notice as you listen to this voice that your hands are becoming numb. . . ." I touched her hands, first gently, then with greater pressure, and Carol didn't respond. By the time I'd been talking for about ten minutes she was slumped heavily in the chair.

"Now, Carol, I'd like to speak with your unconscious mind. And I'd like to speak with it privately, without your conscious mind hearing." Even in deep trance a person's observations can be tainted by defenses. As much as possible I wanted to clear those defenses out of the way and leave Carol's unconscious free and unfettered as it talked to me.

At the sound of my words Carol's eyes opened and she sat up straight in her chair.

"Are you ready to speak with me?"

"Yes." Her voice was warm and friendly, but noticeably more subdued than it had been before.

"I'd like you to tell me anything you think I need to know in order to help Carol. And you will be able to tell me comfortably—even about things that Carol can't discuss consciously."

"She doesn't like herself," the unconscious spoke out quickly. "She thinks she's ugly."

I nodded. The words didn't surprise me—they seemed close to what Carol might admit consciously—but the emotion in them did. They were voiced with a decided note of resignation. "Anything else?"

"She's very irresponsible and sometimes she isn't very kind to others."

An interesting observation, I thought, given Carol's earlier statement about how adamantly she kept her promises. As Erickson had noted, the "little saints" often fail to live up to their own code of honor.

"But sometimes she can be quite kind," the voice went on. "Sometimes she does too much for other people. And then she wants people to pity her." She hesitated. "And she gets angry a lot. She locks it inside and doesn't talk to anyone about it. But sometimes when she's angry she talks about people—behind their backs."

What a perfect description of a psychosomatic family, I thought. The child "does too much" for the other family members as she sacrifices herself to their needs. And the parents, instead of expressing their feelings directly, "say mean things" about each other to the children. They criticize the children when they are angry at each other, and place the children squarely in the middle of their adult conflict. The conscious Carol had alluded to this dynamic, but here was her unconscious virtually spelling it out. And indicating that Carol herself had adopted those behaviors.

"She talks about others quite often," the unconscious continued. "But she expects other people not to talk about her. And she gets upset when she hears people talking behind other people's backs."

Was this more evidence of the "little saint" syndrome? If so, I could guess at its genesis. Unconsciously, Carol probably saw and disliked that behavior in her parents—just as she saw and hated it in herself. So consciously she defended against it and pretended it didn't happen by verbally espousing a rigid moral code. In Carol's conscious universe she *always* kept her promises, *never* talked behind someone's back, because the slightest slip, the slightest deviation from the code, might reveal the truth: that in her family promises were rarely kept, that what people said was not always what they meant.

Now I was curious. Carol had answered my open-ended question by describing her family dynamics. How would she respond if I questioned her more directly. "Do you think the condition Carol came here with has anything to do with her family?"

She grew quiet for a second, then ever so faintly she nodded. "Her mom was always yelling at her for doing the wrong things." Her voice had that same note of resignation in it. Or was it sadness?

"The wrong things?"

"Mom always yelled at me for eating the wrong things or for eating too much, and got mad at me for dieting."

I noticed the change of pronoun. The dissociation between her conscious and unconscious minds had broken down—usually a sign of strong emotion. And no wonder! She was describing a no-win situation: her mother yelled at her for eating too much *and* for dieting. Carol could do no right.

"What about Carol's father?"

"Her father was really kind. But he never said anything. He never got mad at her for . . . for too many things. And then he left. He left her."

Why had she stumbled? Her pause seemed to imply a reconsideration, as if she'd decided that he did get mad—but only when she deserved it. She seemed to be absolving him of responsibility: he got mad, but the fault was hers. And then, as if to prove it, he left her.

"How did she feel about that?"

"Sad. She thought it was her fault. She thought it was something she did when she was little."

"And is that true?"

Her voice softened. "No."

"But Carol doesn't know that, does she?"

"No," she murmured. She sounded genuinely sympathetic.

I was amazed. Her unconscious had shown a remarkable degree of self-understanding. I had merely asked what I needed to know and it had described in detail Carol's family dynamic—and almost everything it said had matched the bulimic families I'd heard about. Suddenly I felt the thrill of discovery. I had been cautiously testing a theory, and Carol's unconscious seemed to have proven it correct!

I had dozens more questions, but for now our time was almost up. So I thanked the unconscious for being so helpful and then gave Carol the suggestions I typically give at the end of the trance utilization phase of an intervention. I told her she would think less of her problem in the coming weeks and would experience an improvement in her mood and outlook; I told her she would remember as much or as little of our conversation as her unconscious mind thought best; and I suggested that in the future whenever I counted from one to five and it was in her best interest she would go back into a trance. Then I awakened her.

Carol awoke feeling relaxed but denied she had been in a trance. I was pleased. Her amnesia verified that what I had witnessed was in fact the workings of her unconscious, observations so close to the core that they were sealed from her conscious mind. But when I asked about scheduling future appointments, Carol expressed disappointment. "This one was so short," she complained. "I really wanted to do it all in one."

I remembered that she had ostensibly come for help in ending her binging and vomiting. Apparently she had expected one-shot behavioral hypnotherapy, the type that's often used for habit control. But unconsciously, I thought, she must have known the truth, that she was here for something more. Given the perspicacity of her unconscious and how quickly it had led me to her family, at a deeper level Carol must have seen the opportunity to extricate herself from the family dynamic: to differentiate herself from her parents, to help her see herself as a whole and separate person.

"I don't know if any more sessions will help me," she hazarded, lamely. "And anyway I don't have a lot of money. I probably can't afford to come back."

I realized what Carol was doing: she was consciously resisting the idea of change. Unconsciously she knew something had happened: we had established a rapport, she had offered important information, major change was possible. But major change is scary, and consciously Carol needed to maintain a sense of safety and control, a sense that nothing precipitous would occur.

Suddenly I had an idea. That afternoon I was scheduled to hold my weekly consultation group with five therapists who were studying hypnotherapy with me. If I could persuade Carol to be a demonstration subject I could work with her again gratis. And if she believed she were doing it to *help* us, rather than as *therapy*, her conscious defensiveness might be lessened. I had a feeling Carol might like this idea because it might appeal to her "saintly" inclination toward helping others.

"I just had a thought," I offered. "I'll be teaching hypnosis to a group of therapists this afternoon, and a number of them are particularly interested in eating disorders. I wonder if you'd like to work with me in front of them as a demonstration? I know it would mean a sacrifice of time, but it would be free, of course. And it would be very helpful to them."

Carol was immediately interested. "You think they'd learn something from me?"

"I'm sure they would."

"You think it would help them help other girls like me?"

"I do."

"Then I'd like to do that."

So we agreed that she would return to my office at four o'clock that afternoon.

I spent the next five hours in nonstop meetings and sessions, but through them I felt that feverish undercurrent of excitement. I was certain that given the incisiveness of Carol's deeper mind and its earlier disclosures, it would confirm the family basis of eating disorders. In fact, I decided to tape-record the session so that I could capture her revelations for review.

But that wasn't all. What an unconscious! What a performance! Most clients, even those capable of deep trance, spend their first several sessions practicing. In four to eight hours of *trance training* we practice going deeper, practice responding to suggestions, practice talking while in trance. Serious trance work, such as the revelation of family patterns and lifelong emotional issues, doesn't come for several sessions. Even in trance, people have defenses, and intimate revelations can be made only when those defenses have lessened. But Carol had walked through my door a stranger, we'd established minimal trust and rapport, and in fifty minutes she had told me her life's emotional story. Her capacity for trance work was truly amazing.

But that wasn't all. Just when she had offered conscious resistance, I had remembered my consultation group, and her own propensity toward sacrifice had encouraged her to attend. What an extraordinary collusion of circumstances!

Throughout the day I knew that something important was bound to happen. I didn't know exactly what, or even how it would transpire, but I knew the potential was there. And, as sometimes happens in hypnotherapy, I sensed that almost anything I did would unleash it.

Five hours later Carol returned. With the therapists already seated in my office I found her in the waiting room, face ashen, knees shaking perceptibly. For a moment I felt stricken: I had manipulated her into doing something she didn't want to do. But when I asked if she wanted to forgo the session and meet privately the following week, she quickly demurred.

"Oh no!" she sang back. "I really want to do it! I'm just excited is all."

So we proceeded to my office where she laid her coat and purse on the floor, and I introduced her to the five therapists. In the tiny space our seven bodies were barely a knee apart, but Carol smiled broadly as she settled into a chair. I realized that, even prehypnosis, there was a hypnotic element to the encounter. Carol was following my suggestion: she was behaving *as if* she were there to help the therapists, rather than as a client, and had indeed split off much of the anxiety that would otherwise accompany the session. When I asked if I could tape record the session, she quickly agreed.

"Well," I smiled at Carol. I noticed that she'd changed her skirt since the morning, putting on a longer, less casual one that must have seemed to her more suited to the occasion. "I wonder if you could tell the group some things about you that you think are important, and why you came to therapy?"

Carol sat up straight in her chair, hands folded in her lap. "Okay," she began shyly, "I . . . well . . . about three years ago I started going through this stage of eating a lot and vomiting. It got me down to ninety-two pounds and I stayed that way for three years. At the same time, my mom and dad separated and I kind of went into a shell. I didn't want to have anything to do with anyone then, just the family."

I was intrigued by her choice of words, *went into a shell.* Immediately I pictured a tiny creature, peering out from a shell, withdrawn from and frightened by the outside world. It was also a perfect metaphor for her body: as a result of her disorder it, too, had become a shell, a thin shell of what it once was.

"And then . . . well . . . let's see . . . I guess about a year ago I overdosed and was put in the hospital. And then after I got out things were going pretty good, I wasn't vomiting as much or anything. And then it started picking up again. You know, candy and stuff like that.

"And then, let's see . . . well, then I found an apartment and started living on my own, and I was very lonely. So I overdosed again because I was eating and that led to stealing. When I got caught one time I just overdosed. Then I went in the hospital again. And now I'm working on trying to stop that because it's been going on too long."

By the time she had finished, her voice had brightened and her speech had quickened. The cheery, matter-of-fact tone of the morning had returned. I looked briefly at the therapists to see if they were as struck as I had been by the dissonance between her words and her presentation. Several returned my glance as if to say, *She's out of touch!*

"Thank you," I proffered. "I know this is difficult for you."

Carol laughed and shook her head no.

"Well then, why don't you just put your hands on your thighs and be comfortable. Do you remember how you were waiting for those hands to go numb this morning? Well, I want you to wait in that same way. Good. Now five . . . let yourself relax completely . . . four . . . you can feel yourself going to sleep now . . . three . . . going deeper and deeper . . . two . . . just let yourself go . . . very, very deep, your whole body loose and limp . . . and one."

As I counted Carol slumped progressively in her chair. Now she sat with her head leaning on one shoulder and her eyes closed.

"Now I'd like to speak again with Carol's unconscious mind

privately. At the count of three your unconscious mind and I will be alone . . . one . . . going deeper and more relaxed . . . two . . . deeper still . . . three."

At the count of three Carol sat up and opened her eyes. She stared sightlessly in front of her, oblivious to the five therapists just a few feet away. Since I had asked to speak with her privately she literally couldn't see them; what hypnotherapists call a *negative hallucination.*

"Hi," I said.

"Hi!" she returned warmly. As it had that morning, the voice of her unconscious sounded older, more mature than did the conscious Carol.

"It's nice to talk to you again. I wonder if you'd be willing to tell me some of the things you told me before?" I wanted the group to hear Carol's description of her family. I wanted them to see what I had seen: how it matched the pattern of bulimic families.

Carol nodded her agreement.

"You can remember exactly what you said to me before and then just say it again. I asked if there was anything I should know about Carol and what did you say?"

One of the remarkable abilities of the unconscious mind is its ability to repeat itself virtually verbatim. And now, using almost precisely the same words, Carol told me what she had said that morning. "She doesn't like herself," she said. "She thinks she's ugly. And she's very irresponsible and sometimes she isn't very kind to others. But sometimes she can be quite kind. Sometimes she does too much for other people. And then she wants people to pity her."

"And then you spoke about anger, too."

"I said she gets angry a lot. She locks it inside and doesn't talk to anyone about it. But sometimes when she's angry she talks about other people—behind their backs.

"And she gets nervous sometimes. She wants things to happen too fast."

I listened closely. The last two sentences were new, and "nervous" was an interesting word. What feels "nervous" to the unconscious may feel like panic to the conscious mind. Apparently we were getting another glimpse into Carol's secret life: a window into her ample garden of emotions that she so carefully screened from view.

"And then I asked if you thought her condition had anything to do with her parents and what did you say?"

There was a pause before she answered. "Yes." Her voice had

a decidedly childlike intonation. Apparently just thinking back to childhood had caused her to regress.

"Can you tell me more about that now?"

Another pause, and then the steady voice of the unconscious returned. "Her mom always yelled at her for eating the wrong things or eating too much, and got mad at her for dieting. And she yelled at her a lot, got mad at her a lot. But her dad was really kind. He never said anything. Never got mad at her for too many things . . . And then he left. He left her."

"And how did she feel about that?"

"Sad. Then she started eating and vomiting to get rid . . . to hide the problem."

I glanced quickly at the therapists to see if they had noted her correction.

"How did that hide it?"

"She didn't have to think about it because she was busy doing something else."

The candor of the unconscious was remarkable! Therapists have surmised that obsessive behavior can be a way of distracting a person from unwanted thoughts and feelings, but here was the unconscious laying it out in black and white!

"And you also told me something she thought about herself in relation to the separation of her parents."

"She thought it was her fault. She thought she did something wrong when she was little."

"Yes. Thank you . . . I think that about covers what we talked about this morning. Is there anything else you think I should know?"

She was silent for several seconds. "She remembers her dreams, easily. She always dreams about food, or she dreams horrid dreams about s-s-stealing, and they seem so real!" Her voice was subdued by trance, but there was no disguising the panic in it, or the fear that had caused her to stutter. Seconds later her voice grew calm but the horror remained in her words. "That just really scares her. She goes to bed at night thinking about breakfast, and then has a scary dream about food and wakes up with a headache." In the compressed speech of the unconscious the words sounded so simple, but the reality they described was anguished: chronic nightmares followed by daily headaches, and the relentless knowledge that bedtime would bring more of the same. I understood now why she had threatened suicide if our therapy didn't work.

"She felt scared a lot when she was little," Carol continued.

"She was scared of the dark. She was always scared her mother would die. Always told her that she didn't want her to die. She thought to herself that if her mother died she would kill herself so she could be with her mother."

Most children feel bonded with their mother and fear their ability to survive her death, but for few is it such a preoccupation. Was Carol's fixation another example of the enmeshment of the family, a symptom of how little sense of self she had, even as a child? And what would have triggered that particular fear? Children who witness spousal abuse often fear their mother's death. Had Carol witnessed such a scene? So far nothing suggested that she had.

I considered asking about her parents' relationship but refrained. Once I've given the unconscious an open-ended assignment it's best to let it roam, to note what *it* chooses to tell me and the order in which it presents. Interposing a question can indirectly suggest that an item is important, and I want to know what the unconscious finds important—not overlay its priorities with mine.

In fact, as I was reconsidering, Carol spoke again. "Her mother promised her when she was little that she would never get a divorce." Her voice lowered in disappointment. "But she did."

"Does Carol remember that promise consciously?"

"Yes! She does! Very strong. It was at night when I was going to bed mom promised me that. 'I'll never get a divorce.' . . . But she did." With the last words her voice became childlike and petulant, as if she still held the child's anger and sorrow. It was interesting to me that at nineteen Carol would still feel those feelings so strongly. While most children feel pain and betrayal at their parents' divorce, by nineteen, when the child is leaving home herself, those feelings are generally dampened. By nineteen most children have begun seeing their parents' lives as separate from their own. Carol didn't seem to.

I remembered Carol's adamancy about keeping her own promises, and the "saintly" rigidity with which bulimics defend against the distortions and contradictions of their parents. Perhaps pain over her mother's broken promise had fueled some of that behavior.

"And she was always scared of getting spanked by her dad. Her dad always spanked when we got in trouble, when the kids got in trouble. He would use his belt. One time she . . ." She paused. Her voice grew quiet and ominous, as if she were witnessing the scene while trying to stay out of sight. "One thing she remembers is her little brother getting spanked with the belt one time and . . . big red welts on him." She grew silent for a moment, then added quietly, "That scared her. It made her sad."

I thought about the escalating portrait she was painting of her father. First she'd called him "kind"; later she'd claimed he didn't get mad "for too many things"; now she'd revealed that he spanked them with a belt. In her successive tellings his image had changed from a benign figure to one who was violent enough to raise welts. Watching the belting had scared and saddened her; her pauses as she talked suggested that even now it was hard to touch this deep material.

"Now Carol has petit mal seizures," I noted. "She's had them since sixth grade. Do they have any psychological meaning?"

There was a long pause before she answered, and when she did her voice was high and diffident, like a child's. "No."

"You didn't cause those?"

"No-o." She whined the word as if fearful of being punished.

I realized immediately that I had erred. By asking if her seizures had psychological meaning, I had asked her to make a professional interpretation of her own behavior. Such a request can frighten a client, who may feel that the therapist has abandoned the role of knowledgeable helper and instead asked her to do the job. In response, the client may regress, becoming tentative, helpless, and childlike—and that's exactly what Carol had done. My mistake was compounded by asking so blatantly if she had "caused" them. A client, especially one in a deep trance, may hear those words not only as a question, but as an accusation: *you caused them!* Feeling blamed, Carol shrank back fearfully, like a child caught before her parent's wagging finger.

I had asked the questions because seizurelike behaviors are sometimes a somatic representation of an emotional problem. In Carol's case, despite her denial, I suspected they were a symptom of unexpressed conflict: conflict between what she'd allowed herself to know and feel about her family and what she'd split off.

To help the unconscious recover from my faux pas I quickly changed the subject. "Is there anything *else* you think I should know?"

Immediately her voice grew more mature. "She's impatient to find a solution to this. And she's tired of being inpatient."

Inpatient? The slip of the tongue had been unmistakable. But why? Carol was no longer an in-patient, at least not in a hospital, although she *was* confined to a group home. Perhaps she was saying she was tired of all that implied: tired of being hospitalized, tired of being suicidal, tired of being anxious and bulimic and unhappy. Perhaps she was saying she was ready to be done with it: ready for a cure.

"She feels dumb a lot of times," she went on. Her tone was clearly disapproving. "Everyone else she sees and associates with is accomplishing more than her, she thinks. She always looks at the bad points, never the good points."

"Any idea why she does that?"

She paused as if in thought. "Her mother," she asserted slowly. "Her mother caused that."

"In what way?"

"She always took her to the doctor, always made her feel sick. She said there had been something wrong with her for a long time."

Was she talking about her petit mal seizures? About her eating habits? I didn't know. But apparently Carol's symptoms had been a family focus since childhood.

"She always favored . . ." she paused. When she resumed, her voice was lower, ". . . my sister. Always favored her. And that, I think, caused a lot."

There was no missing the change in pronoun, the reversion to first person that marked the advent of strong emotion.

"Does Carol understand these things consciously?"

"Partly."

"But not completely?"

"No. She gets confused very easily."

I could imagine Carol's confusion. I could imagine her seeing bits and pieces of the family's dysfunctional patterns—a scary father raising welts, unfavorable comparisons to her sister, the double bind in respect to food, the demand she take sides in her parents' struggles. And I could imagine the pain those realizations would cause. So what would happen? The distressing information would begin to fade, would break apart like fog, and drift away, dissociated from her conscious mind. At times she might recall parts of it, but the whole of it, the patterns, would be too diffuse to see. She'd feel "confused."

And I suspected, too, that she had another means of handling the unpleasant family truths: rationalizing, minimizing, and idealizing her parents' behavior. "She can't help it," she'd said about her mom, rationalizing their "on-again off-again" relationship. "He never got mad at me for . . . too many things," she'd said about her dad, minimizing the instances when he did. "He's kind," she'd said, idealizing her father despite his beltings and his temper. These misperceptions would also lead to her confusion—for while she'd painted images she wanted to believe, a haunting inner voice must have whispered to her the truth. For Carol to recover she'd need to overcome her "confusion." Somehow she'd need to get a clearer picture of her past.

"Do you think it would be useful for Carol to look into her past in order to understand things about herself?"

"She's tried that, but when she does she always looks at the good things that happened when she was little. She can't see the bad things. And she tries to figure out if anything she did caused this. That's why she goes to a therapist, to find out."

I realized suddenly that Carol had the wrong scope on the problem. She wasn't looking at the past to see how family interactions had contributed to her problems. She was looking to see what *she* had done wrong. She couldn't see the "bad things"—the ways the family's interactions had been destructive—because her conscious defenses disallowed it. Instead she examined her own actions, looking for the fault.

Now I knew what to do. In explaining why Carol's previous therapy had been ineffective, her unconscious had told me how to help.

"Would it be helpful for *me* to help her look at her past?"

"Yes."

"Even the bad parts?"

Her voice rose slightly, "Yeah."

"And would you be willing to decide what would be okay for her to remember when she wakes up?"

"Yeah."

"How will you decide?"

She paused for a moment, thinking. "Well, the things I know make her upset, I won't let her remember!"

I smiled; it seemed so obvious. "Then I'll describe to you what I'd like to do, and I'd like your opinion about it, okay?"

She nodded.

"In a moment I'd like you to form a picture of all the significant people you have interacted with in your life, perhaps some that you don't even remember consciously. I'd like you to see those people in a progression over time, from when you were just a tiny, tiny baby to the present. And while you're doing that I'd like another part of your mind to see how, in various ways, those people helped form your personality: how they contributed to your fears, how they influenced your self-image; how they contributed to your ways of living in the world. I'd also like that part of your mind to see how those people interacted with each other and how *their* interactions affected you." I waited a moment to let her mind digest.

"And then, while those two parts of your mind are doing that, I'd like a *third* part of your mind to make mental notes—but without your knowing that it's doing so—about all those relationships and interrelationships." I paused again. "Do you think that would be useful?"

Carol nodded resolutely. "Yes."

"All right. Now you can close your eyes and go deeper to sleep while I talk elsewhere for a moment. When you feel me touch you on the knee like this," I leaned forward and touched her gently on the knee, "you will know that I am talking to you again. When I do, I will count to three and at the count of three your eyes will open and you will begin the assignment we just discussed. When the progression is over, the part of your mind that has been making mental notes will show you a whole new scene. It will be of you, some time in the future, but taking into account all the new learnings you've made. Do you understand?"

Carol nodded.

"Good. Now you can go deeper . . . deeper . . ."

Carol closed her eyes and slumped slowly to one side.

My assignment to Carol was extraordinarily complex. Had she been less remarkable a trance subject I never would have attempted it so soon. But her unconscious had been so forthcoming, and so seemingly insightful, that I believed she could carry it off.

I was configuring her unconscious mind to simultaneously accomplish three different tasks. One part would, in essence, create the movie of her life: it would revisit the significant events as they unfolded and mentally relive them. But that alone wouldn't help Carol see her past anew, for she would simply experience her life the way she already had. The events she witnessed would trigger the same feelings they had the first time, and lead to the same misinterpretations. To see her life differently—from a family systems perspective—she would also need to see the movie at some remove, distanced from the feelings those events would evoke. Only that way would she be open to new interpretations. I therefore asked *another part* of her mind to watch the progression but not relive it. This part would feel the feelings in diluted form, as if they were happening to Carol on a screen rather than in real life. This emotional distance would enable Carol to see her life from a less subjective perspective.

In asking her to use a *third part* of her mind to make mental notes about what it was seeing I was asking it to step back one *more* time, to assume an observer position in relation to Carol's past, from which it could watch the family interactions in a purely cerebral, analytic way. Completely divorced from feeling, armed with the intellectual knowledge she had gained in her previous therapy, and prompted by my cue that it would use its "new learnings" to show Carol her future, this part would be able to reinterpret Carol's past—hopefully to record a view of a family whose dysfunctional interactions had created a climate in which her problems flourished.

I asked that part to work in secrecy because I wanted its work to be pristine—untainted by Carol's earlier thinking or her feelings. Unlike the conscious mind, the unconscious can think in nonlinear ways. It can view a situation holistically, seeing multiple points of view and multiple points in time. I wanted it to have a free hand, to draw on its inner wisdom, as it reconfigured her understanding of the past. I trusted it to show her what she needed to see.

I talked with my consulting group for several minutes, partly to hear their thoughts, and partly to give Carol's unconscious a chance to "cook" on the assignment. Then I touched her lightly on the knee.

"Where do you think the images will begin to form?" I nudged.

"When I was a baby?" she asked querulously.

"Do you begin to see them?"

"Yeah."

"Just continue to watch them. And I think we should let them move down here." I reached out as if grasping something in the air in front of her and moved it toward her lap. Some clinicians believe that visualizing with the eyes lowered provides greater access to emotions, and I wanted to give Carol every advantage in that area.

"Now just continue watching the progression. And from time to time tell me how old you are." I assumed the images would flash through Carol's mind at lightning speed. There would be no way she could tell me everything she was seeing. Nor did I want her to, for that would be an intensive demand in itself. The unconscious thinks in word pictures, images, feelings, and sensations. To translate all its images into speech would require mobilizing yet another part of her mind. Such a demand might lighten Carol's trance or detract from her concentrated attention. So instead I asked her to recount the images "from time to time."

Carol sat upright in her chair, her eyes focused before her. Her pupils darted rapidly as images scrolled by. "She's playing with her neighbor, her best friend. . . ." she said. "Now she's going to school. It's her first day of school. . . ." Her voice grew childlike. "Her neighbor and her are getting on the bus. . . . Her mom is waving good-bye . . . she's a little scared, but she's with her friend so it's okay."

Interesting, I thought, that she would choose to open with her first leavetaking of the family. It was the same issue that dogged her after her parents' separation and that dogged her now: moving out into the world, growing out of the family and into her self.

"Now she's with her teacher. . . . At the end of the year she decides she doesn't like her teacher because she separated her neighbor and her, wouldn't let them sit next to each other." There was a long pause as images flew past, unnarrated. "Now she's in fifth grade. She had a rotten teacher. He made her exercise every day, twice a day, and run around the field eighteen times. . . . He never saluted the flag. He was a Jehovah's Witness." There was another long pause. "She's going to high school now. . . . She doesn't get along with her sister very well. They're fighting. Her mother is yelling at her. Her sister's a cheerleader and her mother is upset because she's not a cheerleader, too."

I wondered how she decided what to tell me. Some of her comments seemed expected, such as the talk of separation from first her mother and then her friend. And the alliance between her mother and her sister, which both excluded and denigrated Carol, seemed to illustrate the family dynamic. But why dwell as long on her teacher as on her mother and sister? Was she merely annotating as she thought of it? Or was she voicing the things that were most important? I didn't know. Nor did I need to find out, because I didn't need to interpret her past. Her unconscious was showing her what she needed to see; *it* would reinterpret as necessary.

"Now she's getting sick . . . she won't talk to anybody."

I assumed she was referring to the period following her parents' separation.

"She'll talk to her dad. Her mother and her are fighting. . . . Her mom's crying at night. It makes her very sad. . . ." There was a long break. "Now she's talking to her brother at night and tells him how she wants to take an overdose of pills. He thinks it's silly. She goes in and does it."

Now there was a long halt, a full ten seconds. When she began to talk again her voice was quiet. "Now she sees a fuzzy image of her mom . . . she's waving flowers over her face . . . she's saying, 'What's wrong?' . . ." Carol stared at the scene before her, focused on the images that only she could see, and slowly her lower lip began to quiver. She blinked quickly several times but the action couldn't impede the flow of tears. Silently they stained her cheeks and pooled at the corners of her mouth. In deep trance Carol's motions were muted: she couldn't sob, or hide her face, or bend her body to her grief. Just the fact that tears had come signaled very powerful emotions: emotions so strong they had collapsed the three-part dissociation in her mind. The part that was *watching* the scenes like a movie had begun to relive them and was overwhelmed by what it felt.

"*She* had those feelings and *you* don't need to," I urged, hoping to recreate the split between the parts.

Carol snuffled and gradually stopped crying. A moment later she continued. "And then she went away!" Her voice was incredulous as if trying to make sense of what she saw. "Now she's in a different room . . . her dad's there . . . very concerned. She's very weak."

I realized that she had described herself slipping into a coma; that's where she'd been when she "went away." The "different room" must have been another hospital room, out of intensive care.

There was another pause as images raced by. "Her dad takes her into his house . . . so she can find a job. She doesn't want to live with her mother anymore." Another long pause. "Now her dad wants her to move out. She doesn't want to. She's not ready. . . . She moves into an apartment by herself. . . . Things are going pretty good. Now they're starting to go downhill. . . . She tries to explain her feelings to her dad . . . but he just partially understands." There was another long pause, then her voice grew dull. "There's her brother. She's looking at her brother."

I knew from Paul Ellicott that before each of her suicide attempts she had spoken with her brother.

There was a long break before she continued. When she did her voice was soft. "She's in the hospital again. She sees him for two minutes and then she's gone."

Was it another coma? I presumed it was since her words were followed by another long pause.

"Now she sees her mother. Her mother's friend . . . his name is Jack." As she spoke her chin began to quiver again, and once more she began to cry.

Why was she crying? Was it because Jack had replaced her father? Or was she crying over all of it, for the whole sad picture she had painted of her life? She had reviewed nineteen years and mentioned nothing positive. No family vacations, no birthday parties, no quiet moments in the family embrace. Of course she'd probably told me less than a tenth of what she'd seen—but not one warm memory of childhood had been included. Perhaps she was crying because she was seeing her family afresh—and feeling the feelings she had previously denied.

"And you can continue to be calm as you tell me about them," I said gently, once again encouraging the split in her mind.

Carol stopped crying and began to talk again, but her voice was weak and sad, and sounded far away. "Jack and mom come to see her every night at the hospital. She doesn't lose her job. She seems happy. She wants to go back to work but the doctor won't let her." She paused, eyes following the imaginary film. "Now she's found a new family. A better one."

A reference to the group home?

"They don't fight. They're very kind to her. She doesn't want to have anything to do with her other family anymore." She stopped and blinked and then her gaze became less focused. She relaxed back into the chair.

"Does that take us to the present?"

"Yes."

"Good."

More than good, it was remarkable. She had relived and reinterpreted nineteen years of history right there before my eyes, in less than five minutes! And I knew but a fraction of what she had seen. She seemed to have touched emotions that were inexpressible before; did that mean the distancing had worked? Had she made "new learnings" that would result in change? Time would tell: over the next few months we would track her behavior. But what she told me next would be a valuable indicator of what to expect.

I had told her earlier that she would be envisioning her future because that step was needed for her to translate her reinterpretation into action. *Imagining* a future based on her "new learnings" would be a dress rehearsal, a chance to try out a new script in a safe environment before taking it out into the world. Would the script be one of growth? Of emancipation from the family? Of a new sense of self and self-esteem? We were about to find out.

"Now I'd like you to close your eyes for a moment, and when you open them you'll see a crystal ball floating in the air in front of you. . . . And as soon as you see it, you'll know why it's there!" The image of a crystal ball is so potent—so full of magic and power and wondrous possibility—that it would speak far more eloquently to her unconscious than the pallid directive to "imagine your future."

"At the count of three . . . one . . . two . . . three!"

Carol opened her eyes and stared into space.

"That's right," I encouraged. "Can you tell me what you see?"

"I see her," she said tentatively. "She's with her boyfriend now. They're dancing." Her voice grew stronger. "She has lots of friends. She's very active. She does lots of different things!" Her voice was confident now; the pace of her speech had quickened. "She's very artistic . . . she's doing pottery!" There was a long pause as time moved forward in her mind. "Now she's in an apartment by herself again. . . . She's very happy!"

She was imagining recovery! Dating, seeing friends, doing "lots of different things": she was forming attachments outside the family. She was emerging from her shell.

Carol was still staring blindly into space, images unfurling inside the crystal ball. For several seconds she said nothing, then suddenly, joyfully, she cried, "Now she's got a baby in her arms! . . . She seems even *more* happy!"

I waited to see what else she would say, but she was quiet.

"What season is it when she's in the apartment?" The baby image was clearly in the more distant future, but I was curious about her timeline for the more immediate events.

"Winter . . . It's snowing out . . . It's two weeks before Christmas!"

It was now November 11th. Did she mean Christmas of this year? That seemed unrealistic.

"How much does she appear to weigh?"

Joyously, "115!"

"What else about her is different?"

"She's very pretty! . . . She's happy!" She beamed and her face took on a radiance that her morning's superficial cheerfulness had not even approached.

"Is there anything else about her?"

Carol stared for a long time, then very slightly shook her head. Then she blinked several times and relaxed in her chair. Even with her eyes unfocused and her mouth agape, she seemed to radiate happiness.

She had done it. She had visualized a complete recovery. Breaking away from the family; seeing herself as pretty; weighing—joyously—115 rather than her current 92; she seemed to have incorporated a wholly new self-image. And the baby: I took that as the ultimate sign of health, for it presupposed two things. It meant that her period would return, marking an end to her bulimorexia, and it meant that in mothering someone else, she would cease needing to be a child.

"Okay," I directed softly, "you can let the crystal ball go away."
Carol closed her eyes.

"That's right. . . . Now you can open your eyes again and look
at me . . . still deeply asleep." When her eyes were open I smiled at her
warmly. "You can handle it from here, can't you?"

She answered immediately. "Yes!"

"Okay. Go to sleep now."

She closed her eyes and slumped slowly to the side.

"Just sleep deeply for a few minutes. . . . You've done a lot of
work. . . . You deserve a rest. . . . I'm going to talk elsewhere for a
moment and I won't be talking to you again until I touch you on the
knee."

I spoke with the consultees for several minutes, reviewing what
we'd seen and giving Carol's mind time to process its operations. Then
I turned back to her. When I touched her knee she sat up and opened
her eyes.

"That's right. . . . You can look at me . . . deeply asleep. . . . Do
you think you're ready to take it on your own?"

"Yes!" The confidence and eagerness in her voice were hard to
miss.

"Do you need anything else from me?"

She shook her head.

"How would you like to let Carol know *consciously* that she's
going to do what she needs to do? I don't think she needs to remember
all of this." I wanted the unconscious to allow some of what she'd done
into her conscious mind, for conscious awareness would help translate
her new learnings into action.

"I'll let her remember the happy parts."

I enjoyed how simple it seemed. "Good. You'll take care of
that?"

"Uh-huh."

"You've considered all the things you need to consider?" I
wanted to make sure she had reviewed and reinterpreted everything
she needed to before I woke her up.

"Uh-huh."

"All right. I'm going to wake you up now. You can close your
eyes."

Carol did so and leaned heavily to the side.

"In a moment I'm going to count from five to one. At the count
of one Carol will be wide awake, remembering only what her unconscious mind finds useful and productive. . . . And you won't be sur-

prised to find other people in the room . . . as a matter of fact, they'll seem very warm and friendly to you." I didn't want her to be alarmed or embarrassed by the presence of the five consultees.

"You'll feel positive and refreshed and you'll have an idea that you're going to have a very pleasant surprise sometime later. . . . You may or may not know that you have to see me again. . . ."

I stopped quickly. I had meant to say, "you may or may not have to see me again," indirectly suggesting no need for further therapy, but I had actually suggested the reverse. Why? I realized that a part of me was actually a bit incredulous about Carol's performance. She had been so accommodating. She had done it so well, exactly as I had asked. Was it too good to be true? Hilda Bruch, one of the pioneering interpreters of eating disorders, had noted the "enormous compliance" that women with eating disorders often show in treatment. They agree with everything that's being said, even fabricate material they feel the therapist wants to hear. Is that what had happened? In the space of a second I developed a fantasy that Carol would leave my office not to be seen again and chuckle over how she'd put one over on me and my consultees. I realized as I heard my slip of the tongue that I wanted Carol to come back so I could verify her changes.

"With each count you're going to feel better and better . . . very positive. . . . And you'll probably want to learn self-hypnosis in the future." With that suggestion I could encourage her to come back. "Now, five, you're beginning to feel a sense of well-being . . . four, it feels better and better . . ."

Carol began to smile and sit up.

"That's right . . . it feels good! . . . three, it's going to be hard to resist a smile . . . two, almost back in the room now, feeling wonderful . . . one!"

Carol sat up completely, opened her eyes, and began to grin.

"Hi," I greeted her.

"Hi!" Her manner was effervescent.

"Did you have a nice sleep?" I wanted to reinforce whatever degree of amnesia her unconscious had chosen.

She laughed. "Yeah!"

"Good! Are you comfortable?"

She nodded.

"Just take a couple of seconds to gather yourself together."

I realized as I heard myself say those words that I had made another error. During the trance I had asked her unconscious to split into three parts, but then I had failed to reunite the parts before awakening her. I was completely unaware of my error—until I heard myself talk. Unconsciously I'd chosen the phrase "gather yourself together," which gave Carol a chance to reunite the parts herself, unconsciously.

As Carol gathered up her coat and purse she noticed the consultees. One smiled and said hello and Carol grinned back.

"They don't seem too weird, do they?" I asked, gesturing toward the group.

Carol radiated cheer. "Nah." She seemed truly unfazed by their presence.

Amazing, I thought. If I had just awakened from a trance with at least partial amnesia and found myself facing a group of strangers, I'd be anxious: I'd wonder what I'd revealed! But Carol seemed perfectly calm; in fact, more than calm. She seemed positively giddy, grinning from ear to ear as she donned her coat and bag. Her giddiness rekindled my concern about the authenticity of her performance. Suppose she hadn't really reinterpreted her past? Suppose she was merely feeling good because I'd suggested that before awakening her? Suppose she got home, grew increasingly despondent, and killed herself? I'd trusted that she wasn't suicidal earlier in the day, but that was before the intervention. What if the failure of the intervention had drained her hope? I needed to hear from her again quickly.

"What I'd like you to do, if you would, is call me in two days— just to let me know how things are going." If the intervention *had* worked, two days would let her feel some positive changes; if it hadn't, I'd catch her before she succumbed to despair.

"OK," Carol agreed.

She had mentioned earlier in the day that she would be going out that night with friends from the group home. "Have a good time tonight," I offered.

"I sure will!" she giggled and waved graciously at the group. "It was nice meeting y'all." Then she sashayed out the door.

Two days later, despite my fears, Carol called to report her progress.

"I'm doing okay," she said quickly, "but I'm worried it's not working because I can remember most of what you told me."

I was intrigued by her phrasing, since I had told her nothing. Apparently she'd recast the experience as a dialogue with an authority, rather than as a trialogue within her own mind.

"What can you remember?"

"I've been fighting against remembering, but I remember looking in the crystal ball, and I remember some things from my childhood. Does that mean the hypnosis won't work?"

I assured her that it didn't, that her unconscious was allowing her to remember because she was ready to. She protested several times, and finally I suggested that she ask her unconscious if *it* thought remembering was a sign of progress. The phone grew quiet for several moments, then she exhaled loudly.

"I guess it *is* working," she said. "Now I feel more relaxed."

"Good," I reassured her. "So tell me how things have been."

"I haven't binged or vomited since I saw you."

"That's great!"

"Yeah, and I think I've been getting full more. It's like at the end of the meal I don't need to keep eating."

That was music to my ears. People with eating disorders typically don't feel full after meals. Often they've dissociated the sensations of the body so they are unaware of the fullness signal; often they so crave emotional nourishment that its physical counterpart, the demand for food, becomes insatiable. I wasn't surprised that Carol dissociated bodily sensations: that would be a reasonable response to repeated beltings. But if now she was beginning to feel full after meals, did that mean she was ending that dissociation? And if so, would she also bring back other feelings and knowledge she had split off?

"And I don't feel like the problem is nagging at me so much anymore."

Again I was intrigued by her choice of word. Did that mean she was beginning to free herself from her family, from *their* nagging voices?

"I've been thinking about food less," she went on. "I haven't felt like I need to eat every time I *see* food. And, oh yeah, I haven't had any nightmares since I saw you!"

"Wow!" I said. "That's quite a report!"

"Yeah!" She sounded quite pleased, as if she were tallying her progress for the first time.

We then arranged to meet in nine days to review her progress, with the proviso that she call me earlier if she experienced concerns. When I got off the phone I wondered: Why had I thrown out that proviso? Was I *expecting* Carol to have concerns? Or was I expressing concerns of my own? I realized that part of me still questioned the efficacy of the intervention. Treating eating disorders can take years, I knew, so how could I expect to see healing after an hour's session? It was with nervous anticipation that I awaited her next visit.

When Carol arrived nine days later she waltzed into my office with the same upbeat manner she'd worn the first time, but the minute she opened her mouth I sensed a change. Her voice seemed older, a bit more sober—closer to the voice she'd had in trance.

"How are things going?"

"Good!" she proclaimed eagerly. "I've only binged and vomited once. It was after talking to my mom."

"What happened?"

She grimaced. "She told me I was stupid to do hypnosis."

"What did you say?"

"I said it was good for me. But then I got upset." She paused and wrinkled her nose. "But that was a week ago and I haven't done it since!"

I was delighted. A client's truest measure of recovery is her ability to recover from a relapse. Until we've seen that happen—repeatedly, with the recovery period shortening over time—we don't entirely trust the recovery process. So both Carol's binge and her recovery were welcome news.

"How are you getting along with your folks?"

"I'm trying not to see them too much. I think it's better that way. They just make me nuts." She paused. "But even though I vomited that once, I still managed to gain a pound!"

She'd *managed* to gain a pound? Less than two weeks earlier she had adamantly refused to gain weight.

"I think I've also been feeling better about myself," she continued. "I mean, more confident. I'm trying not to be so hard on myself all the time."

"That sounds great."

"Yeah." She nodded pensively. "And I think I've been feeling better about other people, too."

"In what way?"

"Oh, just less critical. Like it's okay if they're not perfect. Like Lisa, my roommate, she borrowed my brush and didn't give it back and then when I needed it I didn't know where it was. And in the past I would have really gotten on her case about that—you know, I'd be really pissed and give her a lecture about how you always have to return things. . . . But for some reason I didn't. I just thought, oh well, I guess she forgot. I mean, it's just a hairbrush."

I smiled. The "little saint's" halo was tarnishing before my eyes. "It sounds like you're making progress."

She nodded, then her eyes narrowed slightly, her gaze grew soft, and I could see her look inside. "You know, I've been thinking about things since I saw you." She spoke carefully as if choosing her words. "I've been thinking about my suicide attempts. And I think I've made a decision to live." She nodded her head slightly as if confirming her own statement. "I think I might have been set up for those overdoses."

"Set up?"

"Yeah. I mean, it wasn't like I really wanted to do it, but at the time I felt I had to. Kind of like a reaction to things. It's hard to explain."

I tried to get Carol to be a little more specific but she couldn't, and after a few questions I stopped pressing. Whatever had motivated that statement was not yet fully formed consciously. Perhaps at a later appointment she could say more. For now I could only guess that she was beginning to understand that complex family interactions had precipitated her actions.

"Well," I observed, after we'd chatted a few more minutes, "it sounds like you're doing everything you need to be doing. How about if I give you a hypnotic 'reinforcement' today and then see you again in about three weeks?"

Carol agreed readily, so once again I induced a deep trance and asked to speak to her unconscious privately.

"Hi," I said as she sat up and opened her eyes. "Nice to speak to you again."

"Hi!" she smiled back.

"How do you think she's doing?"

"Good," the unconscious reported soberly. "She's a lot happier than she was before. And a lot more patient. She doesn't get as upset with herself anymore."

She was confirming Carol's conscious report.

"She misses her parents a little. . . . She's not going to see them for a while. Later she'll see them again, but things will be different."

"In what way?"

"She won't be the same. So things will be different between them."

Was she forecasting a loosening of the family bond? She'd described a period of separation and then a changed relationship. Was this a sign that Carol would later rejoin her family on more self-selected terms?

"What's your assessment of her overall progress?"

"Oh, she's definitely making progress. She has about three-quarters of the way to go. She's going to binge and vomit a few more times—for about three more weeks. Then she won't do it any more. She'll complain about it when it happens—she'll think she's having relapses—but they won't really be relapses. Not really." She looked at me matter of factly, then added, as if for my benefit, "It's better for her to do it gradually."

I had to chuckle to myself. The unconscious was predicting her course of recovery *and* she was doing it according to therapeutic models. People in recovery often experience a period of oscillation while they adjust to the idea of change. In effect, they "try on" their old symptoms from time to time to make sure they want to discard them.

"Basically she'll get better the way she saw it in the crystal ball," the unconscious added with an authoritative nod. "It'll happen just like that."

Of course, I thought. I shouldn't have been surprised. She'd predicted this recovery before. Now she was just translating her images into words.

"Well, thank you. You've been very helpful."

She smiled as if the pleasure had been hers.

"Do you think it would be useful for Carol to learn auto-hypnosis so she could consult you herself?"

"Yes," she assented, "that would be good."

So I gave detailed instructions on the practice of self-hypnosis, plus suggestions about the value of trusting her inner wisdom, and then I awakened her.

Carol awoke feeling relaxed and cheerful, with self-elected total amnesia. I repeated the instructions for self-hypnosis and had her demonstrate a self-induced trance. Then I got out my appointment book to schedule our next appointment. As I found the date on the next month's page a little shiver ran through me. The date we'd agreed on for her final appointment was December 11th, precisely two weeks before Christmas.

*   *   *

Two days later Carol called for advice. Her father had invited her to spend Christmas with him and she wanted to know if I thought it a good idea.

"I don't know," I told her. "But you do, deep inside. Why not use self-hypnosis to consult your unconscious and abide by whatever it tells you?"

Carol agreed that she would, and I didn't hear from her again until her next appointment.

On December 11th she came for her final session. She stood in the doorway expectantly and when I looked quizzical, wondering why she hadn't come in, she twisted her face in mock annoyance. "Don't you *see* anything?" she demanded. "Don't you see a *difference*?"

As soon as she said that, I did. Her face was a little fuller, softening the harshness of her cheeks and chin. Her skin had lost its pasty pallor. "You've gained weight."

She blushed. "Eleven pounds. It was easy."

"Easy?"

"Yeah. I didn't even have to work at it. It just happened."

That's pretty remarkable, I thought. Five weeks ago she was adamant about not gaining weight; now she's impressed with her ease in gaining.

She flopped casually into the chair. "I've been weighing myself once in a while. I think that's a good sign."

Apparently for years she had weighed herself obsessively, several times a day. Then the mental health center had prohibited her from weighing herself at all. So the fact that she was now weighing herself occasionally suggested a normalization.

"How does it feel?"

"It feels good." Suddenly her face sobered. "But I've binged and vomited twice since I saw you."

"How does that make you feel?"

"I get scared it's not working."

"Do you know what triggered your binges?"

"Yeah. It was after talking to my mom." She sighed. "We're still not getting along."

"What's the problem?"

"She's just so selfish! She always wants me to do things for her. But she never wants to do anything for me."

"What does she want you to do for her?"

"Oh, her and her boyfriend are having a fight and she wants

me to come over to the house. But she won't come to *my* house if I call her and tell her *I'm* lonely."

Apparently the truth about her mother's behavior was seeping into Carol's conscious mind. She would be in for some painful times, I thought, as she began to see her family more clearly. But ultimately, I believed, she would come out stronger.

"Did you decide to visit your father?"

"Yeah." She was surprisingly cheerful. "I did what you said—I asked my unconscious, and it said it would be all right."

I smiled. I was delighted that she had learned to use her own unconscious as a guide.

She went on to tell me that she was thinking about leaving the group home, although she needed a job in order to move out. So we talked about job prospects for a while and about the assets and liabilities of living alone.

"I feel like I'm becoming a new me," she said finally, as if summing up. She looked out the window and I had the sense that she was taking stock of her new attributes. But suddenly her eyes clouded. "But I don't want the new me to gain any weight!" Her voice had that same guarded tone it had had at the beginning when she had warned me against weight gain at her very first session.

I was startled: earlier she'd been so pleased with her eleven-pound gain, and she was still twelve pounds shy of 115. Why this sudden retraction? But then I remembered—it was just as the unconscious had said—Carol would alternately accept and resist the idea of gaining weight.

"I can gain in other ways," she considered, "just not on the scale. I mean, I'm gaining already . . . it's just *proportioning* itself."

I smiled at her choice of words. It was, indeed, proportioning itself. Her body was taking on more womanly *proportions*. Food was being consumed in more appropriate *portions*. And her understanding of herself and her family was growing, in *proportion* to what she could handle. "You're right," I commented. "I think you're gaining in all the right ways."

And after a little more conversation we agreed that Carol didn't need to return, but could certainly if she felt the need.

As she got up to leave I happened to glance out the window. To my surprise it was beginning to snow—not a common occurrence in Seattle.

Carol followed my gaze and saw it too. "It's snowing!" she cried with a child's delight, and with barely a good-bye, grabbed her coat and sped out the door.

It was only after she was gone that I realized: it was snowing in Seattle. Carol had not achieved all of her predicted targets but she was clearly moving in the right direction. And there were two weeks to go before Christmas.

Six months later I called to see how she was doing. The group home gave me a new telephone number at the apartment Carol had rented four months before. When I reached her, her voice sounded cheerful and strong.

"You moved," I observed.

"Yeah!" she exclaimed. "Boy, was I glad to get out of *there*."

"How do you like being on your own?"

"I like it. There's nobody watching over me all the time."

"You're not lonely?"

She hesitated for half a second. "Sometimes I get lonely. But it's okay. It's not like it was last time. I mean, I'm not gonna OD or anything." She giggled a little, as if the memory embarrassed her.

"That's good. What else is new? Give me a report."

She thought for a minute. "I've got a job working in an office. I file things all day. But I like it. The people are real nice."

"Sounds good."

"I've started seeing my family a little bit more. I didn't see them for a long time. But a few weeks ago I had dinner with my dad and it was okay. He started in about how I should be going to college, and how come I don't visit him more, but I just kinda didn't pay attention. I guess that's good. It used to make me really crazy when he said those things." She stopped as if thinking. "I mean, I probably will go to college, maybe in a year or so. But I need to wait until I'm ready."

I smiled. "How are things with your mom?"

"Not so good. I don't think I'm ready to see her a lot yet. She broke up with that guy Jack and for a long time she wanted to be at my place all the time. But I told her I didn't think that was such a good idea."

"How did she deal with that?"

"She got upset. She called a lot. She got my sister to try to change my mind. But now she's kind of calmed down. She calls me every once in a while, but that's about it. I guess she figured out she can't make me do it." Carol was silent for several seconds. "But you know what?" Suddenly her voice was cheerful again. "I haven't binged or vomited in months! Not once!"

"That's terrific!"

"Yeah. . . . And I'm still doing self-hypnosis."

"How's that going?"

"It's pretty cool. I was just having a problem with my sister and I decided to hypnotize myself and see if I could dream a solution. And I did."

"That *is* cool," I agreed. In fact, it was more than cool. Just months before, Carol had been deliberately out of touch with her inner mind; now she was soliciting its advice. That was the strongest sign of recovery yet.

We chatted for a few more minutes, then Carol announced that she had to go: her boyfriend was waiting. Warmly I told her how pleased I was to have known her, and then we hung up. Afterwards I thought about what she had said.

Her recovery seemed virtually complete. She had stopped binging and vomiting. She sounded happy and confident in her life on her own. She was forming a new relationship with her parents. It was, in fact, unfolding as her unconscious had predicted. But something else struck me, something in her description of her mother. Her mother had calmed down, she had said. *She figured out she can't make me do it.* In retrospect those words seemed profound, for they indicated another whole level of change. Carol wasn't the only one to change: her mother had changed too. Faced with Carol's refusal to coddle her, she had eventually backed down and appeared to be granting Carol the autonomy she deserved. Would this island of autonomy extend to other areas? Would her mother begin to see Carol as an "other," whose needs and desires differed from her own? I had a feeling that she might because from now on, I believed, Carol would insist on being treated differently.

And what about her father? Would he, too, change as a result of Carol's growth? Perhaps the signs were already there. Carol had refused to engage him on two chronic issues; how long before he, too, backed down and began to acknowledge her separateness?

I thought about what her unconscious had predicted: after a period of separation, *she* won't be the same, so things will be different between them. That was exactly what was happening. Carol's changes were precipitating changes in the family.

Suddenly I had an eerie feeling. I had never met the family, and yet they had been touched by the process. The intervention with Carol's unconscious had precipitated family change. Suddenly I understood—empirically—the interconnectedness of families. Like a hand whose five fingers are bound by a rubber band, one family member's change causes adjustments in all the others. "Change the child and let the family learn to live with him differently," Milton Erickson would say to me later, confirming what I had noticed. As a result of one member's changed perceptions, family relationships get altered.

Several years after I saw Carol I wrote up her story for a professional book. The editor asked me to discuss my intervention in the context of traditional psychotherapy, so I reread the literature on eating disorders to have a basis of comparison. As I reviewed the articles I was struck by what I found. Carol's course of treatment paralleled the path of long-term psychotherapy patients, but took a fraction of the time. What they accomplished in perhaps two or three years, she did in under two hours, without missing a step. As I read these articles and recognized the parallels, I was filled with awe. Just as Carol's unconscious had collapsed nineteen years into a five-minute review, it had collapsed the traditional treatment process for bulimorexia into a fraction of itself. Once again, the power of the unconscious astounded me.

Yet for all its *similarity* to traditional talk therapy, Carol's case had a fascinating difference. The give-and-take that traditionally occurs between therapist and client took place *privately* between the client and herself. I created the playing field: by suggesting she look at how relationships in the past had influenced her personality; by asking her to use her new learnings to create a vision of the future; by creating the three-part mind split to do the task. But from the moment her unconscious took over I remained mute. I neither prodded nor interpreted; the work of reinterpretation was done wholly within her own mind. In a sense her unconscious played two roles—hers and mine.

What enabled the unconscious to perform these dual roles, and in such an abridgment of time? Part of the answer is definable. In trance we were able to dissociate many of Carol's conscious defenses, enabling her to perceive core material quickly. We were also able to create a meta-position *outside* the family, from which she could see her family interactions more clearly. But that doesn't entirely explain what happened, for something *else* was at work as well: something that enabled the unconscious to work constructively with what it saw, to choose a path of healing over one of stasis. What enabled *that* to happen I don't really know, for that part of the unconscious is a mystery. Western culture has no words or concepts for the kind of higher intelligence that I regularly see at work in my clients' unconscious minds. Eastern religions believe that each of us has "a face that we wore before we were born," an intuitive wisdom broader than any we acquire in our lives. I believe this wisdom is contained in the unconscious. I believe it, too, helped Carol see herself and her family in a different way.

Carol's was a once-in-a-lifetime case. The constellation of events that enabled her healing—her remarkable capacity for trancework, the intellectual knowledge she'd gained at the mental health center, the serendipitous timing of my consulting group and her disposition toward helping others, her own "inpatience"—these factors precipitated healing that was faster and more "miraculous" than any I may see again. But Carol is not unique. The process that was available to her is available to each of us. We are each capable of some degree of trancework. We can each bid our unconscious to see ourself anew. For some the view into the crystal ball is more easily found than others, but for everyone it is possible. We all have an unconscious healer within.

Part III

When Mind and Body Talk

Chapter 7

The Place Where There Is No Pain

TERRY YEAKEL HAD BEEN MY CLIENT FOR ALMOST THREE YEARS. TWICE A week she came into my office, and bit by bit, as water erodes granite, exposed the sad, brutal truths of her childhood, which had been marked by chronic sexual abuse. To survive, Terry had massively dissociated. She had pushed away the pain, the fear, the unacceptable truth that her parents would permit such a thing to happen, to a place where they were almost out of mind. In this way, she could still feel safe. This mental splitting—into owned and disowned, conscious and unconscious—is a form of trance. It is the primary coping mechanism for those who endure chronic abuse.

Terry had emerged from this history with an acerbic sense of humor; what she lacked in self-esteem she more than made up for in personality. Her characterizations of people and situations had the bite of editorial cartoons, and her strongly held opinions were offered as surely and theatrically as if to a claque of reporters. Many times Terry's ready, raucous laugh moved me to laugh along with her, and over the hundreds of sessions in which I had come to know her we had developed a strong and mutual respect.

Over the years we had steadily penetrated her protective trance and brought many of her disowned experiences back into awareness so that she could integrate and move beyond them. But ironically, during a brief detour in our therapy, that ability to split off experience came to protect her once again—by enabling Terry, who was allergic to chemical narcotics, to endure a five-hour surgery without anesthesia.

*   *   *

It was a hot day in June when Terry came into my office, more edgy and distracted than usual. Her dark eyes avoided mine; her over-weight body shifted uncomfortably in the chair; her round, full face seemed flushed. We had been tackling a difficult issue in the previous sessions and I attributed her discomfort to that, so I was surprised when midway through the session she suddenly blurted, "I have a favor to ask you."

"What's that?" I asked, wondering what she could possibly have in mind.

"I have to have surgery. I have a growth. Here . . . ." She touched her right jaw. "And I need you to do hypnoanesthesia."

I scanned her face, seeing it freshly now, as if for the first time. Her narrow, shapely lips in their signature ruby lipstick; her fine, winged nose; her long-lashed, deep-set eyes seemed incongruous with the plump cheeks and padded neck from which they rose, as if a sculp-tor had carefully chiseled the most delicate features from a lump of clay and then grown bored. I realized that the fleshiness of her cheek and jaw could easily obscure a tumor.

"I'm sorry to hear that." I felt genuine sorrow, for I knew how frightening this would be. Only two years before, Terry had had a life-threatening experience in surgery when her trachea collapsed in reac-tion to anesthesia. And now, as then, the prospect of being cut and sewn by a male doctor while feeling largely out of control was apt to engender painful associations to her past. "I'd love to help you, Terry. We can certainly talk about hypnoanesthesia. It would take us several sessions to prepare, but it's probably possible. We can talk to your doctor. . . ."

"No, I've already talked to him. He said it's okay."

"You've already talked to him?" It seemed odd that Terry would talk to the surgeon before consulting me. Our relationship was strong and intimate, and she routinely shared her concerns with me.

"We had to schedule it. . . ."

"Oh?" I was suddenly wary. "When did you schedule it for?"

"Tuesday."

"Tuesday!" Tuesday was four days away. I tried to control my dismay. "Why so soon?"

She raised her shoulder in a defeated little shrug, and as she did I understood: Terry had known about the surgery for some time, but as was her custom with uncomfortable truths, she had pretended it away.

Now bit by bit the truth came out. The growth that was invading Terry's face had been developing for at least a year. Months before, her doctor had pressed her to have it removed—a biopsy had determined it was benign, but its continuing growth would be problematic—but Terry had refused. She'd already been "carved on too many times," she said; there was no way she was "going under the knife" again. Besides, in case the biopsy was wrong and the growth was malignant, she didn't want to know. So the tumor had continued to grow, and it wasn't until this week, when it had begun pressing a facial nerve, that Terry had resigned herself to the surgery.

And now, because of her allergy, she needed hypnoanesthesia.

It was hard not to feel alarmed. I'd done other hypnoanesthesias: dental surgeries, natural childbirths, a C-section. But this procedure would be far more challenging. The surgeon, Terry explained, would be peeling back both sides of her face, separating the underlying layers, scraping the growth from her delicate facial nerves, then sewing her back together, in an operation that would last five hours—four more than any of my earlier procedures. And while those surgeries had been done with posthypnotic suggestion—I'd had the patients practice ahead of time, then hypnotized them in my office and given them suggestions to follow during the procedure—this one would be done in the hospital. We wouldn't have the quiet, protected environment in which I was used to working, or the exclusive, one-on-one interaction that is desirable for hypnotic rapport. Could Terry and I maintain a trance for five long hours? In that distracting environment? Or would my own fascinations and anxieties pull my concentration aside and jeopardize our rapport?

And then there was the issue of Terry's anxiety. Because the situation might trigger a traumatic association to her past, I'd have to "hold" her psychologically, help her feel calm and protected before and throughout the event.

Could we prepare for these demands in the tiny amount of time we had? Normally for a procedure of this sort I'd spend several sessions getting ready. I'd have Terry talk to the surgeon, learning the procedure in detail, so we could tailor suggestions to her specific concerns. I'd talk to the surgical team myself, explaining how suggestible and literal-minded Terry would be, and how they'd have to watch their words. We'd do a mental rehearsal so Terry would feel confident at the actual event. But we'd never have time for all that now.

I evaluated the situation. Terry was an extremely adept hypnotic subject—clearly capable of the depth of trance necessary for this level of work. And there was a strong bond of trust between us, which suggested we could achieve the necessary hypnotic rapport. If I arrived at the hospital early I could talk to the surgical team ahead of time. And if I spent an hour with Terry before the surgery I could induce a trance and still have time to give elaborate suggestions for pain control, anxiety management, and healing. . . . It *could* work, I decided. It would have to.

So Terry promised to arrange for the surgical team to talk with me ahead of time, and I agreed to meet her in the hospital waiting room at six o'clock on Tuesday morning.

When I arrived, the waiting room was empty. I announced myself to the nurse at the desk. She knew nothing about Terry's hypnoanesthesia.

"Is the surgical team here? We were supposed to meet ahead of time."

"I don't know anything about that, sir."

"Is Ms. Yaekel here?"

"Yes. They've taken her back to prep."

"But I'm her therapist," I explained, trying to remain calm despite the fact that our plans were unraveling. "I have to prepare her for hypnoanesthesia."

"I'm sorry, sir, but the patient is preparing for surgery and visitors are not permitted."

I explained again and yet again, and finally, as much to quiet me as anything, the nurse agreed to bring Terry to the waiting room.

She emerged pale and awkward in her surgical gown.

"David!" she cried, visibly relieved to see me.

I put my arm around her and guided her to two chairs in the corner where we huddled for a moment. We were about to request a private room when another nurse appeared, telling us it was time for visitors to leave.

"He's not a visitor, he's my therapist."

"He'll be able to see you later."

"No, he needs to work with me before I go in."

"I'm sorry." The nurse smiled patronizingly. "But the doctor hasn't given us any special orders and it's time to take you back."

Terry looked at me in alarm.

"I'm sure if you talk to Dr. Radke he can straighten this out," I said. "We've worked this out with him. I'm going to be in the operating room with her."

The nurse looked at me skeptically. "Well, I have to take her back now. But I'll check with the doctor." And she led Terry off, paper sandals flopping, trying once again to explain.

Ten minutes later the nurse reappeared. "You can have five minutes with her," she directed rather tartly, "then you have to prep for surgery too. They're getting ready to start."

I felt a jab of anger. *You want my help,* I thought. *Your patient's allergic to anesthesia; I'm here to provide a safe alternative, but then you thwart me!* It was anger I'd felt before when dealing with the allopathic medical community: back in the 1970s they were so ignorant about hypnotherapy that instead of regarding me as a professional, they saw me as a crank. But on the heels of the anger swept another feeling: the knowledge that anger was counterproductive. If I raged against the hospital or focused on my irritation I'd only jeopardize our work with Terry. So I decided instead to teach them a lesson: I'd *prove* the value of hypnotherapy—and my own professionalism—by doing an excellent job. So, biting my tongue, I thanked the nurse and followed her directions to the prep room.

Terry was lying on a gurney, covered from her neck down by a white hospital blanket. I could see from her hand position—palms up, at her sides—that she was trying to self-hypnotize: the meditation-like pose was one she used in my office. I could also see that her efforts were futile. Her eyelids were fluttering; her breathing was shallow; her face was knotted with fear.

"Terry," I said gently.

Immediately her eyes flew open and she turned toward me.

"You're really scared, aren't you? And I bet you're wondering if we have enough time. Well, if we start now we'll have all the time we need. All the time in the world for your unconscious mind to prepare. We can do this."

Terry nodded, her eyes slightly calmer. By giving voice to her feelings I had assured her she was understood. I'd created a *yes set— yes, you understand!*—which would help her follow my next words as they led her toward trance.

"All right now, Terry. Just listen to me and nothing else matters. You are just here with me now, listening and breathing, and wanting very much to disconnect from any stress or pain, worry or fear, and because you greatly desire to *put aside any concerns,* you'll be able to focus deeply on this voice, on these words, and go into a trance *now.*" I had said those words to Terry countless times before. This time, because of the demands of the moment and her familiarity with the procedure, she slipped into medium trance almost immediately. Now I needed to deepen and stabilize that trance. To maintain the anesthesia, to handle the spontaneous demands of the surgery, to stay in communication with the doctor while remaining "inside," to manage the stresses of the situation, Terry would need to be very, very deep. "And with each and every breath you will feel yourself relaxing deeper and deeper, letting go completely. . . ." I counted slowly from one to twenty. As I did so, Terry's breathing grew slow and even, signs the trance was deepening.

But that didn't relieve my discomfort. The day before I had thought a bit about my hypnotic approach. Drawing on what I knew about Terry—her personality, her history, her feelings about herself and the surgery—I had outlined six key points to cover. These were Terry's relationship with me (her need to stay in close hypnotic rapport so my voice could guide and comfort her throughout); her relationship with her self and body (her need to feel a sense of participation and control, while relinquishing conscious control of her head); her relationship with the team (her ability to hear and respond to them when appropriate, and to trust in their expertise); managing her pain (helping her distance from it through numbing and distraction, and helping her reinterpret it as heat or cold or pressure); managing her anxiety (by helping her relax and reminding her that she was safe and in capable hands); and healing (suggesting that, through its own experience and wisdom, Terry's inner mind would heal her incision rapidly and surely). I had sketched these thoughts in my mind, then put the matter away. I trusted that over the ensuing hours, the intervention would "brew" and that when I faced Terry at the hospital, the words I needed would come. Now I had little doubt the words would find me: what I lacked was time to deliver them! In the five minutes left us I had just enough time to give her the most basic outline of these suggestions.

"There . . . now your body is resting comfortably. . . . Because you desire to have a comfortable and successful procedure, because you desire to heal quickly and easily, because you trust the team and want them to be able to do their work under the best conditions, you'll be able to respond to this voice and be very successful at what you're doing . . . and because of your trust and faith you won't mind letting the doctor be in charge of the body from the neck up, and you can stay fully in charge of it from the neck down. . . ." For this woman, who had been brutalized as a child, it was particularly important to guarantee lower body control.

"But there's really no need to have to pay any attention to it at all because the doctors and nurses here are perfectly well equipped to take care of everything while you rest. . . . And all you'll need to keep track of is a deepening sense of relaxation and quiet calmness, while at another level you'll be gathering the resources from the deep healing wisdom of that bodymind . . . and you'll be looking forward to tomorrow when you will already be far along in healing. . . . And as that body heals it will do so with very little discomfort, and the healing energies of the body will go to the sites of the wounds, helping them to heal and mend seamlessly and smoothly so that within a very short time it will be hard to even know they were operated on. . . . And now just let your mind drift away into the possibilities of tomorrow . . . you can enjoy just listening to this voice and drifting . . . and while you are drifting, and feeling so relaxed, if necessary you will be able to hear and see the doctor and be able to respond."

It was important for Terry to be in hypnotic rapport with the doctor in case he had to give her directions, but I had learned through experience to use a suggestion that would filter out anything that was not in her best interest. At one point during my first dental hypnoanesthesia the dentist had marveled, "That's amazing! That should really be hurting!" and the patient had taken his words as a suggestion and just about leaped out of the chair. The dentist had had to call me in my office so that I could calm her, deal with her fear and sense of "betrayal," and then reinduce the trance over the phone.

"And as we proceed, you will be well aware of my presence even when I am not speaking to you. And when I do speak to you you will be very open and attuned to the suggestions, knowing that they will soothe and comfort you. . . . Now in a few moments you will find yourself moving on the gurney, and as you do you will go even deeper within, to a place of centered calmness . . . and when you feel the gurney stop moving and you sense the doctors and nurses around you, you will be twice as deep as you are now and only mildly interested in what is happening around you, preferring instead just to drift and perhaps dream a pleasant dream."

When I finished the induction and Terry was resting comfortably on the gurney, I went to the surgical team's prep room to scrub for the procedure. I had planned to use our scrub time to talk to the team—to tell them what I'd be doing, to warn them about inadvertent suggestions, to explain that Terry would reflect their mood so that regardless of what happened they'd need to stay calm—but by the time I got to the prep room the doctor and nurses had left. So, with a nurse assisting me, I hastily washed and put on my mask and gown.

As I was leaving I caught my reflection in the mirror above the sink, and suddenly, as the eyes above the mask made contact, I became transformed. I ceased being David Calof, hypnotherapist, and became instead Dr. Kildare or Ben Casey, one of the heroic doctors I'd idolized in my youth. Standing there amid the bright lights and shiny tile, my entire reality shifted. I imagined, as if they were real, the thrill of my life-sustaining work, the challenge of my next perplexing case, the accolades that would herald my success. And with my scrubbed arms up, ready for their gloves, I strode into the operating room.

The first thing that hit me was the smell. The acrid odor of disinfectant stung my nose, and instantly the fantasy crumbled. *I'm no Dr. Kildare*, I realized; *I'm David. And I'm attending my first operation.* A wave of apprehension hit me and I realized what I'd done: I'd retreated to fantasy to escape my own anxiety! I shook my head to clear it, and looked around the room.

Terry was reclining in a surgical chair in a bright circle of light in the center of the room. Her eyes were half-closed; her facial expression dreamy. She looked as if she had just taken 40 milligrams of Valium. A nurse at her side was busy arranging sand packs around her head to keep her face from moving. A second nurse, outside the circle, was arranging instruments on a tray; their metallic thuds and clangs formed a percussive counterpoint to the Bach fugue that emanated softly from hidden speakers. Behind the chair two men in gowns and masks were chatting. One looked up as I came in.

"The hypnotist?" he asked.

"David Calof," I answered, "hypnotherapist."

"Dr. Radke. Nice to meet you."

I started to hold out my hand, then remembered that we were sterile.

I had anticipated this meeting with the surgeon. I knew him by reputation as an older man with a well-respected practice—the antithesis of me—a long-haired, twenty-nine-year-old "alternative healer." What would he make of having me on his team?

Dr. Radke nodded noncommitally. "This is Dr. Chan, our anesthesiologist. He'll be monitoring vital signs." He waved his hand toward a set-up of masks, tubes, bottles, and gauges. "We have anesthesia ready . . . in case we need it."

In fact, as he spoke a nurse inserted an IV into Terry's hand and taped it down. Terry had rejected a presurgical sedative: she'd need her powers of concentration to maintain her trance, and a sedative that dulled her mind might interfere. Nonetheless, they were prepared to give her one if necessary.

I realized what a paradox the surgeon was facing. Because of Terry's allergy, he really hoped the hypnosis would work—but with an outsider's understandable skepticism, he had no real expectation that it would.

"Are we ready?" he asked, looking at each of the nurses, the anesthesiologist, and then at me. His tone was light, as if he were initiating a golf game rather than a delicate surgical procedure.

We all nodded.

"Well, let's go." He motioned me to a spot on one side of Terry's chair. The team took up positions on the other.

"Terry," I said softly, "I'm here now. Can you hear me?"

"Yes." Her voice was soft and muffled.

"And are you resting comfortably?"

"Yes."

"Good. All right. I think it's time to go a bit deeper now. Are you ready?"

"Yes."

"You're doing a wonderful job . . . and now that I'm here with you again you can let your attention *go more fully inside* . . . deeper and deeper into that state of relaxation . . . letting go of any remaining tension anywhere and everywhere . . . all you need to focus on is that ever-deepening sense of comfort, safety, and security, and drifting even deeper as I speak with you. . . . And if you are ready to begin, then one of the fingers on the left hand will lift automatically to let us know. I'll wait patiently for your response." By calling on Terry's finger I obviated the need for a vocal response, which could lighten her trance.

Slowly her left index finger jerked into the air.

"All right." I nodded to the doctor that he could begin.

The nurse handed him a scalpel and he leaned over Terry's face. Gingerly he touched the blunt edge of the scalpel to her jaw. "Can you feel that, dear?"

Immediately I shadowed his voice with my own. "You can feel pressure but nothing else, right?" We manage pain in hypnoanesthesia not by telling the patient it isn't there, which wouldn't be credible, but by suggesting she feel it as something else—pressure, tightness, heat, or cold. The surgeon had effectively suggested to Terry that she could *feel*—which meant she might feel pain. I wanted to alter that suggestion by defining her feeling as pressure.

In response to my question, Terry murmured groggily, still appearing comfortable.

The surgeon touched her again, this time with the sharp edge of the tool. "How's that?"

Again I covered him. "You feel some pressure again, but nothing else, right?"

"Nnn."

He touched her a third time, nicking the skin slightly. A bright bead of blood appeared. "Is that okay?"

Her voice was drowsy. "Okay."

He looked momentarily at me.

"Okay, dear, I'm going to do a little test." Once more he touched the scalpel to her jaw, this time drawing a faint one inch line. Tiny drops of blood oozed out.

Terry didn't move.

The surgeon's eyebrows raised slightly and he looked over at the nurse. "Well, dear," he said, uncertainty riding just under the surface of his voice, "I see you're doing just fine. So, uh, you're ready to begin?"

"Yes."

"Well . . ." he breathed in deeply and looked quickly at the nurse. "Let's go then." And with a mental adjustment that was as visible as if he'd rolled up his sleeves, he bent over Terry's head.

"And that's your sign, Terry, to just simply go deeper and to know that everything's going fine. . . ." My voice, warm and soothing, colored the surgeon's words. By saying "let's go" he'd alerted Terry that he was about to start—a warning that might draw her attention to the outside. I needed to counter that warning, to *reframe* it as a signal to go deeper.

Terry breathed in deeply, releasing the air in a slow, steady hum. When she'd finished, the surgeon placed his right index finger against her jaw and traced the line he planned to cut from the top of her ear to her chin.

I realized suddenly that he was in an interesting position. The hypnoanesthesia was working—and now he had to trust me, just as Terry trusted me, just as she trusted him. The three of us were now locked together in a circle of mutual dependence—and the fulcrum on which that circle balanced was Terry's state of hypnosis.

"We'll start by making a nice little incision right here by your ear. . . ." the surgeon murmured, as much to himself as to her.

"Yes," I jumped in, "but you don't really need to attend to that right now because you're in safe hands and what matters most is how you are already beginning to summon healing resources . . ."

The surgeon glanced at me momentarily as if to read the intention behind my words. I had the sense that he finally understood what I was doing, counteracting *his* unhelpful suggestions. Then he turned his attention back to Terry and for the rest of the surgery was largely silent. A moment later he placed the scalpel in front of Terry's ear, spread her skin between the thumb and forefinger of his other hand, and pressed the blade into the tightened flesh. Blood, brilliant under the operating room lights, pooled up on her cheek.

Suddenly a wave of nausea and anxiety overtook me. It wasn't the blood: I'd seen deep wounds before and the sight of blood had never bothered me. Rather it was the whole of it: the full realization of where I was, of what was happening, of just how responsible I was. *What if I failed?* A certain knowledge of the consequences washed over me: Terry would become hysterical, leaping fully conscious from the chair, her face wide open . . .

Rationally I knew this wasn't true. Even if something happened to me, Terry would remain in trance: her self-interest would demand it. But I couldn't hear that rational voice. I could only hear my panic. And as it spread, I felt my eyes roll back, felt my knees grow weak.

But suddenly, as quickly as the image had overtaken me, it lifted. I felt as if pins and needles were leaving my body: my skin felt prickly, I felt lightened. And with the pins and needles went the nausea and panic. Suddenly my field of vision was acute—for just the operating arena. The room was gone. The smells were gone. The chatter of the team was gone. All was crystal clear and quiet. Inside I was quiet too, my internal dialogues stilled. All that existed was the circle of light and what I needed to do within it.

After that, watching the surgery was like watching a movie in which I had a purely cognitive fascination. I followed the careful movements of the doctor as if it were an anatomical model rather than a human face he was carving and dissecting. His first incision had taken him through the layers of skin. He now inserted a fork-like tool and lifted them, revealing the yellow, pulpy fat beneath. Under the fat I could see purple strands of muscle.

As the surgeon worked I kept up a constant suggestive monologue. "You're doing fine, everything's going perfectly well . . . and you can continue feeling confident and calm and just drifting. . . ." I monitored Terry's breathing, the movement of her hands, the small changes in her facial expression, looking for signs of tension. When occasionally she knit her brow or her breathing grew irregular and shallow, I gave her additional suggestions for deepening and detachment. "And still deeper now . . . sink below it all and leave behind any concern or discomfort completely. . . ." When at one point a pan clanged harshly against a metal table, I incorporated the sound. "And even as that jarring sound fades away, so will any other jarring sensation, thought, or feeling . . . and as they do you will remember that nothing really matters but your ability to float comfortably away from it all, knowing this voice will follow you no matter how deep you go. . . ."

With the skin lifted, I could see what I thought was the tumorous growth underneath. Gray and doughy, entwined with fat and muscle, it seemed at once part of and foreign to the healthy tissues. Now the surgeon began to peel back Terry's face in order to expose its mass. I was shocked at the force he used. He sawed with a spoonlike instrument, prying at the tissue as if severing a tendon from a breast of chicken. When he'd released the layer of skin, he rolled it up like a piece of paper from her jawline toward her nose. Suddenly a new wave of anxiety rose in me. The plastic model had disappeared and now I saw Terry in the chair: Terry of the infectious laugh, Terry who had opened her soul and trusted me with her past. And Terry's face was literally disappearing. Faces, I understood then, are what distinguish us as human. And now Terry's face was virtually gone. Once again my knees weakened and I looked for something to grab.

But as it had before, something inside me took over. In the blink of an eye the scene before me changed: the images remained the same, but were drained of emotional charge. Terry became once again a model; the surgery once again a science project in which I had a fascinated objectivity. I was back in the protective circle and I remained there for the rest of the procedure.

For the next period of time—and I had no sense of time—the surgery proceeded uneventfully. The surgeon carefully cut and scraped the growth from slender nerves and muscles. Terry sat quietly, seemingly asleep and unaware. I spoke nearly constantly, a soft background hum of suggestions.

Since the initial incision there had been very little bleeding. As the surgeon sculpted the underlying layers, blood flowed only when he deliberately cut one of the tiny vessels feeding her cheek. Each time he did, he applied a cauterizer to staunch the flow. But as I watched, it occurred to me that Terry could do that for herself. So the next time the doctor cut a vessel I began to talk, raising my voice slightly in a signal for him to listen.

"Terry, I'm going to ask you to use your imagination now to help us. In your mind's eye I want you to imagine the cut ends of those little blood vessels closing down, safely sealing to contain their precious fluid. . . . See it happening strongly and vividly, sealing closed . . . and just do that *now*. And as you do, perhaps you will feel a pleasant coolness coming into the area." By imagining coolness in the area, Terry could direct her blood away from the incision.

Almost as I spoke the words, her bleeding slowed. Seconds later it stopped completely. The nurse who was holding the cauterizer stared in disbelief. Her eyes glazed over as if she, too, were in a trance. Then she turned to look at me.

I met her gaze. *Yes!* It *is* miraculous, I wanted to say, but look at *her*, not me. *She's* the one who's doing it.

I followed her eyes back to Terry, and suddenly I, too, felt awestruck. In my career I'd often seen clients cure persistent headaches in a single hypnotic session; seen others permanently banish chronic pain; helped others open the airways of their lungs to halt an asthma attack or increase circulation to their fingers to reverse the uncomfortable whitening of Reynaud's Syndrome. Psychophysiological phenomena were almost routine to me—yet I was humbled by Terry's ability to stop her bleeding on demand. This ability of the body to heal and self-control struck me as so profound, so generative, that it seemed to have a spiritual dimension—and I believe the potential for it resides in the core of every human being.

The surgeon's eyes met mine above our masks. I knew he'd seen something he'd never seen in thirty-five years of practice. What did he make of it? Would he find a way to make it fit his medical frame of reference, perhaps logging it as a curious anecdote in the annals of unexplained healing? Or would he reach outside his paradigm and acknowledge Terry's self-control, her deliberate willing it to happen, the oneness of mind and body? His eyes searched mine for half a second—and then they telegraphed a smile. And for the first time in the surgery I felt a sense of kinship.

As the surgery proceeded, Terry continued to stop her bleeding while remaining calm and drowsy. The surgeon, with the precision of a jeweler, pried the spidery tumor from its healthy support. But as his tiny wedge-shaped tool appeared to scrape a nerve, Terry suddenly

moaned and turned her head slightly from his hands. Quickly he nodded to the nurse who plucked a novocaine needle from the tray.

"Okay, dear, we have an injection ready," he said, holding it
over her face. "We'll help you now. You'll just feel a little prick."

Quickly I held up my hand to stop him. "Yes," I added, "in just
a moment you'll be feeling comfortable again . . . yes, you can feel it
now . . . there's the prick. . . ."

The doctor froze, syringe still poised above Terry's face, and
looked at me. Seconds that felt like hours passed between us, and in
those moments his eyes were intimately transparent. I read them like
a confession: first his confusion, then his understanding, then his inde-
cision. And then, deep and soothing as steady rain, his voice joined
mine. "That's right, dear," he said. "There it goes. You can feel it infus-
ing now. Can't you?"

Almost immediately Terry relaxed in the chair. Her breathing
deepened and grew even. The lines that had pleated her forehead disappeared. The surgeon studied her intently for several moments, eyes
narrowed, eyebrows furrowed, apparently assuring himself that she
was as painfree as she appeared. Then without a word he handed the
loaded syringe back to the nurse.

Once again he bent over Terry's face, fully given to his task. As
he removed the last of the tumor from her cheek, several capillaries
began to bleed.

"And now you can just close those capillaries down," I told her.
"Just see the ends sealing."

The bleeding stopped for several minutes, then began again.

"Now we need to stop that bleeding, dear."

The nurses and I looked up, surprised. It was the surgeon who
had spoken. But he didn't return our looks. His head was down, fully
engaged with the procedure, as if he found nothing odd about his own
behavior.

Seconds later the bleeding stopped, and thereafter, whenever
it began again, the surgeon directed Terry to contain it.

Once the growth was gone from her cheek he pulled the skin
taut and tacked it in front of her ear with several running stitches. An
inch of extra skin hung over the seam, and he quickly snipped it off.
Now Terry's face was lopsided—its right side newly taut, the left still
pouchy and round as it had been before. Without hesitation the
surgeon walked to Terry's other side and made a parallel incision along
her left jaw. Tugging strongly, he pulled the skin up until the left side
of her face roughly matched the right. Then he tacked that skin in

place in front of her left ear, creating another one-inch overhang. Now he came and stood in front of her, eyeballing and measuring the two sides. After making small adjustments on either side, he again cut off the excess skin that had been pulled up in front of her ears, then used tiny internal stitches to close the wounds. On the surface, he placed surgical tape to seal the uppermost layer of skin.

Instantly Terry had a new face. The rolls of fat that had padded her chin and jaw were gone, replaced by a single, firm, smooth curve. Against this curve, her features, sharp and delicate, stood out. I almost gasped. It was Terry—but something significant had changed. It was as if the sculptor had returned to work and taken up where he'd left off. By finely chiseling the surrounding rock, he'd revealed an unexpected beauty in the stone.

Inarguably this unexpected facelift greatly improved Terry's appearance, yet I found myself feeling wistful. *I'll never see that old face again,* I thought. *How will Terry respond to the change?* Our image in the mirror and our sense of our self are so intimately bound. How will this external alteration affect her inner self?

When Dr. Radke had finished and was packing Terry's face with medicated gauze, I gave her postsurgical suggestions. "Even as the soothing gauze touches your cheek, your body is already hard at work healing . . . and because you seek a speedy and complete recovery you will drift even deeper now, freeing all your energy for healing . . . and we are calling upon the body's deepest wisdom to accelerate this healing process . . . now you can just drift . . . there is nothing outside of you that requires your attention . . . everything that needs to be attended to is being attended to by capable hands . . . you can just drift into a natural state of sleep and wake up when it's time for your body to awaken . . . and now nothing need disturb that restful state. . . . Should any discomfort occur you will be able to go beneath it and leave it behind you as you go deeper."

I continued my suggestions as they transferred Terry to a gurney and then watched as an attendant wheeled her through the double doors to the recovery room. As soon as she was gone the surgical team peeled off their masks. I looked at the surgeon expectantly. But to my surprise he talked briefly with one of the nurses about an upcoming surgery, joked about an unrelated matter with the anesthesiologist, and then headed for the dressing room. The anesthesiologist followed and I was left to do the same.

In the dressing room, with a swift economy of movement, Dr. Radke removed his hat and gloves and began dictating surgical notes into a machine. In terse, cryptic phrases he established the particulars of the case: a description of the growth removed; the nerves and muscles it had ensnared; the types of incisions he had used. As he neared the end of his report he turned to the anesthesiologist. "Jimmy, what sedative did you give her beforehand?"

The anesthesiologist looked at him surprised. "I didn't give her one."

The surgeon stared at him blankly, trying to make sense of this anomaly. *Patients always receive a sedative before surgery. How else could she have remained so calm?* Then slowly his face softened, his mouth broke into a wry smile, and for the first time since we'd left the operating room he turned toward me. He didn't say a word, but as our eyes met I felt that same sense of intimacy that I had felt when our voices merged to suggest that Terry feel the prick of the novocaine needle. Slowly he shook his head—in wonder? In admiration? I couldn't tell. Then abruptly he turned back to his dictation. "No presurgical sedative given. No anesthesia . . . uh, make that *hypno*anesthesia." He paused. "Everything else uneventful." Then he placed the microphone back on the machine.

"Well," he said, clapping his hands together and looking at no one in particular, "I'm going to grab a cup of coffee. I've got another surgery in an hour."

He clapped me on the back and started off. "Take care."

"You too."

Then with a wave of his hand he was gone.

As I left the hospital and walked out into the parking lot I was still under the spell of what had happened. I was pleased with my own performance, but even more, I was overwhelmed by the beauty of what I had seen and by a sense of privilege that I had been both its catalyst and witness. As I reached my car I turned to look at the hospital building behind me. Suddenly, as if its white wall were a giant movie screen, the sensations and images of the morning played out before my eyes. The lack of preparation time; the pressure to perform; the smells; the Bach; the unexpected wave of nausea; the horror of seeing Terry's face rolled back. . . . The reality of it all, everything outside my circle of concentration, came rushing back and struck me in the gut. My knees crumpled and I had to grasp the door handle to stop myself from falling. I clung to the car for several moments until I could steady myself enough to stand.

But even as I hung clinging to the car, a part of me stood back. I was aware of a voice inside me chortling, "You were marveling at *her*, Calof, but *you* are just as much the marvel. You did just what she did—used trance to split off the parts you couldn't bear!"

And the voice was right. I *had* gone into trance, and in that state I had dissociated—feelings, body sensations, the knowledge that it was *Terry's face* that was being carved. All the aspects of the experience that could interfere with my performance had fallen away, as cleanly and absolutely as ice calves from a glacier. Left were the aspects that would enable me to perform the task with utmost concentration and precision.

Now I had to laugh out loud. I had tasted my own medicine completely unaware! I, too, had been in trance, and it wasn't until now that I'd reawakened that I realized how much I'd depended on it.

I had been back at the office for about an hour when a nurse from the hospital called.

"Mr. Calof? Can you talk to Terry Yeakel? She's in some distress."

Terry got on the phone almost delirious with pain and frustration. Apparently she had begun to feel some discomfort and was working to deepen her trance and go beneath it when the recovery room nurses heard her moaning. They had quickly come to inject her with pain medication and were unswayed by her garbled refusals. The resulting argument lightened her trance, bringing the full intensity of her pain to conscious awareness. Her incisions, which had begun to seal, began to bleed, and Terry, now fully awake, was inconsolable.

Over the telephone I used a reinduction signal to reinstate the trance and reinforced my earlier suggestions for pain control, control of bleeding, and healing. To guard against further mishaps, I told her she could screen out intrusions that were unhelpful and that if something broke her trance she would be able to go back into it quickly by herself. I then reminded her that she would wake up when her body was ready, feeling comfortable and rested, secure in the knowledge that the nurses now understood her situation and would act in her best interest.

After I hung up the phone I reflected on what had happened. On one level it was my fault that the mishap had occurred. I had planned to brief the nurses ahead of time; the hospital's refusal to admit me and the resulting lack of time had prevented that. But as

Terry's therapist I was nonetheless responsible for the safety of her experience. By allowing them to invade her "boundaries," I had breached her trust.

But on another level there was a very different dynamic at work—a dynamic that seemed classically hypnotic. The nurses had known that Terry was in a trance and that she had had successful hypnoanesthesia, and when they had offered her pain medication she had refused. So why had they persisted in trying to give it to her? The simplest answer is that they were trying to help. But a more *systemic* answer is also possible: they persisted because they were limited by their own view of healing. Their training and experience allowed them only one way to look at the situation, even when contradictory evidence was right before their eyes. They *literally couldn't see* that Terry didn't need their help—just as a trance subject cannot see what a hypnotist tells her isn't there. In effect, the beliefs transmitted by the traditional medical model had the force of hypnotic suggestion. The nurses were merely following along.

Terry remained in the hospital overnight, at some point shifting from trance into regular sleep. When she awoke the next morning she was in mild discomfort, but was able to reinstate the trance and eliminate the pain. When she left the hospital that morning she refused a prescription for pain medication.

Ten days later she appeared in my office for her regular appointment. I had seen other women postfacelift whose faces were so distended and discolored that they had contrived elaborate methods of concealment, so I had an idea of what to expect. But I was not prepared for Terry. There was virtually no sign of surgery. Her face was neither bruised nor swollen, and she had a scar so faint that I could barely see it. But even more startling, she looked radiant. As she stood before me, glowing, this woman—who had never taken pride in her appearance, whose self-esteem hovered just above the gutter—seemed genuinely, confidently, pleased with herself.

"You look like a million dollars," I exclaimed.

"I *feel* like a million dollars!" she crowed. "Can you believe it? Dr. Radke said he'd never seen anyone heal this fast. Can you believe it? I did it!"

I grinned. Terry was apparently as impressed by her ability to heal as she was with her new appearance. And that seemed fitting: for someone who never expected to excel, this was a notable achievement.

Her sense of mastery and self-esteem grew rapidly afterwards as she took giant strides in therapy. We worked together for another year, during which Terry controlled her diet and initiated a sensible exercise program. By the end of therapy, she had dropped over thirty pounds. These changes, plus a promotion at work, spawned a new interest in her wardrobe, and by the end of the year she said with characteristic brio, "Now my insides match my outsides: new, improved, and under new management!" It was an interesting choice of phrase, I thought, for she'd pinpointed an essential truth—that work on the inside and work on the outside are inseparable. What happens in the psyche is always reflected in the body, just as bodily events cast shadows in the mind. Terry's remarkable healing and her changed appearance reflected the processes that were taking place within: the healing of her childhood trauma, and the shaping of a "new Terry" who was no longer scarred by her past.

I never spoke to Dr. Radke again, although I've often wondered what he made of the case. Those few seconds when he took over the anesthesia suggestion stand out in my mind, for in that moment we were stripped of our differences and became joined in a shared vision of healing. In that moment, he did what the nurses had not: he transcended his experience and training—cast off the suggestion, as it were—and saw new evidence about the body's ability to self-control and heal. His awareness may have been as transitory as the surgery—gone before he reached the dressing room. But I have to believe that somewhere in his mind this experience lives on. Were this his only such experience it might be permanently banished from consciousness, the dissonance between his normal practice and what he had seen too great to contain. But most surgeons keep mental notes of medical anomalies: patients whose attitudes have swayed their recoveries; patients whose tumors have unexpectedly shrunk or disappeared. As he slipped this case into that mental file, wouldn't the file have thickened considerably? Wouldn't its sheer size now make it harder to conceal?

Will Western medicine find a way to incorporate our power to self-control and self-heal? I wonder. I think about the surgeon's smile as he left the dressing room, and about that curious shake of his head. Perhaps he saw, if only for a few moments, that our paradigms needn't be contradictory, or even mutually exclusive. Perhaps he saw that they can work together, just as he and I did.

Chapter 8

Washing Away Disease

NANCY SHEPHARD FIRST CAME TO SEE ME WITH HER BOYFRIEND, PAUL. Twenty-three years old, she was small, with a heart-shaped face and auburn hair that fell in unruly waves past her shoulders. Bright and eager, with a wide-eyed innocence that seemed almost childlike, she seemed sometimes to lose herself in conversation much as a child might get lost examining the reflective facets of a crystal chandelier. This capacity for fascination is a trance phenomenon, so it was no surprise to me that Nancy was a good hypnotic subject. Apparently she had learned in childhood—with her alcoholic father and passive mother—that it was possible to lose herself in fantasy and escape the pain of home.

Two months after we began therapy, Nancy broke up with Paul but continued to see me alone. In fairly rapid succession she moved from Paul to Brad to Todd before realizing that all her relationships were colored by the same unhappy patterns. She chose men with whom she had little emotional rapport, slept with them without much pleasure, and allowed them to make her feel bad about herself. As this pattern took shape, we began to discuss her relationship with her parents and siblings, for in many ways it seemed she was recreating those relationships elsewhere in her life. During one session, however, she seemed uncharacteristically distracted.

"I sense that there's something else going on for you right now," I finally brought up, two-thirds of the way through the session.

She looked me in the eye for a second, then looked away.

"You don't seem fully here. . . ."

She clamped her lips together and I realized she was trying to hold back tears. In the ten months I'd known Nancy, despite the roller coaster of her love life and our often painful discussions about her family, I had never seen her cry.

"Is it something you can tell me about?"

A single tear rolled down her face. She brushed it away with her hand. "I just found out. . . ." But speaking unleashed the momentum of her tears and she broke down. For a long moment she wept silently, her head turned away. Then with a deep sigh she blew her nose and turned back toward me. "I just found out that I might have cancer."

"Oh no." I kept my voice even, but her words were shocking. "What's going on?"

"Right before I came here I got a call from my gynecologist. My pap smear came back really bad. And now I have to have a biopsy and I might have to have surgery and it might be cancer." She spewed the words as if the pressure of knowing without telling had forced them out.

My knowledge of gynecology was slim, but from experience with other clients I knew something about cervical abnormalities, and as Nancy reported her conversation with the doctor I pieced together the situation. Apparently her pap smear had come back from the lab with a diagnosis of *carcinoma in situ,* a condition in which a large number of precancerous cells are growing on the surface of the cervix. The doctor wanted her to come in the next day for a colposcopy during which he would remove some cervical tissue for a biopsy. If that tissue was also precancerous Nancy would be scheduled for a cone biopsy, an outpatient surgery done under general anesthesia, during which the doctor would remove a cone-shaped piece of cervix, hopefully removing all the precancerous cells.

"I said I didn't think I could do it tomorrow and he told me I had to. He said it couldn't wait." Her voice started to crack again. We both knew what the doctor's urgency meant.

"He said it comes from having lots of sexual partners." Nancy looked down and her chin began to quiver.

"Nancy . . ."

But before I could finish she began to cry, hiding her face in her hands. "I feel so dirty," she moaned. "I feel like it's my fault."

The doctor's words could not have struck a more sensitive vein. Nancy slept with men to secure their affection, not because she truly wanted to, and she felt guilty and vaguely dirty for doing so. Now her doctor had essentially affirmed her feelings. It was as if he'd wagged a moral finger telling her she'd received her just deserts.

"Nancy, I know that you're feeling very scared and over-whelmed. You've just been told some very upsetting news. But I wonder if I can tell you some things I know about your condition?"

Snuffling back her tears, she looked to me.

"I'm certainly not an expert on cancer, but I do know that there are many reasons why women get abnormal cells in the cervix. Multiple sexual partners is only one. I also know that there are several steps between your condition and cancer. You have some cells that are growing abnormally. Sometimes abnormal cells progress to cancer and sometimes they don't. Sometimes all the abnormal cells slough off and the cervix goes back to being normal. Did you know that?"

She shook her head.

"Some people believe that cancer, and precancers, happen when a person's immune system is depressed. When the immune system can't fight well, abnormal cells are allowed to grow. But there are ways to boost the immune system, to make it fight better." I paused. "In any event there are some things we can do hypnotically to help you take whatever steps you'll need to."

Her eyes widened.

"Would you like that?"

She nodded.

"Okay. There are several things we can do. . . ." I thought for a moment. "But you have to understand that I'm not telling you not to go back to the doctor, or not to follow his advice. You should still get your colposcopy, and you may still need to have surgery."

"You mean it might not work?"

"I'm not saying that. I'm saying that our role is to work to-gether adjunctively with whatever medical treatment you may receive."

"Do you think maybe I won't need surgery?"

"I'm hoping you won't. But you need to keep working with your doctor, too. His advice may disagree with mine—and then you'll have to decide what to do. I can't recommend that you go against your doctor's advice."

Nancy eyed me anxiously. "But this could help me, you think?"

"I think there's a very good chance. It wouldn't be the first time that hypnosis made a difference in treating a medical condition."

In fact, I believed there was an excellent chance that hypnosis could help Nancy. At the least, I thought it could help her with pain and anxiety if, in fact, she needed surgery. But for two reasons I was also optimistic that it might help her with nonsurgical healing. One was that Nancy's capacity for trance work was very good. The second was that she was a survivor: she had learned in childhood to wrest the best outcome from a difficult situation. By contrast, I once treated a woman with breast cancer who was a lovely person, warm and bright, but whose personality was so accommodating that she had trouble marshalling unconscious resources on her own behalf. We worked for a long time before she was able to see the value of winning rather than giving in, and only then was she able to start fighting her disease. Nancy would not have that problem.

"I have an idea for something we can do," I submitted, "but I think it will actually work better if I don't tell you exactly what it is. It's something that would have to take place outside this office."

Nancy wrinkled her face into a question mark.

"I sometimes see clients outside the office when I think it will be helpful and appropriate. I've visited clients in the hospital. Once I helped a client with a driving phobia by working with her in a car. Once I even did a session at the airport with a client who was afraid to fly. . . ."

Nancy gave a little laugh.

"We would do this within the client/therapist relationship and it would take just about an hour, so it would be basically a regular session."

I saw her weigh the idea; saw her spirit of adventure surface. "Okay, I'm up for that."

"Now, this isn't the only thing we could do. There are several other options we could choose instead."

"No," she insisted firmly. "I want to do this one."

"If it would make you feel more comfortable I can tell you what I'm thinking of doing . . . but I think it will work better if I don't." I wanted to reassure her by giving her a sense of choice and participation, while steering her toward the better option.

I sometimes use this "mystery" device with clients—suggesting a potent intervention without disclosing what I'll do—because it builds their expectation that something especially helpful will happen. Since positive expectation plays a major role in treatment, the client does a large part of the work herself before the intervention even starts.

Once I treated a woman who was trying to quit smoking for the "fourth and final time." At our first session I sat silently for a long time, apparently engaged in serious contemplation, then announced that I knew exactly what to do: an unusual cure, used only in the toughest cases, but one that I thought might work with her. The caveat was that I couldn't tell her in advance what I would do. The woman's face lit up and she immediately agreed. At the following session, I told her I didn't think she was ready: stalling built her expectation further. At her third session I sent her away again. By the fourth week the woman came in on pins and needles to hear what I would do.

Now, I told her, she was ready. I put her in a trance and asked her to imagine getting an ice cube from the freezer, dipping it in lemon juice, then holding it in her mouth until it melted. When she'd done that I told her she would repeat that procedure with an actual ice cube each time she craved a cigarette over the next two weeks. Then I woke her up and sent her home.

Now, this "cure" is not as strange as it sounds. When a person craves a cigarette, certain images, emotions, and physical sensations combine to create that desire. By asking the woman to suck the ice cube when she wanted a cigarette, I was altering part of that equation. The coldness and taste would overwhelm her mouth and taste buds, short-circuiting the oral sensations that were part of her cue to smoke. With that part of the equation disabled, her drive for a cigarette would be lessened.

Three weeks later she called to say she hadn't smoked in a week and felt only the slightest cravings. Six months later she reported that she hadn't lit up once. After all her false attempts the woman thought the cure miraculous. In truth, given the amount of positive expectation she'd built up, almost anything would have worked.

Like this woman, Nancy seemed already committed to the mysterious idea. "No," she waved her hand. "You don't have to tell me."

"When are you scheduled for your colposcopy?"

"Tomorrow at eleven o'clock."

"Will they give you the results of the biopsy right then?"

"Uh-huh."

"Is anybody going to pick you up afterwards?"

"No, I mean, I haven't thought about it. I guess not."

"Would it be all right if I picked you up? We could do what I'm thinking about right then. Or would that feel too awkward?"

She considered the idea. "I guess that would be okay."

So we agreed on a time and a place to meet.

Before she left, however, I wanted to give her suggestions that would make the colposcopy procedure more tolerable. Several months before, I had taught her to use self-hypnosis to relieve severe menstrual cramps and now, after quite a bit of practice, she was able to touch spots on her thigh and upper abdomen and feel painfree in between. Now I helped her into a trance and suggested she use that same ability to disown the sensations in that part of her body the following day.

"And I want you to know that the procedure will go by so quickly you'll hardly notice that it's happened," I added. "I want you to imagine yourself at the end of the day . . . putting your head on your pillow, putting the day to rest . . . already well into the process of heal-ing, which we're going to begin calling on right now . . . calling on the deep healing powers of your body to focus their energies where they are needed most. . . . And the next time you see me, your unconscious mind will already have prepared to take the next healing step. . . ."

Nancy awoke feeling rested and relaxed. I wished her well until the following day.

Had I not known Nancy quite well by then, and had we not had a trusting relationship, I never would have suggested meeting out-side the office. But our relationship was carefully bounded and our therapy task well defined. I believed we could safely meet out of the office without jeopardizing our future work.

My suggestion had been prompted by an idea that had oc-curred to me while she was discussing her diagnosis. I had been re-minded of the work of Carl and Stephanie Simonton, who in the late 1970s had advanced a theory called the *surveillance model* of cancer. The human immune system, they maintained, is like a small town. Just as a town is subject to crime and fire, the body is subject to cancer. And just as police and firefighters maintain control by engaging in ongoing maintenance and repair and by tackling crises as they arise, the im-mune system constantly repairs cells and fights invaders to suppress malignant outbreaks. In towns, however, a fire or crime spree occa-sionally spreads. When that happens, emergency crews recruit rein-forcements from outlying areas. So it is with the immune system, which calls on deeper reserves to attack the invading cells. It is only when the reinforcement crews are inadequate to the job—when the available immune resources are insufficient—that fire, crime, or can-cer spread. The question then is how to help the immune system use its existing resources most efficiently and how to help it marshal *further* reinforcements to fight off the invaders.

The Simontons established a healing center where they used

imagery as an adjunct to chemotherapy and radiation to help patients boost their immune response. And although they worked with patients with advanced cancers, they produced impressive rates of remission. But as Nancy talked I had begun to wonder what would happen if we applied the surveillance model more literally. What if we used the city to create an unconscious metaphor for Nancy's body? What if we tackled Nancy's putative "dirt" the same way a city would tackle its own?

I knew that whatever I did I would have to do it quickly. Abnormal cells spread rapidly, and we'd have to match her doctor's aggressive schedule. When Nancy had mentioned that she would hear the results of her colposcopy the following day, I realized that that would be the time to act. If the results were bad she would be hypersuggestible: like anyone whose world has been turned upside down, she would be frightened and grasping for an answer. She would also be highly motivated to avoid another invasive procedure, making her especially open to my suggestions.

By working with her then I would also be able to circumvent her negative autosuggestions. Left alone, Nancy would imagine the worst scenarios. Not only would she elaborate on the cancer, but given her doctor's remark she might convince herself that she was unable to get "clean." By moving quickly, I could interject suggestions to the contrary—in effect, hard-wiring "circuits" with the power to heal.

The next day I pulled up outside the medical center where Nancy's doctor had his office, got out, and leaned against the car. Fifteen minutes later she emerged, visibly pale and shaken. The biopsy results were apparent.

She walked over to the car and I gently touched her on the arm. Her lips were curled tight in an effort not to cry.

"All right," I stated. "Looks like plan B."

She managed a half-hearted smile.

"Okay now, all you have to do in this session is let your unconscious mind be receptive to a new way of thinking. . . . I'll get us back here in just about an hour, and between now and then I'll drive us safely and attentively so you don't need to pay attention to anything outside yourself." My voice was slow, the cadence of trance induction.

She blinked, then got in as I held her car door open. I slid into the driver's seat.

"Now I'm going to ask you to do something that may not make

a lot of sense to your conscious mind . . . but your unconscious mind can understand that it has the potential to help."

She nodded.

"Are you ready to begin?"

"Uh-huh." Her eyes were focused straight ahead, but I could feel her mind keenly tuned to my words. We were building hypnotic rapport.

"All right then, what I'd like you to do now is close your eyes and keep them closed until I tell you to open them. Are you willing to do that?"

With relief she closed her eyes. At that moment trance was an escape from her worry, a journey to a place where hope was possible.

"Good. Now as you feel the car pull away from the curb you can just sit there and be in timeless time and let the tensions of the day melt away. . . . You can be reminded of other times when I spoke to you in this fashion and you didn't need to move or think . . . and you can do that now even as we drive. . . . And now as I count just let yourself go deeper . . . one . . . that's right . . . two . . . more and more relaxed . . . and three . . . just letting go completely."

Nancy breathed in deeply, exhaled, then her head slumped forward. She was in a moderate trance.

With Nancy resting quietly beside me I drove a mile and a half to a rough part of town. Here the street fronts were lined with bars and missions, masking bleak alleys in the rear.

"You can open your eyes now," I said as I turned into the slice of darkness between two buildings, "but you needn't wake that body resting there." The rutted alley was strewn with garbage. I drove slowly. On one side two men with bruised and swollen faces sat leaning against a building. An empty liquor bottle lay between them.

"Just look," I said. "Just take it in."

She blinked but didn't turn away.

Toward the end of the alley I told her to close her eyes: I wanted to restrict her vision to the alleys. In the darkness of the adjoining alley I told her to reopen them. Here a man lay spread-eagled under a sheet of newspaper, two mismatched shoes and a bundle of clothes beside him. A stream of water running from a gutter ran within inches of his head. As we approached the end of the alley I again told Nancy to close her eyes, only to open them in the canyon of the next one. There, a man urinating against the side of a building glared at us as we drove past. I rolled down my window and asked Nancy to do the same. The stench of garbage heated by the warm spring sun filtered into the car.

As we threaded the alleys Nancy sat wide-eyed. I could hear her mind as if it were speaking: *This is horrible; why are you bringing me here?*

"Just look," I directed. "Just take it in. You don't need to understand." I didn't want her musing consciously on what we were doing: conscious thought would lighten the trance. I just wanted her absorbing the images of filth.

We drove slowly for fifteen minutes, which felt like an eternity. Finally I pulled out of the narrow alleys onto a main thoroughfare. Nancy's face was gray and pained.

"And now you can close your eyes again and drift . . . there's nothing you need to think about . . . nothing you need to do. . . ." Nancy's head sagged and she returned to a sleeplike state.

Now I drove to a park that sat high on a hill overlooking the city. We got out and, with Nancy's eyes still closed, I led her to an observation point with a panoramic view.

"In a moment," I said, "you will open your eyes. You will remain deeply in this comfortable state in which you can forget about your body completely and instead become transfixed by what you see."

Nancy opened her eyes, then followed my pointing finger. Spread out before us were the downtown and adjoining neighborhoods, the harbor and outlying islands, and the freeway. All sparkled in the springtime sun.

"Just look . . ." I told her. "Isn't it beautiful? From here we have such a wide view of the city . . . we can see how big it really is . . . so many neighborhoods . . . so many roads . . . so many big buildings . . . it seems so solid, doesn't it? . . . All those elements working together, the port and the freeway and the roads all coming into downtown . . . and so many buildings . . . from downtown you don't realize just how big the city is, how far out it spreads . . . and see all the construction cranes? . . . Why, they're putting up even more buildings . . . what a sparkling, vibrant city. . . . You know it's easy to think that a fire or some kind of disaster could do a lot of damage to the city, but from up here you can see that it really couldn't, because the city is so vast . . . and it's been here for so long . . . it's already had lots of disasters but none of them has had a long-term impact . . . the city always recuperates. . . ." I talked slowly, hypnotically, and as if my voice were a pointing finger Nancy followed it around the perimeter of our view.

"Oh . . . and there's where we just were. . . . Isn't that funny, from up here it looks so much smaller than it did down there . . . when we were there it felt so horrible . . . so overwhelming . . . it seemed to surround us and be everywhere. . . . But from up here you can see that it's not everywhere. . . . It's local, just one small area.

"From down there it seemed like, how could anybody clean that up? . . . But from up here you can see that it's easy. There are all kinds of things you could do. . . . Garbage trucks can come in and pick up all the filth and cart it away . . . and then street sweepers can come in and wash the streets, *wash all the dirt and filth out* of those alleys. . . . And if that neighborhood ran out of garbage trucks they could bring in trucks from Ballard, or from Capitol Hill, or from Queen Anne. . . . Those alleys are small . . . perhaps the garbage trucks would have trouble squeezing in . . . but I'm sure city engineers could find a way . . . or they could ask shop owners to roll their dumpsters to the corners, like they do in other neighborhoods. . . ."

In the loosest metaphorical way my images could be construed to be related to the body, but I didn't need to make a one-to-one correspondence. In fact, I couldn't have had I wanted to. I have only a rudimentary knowledge of biochemistry and physiology, not enough to prescribe even a metaphorical course of healing. But prescribing was not my plan. I needed only to suggest material to Nancy's fertile unconscious. Its own inherent wisdom would extract what was useful from my rambling speech and turn those images into tools for Nancy's healing. I might learn later if the strategy had worked—but I would never know precisely which of my words had been the triggers.

"Some of those buildings we saw looked like firetraps . . . but even if some of them caught on fire, the fire trucks could get there easily . . . there are fire stations all over the city and they can all send trucks within minutes to fight any fire . . . even a really big one. . . . And the fire equipment these days is so powerful . . . the water sprays from their hoses in such powerful streams . . . it's so much easier to contain and eliminate fires than it used to be. . . .

"And it's so easy to get to that neighborhood because it's so central . . . why, equipment and services can come from all over the city in minutes . . . look at all the roads and arteries that feed it. . . . Look at all the cars flowing down the highway toward it now. . . . And people wouldn't even need to come in cars . . . they could come by boat. . . . Look, there's a ferry bringing people now . . . and a tanker pulling into the harbor . . . even the airport. . . .

"Some people think that area is dirty and a wasteland, but it's actually a very valuable part of the city . . . it has some of the most beautiful architecture in the city. . . . Some of those beautiful old buildings need some renovation, but that's very doable . . . some structural repairs, some paint and cleaning . . . some new plumbing . . . those old buildings can be made like new. . . . Architectural firms can develop renovation schemes . . . carpenters and plumbers and painters and drywallers can come and help restore it. . . ."

I talked in this vein for about twenty minutes, and throughout Nancy listened raptly, as if her mind were wired to my voice. Then it was time to go. Before leaving, though, I wanted to encapsulate the experience in her unconscious, tuck it away out of the range of conscious intrusion, enabling it to "cook" in the back of her mind.

I raised my voice slightly to indicate a different line of thought. "Now, this has been a very important experience for you, although there's not really much need to have to think about it now. . . . Your unconscious can derive its own meaning and value . . . and besides, it would take so much energy to have to think about that when your energy is best directed toward other matters. . . . And over the next days and weeks and even months you will know that in the back of your mind and in your body you will be doing a great deal of work . . . and your unconscious mind will see to it that you take these learnings and apply them in just the right ways, at just the right times, for your benefit and for your healing growth. . . . In fact, you are already doing that even as we stand here now.

"Now you can put these matters out of your mind. . . . And if you ever need to think about them in the future, or if your unconscious mind thinks it is desirable, you will be able to do so. . . . And certainly if it were ever in your best interest to discuss them with someone you would be able to." I didn't want Nancy to feel bound to secrecy about this experience or about her condition. I wanted her to be able to talk to friends, family, and certainly her doctor if she wanted to, while also preserving the possibility of complete amnesia.

"Now, in a moment we will turn around and get into the car . . . and when you are again seated in the car you'll be aware that the appointment time is almost over, and you'll be needing to think about driving and about getting ready to go back to work, completely alert and refreshed. . . . And why don't we do that *now*." My words were an indirect suggestion to wake up—slowly, at her own rate. They would also distract her from what we had done, permitting our work to brew, unquestioned by conscious logic, in her unconscious. I then turned toward the car and Nancy followed.

We drove back to the medical center in quiet, and as we drove Nancy grew more animated. Life came back to her eyes and the signs of trance disappeared.

"Well, we made it back in just over an hour," I commented lightly as we pulled into the parking lot. By invoking the promise I'd made to her before she went into the trance I hoped to consciously bridge that conversation to the current moment, further encapsulating the intervention in her unconscious.

She looked at her watch. "That's good," she remarked. "I have to get back to work. My boss'll kill me if I'm late again." Her tone was upbeat; it lacked the undercurrent of someone who is harboring bad news.

"Would you like to come in the day after tomorrow at five o'clock?" I wanted to schedule extra appointments to keep on top of her condition.

She looked surprised for a moment, then agreed.

"Good." I smiled. "What do you say we meet in the office this time?"

A brief look of confusion crossed her face as if, despite the fact that we were sitting in my car in the parking lot of her doctor's office, she were unaware that we had ever met elsewhere. Then she smiled uncertainly and said, "Okay," climbed out, and closed the door behind her.

Two days later Nancy returned to my office. On arriving she threw herself into the chair, complaining bitterly about her boss. I let her talk for a few minutes until she ran out of steam. Then I tried to broaden the conversation.

"So, what else is happening with you?" I ventured. I was eager to hear her response to our previous session.

"Not much. I talked to my mom. She gave me a hard time about not coming home for my dad's birthday. . . ." Nancy was returning to one of her ongoing issues, dissension with her parents.

I followed her on that tack for twenty minutes, then tried to broaden the discussion once more. "And what else? What else have you been feeling this week?"

She shrugged. "I don't know. Not too much else, I guess. That

224 The Couple Who Became Each Other

guy Jeff called me up and wanted me to start seeing him again but I don't think I will. I think he's not so good for me. . . ." Once again she settled into an ongoing issue.

Despite several more openings Nancy never mentioned our previous session or her cervical condition. We ended the session by acknowledging that we would see each other four days later, at her regular appointment on Tuesday.

When she returned after the weekend it was like a replay of the previous session. She opened with a harangue about her boss, then segued into her parents. This time, however, I was unwilling to let her go. Time was passing; her condition was possibly deteriorating; she was under pressure to have surgery. If *she* wasn't going to bring it up, I would. But still I wanted to do it gingerly. If she had truly forgotten our session in the city I didn't want to remind her, for amnesia would be a sign that it was brewing unconsciously. But I at least wanted reassurance that she was continuing to see her doctor.

"I'm wondering how the next to the last session has been sitting with you?" I asked.

Her eyes narrowed slightly as if searching an interior database, but she said nothing.

"We really haven't had a chance to talk about those things *in the office.*"

"Yeah . . ." she looked confused. "I mean, it's good for me to talk to you about them." Apparently she'd completely missed the allusion in my remark.

"Isn't it good to know your unconscious can consider every *viewpoint* without your needing to pay a great deal of attention?"

She looked at me blankly. "I guess." It appeared she had no idea what I was talking about.

I felt a thrill. The fact that our entire excursion was missing from her conscious mind meant that she'd been in a very deep trance: the suggestions had been profoundly taken in. That gave me great hope that the intervention on the hill would work.

I decided to probe her thoughts on her cervical condition. "How have you been feeling this week, physically I mean?"

She perked up. "Fine."

"Sleeping well?"

"Yeah."

"Any intrusive thoughts?"

A sly look flitted across her face, then she shook her head.

I looked at her closely. *What was that look? Why the sly smile?* Suddenly I understood: our conversation was occurring on two levels! On a conscious level we were talking casually as if nothing unnatural were going on; on an unconscious level we were communicating the truth. Unconsciously Nancy knew we were talking about her cervical condition as much as I did; her subtle gesture was her signal that this was so. But by keeping knowledge of the intervention out of her conscious mind, she was protecting it from conscious intrusion. The conscious mind operates in a linear way, and its dot-the-*i*, cross-the-*t* kinds of demands can interfere with the more circular, holistic unconscious process.

"Well, since you seem to be doing very well," I suggested, "I wonder if you'd like to take another step? There's something I can teach you to do on your own that will make what we've already done even stronger." It was time to teach Nancy to use imagery to augment her unconscious efforts. This double-pronged approach would strengthen her fight against the precancerous cells and would make her a participant in rather than just a passive recipient of the intervention. I'd have to raise our hidden subject to the conscious level to do that—for imagery to work we'd have to be explicit—but I felt the potential reward was worth the risk.

"Yeah," Nancy asserted. "I'd like to do that."

"Then I'll teach you to use imagery. You can learn to direct your imagination, and your imagination can direct your immune system to kill off those abnormal cells."

I watched her face for any sign of discomfort at my mention of the cells, but Nancy merely nodded.

"In a minute I'm going to ask you to come up with imagery that depicts your bad cells. Then you'll come up with imagery of your immune system. You'll see images of your immune system attacking and killing the bad cells and flushing them out through your breath, sweat, and other processes of elimination. Do you understand what I mean?"

"Yes."

"Good. Then right now you can just relax and close your eyes and go inside . . . that's right . . . now one . . . deeper and deeper with every count . . . two . . . more and more relaxed . . . and three . . . just letting go completely."

Nancy's head slumped forward.

"Now I want you to let images come into your mind the way I just described. . . . Take your time . . . there's no need to hurry. . . . Just nod your head to let me know when they've come."

After twenty seconds Nancy's head nodded slightly. Unlike the conscious mind, which might take minutes to find an image through linear, trial-and-error sorting, the unconscious can conceptualize an image almost instantaneously.

"Are they there?"

She nodded once again.

"Good. . . . Take a moment to be sure these images are exactly right, that they're exactly the ones you want, exactly the way you want them." By asking Nancy to approve the images I was asking her to fully commit to the imagery program. In effect she would be saying, *Yes, these are images I can work with.*

After a moment, she nodded again.

"Good." I gave her suggestions to let the work brew in her unconscious mind, then brought her out of trance.

"Can you tell me what you saw?"

"A fire hose."

"Tell me about it."

"It's big."

"How much does it weigh?"

"*A lot.*"

"But you can carry it by yourself?"

"Uh-huh!" She had started off unemotionally, but now her enthusiasm was growing.

"And tell me about its blast."

"It's strong."

"How strong?"

"Strong enough to knock over a building."

"Strong enough to knock over anything in its path?"

A wide grin lit her face. "Oh yeah!" she exulted, and her voice conveyed absolute conviction.

"And what about those bad cells? How did you imagine them?"

"Leaves. Little green leaves."

"What happens when you turn the hose on them?"

"They fall off the trees and land in the gutter and then they turn brown and dry up. And then I can use the hose to wash them away!"

Nancy's imagery pleased and heartened me. The Simontons had noticed that a cancer patient's image was often a reliable indicator of the person's orientation toward healing. Patients who imagined their bad cells as weak and their immune systems as strong typically had better recovery rates than did those whose images were tilted in the opposite direction. One man, for instance, imagined his throat cancer cells as obdurate chips of granite, but he also saw his white cells as purveyors of powerful acid; his cancer went into remission. Another man, who imagined his throat cancer cells as tar and his white cells as snowflakes, died quickly. When the Simontons encouraged patients to alter their images, they were not always successful. Apparently people's images and their willingness to change them were true indicators of their stance toward healing. Those who strengthened their immune-system image and weakened the image of their cancer cells had better rates of remission. Those who refused to alter their images usually worsened. So the fact that Nancy had imagined her bad cells as flimsy leaves and her attacking white cells as a powerful fire hose was a positive and reassuring sign.

I was also delighted by the parallel between her imagery and our city tour. I had talked on the hilltop about fire trucks and sewers. Her adoption of those images suggested that her unconscious had incorporated the metaphor and was using it to her benefit.

"Now, as you imagine yourself hosing away those leaves, I'd also like you to imagine that part of your body growing warm. Let's practice a few times. Just close your eyes and imagine yourself hosing away those leaves while that part of your body grows warm." I had no medical knowledge to back me up, but it seemed logical that imagining warmth would be a way of increasing blood flow to the cervix. And blood, I assumed, would carry necessary healing agents and would wash away the toxins. In the surveillance analogy, the blood would be the vehicle carrying reinforcements to the crews already working to contain the emergency.

When Nancy had practiced her imagery several times, I suggested that she do it outside the office in two different ways: in self-hypnosis sessions two or three times a day, and also "in spare moments throughout the day—perhaps while waiting at a stop light, taking a shower, or eating a meal." These impromptu sessions would constitute *waking suggestions,* for the evocative images would tend to bypass her conscious thinking just as hypnotic suggestions did. Through this combined use of autohypnosis and autosuggestion, she could extend the reach of our work.

"When do you have to go back to the doctor?" I asked as she was getting ready to leave.

She wrinkled her nose. "He wants me to have surgery as soon as possible. I told him I wanted to wait a while. He said two weeks max."

"Well, that gives us about ten days to see how well this is working. Do you want to wait for your regular appointment or would you like to schedule something sooner?"

"Sooner!"

So three days later Nancy returned. She was aglow.

"I don't know what's happening down there," she announced even before she sat down, "but I'm hosing those leaves!" She held an imaginary fire hose in her hands and rotated it in front of her as if power-spraying the leaves.

"Way to go! Do they go down pretty smoothly? What's it like?"

She flexed her arm muscles like a weight lifter. "Piece of cake." Then she grew more sober. "At the beginning it was kind of tricky. The hose was really heavy and with all that water coming out it was hard to turn. And sometimes the leaves were real sticky. They just wouldn't move. But now, the last day or so, it's gotten a lot easier. I think I'm really getting the hang of it."

"That's terrific. Are you feeling warmth?"

She nodded assiduously. "Definitely."

"Great. Well let's do a little reinforcement. In fact, why don't I make you a tape of us doing this so you can play the tape for yourself at home?"

Nancy agreed, so I turned on the tape recorder and helped her into a moderate trance, and then while she relaxed I made suggestions. "We're calling upon the healing capacity of the body to increase . . . for the systems of the body to operate in perfect harmony and balance . . . for all the raw materials you take in each day as you breathe and as you eat to go directly to the place in the body where they will do the most good . . . for all the toxins in the body to be washed away . . . and for all the abnormal cells to be killed and sloughed off. . . ."

I watched Nancy's face and body for signs that she was listening and relaxed, but as I talked a part of my mind was elsewhere. Nancy's report had been optimal; I couldn't have asked for anything better. But what if things weren't really what they seemed? What if she wasn't *really* washing away her precancerous cells? What if her buoyancy was caused by denial? What if, while wielding her imaginary hose, she was actually getting *worse*?

Suddenly I was scared. Despite my faith in our unconscious ability to heal, despite the scores of cases of self-assisted healing that I'd read about or witnessed, I now imagined a scenario in which that healing failed and Nancy's condition worsened.

"Nancy," I said when we had finished the reinforcement tape and she was out of the trance, "when are you planning to talk to your doctor again?"

She cocked her head to the side. "He said two weeks and that's next Wednesday." Four days away.

"You know if he tells you that you really need the surgery I won't advise you not to do it."

Nancy nodded. Her voice grew resigned. "I guess if he tells me I have to do it I probably will. . . . But I sure don't want to."

"I know."

We were both silent for a moment.

"But I don't think I should have surgery without them checking me again first!" Nancy had grown animated. "I mean, all this hosing has probably helped. So I think I need to have another pap smear to see if it's gotten better before they operate. Don't you?"

"Absolutely. They may be reluctant to do it since they think you need the surgery. But I think you should push for it."

So Nancy vowed to request a second pap test and we planned to meet again at her next regular appointment on Tuesday.

On Tuesday she raced breathlessly into my office. "They're better!" she shouted, "It's gone from *carcinoma in situ* to *severe dysplasia!* It's a whole classification better!"

"You had your pap? That's terrific!"

"I had it this morning and they just called me with the results! Can you believe it! It's working!"

Pleasure for Nancy merged with my own relief.

"The doctor said this is very unusual. And he said I still need to have surgery immediately. But I said I just wanted to have another pap smear in two weeks." She sounded giddy, like a schoolgirl who had just aced a difficult test.

"And he agreed?"

"Yeah. He didn't have any choice!"

I relished her enthusiasm: it would only aid her unconscious efforts. But I winced slightly at the idea that Nancy was countering her doctor's advice. Still, her doctor had agreed. . . .

"Well, since you're doing so well should we go ahead and have a regular session and then maybe do a booster at the end?"

"Yeah!"

So we talked about Nancy's family and she tried to stay on track, but throughout the session I could see her mind wander. Finally we did a brief imagery booster in trance and then agreed to meet again in a week at Nancy's next regular appointment.

The following Tuesday Nancy's mood was quite a bit more somber.

"I think I'm doing a good job of hosing," she said with obvious anxiety in her voice, "and it keeps getting easier and easier, but, I don't know . . . I'm just kind of worried. What if . . . ?"

"What if you're tested next week and it's not better?"

"What if it's *worse*?"

"Probably if it's worse you'll need to have the surgery," I voiced gently.

"I know."

So we talked about her fear for several minutes, and about the mechanics of a cone biopsy so she would have a sense of what might occur. But then I wanted to remind her that she had unleashed a powerful healing force in her body and that she needn't focus on the negative. "You know, you've been working very hard on your imagery," I observed. "I think you're doing an excellent job."

"I sure hope so," she answered, and her voice was as plaintive as I'd ever heard it.

Nancy's third pap was scheduled for the following Friday afternoon with results to follow on Monday. All day Monday I anticipated her call. When it finally came I was in session with another client and had to call her back.

The minute she heard my voice on the phone she shouted into my ear, her voice so loud I had to move the receiver. "They're gone!" she yelled. "I'm clean!"

"Your pap was normal?"

"Normal! Like they'd never been there!"

I could feel her grinning through the wire.

"That's fantastic!" I rejoiced. "You did it."

"I know." She sounded very pleased with herself. "I hosed them all away."

On Tuesday she returned for a regular session. We talked about her victory and I suggested that she keep up the imagery for several months to guard against a recurrence. But I was curious if, postrecovery, she had remembered our travels through the city.

"Do you remember that day I met you outside your doctor's office?"

"Kind of," she murmured. "I remember sitting in your car. . . . Did we go somewhere?"

"To the top of Queen Anne hill."

She squinted. "Yeah? I kind of remember that. What did we do up there?"

"Just talk."

"Hmm . . . I guess I don't remember too well. It's pretty foggy."

I waited.

"What did we talk about?"

"Oh, about the view and stuff." I didn't really want to recount our conversation. If Nancy's unconscious had chosen to keep it out of her conscious mind, I saw no reason to counteract that. Obviously her unconscious was doing an excellent job.

Nancy looked at me expectantly for a second, but when she saw that I would say no more her expression changed to indifference. "That's funny I can't remember," she remarked without much interest or conviction. Then she shrugged, letting the effort to remember go.

Nancy remained a client for approximately another year. Toward the end of that time she began to date again—not leaping immediately into a serious relationship as had been her wont, but seeing several men casually. And, most encouraging of all, she was determined not to go to bed with any of them until she knew the relationship felt right. I applauded her resolve, for it marked a significant change in self-esteem. Nancy's image of herself as dirty had largely disappeared, replaced by a stronger, "cleaner" sense of self.

During that year Nancy also had pap smears every three months so her doctor could keep tabs on her cervical condition. Every one came back normal.

What was responsible for Nancy's healing? Was it the working of the metaphor—the recruitment of immune resources to "clean up" her abnormal cells just as human resources could clean up the dismal alleys we had visited? Was it her imaginary hosing of the cancerous leaves? Or was it the sense of hope and power that those two experiences created? I believe it was all those things—for they are all, really, one and the same. They are all means of marshalling unconscious resources in the service of healing.

How does this seemingly miraculous healing occur? No one knows for sure, although thousands of cases of mind/body healing have been reported. Western researchers have posited numerous theories. Most agree that the body secretes chemicals that carry messages from the brain to the body and back in a never-ending feedback loop. In this model, brain and body become one organism in constant dialogue, rather than the hierarchical duality of brain over body that we have traditionally imagined. Eastern yogis, philosophers, and healers have long understood this mind/body unity, whose inseparability underlies most forms of Eastern religion and healing.

Even in the West we take for granted certain aspects of mind/body unity. We acknowledge, for instance, that the unconscious mind controls the autonomic nervous system: the pumping of heart and lungs, the flow of blood through veins and arteries, the flexing of muscles in the eye, the flood of adrenaline, the digestion of food. We know that we can influence some of these processes with our minds. With biofeedback, for example, we can lower blood pressure, open the small airways of the lungs, disengorge blood vessels in the brain, warm the fingers and toes. We've observed that suggestions to anesthetized surgery patients can enable them to lower their blood pressure and reduce their bleeding, and we know that through mental imagery individuals can influence their heart rate, muscle tension, and galvanic skin response. If with mental effort we can influence these functions, if we can control the flow of blood to warm the fingers or mute a headache, then is it too great a leap to believe that we can also control, as Nancy did, the flow of blood to a particular site in the body?

In the last thirty years we've also learned that elements of immune function are within our control. Complementing the work of the

Simontons, studies of children with cancer have shown that the use of mental imagery can help their cancers go into remission. Other studies have shown that regular calming of the mind through meditation can reduce incidents of illness, and that venting stress through a diary can boost immune response.

Thirty years ago in the West we believed we had no control over these and other physiological processes. Therefore, I can only wonder: What will the next thirty years reveal about how our minds can heal us?

Part IV

Voices Within

Chapter 9

The Woman Whose Eyes Refused to See

"I'd like to bring in a client for you to take a look at," said Carla's voice on the phone. Carla was a colleague and former student who often asked me to consult on difficult cases. "She has an unusual problem. I think you'll be interested."

"Tell me more," I prompted, curiosity piqued.

"For confidentiality purposes I'll call her Jane. She's 37. She came to me a year ago complaining of chronic nightmares, panic attacks, insomnia, and general depression. Right away she began having episodes in which she seemed to be reliving some kind of childhood abuse. But she denies they have any meaning. Whatever it was, I think it's so aversive to her that she can't bear looking at it. And that's what makes this case so interesting."

Carla's voice rose in urgency. "David, Jane is going blind. She has some kind of degenerative eye disease that's got her doctors baffled. They don't know what's causing it, but they can measure the deterioration and they say it's irreversible. It's been getting worse gradually for seventeen years, but, suddenly, over the last year, the rate of deterioration has speeded up. She can't read at all any more and she's almost lost her ability to work. She's an artist."

Carla paused, giving me time to absorb her briefing. "At the same time, we've come to a standstill in therapy. After months of progress, she's completely blocked."

"Uh-huh." I was beginning to get her drift. "And you think . . ."

"Yes! I think there's a relationship there! I think we've gotten close to some material she doesn't want to see, and the aversion is so strong that *she's literally making herself blind.*"

In my years as a hypnotherapist I had seen many cases in which clients unconsciously made themselves ill or created debilitating physical conditions, and in almost every one the physical symptom was a metaphoric manifestation of the client's conflicts. One client, for example, complained about a loud ringing in her ears. When I asked about her marriage she told me her husband was "intrusive," and when I asked how she handled his intrusions she responded, "I tune him out." Apparently she was unaware that her body was doing the same. A teenage girl with an angry and controlling mother developed a debilitating rash on her hands. As she talked about her mother in hypnosis her hands tightened into a stranglehold. When I asked her to look at them and tell me what she saw, she repeated, "I see red, I see red"—a metaphor for her unacknowledged feelings toward her mother. The rash was also a way of punishing her hands for the unacceptable wish they represented.

In each of these cases, the client's issues were played out through the body, and once we resolved the underlying conflict, the physical symptoms abated. Carla was suggesting a similar phenomenon here. But I could hear in her excitement that she was also suggesting something more. Those earlier clients had developed known psychophysiological ailments, disorders that the medical community believed could be psychogenic. In contrast, Jane's deterioration of eye tissues seemed purely physiological. If Carla's theory was correct, in its eagerness to serve Jane's unconscious, her body was destroying *itself*. This ultimate complicity between mind and body was the logical conclusion of our earlier observations, yet was stunning in its indication of the power of the unconscious mind.

But that power immediately suggested a corollary. If the mind/body was capable of damaging itself so severely, would it also be capable of self-repair? If Jane's blinding was a metaphor for her refusal to examine her conflicts, could she regain her sight by attaining a willingness to look? This possibility also fueled the excitement I'd heard in Carla's voice. If we could stop, or reverse, Jane's blinding we would not only demonstrate the interrelatedness of mind and body, we would also demonstrate that the realm of psychophysiological phenomena was far broader than traditionally believed, and we would harness those phenomena in the service of healing.

*   *   *

"What do you think she's resisting seeing?" I was intrigued.

"I think it's maternal sexual abuse. She remembers being abused by her mother's brother, but all the signs suggest that mom was a perpetrator as well. She has experiences in which she becomes childlike and cringes as if she were about to be hit. Sometimes she yells, 'No, Mommy!' or 'Stop, Mommy!' Moments later she 'comes to' and has no idea of what happened.

"She's also had episodes in the office in which she feels as if she's in bed with her mother and feels her mother pushing her down, feels her head being held between her mother's legs. As she experiences this she panics. She has trouble breathing and she yells, 'No, Mommy! I don't want to! I don't want to.'"

Carla broke off to let me register her words. Clients with traumatic backgrounds sometimes have *flashbacks* in which they vividly reexperience the trauma with all their senses, feeling in those moments as if the trauma were still occurring. I'd seen many such flashbacks in my own office, and the behavior Carla was describing sounded horrifyingly familiar: a child being forced to perform oral sex.

"Several months ago she began having these experiences frequently. Sometimes she'd have complete amnesia for them afterward; sometimes she'd be left with vague, uncomfortable feelings. But by the next session she always denied that anything had happened. Then she began deflecting me from her mother altogether, filling the sessions with other things. Now we've bogged down completely." Carla sounded frustrated.

"What does she say about her childhood?"

"She paints the usual picture of an alcoholic family. She says it was rough. Her dad was a late-stage alcoholic and absent a lot of the time. Her mom had a 'short fuse.' She remembers dozens of incidents in which her mother hit her—once with a telephone receiver, once with a rolling pin, once she pushed her down the stairs. And she remembers being yelled at a lot—for being stupid, everything was her fault. Apparently she had her mouth washed out with soap a lot because she'd done something 'bad' or 'dirty.' She doesn't have many strong, coherent memories, just a lot of bits and pieces. But she doesn't connect them into a pattern. Despite the horror of the individual pieces, she denies that anything 'really bad' ever happened.

"But at the same time she's flooded with feelings and dreams that point to more severe abuse. She wakes up at night in a panic, afraid there's someone 'evil' in her room. When we talk about her mother she breaks out in a sweaty panic. And she's brought me some of her artwork. She consistently draws herself as a small dog, belly up. A big female dog stands over her with its genitals near her mouth and its teeth bared in a menacing way. She's terrified that all these sensations and images are coming out of her—but I think she's even more terrified to find out why."

Carla's description was typical of survivors of chronic childhood abuse. Almost always, they deny or minimize the abusive memories. They have to: it's too painful to believe that their parents would do such a thing. So they fragment the memories into hundreds of shards, leaving only acceptable traces in their conscious minds. Rationalizations like "my childhood was rough," "he only did it to me once or twice," and "it wasn't so bad" are common, masking the fact that the abuse was devastating and chronic. But while the knowledge, body sensations, and feelings are shattered, they are not forgotten. They intrude in unexpected ways: through panic attacks and insomnia, through dreams and artwork, through seemingly inexplicable compulsions, and through the shadowy dread of the abusive parent. They live just outside of consciousness like noisy neighbors who bang on the pipes and occasionally show up at the door.

"Any chance she's a multiple personality?" In some survivors of severe chronic abuse, the trauma is so overwhelming that it literally fractures the child's developing personality. The intolerable pain and knowledge protectively split off from consciousness and crystallize over time into *alternate personalities.* Some *alters* form to carry the pain and suffering of childhood, while others form to manage feelings such as fear, guilt, or shame. Others form to carry complex functions for the child: one might enable her to put on a "normal" face at school, while another comes out only at night to handle Daddy when he is drunk. Each alter surfaces in response to life's daily demands. All help her distance herself from the unacceptable aspects of her present and past.

Personality splitting may not cease with the end of the child abuse, however. If left untreated, the compartmentalization of experience may become a lifelong habit, and, rather than develop an integrated adult personality capable of handling a broad range of emotions and performing a wide range of tasks, the survivor may continue to create alters into adulthood. One alter may form, for example, to handle the task of going to college, while another forms to handle parenting. By adolescence a survivor may have a dozen or more alters within, all helping her cope with daily life, all protecting her from the full experience of her past.

"She's not a *multiple*," Carla said, "but she certainly has a *dissociative disorder*. She has many well-formed internal *parts* that influence her behavior, but they don't generally come out and take over. They flood her with thoughts and feelings, and they vie for control to the point where she becomes paralyzed."

"Tell me about them."

"Well, there are probably dozens of parts altogether, but only three you'll need to work with—the three that seem most embroiled in this struggle. One is a 'little girl,' a part of Jane that fixated at about six. She's the one that experiences those terrifying episodes. Then there's the 'teenager,' a part of Jane that's tough and angry, rebellious and self-protective. And there's the 'mother.' She's very angry, and verbally abusive to the others. The three of them are in conflict with each other—they're locked in the same dysfunctional relationships that existed in Jane's family—and they're all determined to keep Jane's deep emotional conflicts out of sight."

"Have you talked with them?"

"I have."

In people with dissociative disorders, parts don't usually come out and take over the way a multiple's alternate personalities do, but they are always there, close to the surface, aware of the outside world—and they can be "talked to" just as any of us might converse with an aspect of ourselves. At times parts can be difficult to engage through the conscious mind, for they house material the person is shielding from conscious awareness. But in hypnosis we can work around the conscious resistance by setting aside the client's conscious mind. With the resistance tied up, the parts can be brought out—and often appear with distinct attitudes, features, and voices.

"I've actually talked with them three different ways," Carla went on. "Sometimes Jane goes into a *mixed state*—she shuttles back and forth between trance and the waking state—and she's able to hear their voices and tell me what they're saying. Sometimes I induce a trance and ask to speak with them directly. At those times Jane's voice will change and I'll have the sense that the parts are speaking through her right to me. And then sometimes—if I press her about something really painful—Jane will develop a spontaneous trance and the little girl part will emerge and take over the body."

"What's Jane's sense of her parts?"

"She's aware of them. I think she feels herself as a collection of voices that push and pull her wretchedly from inside. Her sense of herself is fractured. She feels herself do things that she didn't mean to, as if her body doesn't belong to her. She said once that it's 'noisy inside, like being locked in a small house with a lot of people who are yelling and crying.' "

"Have you discussed the idea that there might be a connection between her worsening blindness and her block in therapy?"

"She's open to the idea. She doesn't buy it completely, but since doctors can't find a medical cause, it makes sense to her that there might be an emotional one."

"What did she say when you suggested seeing me?"

Carla chuckled. "You know how it is when you suggest hypnotherapy. People get this kind of magical thinking. *I'll close my eyes and wake up cured.* She knows that isn't true, but it's appealing to her because she so desperately wants to get better."

"Do you think she expects us to have an impact on her blindness?"

"I don't think she does. She doesn't want to go blind, but she suspects it serves a purpose, and ultimately I think she's more afraid of what it's masking. I think what she's hoping for from you is an end to her other symptoms. Ever since we hit the impasse, her nightmares and panic attacks have been nearly constant, and she's reached the point where she doesn't like leaving the house. That's what she's hoping to fix."

"Well, let's take a look at her." I opened my appointment book.

"Just one more thing. She has these images of suitcases."

"Suitcases?"

"Yeah. It's a mental image: rows and rows of suitcases lined up like graves in a cemetery. They show up a lot in her dreams and artwork, and the little girl and the teenager have mentioned them. They're afraid of them. There must be stuff in there they don't want to see or deal with."

"Sounds like a good way to contain unwanted material."

"Uh-huh."

"But you've been tampering with the locks."

"We have. And now her blindness is getting worse."

After I hung up, I mused about the conversation. I was intrigued by the notion of the suitcases: in all likelihood they were Jane's way of containing her conflicted emotions, her unwanted sensations, and even her painful knowledge from the past. The fact that they intruded as frequently as they did, and that she worked strenuously to avoid them, implied that she might need to open them in order to improve. But opening the suitcases wouldn't be my job. I was merely a short-term consultant and examining the suitcases would be long-term work. My job was to tackle Jane's resistance, to untie the knot that was causing her impasse in therapy. That *might* mean getting her to the point where she was willing to address the suitcases so that later she and Carla could do that work together. But more important would be working with her parts, for it was they who were keeping her in the blind.

From Carla's description, the subpersonalities matched the ones we typically see in survivors of severe abuse. And that wasn't surprising: given Jane's reported history, including sexual abuse by her uncle and brutal punishment by her mother—it was understandable that she would create these "containers" in self-protection.

A "little girl" part often forms in response to the repetitive demand to manage the pain and disown the knowledge of the abuse. Each time a child is abused she spontaneously insulates herself from the event. Some children fixate on a painting on the wall, imagining themselves inside it; others imagine themselves flying on the ceiling; others imagine their experience as a movie that they can watch dispassionately from a distance. Whatever device the child uses, it separates her from the experience. It enables her to split off the physical sensations *(where I am nothing hurts);* it enables her to split off the knowledge that it is a parent or family member who is doing this to her; it enables her to split off the knowledge that it is *she* to whom the abuse is occurring. In this way she can live through the experience and yet not fully know it is happening, for she has relegated much of the experience to places beyond conscious awareness.

This demand to split off the experience is reinforced by her family. Usually no mention is made of the events once they're over, giving them a sense of unreality. Or they are reinterpreted as a "bad dream" or as "a sign of your father's love," adding to the child's sense that her perception was wrong. And the child is exhorted "not to tell," not to betray in any way that upsetting events are taking place, prompting her to hide her bruises or anxieties behind a mask of nonchalance. These demands to pretend the abuse away foster the splitting of her experience. Soon, the child herself has only a hazy, distorted awareness of the truth.

Because this splitting protects the child—both within her

psyche and within the family—she does it each time abuse occurs. Gradually the process becomes well worn, a kind of mind/body habit. The "places" in which the fragments of experience are stored become well-grooved neural patterns in her brain. Bit by bit they coalesce into her parts. Each time present-day experience reminds her of the abuse—by evoking similar feelings or sensations—those neural patterns fire: that child part comes to the fore. Carla had said that Jane's "little girl" was terrified and prone to flashbacks. This kind of child part almost always is, for she knows no reality other than the abuse: for her the torment has never stopped.

According to Carla, Jane also had an angry "teenage part" inside. She, too, would have been formed to contain feelings, sensations, and knowledge that Jane found unacceptable. Parts that fixate during teenage years often hold a person's feelings of sexuality, rebellion, and anger, for teens feel those sentiments strongly but know they are frightening or inadmissible in their families and culture. They're not encouraged to integrate those feelings into their personalities, hence the feelings remain split off, relegated to a rebellious teenage part.

Sexuality for Jane would have been particularly troubling because of the molestation by her uncle; as her age-appropriate sexuality developed it would raise the specter of her past. Did her budding sexual desire mean she *wanted* that childhood sex? Did she encourage it? Such concerns would be completely unacceptable—how could she live with herself if they were true? So she would have *had* to split them off, push them far from her sense of self. If, as Carla suspected, she'd also been molested by her mother, those anxieties would mushroom further, giving even greater impetus to the creation of a teenage part.

Carla had said Jane's teenage part was angry. Most teen parts are, but none more than children who have been abused, for in addition to harboring the age-appropriate anger that fuels separation from parents, they seethe with rage toward their perpetrators. But expressing that rage is forbidden: in most abusive families only the parents are permitted to get angry; children who do so are punished, ostracized, or ridiculed. So the teen must deny her anger. The habitual banishing of these sentiments to a place beyond consciousness etches an ever-deepening groove in the adolescent's brain. And as those neural pathways form, the teenage part solidifies.

"Mother" and "father parts" form because all children internalize their parents. We take in their values, their admonitions, their points of view, and we create multiple internal parents who influence us from within. Invariably we form good internal mothers and fathers as well as bad, representing our dichotomous perceptions of our parents.

Children whose parents have chronically abused them—either physically or sexually—also form good and bad internal parents, but for them the bad internal parents may be far more influential. The inner voices, urges, or images that sway them most persuasively are likely to be punitive and blaming, just like the external parents on whom they're modeled. I've met many of these "bad parents," speaking to them in trance, and it's hard not to recoil when I hear them talk about their children. "She's bad! She's filth!" they'll cry, echoing the actual parents' rage and recriminations. Apparently it was this bad mother part in Jane that was contributing to her impasse.

Perversely, even a bad parent part is formed by the child in self-protection. By telling herself that she is bad, the child maintains the necessary illusion that her parent is good. The parent is *right* to mistreat her: she deserves the abuse. She also gains a sense of control over an uncontrollable situation, for she is able to believe that if she tries harder and becomes "good enough," her situation might improve. In another form of self-protection, the internal parent echoes the actual parent's limits. In this way she protects the child from transgressing those limits and incurring the real parent's wrath. The most profound limit is the one most closely followed: *If you tell what happens to you at home, worse abuse will follow!* So the child, out of fear and self-protection, often carries her secret to the grave.

So these were the parts I'd need to work with in Jane: a child, a teenager, and a mother, each with her own feelings and sensibilities about the past, each with her own compelling reason to keep that material locked up. But that, I knew, was only half the challenge. According to Carla this trio of personality fragments was in conflict, replaying the dysfunctional relationships of the family. So not only would I have to work with them as individuals; I'd have to work with their relationships, with the alliances and antagonisms that bound them in a family system.

From having worked with many abuse survivors in the past, I had an idea of how the parts probably interrelated. Typically, the frightened little girl fears the mother, while the mother castigates the little girl. The girl is often wary of the teen with her explosive anger, yet depends on the teen for protection from the mother. The teenager often blames the child for their victimization (thinking *if she had been stronger, it wouldn't have happened*) and despises the child's weakness, for she sees in it her own; but at the same time she identifies with the child and wants to protect her. Between the teen and the mother lies a bond of muted hatred. The teen despises the mother for what she's done, but is too scared to express it directly; instead she vents her anger on the whole person and on the little girl.

The effect of these conflicts is a tremendously disjointed sense of self but, ironically, even that is protective, for as long as she is so "at odds with herself," the individual can't clearly examine the residue of her past. If Jane had been sexually abused by her mother, the skirmishing of her parts would conveniently blur her awareness of that truth, as well as a host of other issues that the awareness would raise: *Did I cause it? Did I enjoy it? If my mother did this, she must not love me, and if my mother can't love me, who can? I must be bad, unspeakably bad. I must be beyond redemption.* All of those feelings, so painful—so damning—would be kept at bay, subsumed by the conflicts of the parts. Thus, until her part-selves began to interact harmoniously, Jane would be unable to heal.

But how to elicit harmony in this divisive crew? The answer would require all of my skills as a family therapist, for I would need to negotiate with each of them to build a functioning family team. The task would be difficult but not impossible, for while the parts were at odds, they shared a common goal. Despite their often injurious efforts, *they all meant to protect Jane.* If I could remind them of that intent—if I could show them a better way to carry it out—perhaps I could encourage them to forsake their conflicts and become a team. That was my challenge.

Carla ushered Jane into the room and, with the barest touch, guided her to the recliner. I was immediately struck by Jane's air of self-assurance. Despite the thick Coke-bottle glasses and Carla's guiding arm she gave no indication of being unable to see. Tall and slender, with wild, dark hair that fanned out to her waist, she moved with a fluidity and determination that seemed to steer her from within. Dressed wholly in black and devoid of any ornamentation, she reminded me of a warrior or a totem: her posture, proud and defiant; her features, solemn and unforgiving; her hands, blunt and utilitarian like tools. All suggested a steely potency that was at once magnetic and off-putting.

Jane rapidly took her seat, not even glancing around the room. Her posture was taut and erect. I realized that, primed by Carla for our encounter, expecting to be hypnotized, and prone to dissociation because of her brutal childhood, she was effectively in a light trance already.

"What I typically do in sessions like these," I began when the two women were settled in their chairs, "is let you two start. Then I'll just watch, and if I see a place to make a comment or ask a question, I will." By asking them to begin the session in front of me I emphasized that I was a consultant and not a co-therapist. And I gained a chance to see the two of them relate. Before jumping into a consultation, I need to know if the client's impasse is solely within herself or if it stems, in part, from her interaction with her therapist.

Carla smiled warmly at Jane. "Let's review what we're hoping to accomplish here today. It seems like things have bogged down for us. . . ." She left the sentence open for her client to finish.

Jane nodded. Her hands lay open in her lap, palms up, and as she talked she squeezed them into fists. Her voice was deep and husky. "I guess I want to get over this block. My symptoms are getting worse, and I know it's because I'm closing down. But you ask me questions and I just go dead inside. I want to sleep."

"Do you know what you're thinking about, or feeling, just before that happens?"

Jane rolled her head slowly back and to the side and her eyes closed slightly. It was, I suspected, an habitual gesture, but it had an air of recoil, or avoidance. "Thinking about *her*."

"About your mother."

"Uh-huh."

"You've had other kinds of feelings when we've talked about your mother. Stronger feelings. Can you tell David about those?"

"Panic. I get panicked. Sometimes I get the sweats."

"Can you remember what you were thinking or seeing when that's happened?"

Her eyes half closed and she shook her head. Her hair, back lit from the window, made a dark halo around her face. "It's hard . . . it's just images . . . and feelings."

"Can you try to describe the images?"

"Sometimes I see her bedroom, where we lived when I was a kid. Or I see her . . . No, it's not that I see her, I feel her . . . like I feel this sensation of her." Her voice was cool but her face grew pinched. "Sometimes I hear her calling my name."

"And then what happens?"

"Then I panic. I don't want to go in there. I start breathing heavy. And I sweat. It's like what happens to me at night."

"And then?"

"And then it goes away. Then you ask me what's going on and I say 'I don't know.'" Jane looked at Carla and laughed and Carla smiled back. They seemed to share a moment of intimacy.

"You've also had some bouts of anger toward your mother."

Jane nodded ruefully. "Yeah, I want to . . . sometimes I think about hurting her."

"Can you remember what you were thinking about when you had those feelings?"

She sighed. "It's hard . . . the same thing . . . those images."

"Images of your mother and her bedroom?"

"Not even images." She closed her eyes and squinted as if to bring an internal picture into focus. "It's a feeling of her . . . of her being too close. Smothering." A grimace crossed her face and she opened her eyes.

"I told David about your experiences in our sessions in which you seemed to feel her smothering you, holding your head so you can't breathe."

Jane's face twitched, then she let out a harsh little laugh. "Yeah, so you say."

"But you don't remember saying it? You don't remember feeling smothered?"

The blunt fingers tightened in her lap. "Sometimes I do . . . at night." Her voice was halting, as if she were calling the feeling back from a distant place. Suddenly she sat up in the chair and shook her head. "I don't get it."

"What don't you get?"

"Why I get those feelings. I mean, it's not like that really happened, so why do I keep getting those feelings?"

"What do you think those feelings are about?"

"I don't know." Her voice was sharp. "But it pisses me off. I know what it looks like but I know that didn't happen. My mother was tough. She was rough with me sometimes. But she loved me. I know she loved me."

I saw my place to jump in.

"What do you think it would mean for you if those feelings *were* true?" I asked her gently.

Jane turned toward me and for the first time I sensed her failing vision. Her glance was softly out of focus, and seemed to sweep my face as if looking for the person behind the voice. "They're not true."

I nodded. The words were so familiar, spoken by all my dissociative clients—for dissociative disorders are disorders of denial, systematic organizations of a personality for the sole purpose of denying knowledge of one's past.

"I understand. I understand that you hope they're not." I needed to empathize with Jane's adamancy if I wanted to encourage her trust. "But, hypothetically, what if they were? What would that mean to you?"

Her face darkened; her mouth tightened into a grim line. She looked briefly at Carla, her touchstone, then down at the floor. "If they *are* true then I should have stopped it."

I closed my eyes briefly against the futility of that thought. It was a belief held by most survivors—that they *could* have stopped it, despite their powerlessness as children in the hands of grown abusers. (They cling to that thought for numerous reasons: their families often blamed them for the abuse, saying *you're bad! you made him do it!;* a child would rather believe she caused the abuse than believe her parent would willfully harm her; and believing she can stop the abuse gives the child an illusion of control. Unfortunately, what is protective in childhood is damaging to an adult: as a grown-up she reviles herself for having permitted the abuse to happen.)

Jane continued to stare at the floor, brooding and rigid, as if only by sitting still could she prevent her unwanted thoughts from coming true.

Softly, I pushed. "What else would it mean if those feelings were true?"

Her face and body remained still, but her mouth moved rapidly, as if she'd anticipated my question. "That I should die because I'm not worth keeping alive."

Again, it was so familiar: the survivor's legacy, the self-damning double bind: *because I am bad this happened; because this happened I am bad.* Either way the message is the same: I am evil, I deserve to die. It is a helix of despair that sometimes propels survivors to take their lives.

But Jane believed—at least wanted to believe—that her feelings and images weren't true. She'd honored my request—told me what it would mean if, hypothetically, they were. But what would it mean to her if they weren't? I needed to know. "And what if those feelings aren't true?" I wondered.

Still she stared at the floor. Only a faint twitching of her eyebrows indicated that she'd heard me. When she finally answered, her voice was full of contempt. "Then I'm a liar for making it up."

A simultaneous wave of anger and sadness rose inside me—anger at families that wreak such devastation, infinite sadness for their innocent victims. For in Jane's words and voice I recognized another piece of the pattern: the prison of self-loathing to which survivors are condemned. On the one hand, Jane believed she deserved the abuse and damned herself for causing it; on the other, she believed she was despicable for having invented such filth.

I glanced at Carla, and saw a similar recognition.

Suddenly Jane looked up, searching my face. "But why would I make it up? Why would I have those images if they weren't true?"

I caught my breath: she'd walked right to the edge of the abyss. "I don't know. That's certainly worth exploring." I gazed at her silently, letting the question float in the air between us. "But if it *is* true," I asked finally, "why would you want to remember?"

She stared into my face for several long seconds as if daring me to answer my own question. Then with a deep intake of breath she lifted her face toward the ceiling. "Because," she said carefully, releasing the words like wishes, "if it is true, and if I remember, maybe it will reduce my nightmares and panic attacks, and make it easier to go out of the house." She lowered her gaze to mine for a moment, then turned to Carla. "And Carla has this idea . . ."—a faint smile crossed her lips—". . . that remembering might help my eyes."

So Jane had said it. Did she believe it? Was that smile just a patronizing handpat to her trusted therapist? Or a wistful expression of hope? Or was it the visible expression of inner knowledge, a sign that our hypothesized connection was real? I couldn't tell. But perhaps we'd soon find out, for Jane had invited me to help her begin to explore her conflicts.

"Would you be willing for us to do a little exploration now?"

She turned toward me once more. Fear and hope were partners in her eyes. "I guess so. Parts of me are terrified . . . but other parts want to do it."

I doubted that Jane was consciously referring to her parts—the child, the teen, the mother, and the other voices she felt within. But unconsciously I'm sure the word was intentional. Because that's what conflicted feelings are—the battle between parts of ourselves as each part or faction vies for the upper hand.

"I know you and Carla have talked about your inner parts—the little girl, the teen, the mother. What I'd like to do is to ask some questions of those parts. Would you be willing to tell me what they say?"

"You can try. But it usually works better when Carla puts me under."

She was inviting me to hypnotize her, inviting me to explore! I was delighted. Since this was a consultation—we had just one fifty-minute session—moving quickly was important. Jane's eagerness to proceed would buy us valuable time for the intervention.

"I can do that if you'd like. Should we get started now? Are you relaxed and comfortable?"

She nodded.

"Okay. . . . Why don't you take your glasses off? You won't need them with your eyes closed and we don't want them to get in your way." I always ask clients to remove their glasses before going into a trance. I don't want them to hurt themselves if their heads slump forward or if they make forceful gestures. And I want to reduce physical distractions: merely feeling glasses on the face pulls one's attention to the outside world, detracting from internal focus.

"Now you know that once you are in a trance you will do only those things that are in your best interest. . . ." My voice took on the tones and cadence of trance induction. "If I ask you a question that is not in your best interest you can refuse to answer it . . . and if for any reason it becomes not in your best interest to remain in this state you will be able to open your eyes and wake up. Do you understand?"

She nodded slowly. Already her eyes looked glazed. Like most survivors of childhood torment, she was adept at trance: it was a practiced coping mechanism, a means of escaping brutality and pain by drifting into an inner world.

"Now, as you sit there comfortably, I'd like you to look down at your hands, and as you watch them just let them do whatever they want to do. . . . There's nothing you need to do now and nothing you need to try *not* to do. . . . You might find as I'm talking to you and as you continue to relax that your conscious mind has a tendency to drift. . . . That's all right, just let it drift."

By the time I'd finished a brief induction Jane's eyes had closed and her head had leaned to the side.

I needed to move slowly with Jane to build trust and a working alliance. She had already had severe boundary violations and was justifiably wary of letting others take too much control. To avoid triggering her defensiveness I would need to ask her permission repeatedly and move with informed consent and utter caution toward the most sensitive material.

"I wonder," I kept my voice quiet and mellifluous, "if your deepest mind could let me know, perhaps by raising the index finger on that left hand, if it would be willing to answer some questions related to the work here today?" Beginning with a finger was a cautionary move. Parts are easily threatened; when asked to speak they sometimes feel exposed. By asking Jane to lift a finger rather than speak I avoided asking any of the parts to come into the room before we'd had a chance to establish trust, and instead asked for a response directly from the deep unconscious, the place where Jane was one, intact.

Slowly, with the characteristic jerkiness of an unconscious response, the index finger on Jane's left hand rose.

"Thank you."

The finger dropped.

"All right, here is the first question. Does Jane's unconscious mind believe that it would be in Jane's best interest to explore the issues we've been talking about?"

Again the index finger rose.

"Thank you."

The finger dropped.

"Does the deep unconscious believe that if Jane explores the issues around which her therapy has bogged down it might have a positive effect on her symptoms?"

After a pause of several seconds, the index finger rose.

"Thank you."

The finger dropped.

"Is it possible that exploring these issues might also have a positive effect on Jane's sight?"

Jane's hand lay quietly in her lap. Five, then ten seconds passed, then slowly the index finger rose. This time it rose higher, pulling the hand up slightly behind it.

We'd gotten our confirmation: there *was* a relationship between Jane's blindness and her conflicts. I felt a rush of excitement and traded glances with Carla. But immediately a voice sounded in my head: "Wait, there's no empirical proof," and I had to acknowledge it was right. The only way we'd know for sure that Jane's blinding was psychogenic would be if she resolved her underlying issues *and* her vision improved. For that we'd have to wait and see.

"I'm wondering if there is any aspect or part of Jane that would like to speak with me, or bring something to my attention."

Jane sat immobile in her chair, head bowed. Nothing indicated she had heard me.

"And just be comfortable as you listen and watch and feel inside for some kind of response."

Five seconds passed. Jane's eyes began moving behind her eyelids; the rhythm of her breathing quickened. Then suddenly, as if pulled by an inner spring, she curled up in the chair. Her feet tucked up beneath her, her shoulders hunched, her arms circled protectively around her waist. Her eyes flew open, wide as disks, and cased the room in rapid, frightened movements. The change was unmistakable: this thirty-seven-year-old woman was manifesting the body language and facial expressions of a terrified little girl.

I was swept with a wave of wonder and compassion. I've seen this phenomenon hundreds of times—the rapid and total transformation of a client into a different persona—and the remarkableness of it never fails to move me. But as much as awe, I felt compassion for the little girl who now sat in the chair before me. I had no sense of her being Jane. She *was,* wholly, a child of six or seven.

"I'll bet you're scared," I said gently. "But nothing bad is going to happen to you here. Nothing is going to hurt you and we won't let anyone come in that you don't want here." This child, deep in trance, was frozen at the time of trauma. She could see me and see my office, yet for her the time was thirty years before, the time in which the abuse was still occurring. Now she literally feared that someone might see or hear her sitting in my office and report her to the mother. "No one can hear us here, so is it all right that we're talking?"

She stared at me wide-eyed, but gave the faintest nod.

"Do you know who Carla is?"

Another cautious nod.

"And do you know that Carla doesn't want to hurt you?"

Nod.

"Well, Carla thought it would be good for us to talk a little bit. Would that be okay?"

Again she nodded, ever so slightly, but her eyes remained wide with caution.

"And would it be all right if Carla is here with us?" I gestured toward Carla, which brought her into the girl's hypnotic field of vision.

The girl seemed reassured by Carla's presence and nodded again, slightly harder.

"Do you know who I am or what we're doing here?"

She put her right thumb in her mouth.

"You can take as much time as you want to answer. There's no need to hurry and you don't even need to answer if you don't want to."

Her index finger curled snugly over her nose.

"But do you understand that I'm here to help you feel better?"

Without moving her hand she nodded diffidently.

"That's good. Isn't it, Carla?" I drew Carla in for a moment to comfort the child. Carla looked at her warmly and I turned back to the girl. "So do you have anything you'd like to say to me or ask me?"

She stared at me with her cautious eyes but neither moved nor spoke.

It's human to want to tell our fearful and upsetting stories, to find relief by letting out our thoughts and feelings. But parts that carry secrets of childhood abuse are terrified to do so. Usually their aggressors have warned them that if they tell, something they love will be taken from them, or they or someone they love will suffer worse abuse. And they can't imagine giving up their secrets safely, for safety is a condition they have never known. They fear that even the person they tell will be overwhelmed by the knowledge, just as they themselves are.

Thirty seconds passed in silence. Still she eyed me like a frightened bird.

I smiled at her kindly. "I'm proud of you for doing a really good job of being here and checking things out. And we might even meet again, but for now wouldn't you just like to be able to go back to sleep and be left alone?"

She nodded, thumb still glued tightly to her mouth.

"That's right, so why don't you just let your eyes grow heavy and close, and go back to sleep. . . ."

She closed her eyes. A nanosecond later they opened again and gave a last furtive look around. I recognized that look; I'd seen it in children as well as in childlike aspects of adults. Threatened by the unfamiliar therapy situation, frightened they'll get in trouble for having let their story out, they are reluctant to close their eyes, to let down their guard. But a second later the eyes closed again, and then slowly, as if released of air, the body unfurled in the chair. It lay motionless and slack, head back against the headrest, arms splayed loosely at its sides, mouth open. The little girl was gone. And as happens when one part has been dismissed and another has yet to take its place, the body seemed uninhabited.

I exchanged a glance with Carla. It was important that she stay "with" me through the session. My goal was to smooth the communication between the fragmented aspects of Jane's mind and to pave the way for Jane and Carla to continue working with those fragments in their therapy. So it was important that Carla feel comfortable with what was happening. She met my eye and nodded.

"Now," I turned back toward Jane. "I wonder if there is another aspect of Jane that might wish to speak with me or call something to my attention."

The body remained lifeless for several seconds, then suddenly the eyes flashed opened and, glowing like irradiated marbles, stared into the room. A second later the torso jerked to life. The shoulders rose into a defiant slouch, the arms crossed protectively across the chest, the mouth settled into a thin, irascible line. Jane glowered at me through beady, observing eyes. She had become a wary, angry teenager.

"Hello," I opened.

She glared at me hostilely as if through her silence she could take control.

"I appreciate your willingness to speak with me."

She gave a single grudging nod.

"So I'm wondering what it is you may want me to know."

"What I want you to know is, stop messing with that stuff."

"What stuff is that?"

"*She* knows what stuff." She nodded toward Carla. "The stuff she wants us to look at."

"Well, Carla's told me a little about your sessions, but I haven't observed them. And I don't think I should make any assumptions without first hearing from you. So would you be willing to help me understand what's been happening in your work with Carla?"

She eyed me sullenly. "Just back off, okay?" Her voice was threatening, but it ended with a question.

I sat back visibly in my chair to give the impression of backing off. "Look, I'm not here to hurt you or pry into stuff that's really none of my business. I'm just here to see if I can give Carla some help in working with Jane and you guys."

I wasn't surprised at the teenager's blatant hostility. Like any angry rebellious adolescent, Jane's teenage part compensated for her insecurity by adopting a tough, self-assured demeanor. Beyond the usual insecurities of adolescence, she'd been made to feel small and weak by an abusive parent. Her distorted thinking, characteristic of a mistreated child—*I wasn't strong enough to stop it*—only reinforced her sense of impotence. And since she believed that weakness invites abuse, she went to great lengths to hide her terrifying frailty beneath a carefully crafted exterior. To earn the trust of the teenager I'd have to appeal to her preferred self-image.

"I'm impressed that Jane has such a tough part of her to keep her safe."

Her narrowed, suspicious eyes kept me in her sights.

"You must be doing a good job or you wouldn't be here checking me out."

Her eyes flared slightly and she seemed to soften a bit. I'd paid her an unexpected compliment. I'd also caught her in a bind. On the one hand she wanted to thwart the therapeutic process, for we were tampering with Jane's defenses. But the irony of "hostile" parts—parts that may be injurious to the self—is that despite their damaging effects, despite their angry bravado, despite their recalcitrance in therapy, despite their seeming to work against the client, they *want* the therapist's help, for their original intent was protective. The client allows these hidden parts to surface in therapy in order to engage in a therapeutic relationship. The fact that the teenager had shown her face, had engaged me in conversation, was a sign that Jane was willing to risk finding a way to work with me.

"I know you don't trust me," I kept going. "And you aren't sure you like being here. But you don't have to like me to get something for yourself here. You don't even have to like me to trust me."

She curled her lower lip over her teeth and ran her tongue along it as if finely honing a blade. "Yeah, well I heard what you said. I can listen when she talks. Mostly she bores the shit out of me. You want her to see what's in those suitcases. Well I ain't gonna let her. You got it? I ain't gonna let that happen." Her voice was raspy, a shade darker than Jane's, and her eyes darted nervously while she talked.

"Well, I certainly think she *shouldn't* look into those suitcases unless you and the others think it's a good idea."

"Well, we don't think it's a good idea. You got that? So just leave us alone. We got it all handled."

"I'm just trying to find a way I might be helpful to you."

"We don't need any help."

"You do seem to have things under control. . . . Except one thing troubles me. . . ."

She eyed me warily. "What's that?"

"Well, it seems to me that by fighting with each other all the time and keeping the suitcases locked up you're doing exactly what the mother wants."

She sucked in her breath. I'd shaken her: I'd pinpointed the flaw in her strategy. She saw her actions as *protecting* Jane; I'd framed them as *collusion*. She saw her actions as keeping the painful material out of view; I'd framed it as obeying the mother's injunction not to tell.

"That's not true," she hissed.

"Well, she sure doesn't have to kick you guys in the ass any more to get you to do what she wants. You're already doing it for her. It's a shame, really, that in trying to protect Jane you end up being your mother's handmaiden. I'll bet she's pleased with you. You're a very loyal daughter."

Her face had turned pale and she sat stock still. Her eyes wore a mixture of hostility and panic. Behind the panic tears began to form.

"If I could show you all a way of helping Jane come to terms with whatever it is you're so afraid of—a way that doesn't overwhelm everyone and doesn't play into the mother's worst wishes—would you be interested?"

"You couldn't do that."

"Perhaps not."

"You couldn't."

I leaned forward slightly in my seat. "I want what you want. I want Jane to be safe and able to watch out for herself—not to have to live in the dark anymore, for anyone. I think we may be able to work together to find a way to help her get there."

She turned her head to the side and breathed in deeply, then she blinked quickly two or three times.

I waited for her answer.

"I don't know . . ."

I remained silent.

She cleared her throat. "Maybe."

"It might have to involve coming to terms with whatever is in those suitcases . . ."

"No!" She wheeled sharply toward me.

"That's what *she* wants you to say."

She glowered, then turned away.

I waited.

She blinked again, hugging her chest more tightly.

I waited.

A moment later her voice had softened. "What do I have to do?"

My voice took on the cadence of trance induction. "You don't *have* to do anything, but you might be interested to find that you *can* do it slowly . . . so slowly that you hardly notice it at first . . . only as fast as your inner mind thinks best . . . and only as fast as you are ready. . . . So if you're ready to take the next step then just let your eyes close now and drift deeper . . . deeper with every breath."

Her eyelids fell and slowly the tension drained from her body.

"Now I'm talking to all aspects of Jane's mind, at all ages. . . . You may discover yourselves taking the next steps with Carla, but only as fast as everyone inside feels safe and secure. . . . And in that process of discovery you will also find a sense of teamwork growing that will enable you to take the next steps in ways that meet all of your deepest interests. . . . And if you should find that it's in your best interest to open that old luggage you will, but not so fast that it overwhelms you or that you cannot learn or profit from it. . . . And you might find yourself approaching that luggage in random ways . . . one here, one there, maybe the smaller ones first, maybe according to some pattern determined by your deepest core . . . without fully appreciating the steps you've taken until you approach the very last piece." The parts seemed to view opening the suitcases as an "all or nothing" proposition. I wanted to let them know they could do it in smaller, easier-to-manage pieces.

"Only as you make good use of the information in each suitcase, only as you integrate those feelings, will you be able to go on to the next . . . and then the next . . . and then the next. . . . And if you need to close any suitcase temporarily, perhaps to muster strength, or for any other good reason, you will be able to do so . . . and then you will be able to open it again when it's time to do so. . . . And in this way, you will be fully in control of opening and closing the suitcases. . . .

"Now see this possible course. . . . See yourself proceeding only as fast as the least willing part wants to go. . . . And are you seeing that now? If so, let the head nod."

Her head dipped slightly.

"And if there's a deep understanding and a deep willingness to carry out this plan exactly as you've imagined it, then simply let the head nod again."

She sat bowed, eyes closed. Then she gave the slightest nod.

"All right, you can open your eyes now, but remain in this relaxed state."

The teenager opened her eyes. Her hands rested loosely in her lap. She'd lost her hardness and now seemed lethargic.

"So how are you doing?"

Her voice was quiet. "Okay."

"What do you think?"

There was a slight pause. "It might work."

"Do you think there are any parts who might have trouble with it?"

"Just the mother."

The mother, not *my* mother. *My* mother wouldn't do such a thing, abuse survivors think. *My* mother must be absent, replaced somehow by this impostor.

"Do you mean the outside mother?"

"No."

"The inside mother?"

"Yeah."

"I see. How do you and this inside mother get along?"

She shrugged. "We get along fine."

"What do you think of her?"

"Nothin'."

"You don't have any feelings about her?"

She jerked her head to the side dismissively. "She's fucked."

The word was deliberate. The teenager was far too scared of the mother and her promised retribution to tell her story outright. But surrounded now by allies she could let it slip unconsciously.

"Can she hear us?"

"Oh, yeah, she's listening. Probably watching, too. Says she's got eyes in the back of her head."

"Do you think she'd be interested in speaking with me?"

She laughed derisively.

"Would you ask her?"

She shrugged slightly, but as I watched, her eyes rolled up in their sockets and her head lolled. These were signs of deepening trance, natural movements of the body as one goes inside and accesses the inner mind. She was consulting the other parts. Five seconds later she returned.

"She doesn't want to talk to you."

"I wonder if there's a way we can make her feel more comfortable. Could you ask her if there's anything we can do to make her feel safer here?"

The girl shrugged to indicate the pointlessness of asking but once again her eyes rolled back. A second later she returned. "She said forget it."

"Perhaps she'd like to look around the room. It's fine with me if you want to get up and walk around, show her things. . . ." I knew the mother part would be suspicious. Like all dissociated personality parts, she represented the forbidden and intolerable: the stuff that no one wanted, the stuff that Jane and the others were trying to disown. She would fear I wanted to punish her, to wrest her out of Jane, to annihilate her. And because she was identified with the aggressor she would be especially wary: certain I'd find fault with her, certain I'd try to wrest control of her child from her, certain I'd condemn her unequivocally if I knew the secrets. More even than the others, she'd be determined to keep me at a distance.

"No," the teenager said grimly. "She doesn't want to look around."

Despite her refusal, and despite her reasons for keeping me away, I knew the mother was considering working with me. As with the teen, the fact that she'd communicated at all was a sign that she was willing to see what I had to offer. My challenge was to engage that tentative interest.

"Well, I wonder if you could tell her this," I tried. Despised by most of the other parts, the mother would feel maligned and misunderstood. Perhaps if I could "join" her in her sentiments she'd feel more willing to engage. "I know there must be a good reason why she doesn't want to talk and why she may not want you and the little girl to talk. Can you let her know that I respect that? And can you let her know that I want to understand her position better because I bet she often feels misunderstood?"

The teenager's eyes became slits. The last thing she wanted was me siding with the mother. But she said nothing, and once again her eyes rolled back. Seconds later she returned.

"What did she say?"

"Nothin'."

"Could you see her face?"

"Yeah."

"What was it like?"

"I don't know."

"You don't know? Can you describe how it looked, or what she did?"

"It was weird."

"In what way?"

The teenager scowled. "I don't know. It was just weird. She didn't look so angry."

"Huh. That's interesting. What do you make of that?"

She raised her eyebrows uncertainly.

"Do you think she's feeling a bit more understood?"

"I don't know." The teenager had lived her life under the admonition not to tell. She couldn't easily believe that the mother might agree to work with me when I had broached the idea of opening the suitcases.

"What if I try talking to her directly for a bit? If I give her some messages, could you let me know how she responds?"

"I guess." She gave me a look as if I'd asked her to touch her finger to a flame.

"Well, just do the best you can." Then I softened my voice into one of great compassion. "I'm speaking to the mother now. I want you to know that I think you must have one of the loneliest jobs in the world." It *was* a lonely job: she personified the person the rest of Jane most feared and loathed. And while she had initially adopted that role protectively, her genesis was long forgotten. Like the *kapos* at Auschwitz who policed their fellow Jews on orders from the Nazis, she had so identified with the aggressor that she and the other parts saw her only in that light. If I could remind her about her initial protective purpose, perhaps I could begin to melt her armor.

"The others may not understand what you're really trying to accomplish. . . . I don't think they appreciate that, like them, you are trying to protect Jane from worse harm. . . . You help set and keep the rules that keep her out of trouble. . . .You believe that if Jane and the others don't follow your dictates terrible things will happen. Ultimately you are trying in the best way you know to be compassionate and protective. . . . But I don't think the others understand that yet." My words were actually meant for all the fragments of Jane's personality, a way of giving the teen and the child a different viewpoint on the mother, a way of helping them all distinguish this internal mother from the one outside. By saying the others didn't understand her "yet" I was implying that in time they would—a subtle suggestion to the teen and child, and an offering to the mother that I hoped might soften her resistance.

"Tell me how she looks now," I said, raising my voice slightly to signal the teen.

The teenager stirred slightly. "She's listening."

"Is there any response?"

"No. She's just listening." There was a decided note of surprise in the girl's voice—surprise, I assumed, that the mother hadn't raked me over the coals.

I shifted my voice again. "Now I'm speaking to the mother. . . . My hunch is that it's not that you want to keep her blind and cut off from her deep feelings and knowledge. . . . I think you just don't want her to be overwhelmed or harmed. . . . You began as a protector but even you long ago forgot that. . . . Now you must begin to know again that you came to help them and there is still much you can do to bring light and lightness to them. . . . I think if you could find a way to do that you would surely want to. . . . There is still time for you to be the kind of mother they always wanted but never had."

The teenager sat sprawled in the chair, eyes shut.

"Would you be willing to ask her how she's reacting to what I've said?"

A moment later she opened her eyes. "She said you don't understand. It can never happen."

The mother had talked! She had balked, but she had joined the conversation.

I shifted my voice again to speak with the mother. "I appreciate that you feel that way. Perhaps you believe that it has to happen all at once, or that it must be totally out of your control, or that it will unleash terrible consequences. . . . But it doesn't have to be that way. . . . You all can tackle it little by little, in such a way that no one is overwhelmed and no one loses her place and no one is gotten rid of. . . . And you can be in charge of how fast that happens. . . . You can be sure they are not so overwhelmed by the process that they can't benefit. . . . And in this way you can be a better mother than the one they had because you can help them grow. . . ."

I paused. I knew if I pushed too hard for an agreement she'd almost certainly retreat. "I don't think this is the time or place for you to decide. I'd like you to think about this in your own time, and then do what you think is best for everyone."

For a suspended moment the teenager sat motionless in her chair, head back, eyes closed. Then she gave the faintest, almost imperceptible nod.

A shiver ran up my spine. On every earlier occasion the girl had *verbalized* the mother's response; this time she hadn't. Did that mean the nod was from the mother herself, that she had stepped forward to answer me directly? If so, it was an excellent sign: the mother had momentarily joined us, even if in the most tentative way.

"What do you think?" I asked the teenager when she opened her eyes.

"I don't know." She looked rattled. "I didn't think she'd go for it."

I hadn't been sure the mother would go for it either, and even now I partially wondered if she had conned me, given me what I'd wanted just to get me off her back.

"Well," I encouraged, "looks like at least she listened."

"Yeah." She sounded tentative.

"Are you afraid you might have to pay for this later, for agreeing to talk to me?"

"Kinda."

Only "*kinda*"? In the past the teen would have been terrified of recriminations. If now she was only "kinda" scared something must have changed. The mother must have genuinely softened!

I smiled at her with a sudden sureness. "Well, we'll have to see what happens, but I have a feeling that something big has taken place—that things can be different now inside—and that you'll be able to move forward."

She gathered a handful of hair and rubbed it against her face the way a child nestles against a blanket. Then she looked into my eyes and nodded.

Now it was time to turn our attention to the little girl. The mother and the teen had taken the first tentative steps toward teamwork; now I needed to draw the child into the circle. Given the mother's softening I suspected that the teen's hostility toward the child might also have lessened and that her positive instincts might have grown.

"I wonder if you could help me now with the little girl?"

She dropped her hair and raised an eyebrow scornfully. "That pain in the ass? What do you want me to do?" Her words were harsh, but unconvincing. An undercurrent of affection seemed to whisper through.

"I wonder if over the next few weeks you could stick close to her and just help her be more comfortable and less afraid. I think the mother will be picking on her less and you need to do that, too. She needs a big sister and you can be that for her. Don't you think?"

She frowned and rolled her eyes. "I guess."

"Thanks."

She shrugged off my appreciation.

"Now, is there anything else you'd like to say to me or ask me because we're getting close to the end of our time together?"

"Will I be coming back here?" She said it quickly, almost defiantly, hoping to mask the fact that she hoped she would.

"I don't know. That's really between you and Carla, but I'm sure one way or another I'll be hearing about your progress."

She nodded, apparently satisfied by that response.

"You've done an excellent job today. I've asked a lot of you and

I really appreciate your cooperation. And now, if you have nothing else to say, you can just close your eyes and rest. . . ." Her eyes fluttered to a close. "That's right . . . just drift . . . deeper and deeper with every breath . . . and now may I please speak with Jane, still deeply in trance?"

The teenager sat motionless for a moment, then slowly her body straightened in the chair. Her head lifted slightly and the curtain of hair fell back, broadly revealing the face. The face seemed newly soft, as if a warm washcloth had soothed away its tension.

"Hello, Jane."

"Hello." Her voice was cautious; her eyes seemed to search inside as if taking inventory. A faint smile touched the corners of her lips, but then disappeared, as if she were not sure she should trust the feeling that had provoked it.

"I've just spoken with the little girl, and with the teenager, and with the mother," I said. "Are you aware of all those parts?"

She nodded.

"All those parts have agreed to work together in their own way to help you come to terms with the conflicts that are stalling your therapy. Can you sense that?"

Jane was still a moment, then she nodded.

"Can you tell me what it feels like inside?"

She cleared her throat as if she hadn't spoken in a while. "It's quieter." Her distinctive husky voice seemed pleasingly familiar. "Less tense."

"Good. . . . Now just relax and let your mind clear. Your unconscious mind is already hard at work building a blueprint for your progress, and in your work with Carla you will continue to refine this blueprint. . . . And you will continue this work toward creating inner harmony as you shed light on those conflicts that have kept you hidden away in the dark. . . . And with each day that passes you will feel a greater sense of optimism and unified purpose, you will be able to *see at a deeper level*. . . . And you will know, more consciously with every day that passes, that your unconscious mind has been doing a great deal of productive work. . . . Now, if you are ready to return to your ordinary waking state just let your head nod."

Jane's head lowered slightly.

"In a moment I'm going to count from twenty back to one and when I reach the count of one you'll be wide awake, rested, and refreshed. . . . Twenty . . . coming back slowly . . . fifteen . . . the heaviness is leaving . . . ten . . . halfway back now . . . five . . . a good sense of well-being with every count . . . two . . . eyes opening . . . and now, one . . . wide awake . . . wide awake . . . and perhaps you feel like stretching."

Jane opened her eyes, blinked several times, then stretched her arms high over her head, arching her stately back. She looked quickly around the room, stopping for a moment on Carla, then moving her gaze to me.

I was sure she was feeling profoundly different—less tense, less "noisy," with a sense of ease or relief that she'd never previously known. Most likely, she had a vague sense of what we'd done, although she'd lack the details entirely. But I didn't want her focusing on that. I flashed her a mischievous grin. "Have you ever seen a chocolate moose?"

Her heavy eyebrows came together.

"Here." I handed her a box from the corner of my desk.

Cautiously she lifted the lid. Inside was a huge chunk of chocolate in the shape of a cartoon moose. She laughed broadly, and Carla and I joined her.

I keep this box on my desk for precisely that purpose. When a client comes out of a deep trance in which a lot of work has been done, it's best to let the work simmer. I want her unconscious free to process the work, without the meddling of her conscious mind. Jane had arrived in my office with all her parts bent on avoiding the unresolved issues represented by the suitcases. Now they were eyeing the problem differently: *How can we approach them, perhaps even explore their contents, while feeling in control?* They needed room to ponder this question without conscious interference. The moose, confounding as it was, was the perfect distraction.

While I didn't want her conscious musing on our session, I did want Jane to begin listening more closely to her parts. Despite their unavoidable presences, Jane had attempted to ignore them, for they and the sentiments they carried were frightening to her. To heal, she would need to listen to their stories and acknowledge their collective pain. Only by integrating her fragmented mind could she become a whole and healthy person. She needed to listen, too, because *not* listening was exhausting. Tuning out their voices, rejecting their feelings, refuting their knowledge required a great expenditure of effort. Listening would free that energy for healing and for the tasks of daily life.

"And now, Jane, there's one more thing I'd like to ask you to do. I'd like you to listen to your parts and get to know them. Can you begin to do that?"

Jane hesitated. I could see her check inside, confirm the quiet before she answered.

"Yes."

"Good. Then each day for one minute or five minutes, or ten minutes, it doesn't matter how long, I'd like you to sit down and listen to them. As time goes on, perhaps you'll be able to have conversations with them. Doing that will help your therapy with Carla. Do you understand?"

Jane turned to Carla, who nodded in confirmation.

"Yes."

Now that Jane had accepted her assignment, my work as a consultant was done: I had sown the first seeds of empathy and identification between the parts, encouraging the building of a team. And I had helped them see a way of addressing the forbidden material that was acceptable to them. These changes were bound to be productive in Jane's work with Carla. Whether they would have an impact on her vision we could only wait and see.

I next heard from Carla three months later. She'd been seeing Jane weekly, and the work was going well. "She's more in touch with her parts," she reported. "They're showing up in her dreams; she's dialoguing with them daily and writing about it in her journal. She's less depressed and more hopeful than she was. And she's having more traumatic memories of her mother. But I'm not convinced we're over the impasse. It still feels like she's holding back."

"How's her vision?"

"I haven't asked. If it *is* improving it may be happening outside her conscious awareness and I'm afraid talking about it may only interfere. And if it *isn't* happening, well, I don't want to create the expectation that it should be and risk making her feel like a failure."

"I think you're right."

"My impression, though, is it's about the same."

"The same? Not getting worse?"

We both silently considered the import of Carla's words.

"It's encouraging," she ventured, "it's certainly encouraging. But I don't think we're there yet. I'd like to bring her back."

So Carla and Jane came back. Jane entered the room with that same totemic bearing, that same sureness that so belied her failing vision.

Once again I asked them to begin the session by discussing

what had brought them. And once again Carla opened by turning the conversation over to Jane.

"My sense is that you've been working with your parts a lot better and that perhaps things are feeling a little easier inside? . . ."

Jane agreed. "I've been feeling, I don't know, less tense inside. Like someone opened a valve and let some pressure off."

Carla encouraged her to go on.

"And I've been having more memories." She grimaced wryly. "That's been fun."

"You've remembered some difficult things."

Jane was quiet for a few moments. "I guess that's why it's so hard."

"So hard?"

"So hard to keep going. Why I still fight it."

Carla nodded sympathetically.

"What do you think's going on?" I asked her.

She turned to me, rueful. "I don't know. I guess we need more of your help."

"How does it feel to be back here?"

"It feels okay."

"You want to take another step?"

"Yeah."

"Do you want to work hypnotically?"

"Uh-huh."

So using the same induction as before, I hypnotized Jane. When she was in a deep trance I asked if any part of her had something it wanted to say, and as before, the child part emerged. Jane's long legs tucked up tightly in her chair, her arms wrapped protectively around her torso, and her head snugged turtlelike between her shoulders. Her big eyes peered out cautiously. But as I looked closely I realized there was a notable difference between this child and the wide-eyed one I'd met before. That child had been filled with terror; this one was wary, but also curious. Her face contained an element of pride, as if she had mastered her fear and stepped into the room of her own volition. How different from last time! I thought. Last time, she'd been kicked into the room by the teenager and the mother, their sacrificial lamb for checking me out. This time she'd *chosen* to come first and they had let her come: they'd trusted me enough to risk their most vulnerable member.

"How are you doing?" I asked her softly. Despite her bravery, I sensed that a single movement could send her fleeing.

She widened her eyes.

"Is it a little more friendly inside?"

She gave an exaggerated nod.

"Is there anything you want to tell us or ask us?"

She shook her head.

"You just wanted to come here and say 'hi' and check things out?"

She giggled a little. "Uh-huh."

"Well, that's good. I'm glad you did that."

She looked at me with pride and her face took on a radiance that took me by surprise. It was so different from anything I'd seen in Jane.

"Anything else?"

She shook her head.

"Well, if there's nothing else, I wonder if I could speak with the teenage part I spoke with last time?"

Obediently the child nodded and closed her eyes, and in an instant, as if transformed by a gust of wind, uncurled her body and planted her feet firmly on the floor. Her forearms rested on her knees, her hands hung loosely in between. Her face, framed by the mat of hair, tilted chin first, toward mine.

Again I was instantly aware of a difference. Her posture was similar—that same defiant teenage pose—but it lacked the tension of its former incarnation. The intense guardedness, the blatant hostility were gone. She, too, seemed wary, but readier to talk.

"Hi," I smiled. "How are you doing?"

She nodded once. "Okay."

"How do things feel inside?"

She looked around for a second before answering. "Things are better. I mean, the kid's a pain in the ass, crying all the time. I wish she'd toughen up." She paused. "But *she's* not on us so much."

"Has Jane been listening to you better?"

"She tries."

"That's good. Any impressions from our last session?"

"Yeah." She eyed me guardedly. "I've thought about it."

"What have you thought?"

She was silent for a moment. "I don't know."

"Is it still pretty scary to think about the suitcases?"

"Not scary . . ." She winced and shook her head as if trying to jettison a disturbing thought. Suddenly she pounded her fist on her knee. "I'm pissed! I'm so fucking pissed at her. I could . . ." Her eyes were like needles. "I could kill her."

"Kill who?"

"You know who."

"You mean the one I spoke to last time?"

"No. The other one."

The other one. The outside mother. The teenager was differentiating between the two. Another sign of change: it meant the teen had moved closer to teaming with the inner mother, that the mother was less identified with the outside aggressor, and no longer such a target of the teenager's rage.

"Is that what you're afraid of? That you might kill her?"

Her eyes touched mine for a split second. They were filled with fear.

"Is that what you're afraid will happen if you remember more?"

The fear in her eyes became panic. She spun her gaze wildly around the room then back at me.

"Or are you really afraid of what she'll do to you? Of what she'll do to you if you open them, or tell?"

The teen's head dropped to her knees and she began to sob.

I restrained the urge to touch her. She would have recoiled at such a gesture, such a comment on her unmasking. And I wanted her to know instead how much I appreciated what she'd done by letting the bravado slip and revealing her underlying fear. So I soothed her verbally, hoping to communicate that even now, soul bared, she was safe with me. "That's right," I whispered. "It really hurts. And it's good to let it out. You don't need to be quiet any more."

She kept on crying, her head bent over her knees, her mane of hair a protective blanket, and as she did I let my voice drift over her. "That's right . . . that's right . . . yes . . . yes . . ."

After several minutes she sat up, sniffing loudly.

"How old is the outside mother now?"

She blew her nose. "Seventy-two." Her voice was thick from crying.

"What does she look like? Can you imagine her face now? What color is her hair?" I knew from Carla that Jane and her mother were estranged, that the mother was sick, that the father had died some years before.

"Gray," she said tiredly. "Her hair is gray."

"That's right," I reinforced. "Her hair is gray. She's much older now. She's not as strong. She can't hurt you any more."

Her eyes examined mine, looking for a reason to believe.

"She hurt you very badly. You have a right to be angry." I paused. "But being angry doesn't mean you're like your mother."

She recoiled as if my words had stung her.

Most children of severely abusive parents harbor violent, consuming rage, contained in dissociative identities such as Jane's parent and teenage parts. Left to fester out of awareness, the rage grows but maintains its childlike form. Adult anger is tempered—translated into words, modulated with reason, defused until its power can be expressed in socially acceptable ways. But a child's rage is pure, primitively self-protective, and overwhelming: an eye for an eye, a tooth for a tooth, a furious, violent urge to strike whenever the child feels threatened. This is the rage Jane held inside—and she feared the rage almost more than she feared her mother. But even more than she feared its imagined consequences, she feared its meaning: *if I am rageful, I am like the mother; if I am rageful, I am as bad as she.*

Until recently Jane had been able to keep the rage relatively in check. But now that she was listening more closely to her parts, now that they were beginning to lift the lids of the suitcases, the rage had come bubbling to the surface. I understood now what was causing this latest resistance. It wasn't only fear of the conflicts and material from childhood. It was also fear of this roiling, consuming rage. To help Jane move forward we would have to help her metabolize, or process, that rage safely.

"You have a right to be angry," I repeated, "and I know your anger is very frightening to you. If I can help you deal with it, if I can help you release it in such a way that no one will get hurt and you won't be like the mother, would you be interested?"

The girl shuddered as if suddenly chilled. "How could you do that?" It was as much a challenge as a question.

"We can use hypnosis to help you fully express your rage in a safe and appropriate way. You'll create a strong, secure, leakproof container in your mind and once you're inside that container you'll be able to safely express all your pent-up emotion. Even though it will seem very real to you and may even seem as if you are being very loud or physical, the body will be sitting quietly in the chair the whole time." Jane had never learned that it was possible to express anger safely; her parents had shown her precisely the reverse. What I was proposing was in essence a retraining, a chance for her to learn that she could experience such powerful feelings fully without harming anyone. That way, in the future, she would be able to let such feelings go rather than holding them inside, turning them upon herself, or letting them control her.

I paused to let her weigh the idea. "Should I tell you more?"

She gave a single nod.

"Once you get inside the container, you will be able to leave behind all your old fear of getting angry at the people who hurt you. You will feel free to express yourself without inhibitions, and this release of feelings will feel very satisfying. You may feel yourself having much greater strength than normal. You may find that words come to mind more easily and quickly than normal. And throughout, your body will be sitting quietly, resting comfortably in that chair." Again I let her consider the idea. "Does this sound like something you might like to pursue?"

Slowly she gave another nod.

"Whatever you do in your container will be your own business. You may wish to share it with me, or you may wish to keep it secret. You will have three minutes of clock time to complete the task, but it can seem like all the time in the world to your deepest mind. I will tap a pencil to let you know when half the time is up, and then again when there is just a little time remaining so you can finish.

"And because I am very concerned about your safety, as well as my own, I will reserve the right to stop this activity if I think it is not in our best interest to continue. If I say the word 'stop,' the images will disappear instantly and you will relax immediately and go even deeper into trance while remaining in touch with this voice. Do you understand?"

Another nod.

"And before we begin we would consult the others, because we would only want to proceed if they were in agreement. I think it would be best if we asked the mother to watch but not get involved herself." I was afraid that if we unleashed the mother's rage at the same time as the teen's it would be too much for Jane to tolerate. We'd need to address her anger at a later date. "And perhaps it would be best if Jane also watches from a distance. Perhaps we could let her decide how close she wants to be? Do you agree?"

Another nod.

"And perhaps we should show the little girl to a friendly room, a room that's strong and soundproof and filled with toys, where she can play until we come to get her?"

Another nod.

"Do you wish to proceed?"

After just a second, "Yes."

"Okay . . . then what I'd like you to do is to go ask the mother if she would be willing to stand aside and watch, and then ask Jane to pick her own distance from the event. Can you do that now and tell me what they say?"

The teen closed her eyes. Ten seconds later she returned. "The mother said okay," she murmured, "and Jane said she didn't want to get too close. She'll watch from pretty far away."

"Thank you, that's good. Now can you escort the little girl to her room?"

Once again the teenager went inside. Forty seconds later she returned.

"Is she safe?"

"Yes."

"Good, then we can proceed. . . . Now what I'd like you to do, even as I'm talking, is to let an image come to mind of your container . . . a container so strong it can hold all your pent-up rage and feelings without leaking. . . . Some people have used a bomb shelter, some have used a vault, whatever your unconscious mind thinks best. . . . Now just let an image come into your mind . . . take your time . . . and let me know verbally when it is there."

Five seconds passed.

"A cave underground."

"Very good. . . . Now some people, when they go into their containers, prefer to confront their aggressors directly . . . others prefer to see their aggressors restrained or behind bullet-proof glass . . . whatever you need will be there for you. . . . Do you understand?"

A nod.

"Good. . . . Now I'd like to help you reassure yourself that although it may feel as though you're moving violently and making loud sounds, the body will actually be sitting in the chair, quiet, calm, and still."

The phenomenon of separating mind and body is common in hypnotherapy. We use it in inductions when we tell a client that her arm will rise of its own accord, without her conscious effort. We use it in performing hypnoanesthesia when we help a patient manage pain. We use it in habit-control interventions when we help people who are quitting smoking "forget" their cravings. It is a phenomenon of dissociation, central to hypnosis.

"I'm going to count from one to five, and when I reach the count of five I want you to see your body sitting over *here* . . ." I leaned sideways toward an empty chair. "But your mind will still be over *there* with you." I leaned toward the girl. Although her eyes were closed and she couldn't see my movements, hypnotic rapport had her tuned closely to my voice. The voice's changed location would reinforce my verbal message.

I counted slowly. "Can you see your body over *here?*"

She gave a single nod.

"And with it are all the sensations of muscle control and movement. Do you understand?"

Another nod.

"As you watch the body over *here*, I want you to try to lift one of the arms."

Her right arm tensed slightly but didn't lift.

"Did you move the arm?"

"Yes."

"How high?"

"About a foot."

"That's right. . . . Now as you watch and understand that the body is over *here* and you are over *there*, I'd like you to try to stand up over *there.*"

Almost imperceptibly the teenager leaned forward in the chair. A second later she relaxed.

"You can't, can you?"

"No."

"That's because the actual body is over here. . . . So now you can know and accept completely that whatever you may feel over *there*, the body over *here* will just be resting comfortably. Do you understand that?"

A nod.

"Do you have any questions?"

She shook her head.

"Are you ready to start now?"

"Yes."

"Then go into the cave . . . but as you do you will stay in contact with this voice even as you seal the cave tightly behind you."

I waited a second. "Are you inside?"

A nod.

"Can you see the people at whom you are so angry?"

Another nod.

"OK, getting ready now . . . I'm going to count from one to five and when I reach the count of five you will begin . . . one . . . getting ready . . . two . . . going deeper . . . three . . . preparing . . . four . . . almost ready . . . and five . . . begin *now*."

Within three seconds the teen began to breathe rapidly; her skin grew red and her muscles tightened as if pulling isometrically in two directions at once. Beneath her eyelids, her eyes darted from side to side. Occasionally she moaned, a muzzled sound like the whimper of a sleeping dog.

"That's right," I encouraged, "get it out . . . feel it . . . yes . . . get it out . . ."

At one-and-a-half minutes I tapped the pencil. "Half the time is remaining. Look around. See if there are any other feelings you still want to express. See if there isn't more."

Her muscles tightened and her mouth opened, emitting a series of moans.

At forty seconds her breathing began to slow and her muscles started to relax, signs that the intensity of her imagined activity was waning.

"See if there's any more you want to express," I reminded, "because we're getting ready to stop."

Her face tightened again. The beads of sweat at her hairline glistened.

"The time is almost up . . . that's right . . . getting ready to stop in just a moment. . . ." The second hand on my watch swept toward the twelve. "Done! You can let it go. You can stop *now*."

It took several seconds for the tension to leave her body. First her hands stilled in her lap, and then with an exhalation of breath she sank back deeply in the chair. Slowly the color drained from her face. The hair at her temples was wet.

"Now you can rest . . . just rest. . . . You've done important work here for which you can feel a sense of accomplishment and personal mastery . . . and a deep sense of appreciation for all aspects of Jane for making the work possible. . . . The work you've started here today will continue into the future . . . you can expect the positive effects of this work to crop up in your sessions with Carla as well as in daily life. . . . Now you may leave the cave and come back into this room, still deeply asleep . . . and later when you awaken, you will remember as much or as little of this experience as your unconscious mind thinks is in your best interest. . . . Now just take some time to drift and absorb this experience. I'll speak to you again in a few moments." I waited a minute. "Now I'd like to speak with the teenager again, please."

The teenager opened her eyes and slowly focused them in my direction. Then, still panting, she surveyed the room.

"It's not trashed." Her voice was disbelieving.

"No."

"I thought . . ."

"You imagined it."

"Imagined it . . . ?" The words were slow and quizzical as she tried to make sense of what had happened.

"Do you need me to explain anything about what you just did?"

She grabbed a handful of hair and rubbed it against her face. "No."

"Is there anything you'd like to tell me about it?"

She opened her mouth but couldn't find the words.

"Intense?"

"Yeah."

"You think you got some of it out?"

"I told her off." A faint smile spread along her lips. "All this stuff that I'd stored up, you know? It just kept coming out and out and out. . . . And when I couldn't think of anything else to say, I *grabbed* her, and I did this thing that she did to me once. . . ." She grabbed the air in front of her and squeezed, pressing her thumbs like boring tools into an imaginary jugular. "I just kept pressing and pressing and pressing. . . ." Eyes closed, she jabbed her head with every repetition. "I didn't let go." She opened her eyes and looked at me. Her gaze was clear and open.

"How did that feel?"

She reflected, then broke into a smile. "Really good," she said softly. "*Really* good."

"Well, I wonder if you'll be willing to go inside now, to where the others are, and just tell me how things look?"

She nodded briefly, then her eyes rolled back and her head listed to the side. "It's quieter," she reported when she returned.

"Can you see the mother?"

"Yeah."

"How's she doing?"

"I don't know, it's weird again."

"In what way?"

"She looks . . . she looks kind of sad."

"That's interesting. Do you know what she's sad about?"

She shook her head.

"Can you ask her?"

Another head shake, this time quicker.

"Okay, we don't have to go with that right now. But that's an interesting thought. Maybe . . ."

The teen's eyes closed as I talked, then suddenly they popped back open. "I think she's feeling bad about how she treated us," she uttered quickly. Her voice was tremulous, disbelieving.

"Aah," I nodded. "That could be. Perhaps she has a clearer view of what happened."

It made sense that the mother might be remorseful about what she'd seen. Watching the teenager vent her rage on an image of the actual mother would have helped her differentiate herself from her namesake. As a result she might now have a greater sense of who she was in relation to Jane and the others, of how hateful her role model had been, and how tragic her own behavior. Previously she'd seen herself as an individual actor; now she might see herself as an equal victim of the abuse and as a member of the team.

"You know," I pointed out, "you've all focused on your own pain. But like Jane, you're going to have to realize that all of you were hurt, and that all of you were trying to help Jane—even the inside mother."

The teenager stared at me for a moment trying to reconcile my words with her own internal compass. Then slowly, as if fueled by a silent stream, her eyes grew wet with tears. Perhaps she, too, was seeing the mother as a part of them, and was feeling remorse at their mutual antagonism. Perhaps she was realizing that the mother wasn't alone, that she, herself, had been hurtful to Jane. Perhaps, with her defensive armor stripped away, she was feeling the loss and sadness that she'd hidden since her youth.

"That must really hurt," I soothed. "It must really hurt."

She whimpered softly for a few moments, then wiped her eyes with her sleeve.

"You know," I suggested, "I think the mother's been very helpful to us here. I wonder if you could tell her how much I appreciate her help, and see if she has anything she'd like to say."

The girl's eyes rolled back quickly, with none of the concern she'd evidenced the last time I'd "sided" with the mother. Seconds later she sat up and opened her eyes. "She said you ask too many questions." Her eyes had a glimmer of light. "But she said you're okay for such a nag."

I grinned. "Well, tell her thank you. And tell her I think she's okay, too."

The girl disappeared and came back a moment later, the hint of a smile on her face.

"Now," I said, "I think we should check on the little girl. Can you see how she's doing?"

She went inside, then returned.

"She's okay. I mean she looks kinda sad or confused or something. But she looks okay."

"Do you think she saw or heard anything?"

"I don't think so." She hesitated. "But she had to feel it."

I agreed. Jane's entire internal system had just been shaken. Of course the child would feel it. "Do you think it might be good for her to see the mother now?"

The teenager weighed that for a moment, then nodded cautiously. In the past she'd have shielded the child from the mother at all costs.

"Could you help her do that?"

Her eyes rolled back and she disappeared.

"How did she react?" I asked when she'd returned.

"I think she's confused."

I'm sure she was. The mother part she'd just seen was far different from the one she'd always known. "Well, tell her that things are going to be getting better. There's still important work to do, but I think things will be a little calmer and easier inside."

The teen delivered the message.

"Does she understand?"

"I think she understands that something really big just happened."

"Is there anything else she wants from me?"

"She wants to tell you that she's glad she came here today."

"Well, good," I replied. "I'm glad too. Tell her she's done a very nice job and she can feel proud of herself. And now is there anything else you'd like to say?"

The teenager shook her head.

"Then I want to thank you again for all your work today."

She nodded and looked away, and the quickness of her gesture touched me. I felt a flush of warmth for her that earlier I hadn't expected to feel. "I know you must be feeling quite a mix of feelings," I said gently. "They may be hard to sort out for a while, but the best thing you can do is let them come. Carla, if she should need to call you in the next few days will she be able to do so?"

"Of course."

"Well now, if there's nothing else, would you be willing to look inside and tell me if everything's okay in there . . . if there's anything anyone else needs to say before we stop for today?"

She nodded, rolled back her eyes, then shook her head.

"Then do you think it would be helpful to wake up Jane?"

"Uh-huh."

"All right . . . then just let your eyes close and go deeper to sleep now . . . everybody just drifting deeper and deeper . . . and in a moment I'm going to count from twenty back to one and when I reach the count of one you will be wide awake as Jane and feeling refreshed . . . And while there is no need to have to remember everything that has happened here today, you will have a deep sense that you have taken a big step for which you can feel a tremendous sense of accomplishment. And in the days to come you will look for positive benefits to accrue from this work. . . . And now twenty . . . slowly coming back into the room . . . eighteen . . . reconnecting with your body . . . ten . . . feeling relaxed and rested . . . five . . . coming back a little more with every count . . . and one, wide awake."

As I began the count, the teenager's body slackened. As it had each time one part left and another had yet to come, the body seemed depleted. But as I counted, the faintest stirrings began to form, and at the count of "one" the body straightened slowly in the chair. The head tossed back reflexively, fanning the mane of hair, and Jane's face turned, open-eyed, toward me.

I waited for her to speak.

"I must have been asleep."

"How are you doing?"

The corners of her mouth tugged up. "Better, I think. It seems a little easier inside."

"You've taken a big step today. What do *you* think, Carla?"

Carla beamed at her client. "I think that's true."

Jane turned toward her and as their eyes met the two women seemed to share the knowledge that something profound had happened. Jane's lips parted, her hand touched her cheek as if to reassure herself, then she reached up and wiped her eyes.

*   *   *

It was five months before I heard from Carla again.

"Jane's dreaming in 20/20," she said.

"What does that mean?"

"Apparently her whole adult life her dream images have been fuzzy. But for the last few months they've been in focus."

A shiver of anticipation ran through me. If her vision in her dreams was changing, would there be a corresponding change in her eyesight? "How's her vision?"

"I'm dying to know, but I still haven't asked."

I felt a stab of disappointment, although I understood Carla's reluctance. "How's therapy going?"

"Good! She's dialoguing with her parts on a regular basis. There's more teamwork, more crosstalk. A few more memories are coming up about her mother. She's definitely less defensive in sessions."

"Sounds good."

Two months later Carla called again.

"She's *reading*, David! She had to get a weaker prescription for her glasses! And get this. When I asked her how long she'd been aware of an improvement she said that right after the first session with you she noticed it had stopped getting worse, and then, by a few weeks later, she thought it was getting better. But she was afraid to say anything for fear it would go away! And you'll love this, David. I talked to one of her doctors. He was totally baffled. He said there are definite indications of improvement in her eye tissues. . . ." Carla began laughing, "and then he said 'but we know that's impossible.'"

I chuckled too. I'd encountered that before: a doctor's baffled reluctance to accept physiological changes that defy modern medical explanations.

Carla raced on, buoyant in her report. "And the memories are continuing to come. She's remembering some brutal scenes with her mother, real sadistic sexual abuse. And she's been expressing more of her anger. And as the anger goes she's touching some of her really deep-felt sadness." She paused finally, almost breathless. "It worked, David. We're not stuck anymore."

"It sounds like she's found a comfortable way to work with the suitcases, just a couple at a time."

Carla chortled at the other end. "You're right," she said. "That's exactly what she's doing."

*   *   *

Eight months later I ran into Carla at a conference.

"Jane quit therapy," she said.

"No!"

"Yeah." Her voice was dark. "It annoys me."

"What happened?"

"I think she'd had enough. Enough probing. Enough rooting around in all that old stuff."

"Too bad. She'd made so much progress."

"Tell me about it! By the time she left she was so much closer to her parts. She was owning their feelings, their memories; she was *integrating* them. She was more confident and relaxed. Her social relationships were strengthening. She was a lot less angry and so much more in touch with her grief. . . . That's what gets me." Carla scowled in irritation. "We were so close to finishing. I really thought she'd stay."

"How were her eyes?"

"Oh, her eyes were fine."

"Fine?"

"Yeah. They were still improving."

"That's fabulous. That's amazing." *My God, the woman can see again*, I thought, *what more do you want?* But I understood Carla's disappointment. It's hard to have a client leave therapy when you know the work is unfinished.

Carla nodded resignedly. "I guess you're right. It *is* wonderful."

We pondered Jane silently for a moment.

"What's your prognosis?"

Carla answered quickly as if she'd already given the question a lot of thought. "I'm guessing her vision will stay. She's not so at war with herself anymore. And I think she opened enough of the suitcases and dealt honestly enough with her feelings about what she found that she no longer needs so primitive a mechanism of denial."

"You two did good work together."

"I know!" Carla glowered at me in frustration, then a moment later she softened. "You know, at her last session she brought me a couple of her drawings. And I have to tell you, I was pretty blown away. They were self-portraits—and they were amazing likenesses. She really captured her essence, her moodiness as well as her features. But even more than that, David, I was blown away by the *detail*. They were pen-and-ink sketches. You know what those are like: just a web of really fine, fine lines . . ."

Carla looked to see if I got her meaning.

"You mean she'd have to be able to see pretty well to do them?"

Carla nodded slowly. "Jane had stopped *working*, David. Once we reached our impasse, *she couldn't see well enough to draw.*" She paused for a moment, her eyes fixed on mine. "And at the point she left therapy, her improvement hadn't shown any signs of stopping."

Reading the story of Jane one must be struck by a sense of oddness. She caused herself to go blind! What mechanism could permit such profound self-harm, even in the service of self-protection?

Perhaps it will seem less strange if you consider more familiar manifestations. We've all known people who have "worried themselves sick" and people who have "nervous stomachs." Perhaps you've known someone who "died of a broken heart" or who stalled death until a loved one came. Perhaps you're aware of storing tension in your neck; perhaps you get headaches when you're anxious. These phenomena are what I call *body conversations*. They are the ways our bodies reflect and communicate our emotional issues.

At first blush Jane's somatic expression of an emotional conflict seems far more punishing than anything you or I might cook up. But is that necessarily so? A friend of mine, a lifelong smoker, was warned to give up cigarettes when doctors found precancerous cells in his lungs. He didn't, and five years later died of lung cancer. I marveled at his obduracy during those last five years—until I realized that the self-destructive behavior wasn't new. Throughout his life this conflicted man had struggled with life and death issues. Was his disease a somatic expression of a script by which he was living his life—an expression even more self-destructive than Jane's?

For each of us, the body is a stage on which our emotional issues are played out. Our differences from Jane are not in substance, but only in degree.

And what of Jane's parts—that cacophony of voices that ruled her from within? How odd, you think, to be so fragmented, to harbor such distinct personas within? Well, odd, perhaps—but not so different from you or me.

In childhood we all distance ourselves from unwanted aspects of our experience as well as from impulses and desires that are unacceptable. Things that upset us profoundly, that threaten our sense of safety or our preferred sense of self, are either pushed to the outskirts of awareness or disowned. When that pushing aside becomes habitual and is reinforced by our caregivers and environment, the split-off material may coalesce into divisions of our personality, which appear and disappear in response to provocation, each with its own lens on the world.

Our parts differ from Jane's in significant ways. Hers were rigid, personified, and constant; ours are more amoebic, forming and unforming in response to environmental triggers. Like Jane's, however, our parts don't act alone. We all have an inner family of quarreling and cooperating interrelationships. What keeps us from succumbing unduly to mob rule is our *executive self* (what Freud called the *ego*), a kind of *supra part*, that acts as leader and encourages the others to move in a unified direction. This executive balances the competing aspects of our personality so that none plays too dominant a role; it is able to remind the aspects that want to solo that their allegiance is to us.

Jane, in contrast, lacked a strong executive. Because of the demands to split her mind in childhood, she had been unable to differentiate an independent self, unable to embrace her disparate parts, unable to mature. So rather than acting with a common purpose, her parts continually conflicted. Rather than share a common identity, they felt unrelated. Rather than harmonize their voices in a multiphonal song, they bleated a frightened cacophony.

So what distinguishes us from Jane is not the fact or number of inner parts, but rather the harmony between them. We may dislike parts of ourselves; we may quarrel with our inner voices; we may even watch ourselves at times and wonder "what came over us." But unlike Jane we largely understand that each of those voices, drives, or impulses is *us*. For ultimately each of us is no more—and no less—than this fluid firmament of parts, this vast and complex chorus singing the song of self.

Chapter 10

Called from the Grave

IN A SENSE THERE WERE TWO HELENE TOWNSENDS.

One was the professionally cheerful second-grade teacher who stepped into my office each week in her tidy shirtwaist dresses, her auburn hair neatly sprayed in place, her web-soled shoes polished to a gloss. Small and plump and apple-cheeked, briefcase stuffed with children's books and drawings, Helene was nothing if not familiar: she was the smiling teacher in my own second-grade reader.

But as the minutes ticked away, this Helene would gradually dissolve. First the smile, then the sturdy teacher's posture would disappear. Then her face itself would start to sag as furrows carved deep lines around her mouth, and soft jowls drew her jawline downward. She would sink lower and lower in her chair as if the knowledge of what she had come to do had turned her body into lead. This Helene spoke slowly, the march of her words anchored in an inner sorrow. And her eyes, although she rarely cried, seemed permanently close to tears.

Helene had come, she told me, because she was "chronically depressed." Her nights were filled with a "shapeless anxiety" that often kept her awake until morning. When she slept, her sleep was fitful, broken by dreams that frightened and disturbed her. Only daytime was "safe," for during the day she could push aside her depression as she interacted with her pupils. She had tried therapy four or five times, but each time she had stopped after several months. This time she was determined to "see it through"; she hoped hypnosis would make the difference.

It was warm in my office the day of Helene's first visit, and as she talked she fanned the open collar of her pale pink dress. Beads of sweat glistened like pearls around her plump neck. She told me that she had grown up as the only child of an alcoholic father and a "depressed" mother, trapped in a "stormy" marriage. She attributed their problems to her father, a "difficult" man, moody and unpredictable, given to violent, angry outbursts. Both she and her mother were afraid of him.

"How did you know your mother was afraid of him?" I wondered.

"She told me," said Helene. "At night, in bed, she told me he was ruining her life. She called me her dream-baby and told me that I was her only ray of sun."

The bed, it turned out, was a bed that Helene and her mother shared. Helene's father slept alone in an adjoining room.

In contrast to her father, Helene recalled her mother as a "saint" who quietly endured her difficult life. "She was beautiful," she extolled. "If it hadn't been for us, she really could have been something."

"If it hadn't been for 'us'?" I asked, surprised she was including herself.

She nodded. "My father and me. We just weren't the life she was expecting to live. She deserved better." And she looked longingly into my eyes as if hoping to retrieve there a better life for her mother.

Despite the sad state of affairs inside Helene's home, her family's image was one of rectitude. Her father owned the only car dealership in their small town, which gave the family prestige and respectability. He was active in fraternal organizations, her mother in church groups. Beyond these activities, however, they apparently had few social connections.

The concern with image apparently extended to appearance. Helene reported that her mother spent "hours" in front of the mirror, fine-tuning her clothes and makeup (although she also hibernated for days at a time, never getting out of her bathrobe). Helene loved the clothes and makeup sessions, remembering them as some of the closest times they shared. She liked less the fact that her mother was equally vigilant about Helene's appearance. A hair out of place, unwashed hands, or a skirt with wrinkles could unleash maternal vitriol.

"Did that happen often?" I wondered.

"All the time," she sighed. "I was never very neat."

Given the care that was evident in Helene's hair and outfit I was skeptical of that statement. "What kinds of things would she find fault with?"

"Oh, she'd find a spot on my shirt and she'd accuse me of putting on a dirty shirt on purpose."

"And why would she think you had done that on purpose?"

"To embarrass her in front of her friends. Or to make her late." Helene looked at me as if the answers were self-explanatory. "She had a lot of reasons for why I would do that."

The image of Helene's mother that was forming in my mind was not quite as saintly as the one her daughter held. This mother was, on the contrary, selfish and immature, one who eclipsed her daughter's needs with her own. She kept her daughter in her own bed, denying Helene the autonomy that comes from learning to sleep alone. She saddled her daughter with unrealistic responsibility, telling her she was her mother's only ray of sun. She fussed for hours over her own appearance, as if her relationship with her own face in the mirror was paramount. And she interpreted her daughter's actions as having been directed toward herself, as if indeed she were the sun and Helene a revolving planet.

Helene seemed to read my thoughts, for she suddenly added, "That makes her sound mean, and she wasn't. She just had a hard life. Sometimes it got too much for her and she took it out on me."

I'm always wary when I hear the words "she took it out on me." Since children tend to gild their childhoods out of self-protection, those words often mask a history of emotional, verbal, or physical abuse.

"Can you say a little more about that?" I probed.

"Oh, she would have a hard day, and then I'd come home and she'd yell at me."

"What kind of things would she say?"

"She'd say I was trouble, or I was in the way, or I didn't understand how hard it was for her. Sometimes she'd say if it weren't for me she could leave and get a good life." Helene looked at me as if her mother's words were perfectly justifiable. As if to prove them so she added, "I was bad. I tried her patience."

"But the rest of the time she was very loving," she continued quickly. As before, she seemed to have heard the condemnation in her words and wanted to correct it. "She told me all the time that she loved me and needed me, that I was all she had. We were very close." She paused and for several moments dropped her gaze. I had the sense that she was looking inward. "My poor mother," she murmured finally. "Such a lost soul. She had such a sad life . . . and so short."

"So short?"

"Yes," Helene looked surprised. "Didn't I say that? She died when I was nine."

"How did she die?"

"She killed herself."

I try to keep my personal reactions from contaminating my sessions with clients, but my eyes must have reflected my surprise, for Helene added quickly, "Well, my dad was so hard to live with, and I was such a burden. . . ." As if her logic were self-evident, she pinned my gaze with hers.

I tried, but failed, to read behind her eyes.

"What can you tell me about her death?"

Helene looked down for a second. "I found her."

"Oh." The sound escaped involuntarily as the horror touched me. A nine year old finding her mother dead . . . Overdosed? Asphyxiated? Hanging? I could only imagine what she'd seen, could barely imagine what she'd felt.

"What was that like for you?"

Helene smiled slightly, her eyes clear. "It was her way out. Her misery was over."

"Yes. And what did it feel like for *you*?"

"For me?" She gave me a vacant look, as if she had never considered the question before. "Well, it was hard of course . . . but maybe she was better off."

Again, a response about her mother. Where were her *own* feelings about her mother's death? And her adamant view that the suicide was a solution: did that mean she might envision such a solution for herself? People who are depressed, and whose parents have modeled suicide, often do.

"Do you ever think of killing yourself?"

"I've thought of it off and on." She looked away, then looked intently back at me. "Sometimes . . . when I hear the voices."

"The voices?"

"Yes."

"Can you tell me about them?"

"There are two of them. One's a child." Helene narrowed her eyes. "She's scared. I hear her crying." She looked me in the eye to see what I made of that. When I nodded she continued. "The other one is a grown-up. A woman."

"You say you hear the child crying," I said. "What about the woman? Do you ever hear her? Does either of them ever say things to you?"

"Yes."

"What do they say to you?"

"The woman says bad things." The line had a curious childlike intonation.

"What kinds of bad things?"

"That I'm dirty, or messy, or good for nothing . . ." She stopped as if the list of qualities were too long and obvious to relate.

"And does she say anything else?"

"Sometimes she tells me I deserve to die."

"What do you think about that?"

"Oh, sometimes I think she must be right. I mean, I think how nice it would be to not have to go on, to just stop trying, you know?" She peered searchingly into my eyes, seeking a sign of understanding, then quickly: "But I wouldn't really do it. Who would take care of Dulcy?"

Dulcy was Helene's dog, and, from what I'd gathered earlier, her only love and close companion.

"I'd like you to promise me something, Helene. I'd like you to be sure and tell me if those thoughts change in any way while we're working together. Would you be willing to do that?" When a client reveals thoughts of suicide, I may need to negotiate a suicide contract. Its purpose is to obtain the client's guarantee that she will take certain agreed-upon steps—for instance, calling a friend, listening to a relaxation tape we've made, or calling me—before acting on her thoughts. I also specify my availability to her after office hours, and request her agreement to be honest and open with me about her suicidality.

As I outlined these elements, Helene nodded. Involuntarily, it seemed, a tiny smile spread across her lips.

Our next several sessions were spent getting to know each other. Like many clients Helene needed to test me—to make sure she could trust me, make sure my responses would be consistent, make sure I would be supportive and nonpunishing—before she revealed her innermost thoughts and feelings. To this end, her answers were often halting; she offered information cautiously and maintained a rather stiff and guarded manner. But as we talked about her past and about her nighttime terrors she gradually warmed. A turning point came during our sixth session, when she told me about her previous therapists. Apparently she'd had "episodes" in their offices in which she'd experienced disorienting feelings and sensations, times in which unwelcome, dreamlike images had exploded in her mind as powerfully as if they were real. These episodes were frightening to Helene, but rather than support her through them, her therapists had "criticized" her, demanding she stop and "come back to reality" each time. "They made me feel like I was bad," she said. "They wanted me to control them—and I couldn't." So feeling maligned and misunderstood, she'd abandoned her efforts to get help.

I suspected that what Helene had experienced was a series of *flashbacks*—intrusions of images, feelings, and sensations from the past as material buried in her unconscious came to the fore. This happens both in and out of therapy, particularly to clients who have experienced and buried trauma. Therapists who aren't familiar with traumatic aftereffects may see these episodes as pathological problems that the client must be taught to suppress, rather than as expressions of unprocessed experience that must be worked through. They generally try to bring the client back to reality, rather than engage with her in the realm of the unconscious where the charged material is stored. Hypnotherapists, on the other hand, comfortable with unconscious process, tend to see these episodes as valuable additions to the therapy. I assured Helene that if such episodes occurred in our time together I would regard them as important messages from the unconscious and that I would give them a great deal of attention and respect. She seemed visibly relieved at my words.

The following week, as if my assurance had triggered a sudden commitment to our work, Helene arrived with both a new demeanor and a revelation. Dropping her prim schoolteacher manner as quickly as she'd dropped her briefcase to the floor, she sank heavily into the chair and blurted that she'd had a nightmare she wanted to discuss—a terrifying return to her childhood home in which she was met by a "psychopath" who threatened to kill her if she didn't do therapy with him.

"What do you make of that?" I solicited.

"I think the psychopath was my father."

"Your father? Why do you think that?"

She massaged her hands. "I think he's threatened by my doing therapy with you."

I was intrigued by her response. She had phrased the sentence as if her father himself were threatened, as if he were speaking through the medium of Helene's dream, rather than the dream being an expression of Helene's own feelings. This suggested to me that Helene was fused with him. In some sense he was still living inside her and she hadn't developed a full sense of self.

"What does he have to be threatened about?"

She continued to massage her fingers. "He's afraid I'll expose him," she said quietly.

"Expose him?" This struck me as an interesting choice of words.

"Oh, you know," she demurred. "Tell you the truth about how difficult he was to live with."

I cocked my head as if to ask her what she meant.

"He was such a pillar of the community and all. They didn't know . . . they didn't know how difficult he was at home."

"You told me you were afraid of him."

She nodded slowly as if remembering our conversation.

"Can you say more about that?"

Unlike most clients, whose gazes wander, Helene had the uncanny habit of looking directly into my eyes, imprisoning my gaze for long, unblinking stretches. Now she peered steadily into them as if looking for an answer to the question. Finally she shook her head. "I have very few memories of my father from childhood. Just little bits and pieces. Nothing very substantial."

"What *do* you remember?"

"I have a few memories of going places with him—to the car lot, to luncheons."

"Nothing of home?"

"No."

"Nothing?"

She sighed and closed her eyes. Her mouth tightened, then pursed, then tightened again, as if she were working to retrieve the past. Gradually it came to rest. A moment later her breathing deepened noticeably. "I see our house," she said slowly. "Our kitchen." Her voice was higher than usual, a monotone. "I'm in the kitchen, doing homework." Helene was having a flashback; she had gone into a spontaneous trance.

Now, spontaneous trance is not uncommon in therapy, even nonhypnotic therapy. Whenever a person "goes inside" to retrieve a memory or to engage a feeling, she leaves the outside world behind. She splits off her awareness of the external environment, just as a subject does when following a hypnotherapist's suggestion. But generally these spontaneous trances are fleeting and light: the client is just a tiptoe away from the outside world. Helene, however, seemed to have entered a deep trance. Her posture, her breathing, her voice quality were all typical of deep trance behavior, and she seemed to be hallucinating the scene in front of her as if it were really there. Spontaneous deep trance is unusual. It occurs primarily in clients with an extremely high capacity for dissociation and mental absorption, those who can easily disappear into an inner world. Children are good dissociators, for they readily engage in fantasy play; only children, who in childhood developed imaginary friends and rich inner worlds, often remain strong dissociators in adulthood. But the bulk of my clients who are capable of spontaneous deep trance are survivors of chronic childhood abuse, for they used trance as a mechanism for removing themselves from their trauma.

"My father is in the house," Helene went on. Her new voice, in its childlike higher cadence, had taken on an edge.

"What is he doing?" Despite the fact that a part of Helene was regressed in time watching herself as a little girl, another part was with me and could hear my voice. Most likely she would incorporate my voice into the logic of her trance, hearing me as a friendly stranger in the house with her, rather than as the therapist she'd hired as an adult.

"He's roaring again. He's waving his arms and yelling. . . . I hope he doesn't see me."

"Why?"

She shook her head strongly. "It's better if he doesn't."

"What will happen if he does?"

She shook her head again, then suddenly her eyes flew open. She quickly scanned the room.

"Helene?" I asked gently.

She looked at me vacantly for a second as if unsure of where she was, then her eyes grew focused.

"Can you tell me what's happening?"

She exhaled deeply and let her head fall back against the chair. "I was thinking about my father."

"What were you thinking?"

"About . . . just about how he was." She looked at me and

sighed, then raised her head and straightened herself in her chair. When she spoke, her voice had regained its polish. "He was a difficult man, my father. Unhappy. He could be heavy-handed at times."

"In what way?"

"He hit me from time to time. Not a lot. Nothing I probably didn't deserve." She spoke unapologetically. "When my mother died he was stuck with me. It wasn't easy being father and mother, especially when I became a teenager."

"And how was it being his teenage daughter?"

Helene looked down. It was the first time I felt her avoid my eyes. "It was okay."

"Just okay?"

She looked back at me and smiled. "Well, you know, we didn't always see eye to eye. And there are some things you just don't want to share with your father."

"Like what?"

She seemed embarrassed. "Oh, you know, your privacy. Parts of your *self*." She averted her eyes again, as if also afraid of exposing those parts to me.

I knew what she meant—certainly I had denied large parts of myself to *my* father. But I realized I had expected a different answer. I had expected her to say "getting my period," or "dating," or adjusting to the changes in her body—the kinds of things girls share more easily with a mother. But Helene's answer suggested something more profound, that her father had in some way asked her to share her *self*. Was this a figurative sharing, as in too many questions asked, too much prying about her life and thoughts and feelings? Or was she suggesting something else, a physical sharing, as in physical or sexual abuse? I had to be careful not to jump to conclusions, and not to lead Helene's thinking in any way. The only way to know would be to listen to Helene's responses as they came.

When Helene arrived for her next session, her walk was brisker than usual, her professional persona even more firmly in place. Laying her briefcase on the floor she sat stiffly in the chair and looked me in the eye.

"I've had two memories," she said crisply. "I don't know why, but these two memories came to me after our last session. I don't make much of them but I thought I should tell you."

"Please."

"The first one is from when I was eight. A neighbor boy invited me to ride on his bike. It was a boy's bike and I was afraid I would hurt myself on the bar. And when I got home I saw . . ." She paused, and for the first time her voice faltered a bit. Whether in embarrassment at discussing this with me or at the memory itself I couldn't tell. "When I got home I saw that I had a spot of red on my panties. . . . I think it was blood." She blushed and looked away, then continued quickly, as if in rushing on she could spare herself further embarrassment. "The second memory was from when I was seven. I found another . . . blood stain. And my mother yelled at me for not wiping myself all the way." She looked at me very briefly, then said, "that's all."

"What do you make of them?" I was doubtful that even landing hard on a boy's bicycle bar could damage the hymen and cause it to bleed, and I couldn't imagine how not wiping could have caused blood stains on her underpants. But Helene seemed wholly satisfied with her logic.

"It's just things that happened," she commented. "I don't know why I remembered them now. My mother warned me about riding that bike and she was right."

"And the other memory?"

She rubbed her fingers. "I guess that happened a few times. I guess I wasn't very clean."

"What does that mean to you, not to be clean?"

"I don't know . . ." She wrung the fingers of one hand with the other. "I guess I wasn't very careful."

"What does that mean, not careful?"

Helene closed her eyes as if shutting out my question and breathed in deeply. The sigh seemed to relax her for as I watched, the stiffness drained slowly from her body. Her face softened until her chin rested inside the open collar of her dress. Her hands lay limply in her lap. "I don't know," she voiced after a few minutes. "I don't know why I thought of this right now, but I thought of my father. I thought of him on his deathbed. Did I tell you how sick he was? He died of cancer just a few years ago, and I took care of him until the end. It was very, very hard." Her voice broke and she began to cry quietly. After a few minutes she blew her nose and looked at me. "Isn't that funny?" she said quietly. "Why would I think about that now?"

Several weeks later Helene arrived in that same heightened professional state. I had come to recognize that state as a signal, an indication that she was bringing charged material to share. It was as if she were buttressing herself against the discomfort that she knew would come from the ensuing discussion. This time she said she had been watching a television movie, a "silly drama" in which a young girl gets locked in a carnival funhouse. For some reason that scene had reduced her to tears.

"What did you feel as you watched it?"

"It was her screaming. She was screaming to get out, but no matter how loud she screamed no one came to get her."

"What does that bring to mind?"

"I don't know. I felt so frightened and claustrophobic."

"Have you ever felt that way before?"

She shook her head in confusion. "I don't know . . . I don't think so . . ." She closed her eyes as if to probe her own memory, and as she relaxed the familiar transformation occured. Her face sagged and her soft double chin disappeared inside her collar. Her breathing grew deeper; her eyes darted behind her lids. Once again my deliberate request that she think back to a time when she might have felt that way had triggered a spontaneous trance.

"I see my bedroom," she began slowly after several seconds. Her voice was high again, girlish.

"What do you see in the bedroom?"

"I see a girl."

"What is she doing?"

"She's on the bed."

"Would it be okay for you to talk to her?"

Helene leaned forward slightly as if approaching the girl. Behind her closed lids her eyes seemed focused, staring. Then slowly her face began to tense. "Something's happening," she said. "She getting scared. She's scared of something. . . . There's something coming in the door. What is it?" The question was sharp with fear. "I don't like it. Don't let it come. Please don't let it come! I'm scared! Please stop it. Please, somebody stop it!" Her voice rose in pitch; her breathing grew harder, faster. "Help her, somebody! Help her! Help her, please, somebody . . ." Suddenly she began to sob. Her hands wrapped around her face like a protective mask, and her fingers glistened with her tears.

I noted her change from third person to first, referring to the girl as "she," then as "I," then back again to "she." Apparently Helene had regressed in time, seen herself on her bed, as if she were a third person in the room. But as her emotions had mounted, as the experience had become more real, she had "fallen into" the image, reliving it completely. Moments later, in an effort to distance herself from the terror, she'd pulled back again, seeing herself from the outside.

"Yes," I soothed. "She is very scared. And what is happening now?"

But Helene couldn't answer. She continued to sob, hunched forward, her face and hands cradled in her lap. Slowly she rose to a sitting position and looked at me. Her eyes were red, her cheeks lined with tears.

"Helene?" She was still partly in trance.

She shook her head, just barely, as if the act required too much energy. But started, the motion seemed to take on a life of its own. It grew harder, faster until it had metamorphosed from a gesture of incomprehension into a movement of denial. The movement seemed to bring her fully out of the trance.

"That wasn't me," she avowed. "I don't know where that came from, but it wasn't me."

"What does it mean to you?"

The shaking continued. "I don't know. It came from that movie. That little girl looked just like the girl in the movie."

"Can you tell me about her?"

"She was just a girl in a movie," she repeated. Her voice permitted no dissent.

"I wonder if there's any relationship between that little girl and the voice in your head, the one you've mentioned to me before?"

Quickly Helene shook her head. "No, what do you mean? It's just a movie."

"Well, I wonder if you'd be willing to listen inside your head for a moment and see if you can hear the little girl you sometimes hear?"

Helene tensed her lips. "I don't see why . . ." But she closed her eyes. A moment later they flew open. "I hear her. She's still screaming."

"Still?"

She shook her head, flustered. "I don't mean still. I don't know why I said that. She's screaming. I just heard her screaming."

"It's not the same screaming?"

"No. Maybe it is. So what does that mean?"

"I don't know. Maybe that's something worth thinking about."

Helene stared into my eyes as if daring me to draw a tighter connection. But her teeth gnawed her lip as if she were chewing on my words.

*   *   *

The following week Helene arrived early for her appointment. When I opened the door to the waiting room she was sitting tightly on the edge of a chair, a sheet of paper clasped in her hand. Her professional demeanor seemed frayed.

I escorted her into my office where, without speaking, she handed me the paper. On it was a pencil drawing of a young girl, naked, spread-eagled on a sofa. In the foreground floated two monstrously large hands.

"I drew that," she noted coolly. "I have no idea why."

"What do you feel when you see it?"

She drummed her pudgy fingers on the arm of the chair. "It's horrifying. I find it repugnant."

"Does it have any meaning for you?"

"Of course not. It's about that little girl. . . ." Helene caught herself as if she had said something unintended.

I waited for her to continue.

"That little girl from the movie. I think it's the same one."

I waited silently.

"It's not me." She looked penetratingly at me to make sure I believed her. "I don't know why I would do a drawing about that little girl, but I know it has nothing to do with me."

"Do you think any part of you knows more about this?"

Helene observed me with irritation, but closed her eyes. "I can't imagine I'm going to find anything." But she leaned back and breathed in deeply. For several seconds she breathed and exhaled, her nostrils flaring slightly, a small gold cross flickering in the sun as it rose and fell with her chest. Then gradually her breathing gathered speed. Her breaths grew shorter and more shallow, became a staccato panting laced with fear. Again, my request that she probe inside had triggered a deep trance, without need of a formal induction.

"What is it? Can you tell me what's happening?"

"He's coming! He's coming! Make him go away, oh please, make him go away!"

"Who's coming?"

"My daddy! My daddy is coming, oh don't let him come, please don't let him come, I don't want him to!" Her arms pushed at the air in front of her.

"What's happening now?"

"I don't know, it's dark, it's so dark I can't see, oh no, Daddy, no!" She flailed helplessly against the apparition before her.

"Yes, you're frightened, but even as you're there you sense my presence with you. And you know that you are also here with me." Phrasing the sentence both ways allowed Helene to be in both places at the same time—inside the image, yet also safe in my office.

Helene's arms wrapped her body like a blanket and gradually her breathing slowed. Silent tears seeped from under her closed eyelids and she brushed them away with her hand. But as if touching the tears renewed the trauma, she suddenly buried her head in her lap and sobbed.

"What's happening?" I asked.

Still curled into a ball, she shook her head.

"Do you still have images?"

She nodded.

"Would you like help in getting some distance from them?"

Another nod.

"Okay." My voice took on the fluid tones of suggestion. "Perhaps you can imagine taking the child out of the house with us right now. . . . Do you know a safe place where we can take her?"

Diffidently her head moved and a frightened voice emerged. "Under the stairs."

"Well, why don't you take her there right now. . . ." I waited a few moments. "Does she feel safer now?"

"Yes."

"Good. Do you think it would be okay for us to come back and talk with her another time?"

"She's afraid he'll hear us."

"Would he hear us under the stairs?"

"No."

"Then perhaps we could speak with her there? Would that be all right?"

"Yes."

"Well, good. . . . And now you can just relax . . . you've worked very hard . . . and when you're ready you can open your eyes."

Several moments later Helene sat up in her chair. Her face was drawn, her eyes half closed as if their sheer weight were oppressive. Slowly she shook her head. "It's not true, it's not true, it's not true."

"What isn't true?" I broached gently.

She touched her forehead as if to indicate the pictures in her mind.

"You know, the way you insist those images aren't true makes me think you're at war with yourself over their meaning."

She stopped chanting. Slowly the firmness returned to her face. "It can't be true. I know it can't be true because he wouldn't make me kiss him there."

"Helene," I said delicately, "our hour is up. But what I'd like you to think about between now and next time is why you would make up something that you don't want to believe is true."

Helene didn't answer, nor did she look me in the eye.

Despite Helene's earlier insistence that the girl in her flashbacks was not herself, we both knew that she was. She was a *part* of Helene—a part of her personality that had split off in childhood. And her resemblance to child parts I had seen in so many other clients made the circumstances of her creation all too clear. Child parts who live in constant terror as this one did are the containers people form to hide and house their experience of chronic abuse.

Because the experience of chronic abuse is so traumatic—so terrifying, so painful, so damaging to the sense of safety a child needs from her parents—she fragments her sense of the experience and pushes the fragments into her unconscious mind. However, the unconscious is not airtight, and when a present-day event triggers an association to the trauma, the fragments leak out: the person experiences anxiety, nightmares, and unwanted images and sensations. In the extreme, she "becomes" again that little girl to whom the trauma is still occurring. A dream, a TV movie, even the smell of her father's cologne in a crowded elevator could trigger the emergence of Helene's "little girl" and an instantaneous descent into terror.

Had Helene been able to talk about the abuse when it was going on (had she been given room to express her anger, sorrow, and sense of loss), had she had a supportive family that gave her room to do the normal tasks of development (experimenting with independence, learning to love and trust, forming a separate self), she might have been wounded by the knowledge of what her father was doing, but she would not necessarily have buried the experience in the form of an inner part. But with a father who was chronically abusive, and with a mother who eclipsed Helene's needs with her own, Helene was denied the chance to talk about and process the trauma. As a result, that trau-matized part of Helene remained a terrorized little girl. And now, in the safety of therapy, that little girl was coming out to tell her story.

I knew that as we continued to listen to her terror, Helene would begin to accept that child as part of herself. And by doing so, she would *process* her history of abuse: she would allow the knowledge of what had happened to seep into her conscious mind and would ac-cept the associated feelings. Gradually her *flashbacks* would give way to *memories,* episodes she could recall in words, without reliving their emotions, body sensations, and behaviors.

"Did you have any thoughts after our last session?" I asked at our next appointment.

Helene eyed me cautiously. "I've been hearing her."

"What have you been hearing?"

"She's crying—she's always crying. But now she has words, too."

"What is she saying?"

Her voice shriveled to a whining whisper. " 'It's all my fault . . . it's all my fault . . . it's all my fault . . .' " She shook her head angrily. "She says it over and over again."

"Why do you think she would say that?"

"I don't know!" Her eyebrows knit together in irritation. "I wish she'd stop."

"What do you think she thinks is her fault?"

"Everything!" The answer flared with the force of a bullet. "Ev-erything is her fault . . . all this . . ." She waved her arm. "This mess."

"What mess is that?"

"This life of mine. The fact that I'm here. That I can't . . ."

"Can't what?"

"Can't do anything right . . . can't . . ." Helene's hands dropped dejectedly into her lap and the corners of her mouth turned down in sorrow. "I don't deserve to live."

"What makes you feel that way?"

"She tells me."

"She?"

"The other one."

"Do you mean the older woman's voice you hear?"

She nodded.

"What does she say?"

Helene gave an involuntarily shudder. "That I deserve to die. That I'm no good. That I shouldn't be alive."

Strong sentiments coming from inside. "I wonder if you'd be willing to go inside your head for a moment and see if you can hear that voice right now?"

Her mouth settled into a hard line. "I can't do that."

"Why not?"

She shook her head. "She scares me."

"I'll be here with you."

"I don't like to hear her. I hear her too much already. I don't want to encourage her."

"I know that voice scares you. But I think it's important to know more about it. To know where it's coming from, so you can come to terms with it."

Helene's eyes roved the floor. "I hate her."

"I know you do. But perhaps you could do that for just a moment. And then tell me what she says."

She wrung her hands. "For just a minute." She closed her eyes. Her eyelids fluttered and her hands grasped each other tightly in her lap. Several seconds later she opened her eyes. "I couldn't do it."

"What happened?"

"I just kept hearing . . ." She shook her head, as if to dismiss the sound.

"What did you hear?"

Her voice narrowed to a hiss. "Don't listen to him. He doesn't understand. *I* know what you need."

"It sounds like you did hear it."

"I hate it!"

"I know you do. And I think it took courage to do what you just did—to willingly go in and listen."

Helene slumped. Her posture and features looked suddenly older and tired.

Based on what Helene had told me about her mother, I had little doubt that the older voice inside her head was the voice of her "bad internal mother," the part of Helene that had internalized the critical words, attitudes, and values of her actual mother (just as a separate "good internal mother" held her mother's nurturing attitudes and words). Knowing how abusively the voice attacked her, I could guess that this "bad mother" was a repository of rage. Children in abusive families are punished when they show their anger, so Helene would have channeled her rage inside. Her rage at her parents for permitting the abuse to happen, her rage at her parents for not being her protectors, her rage at life for the injustice it had served: all would be housed in this bad internal mother.

Under the anger would be a gaping wound containing Helene's grief at what had happened and her sorrow at the loss of the parents and childhood she deserved. But like a bandage that has crusted to the oozing skin below, her anger would be resilient and protective and painfully difficult to remove.

Apparently, as our therapy had progressed, this bad mother's voice had grown stronger. Instead of intruding intermittently into Helene's thoughts as it had at the beginning, it was now a constant companion, dark and damning, inside her head. And its messages, addressed to both Helene and the little girl, were vile and never-changing. *"You don't deserve to live. . . . You're a wicked little slut. . . ."*

I understood now the child's mournful lament. As so often happens in families with abuse, Helene had been told the assaults were her fault—as were all the other family misfortunes. This continual battery of slurs had shaped the child-Helene's self-image, and now, the child part of Helene continued the refrain inside.

This continual song of self-reproach would play a significant role in Helene's troubles. It would make it hard for her to process her father's sexual abuse, because as long as Helene held herself responsible she couldn't blame her father or fully feel her anger. And it could also be responsible for Helene's suicidal thoughts. Not that the child or the bad mother were telling her to kill herself (they told her she "deserved to die," but not to take her life), but the constant recriminations would contribute to her depression, and, given the suicidal modeling, that unrelenting depression could easily spur an urge toward death.

To help Helene heal, therefore, we'd need to tackle the source of the self-blaming, the now irrepressible bad mother. If I could give the mother another outlet for her anger—if I could help her talk it through with me, rather than savage it on Helene and the child—perhaps I could help her move beyond the anger to the pain below. That pain was Helene's pain, pain the mother part had been formed to deny. And once she felt that pain, her need to role-play the bad mother would cease to exist. She could see herself as she really was—a sad and vulnerable part of Helene.

So I began a campaign to talk to the bad mother, hoping to

draw her into dialogue, hoping to win her trust. At every session I would ask Helene to go inside and listen; she would reluctantly agree, then report the standard litany of blame: *"You're not worth the air you breathe . . . no better than an ass . . . don't listen to him, he doesn't understand."*

After several weeks of these epithets I decided to approach her with a suggestion. "I wonder," I submitted to Helene, "if you could listen inside, after I say these words, and tell me how the voice responds?"

Helene agreed and closed her eyes.

"I can see," I started slowly, lowering my voice to show I was addressing the mother, "that you're very angry. You feel you've been badly mistreated." I hoped that by empathizing with her I could encourage her trust.

Helene's eyes remained closed for twenty seconds, then she opened them halfway. "She said, 'I don't *feel* it; I *know* it.'"

I nodded to show I'd heard. "Could you tell me what she says now?" Again I lowered my voice. "I'm sure you feel like no one understands."

Helene closed her eyes again. A moment later she opened them and sighed. "She said, 'They'll never understand, and neither will you.'"

"I might understand more than you think. For instance, I understand that you've been in a lot of pain, and I think you've been trying to express that pain for a long, long time. That's why you're so rough with them. I don't think it's that you mean to hurt them. I think it's because *you* hurt."

Helene closed her eyes, listened inside. Her report came quickly. "'Hey, you can quit the psychology, OK? *She* came for that, not me.'"

I thought about pointing out that she had come, too. Had she not wanted to communicate with me, she could have remained silent. But doubting she'd be persuaded by that remark, I pursued a different tack. "You know, you've been beating up on them for a long time now, trying to get them to listen. But I can't imagine that's brought you a lot of satisfaction."

"'Oh yeah? They're getting the message good enough.'"

"But that's not the same thing as listening. As giving you what you need—someone to talk to, someone to tell your story to." Tough as the mother part was, she was just a wounded part of Helene, and like all wounded souls she hoped to find some solace by telling someone nonjudgmental—someone who wouldn't exploit or abandon her—how badly she'd been treated. I wanted her to see that I could be that person.

Helene sat silently, eyes closed. After a minute she opened them and shook her head. Apparently the mother part hadn't responded.

I tried again. "You know, I'd like to hear what you have to say. I know how pressing it must feel inside, and I'd like to listen—if you'd be willing to talk to me."

Helene closed her eyes. I noticed for the first time how furrowed her face had become. Deep channels lined the space between her nose and mouth, far more prominently than they had just months before. A full minute passed. Was the bad mother considering my offer? Finally Helene opened her eyes. "She didn't say anything," she reported tiredly. "She just laughed."

"Well, at least she didn't say no."

"No," Helene said quietly, "she didn't say no." She didn't look reassured.

Over the next several weeks, Helene shuttled similar dialogues between the mother part and me. The part began each dialogue ragging on Helene and assuring me I'd never understand; she ended each in silence, as if my offer were being considered. But as the sessions went on she seemed increasingly interested in what I had to say. I sensed that she was beginning to get some pleasure from our relationship. After several weeks, I felt that I had a little leverage.

"I sense that you've gotten some satisfaction out of talking to me," I put forth one day. "I'd like to continue these dialogues. I wonder if in exchange you'd be willing to lay off Helene and the little girl?"

Helene closed her eyes and took my words inside. For forty-five seconds she sat silent, hands kneading each other in her lap. Finally she opened her eyes. "She said," Helene whispered, "that she can't make any guarantees."

I weighed the mother part's words. "That sounds like she'd be willing to try."

Helene's brows knitted, as if in response to my comment she was reconsidering what she'd heard. Then her lips curled up in a faint and cautious smile.

*   *   *

The minute Helene appeared in my office the following week, I could see the difference. She looked less tired, as if she'd finally gotten a good night's sleep, and the lines in her face seemed less graven.

"How have things been?"

"Better, I think. I haven't had nightmares. I haven't been feeling as anxious." He words sounded like questions, as if she found them hard to believe.

"Have you heard her?"

She narrowed her eyes, searching inside for the answer. "It's different. I hear her . . . but it's different . . . she isn't as severe. Once or twice she started to come down on me, but then she stopped."

"Well, good." I was truly delighted with the news. "Should I try to talk to her now?"

Cautiously Helene nodded.

"Would you ask her if it would be all right with her?"

Helene closed her eyes. Ten seconds later she reopened them and nodded.

"Okay, then, why don't you take my words inside?" I slowed my voice to show I was speaking to the mother part. "I wonder if you can tell me how it's been for you this past week?"

Helene listened for several seconds, her face drawn tight. Then she opened her eyes. "She said, 'Shitty. How would you like having your mouth bandaged for a week?' "

I nodded, and once again motioned her to carry my message inside. "I appreciate your ragging on them less. I know how hard that must have been."

Helene closed her eyes, reopened them. "She said, 'You don't know the half of it.' "

"What don't I know?"

Helene listened inside. " 'What it's like to be bound and gagged in front of your own child.' "

"Can you tell me . . ."

But before I could finish, Helene closed her eyes, then violently flung them open. " 'To be bound and gagged and have to watch while your kid screws up!' " She voiced the words so forcefully that I sat back slightly in my chair.

Her emotion was so strong, and the language so graphic, that it made me wonder: Is that how she'd felt—bound and gagged, unable to intervene—when her daughter had "screwed up" with her father? "In what way was she screwing up?"

Almost before she closed her eyes, Helene spat out the answer. " 'That's what she does—screw up. The screwed up little slut.' "

"What makes you say that?"

Helene's eyelids dropped heavily and her hands gripped each other in her lap. When she raised her eyes, her voice was a derisive hiss. " '*You* know what she did.' "

"I know what happened *to* her."

" 'She made it happen.' " The answer was quick, out even before the eyes had shut.

"How did she make it happen?"

" 'How does anyone make it happen?' "

"But why would she make it happen? Why would a child want such a thing?"

" 'If she didn't want it she should have stopped it.' "

"Tell me how."

" 'She should have said no. Pushed him off. Same as anybody.' "

"Didn't she try?"

" 'If you call that trying . . . Not very hard.' "

"And what happened when she tried?"

" 'What do you mean?' "

"Didn't he make it worse for her?"

There was a long pause before she answered. When she did her voice was surprisingly resigned. " 'Uh-huh.' "

"So she learned, didn't she, that if she just stopped fighting and went along he wouldn't be so bad to her?"

Helene closed her eyes. Twenty or thirty seconds passed before she opened them again. When she did her voice resumed its defensive tone. " 'So maybe she couldn't push him off, but I know she liked it. The way she danced around in front of him. She encouraged him.' "

She was still determined to fight—but I knew she'd gotten my message.

Our next several sessions were electric, as the mother part excoriated the little girl for seducing her father and railed at the life that had been so unfair. I continued to empathize with her rage and pain and then to "reality test" her ideas, pointing out the girl's powerlessness in the face of her father. Gradually the ferocity of her arguments waned. As her sureness ebbed, I introduced a new theme.

"I know," I ventured one day, after she put up a now-weakened argument about the girl's seductive wiles, "that you feel these things very strongly. But it might be important for us to find out where those feelings come from. It might be that those feelings weren't originally yours. It might be that they come from someone else." I wanted to help the mother part differentiate herself from the outside mother, to realize she was merely a likeness of the mother, not the mother herself, and that while the external mother held those feelings, she didn't have to.

" 'That's a joke. What do you mean?' " Her tone was scornful.

"I mean it might be that you've modeled your feelings after someone else, someone outside. . . ."

Helene sat quietly for several seconds. When she answered, her voice was harsh. "She said, 'You're telling me I don't know my own mind?' "

"No. I think you know yourself very well. I'm just wondering if you're carrying some baggage for someone else, stuff you don't really need to be lugging."

Again she was quiet for almost thirty seconds. Then Helene's voice, doleful, almost a whisper, "She said, 'I got a lot to carry, that's for sure.' "

I felt a part of me relax. The mother part hadn't denied that there might be some truth to what I'd said.

Over the next several sessions the tenor of our dialogues softened. As if my words had blown a hole in her cover, the bad mother argued less strenuously that the little girl was to blame and instead began to show some understanding, even sympathy, for the child. She began to acknowledge, even before I pointed it out, that the girl couldn't have enjoyed the acts that were committed, that in fact she must have been a victim. Bit by bit, she began to understand that she was not the outside mother, but rather a part of Helene. Finally, one day she began to sob—loud, wracking sobs of grief—for the pain that had been perpetrated on the child, who she now understood was herself. Over the next several sessions I talked to her about ways she could nurture Helene from within, and by Helene's eleventh month in therapy the bad mother part had become benign.

*   *   *

Interspersed with our sessions dialoguing with the mother part, we had continued to talk about Helene's father. She'd brought in occasional memory shards, had occasional flashbacks. But now, freed from the constant refrain that *she* had invited and enjoyed the abuse, Helene was able to see the situation objectively. For the first time she saw that she'd been a powerless victim of her father's violence. And as that realization dawned, the banished experience slowly began to surface.

Now our sessions began to take on a pattern. Helene would arrive early for her appointment, bearing a memory fragment, a drawing, a journal entry, or a dream that she felt bound to share. Each sharing would begin reluctantly; each would give way to a spontaneous trance in which she experienced flashbacks. Over time the experiences painted a clear and incontrovertable picture of repeated sexual abuse.

And as the conscious and unconscious pictures of her father began to mesh, Helene began to grieve openly—for the father she wished she had, for the childhood she was denied, for the child inside who had endured such pain. And as she processed those feelings, the little girl's voice changed. Freed from the need to store those emotions for Helene, she grew quieter, calmer, more secure. Freed simultaneously from the bad mother's recriminations, her voice grew less insistent and less oppressed.

Not surprisingly, as Helene made progress, the symptoms that had brought her into therapy grew worse. Not continuously—a steady decline would have had me worried—but episodically. She reported increased sleeplessness and nighttime anxiety, as well as periods of oppressive lethargy and despair. I anticipated these downturns as part of the natural course of change: clients often get worse before they get better as they let in the full extent of their suffering, pain, and loss.

I even anticipated an increase in suicidality. Survivors of severe abuse carry a pain so deep that often only death seems able to ameliorate it. They hold a secret so terrible that often only death seems able to bury it. And they carry guilt so damning that often only death seems able to exonerate them. They carry these feelings inside, buried with the unconscious knowledge of their abuse; as awareness of the abuse becomes conscious, these feelings flood to the surface. Suicidality often intensifies.

In Helene, the pull to suicide would be even more potent because of the suicidal modeling of her mother. A parent's suicide will not, by itself, move a person to take her life. But if the person has motivating factors of her own, such as severe depression or parental abuse, the parent's use of suicide to solve an apparently insoluble dilemma may inspire her to do the same.

And sure enough, as we talked through her father's abuse, Helene reported that her suicidal thoughts were increasing. Whereas initially they had intruded once a week, they were now frequenting her almost daily. They were also more demanding. Whereas earlier she'd been able to shake them, they now commanded her attention.

What did surprise me, however, was that as the weeks wore on, the suicidality didn't wane. Ordinarily, as a survivor works through her feelings, suicidality decreases. She accepts the irrationality of her guilt and shame and builds a healthier self-image in which death is not a necessary companion. Helene was clearly working through her feelings. She had cried and mourned, whimpered and screamed, and had acknowledged that while accepting her past was painful, she no longer felt the need to escape it by taking her life. Yet the pull to death grew. By her fourteenth month of therapy it was the primary focus of our talk.

And as the pull intensified so did her symptoms. Her anxiety increased, her sleeplessness grew, her energy level declined. I didn't fear for Helene's safety—she hadn't formulated a suicide plan and she acknowledged that she wasn't close to action—but I was concerned and perplexed. Why, after coming to terms with her father's abuse and the bad mother's accusations, would her suicidal fantasies be escalating?

"It's in the fiber of my body," she said to me bitterly one day as we discussed her gnawing thoughts of death. "It's like a script I've been chosen to play."

As the weeks wore on Helene continued to decline. She now reported that she had barely enough energy to cook dinner and sometimes skipped it entirely; some weekends she barely got out of bed. And her attention to her appearance, which had always been fastidious, was starting to slacken. Her shoes and briefcase were now scuffed; her hair was visibly graying at the roots; the scarf or pin that had lent style or whimsy to her simple dresses was now missing.

"What's happening, Helene?" I asked one day, after she'd dropped heavily into her chair and turned a doleful face toward me. "You're looking more troubled than I've ever seen you."

She exhaled deeply and massaged her neck with her hand. "I don't know. I feel tired. Lost."

"Can you say more about that?"

She closed her eyes and leaned her head against the chair. Her hand continued to rub her neck as if it could wrest the words from her throat. "I'm not sure why I'm here. If I need to be here. Maybe I should go."

"Here? Where is 'here'?"

"Here . . ." Suddenly she opened her eyes, looked at me and smiled. "I don't mean here in your office, David. I know why I'm *here*. If it hadn't been for you I'd have let go long ago." She paused, then her voice resumed its weary tone. "I mean *here*. In this life. *Here*."

"Can you say more about that?"

She fingered her dress but didn't answer.

"Is it the voices?"

"No." She looked at me directly, her voice and face puzzled. "Not voices. Not like before . . . It's different . . . stronger. It's like a pull. I feel it everywhere . . . in my skin . . . in my pores. . . . It's all through me, David, like a cancer."

"Helene, I wonder if it's worth asking inside. Perhaps the mother part knows something about this feeling."

Helene closed her eyes and lifted her face toward the light, as if inviting the mother part's voice to speak. Several moments later she opened her eyes and looked at me. "She said, 'It's a dark cloud. It settles over us.' "

I lowered my voice to speak directly to the mother. "Tell me about this cloud. What happens when it comes over you?"

Helene closed her eyes, reported the mother part's words. " 'We want to sleep. To not go on.' "

"You want to die?"

" 'It's black. We want to not go on.' "

"Do you know where it comes from?"

" 'No.' "

So it wasn't the mother part. It was something larger, something deeper, something that was affecting her, too. But what? I didn't feel alarmed, exactly: I knew eventually we'd find the force that was pulling Helene toward death. The arduous journey we'd already made had given us the trust and rapport we needed to best this obstacle.

But I was frustrated. What was left? What was I not seeing? Her case reminded me of one of those three-dimensional wooden puzzles in which the pieces refuse to go together until you find the one piece to which all the others hinge. I turned Helene's story over in my head, the way I'd turned those puzzle pieces in my hand as a boy, looking for the telltale clue. Surely I had all the pieces before me. But which was the key to the design?

Over the next few sessions, my frustration only grew. Helene became increasingly hopeless and despondent, and she wore her agony like a shroud. Her face aged by a decade, her walk slowed to a shuffle, her appearance reflected only minimal care. Until now I'd been sure that Helene's thoughts of death were merely *thoughts;* now I worried that she was near the point of action. I ended every session by renewing our suicide contract, asking her to promise to call me first if she felt the urge to act. Every time my phone rang late at night, I prayed it wasn't news of Helene.

One day she appeared in my office more morose than I had ever seen her.

"There's no use," she muttered, sinking glumly into the chair. "I don't see the point of going on."

"Tell me what you feel inside."

She looked distractedly around the room. "What's that?" She pointed to an aboriginal mask that I'd long had hanging on the wall.

"Why does that interest you?"

She looked annoyed, then turned her attention to the window. "I could jump." She seemed to be stating an abstract possibility, rather than an immediate intent.

"You seem particularly unhappy today."

She faced me for the first time. "I can't fight it any longer."

"Are you thinking of ways to take your life?"

"I need to go there."

"Where?"

"There's a realm where I have to go. It's like a cemetery. A cemetery of lost souls."

I was struck by the image. I could see the place in my mind: a cemetery shrouded in fog where ghostly apparitions walked. But there was something else about her words: in what context had I heard them before?

That night, after eliciting Helene's promise that she wouldn't try to kill herself without consulting me, I took her case notes home and reviewed them. Her folder was thick with pages half-typed, half-scribbled, containing write-ups of each of our sessions. After two hours of reading I found what I was looking for: on September 12, 1986, Helene had called her mother a "lost soul."

Of course! Of course her mother was a lost soul: Helene had literally *lost* her! Suddenly the multiple meanings of "lost" swam before me. Helene had *lost* her mother when she was nine. In therapy we'd talked at length about Helene's bad internal mother, but had virtually ignored the real one; in essence, we'd *lost* the real mother in our sessions. *I* felt lost: I'd tried everything I knew to make sense of Helene's suicidality and was now at a *loss* as to where to go. And then there were Helene's feelings of *loss:* Helene's mother had not only died; she'd killed herself and Helene had found her. What feelings of loss—and guilt—would that have caused? I realized this was a universe we needed to explore.

It wasn't unusual for us to have left this issue unexamined for so long. Clients typically work on one parent at a time. While unearthing powerful feelings from childhood they need the sense of having one protective parent to lean on; stripping the veneer from both simultaneously would be far too hard. Since Helene had first brought in the issue of her father, we had focused on that, and once that was done, the work had segued naturally to the bad internal mother. I'd known throughout our time together that we'd need to return to her mother's death; in fact, scribbled in the margins of my case notes were reminders: "go after mother," "mother's death?" "what is unfinished with mother?" But with our plates full with other matters, it had easily gone unaddressed. Now it was time to bring it up.

At our next session, however, Helene once again threw me for a loop. I barely recognized her in the waiting room. For the first time since I had known her, her hair was unstyled and stood out from her head in unruly tufts. Her belt loops were empty. Two coffee-colored stains bloomed across her chest where one of her buttons was missing. It struck me that Helene hadn't changed her clothes in days. At her feet her briefcase lay sideways, spilling its contents on the floor. A pair of stockings and a roll of gauze bandage lay tangled together. A similar bandage swaddled her right arm.

"Helene," I tried to keep my voice level. I couldn't imagine she'd gone to school that way. Or had she gone and been sent home? "Come in."

Like a ninety-year-old woman dazed by catastrophe, she pushed herself from the chair and shuffled toward my office.

"Your things?"

She turned to follow my pointing finger. "Oh." With a great outlet of breath she bent and shoved the items absently into the brief-case.

"Helene," I entreated when she was seated in my office, "what's going on?" I was especially concerned about the bandage but I didn't dare ask: asking might prompt Helene to flee. Instead, I needed to wait, at least for a while, and see what she had to say.

"I am in despair."

"What's happening?"

She merely shook her head.

"It looks like things are a little rough for you."

"Yah." It was more a release of breath than a word.

"Can you tell me what's been going on?"

"It's been a bad day. A bad day. Today is Monday, right? I had a bad day."

"What made it bad?"

"I lost the scripts for the spring play, so I couldn't go to school. What will the children say?"

"What have you been doing all day?"

She looked through me as if I weren't there. "Driving around."

"Helene, it looks to me like something pretty important is going on."

She gave no sign of having heard me.

"Did you injure yourself?"

She glanced at her arm then waved my question away. "I burned myself," she said. "It's nothing."

"Have you seen a doctor about it?"

"No."

"Does it need medical attention?"

She sighed as if I were pursuing an irrelevant detail.

"Helene, I want your assurance that if this needs medical atten-tion you will get it. May I have that?"

"Yes," she said wearily.

I had to trust her. Touching a client is discouraged in most therapy, and as an abuse survivor Helene's physical boundaries were particularly sensitive: even an affectionate pat on the back could seem threatening. To examine her arm would certainly breach our trust.

"How did you burn yourself?"

"I was cooking dinner."

"Usually you're quite careful. It's not like you to burn yourself by accident."

For a moment she looked me in the eye, then half closed her eyes and looked away.

"Helene, I'm concerned about what's going on. Would you be willing to close your eyes and listen inside and tell me what you see, or hear, or feel?" Consciously, Helene seemed determined to remain detached. Perhaps if we went deeper we'd find something that could give me a response.

Helene rolled her head and sighed in irritation, but she closed her eyes. For several seconds her head lolled and her hands kneaded each other in her lap, but gradually her movements stilled. Her chin came to rest against the dirty dress. A moment later she began to cry, short sharp exhalations of breath conveying the intensity of her sobs.

"Helene?"

She seemed not to hear.

"Helene?"

She moved slightly as if my voice had barely breached the space between us.

"Helene. It's David."

She stirred again. Without opening her eyes she seemed to be looking for my voice.

"Can you tell me what's happening?"

Her voice was hollow as if she were speaking from a tomb. "Today's the day."

"The day?"

"The day she died."

I felt my breath catch in my throat. Helene had known, at least unconsciously, this day was approaching! The anniversary of a significant event often causes a powerful unconscious reaction, and deep inside Helene had been getting ready. That explained her rapid deterioration. She was preparing to memorialize the day by following her mother.

"How does that make you feel?"

"I am in despair," she moaned. "I am full of grief. I'm hopeless."

"What else? Just let it come."

"I want it to end. I don't want to go on living this way. I'm so tired of this life."

Through her words I heard her mother's voice: the despairing mother who felt caught in a lethal trap. Would she have said the same? "I wonder if your mother felt that way?"

Helene started slightly.

"You know, we've spoken very little about your mother's death."

"Aah," Helene moaned.

"Can we do that now?"

Resignedly, she nodded.

"Can you tell me about the day your mother died?"

She shook her head slowly, as if it were anchored by a leaden weight. "I told you. I found her."

"What was that like for you?"

"I told you, I . . ." Her voice trailed off. Behind her closed lids her eyes were moving, seeing something.

"Can you tell me what you're experiencing?"

"Nnhh. Nothing."

But her breathing speeded up.

"It looks like something's trying to touch you. I wonder if you would be willing to let it touch you."

Her eyes closed tighter and her shoulders drew up against her chin, a girding movement. But it was useless against the force of the image. Behind her eyelids her eyes were almost still, peering intently forward.

"Are you seeing something?"

"Yes." The voice was the little girl's.

"Can you tell me what you see?"

"I see my mommy . . ."

"What is she doing?"

"She's talking to me. She's yelling at me."

"What is she saying?"

"She's waving her arms. . . . She looks angry . . . sad and angry . . . she's yelling. She's yelling, 'I can't take it any more. . . . I can't take it any more . . . this is all your fault'. . . ." Helene paused, then suddenly recoiled in her chair. "She has the gun! . . . That shiny gun from the kitchen drawer. . . . She said never touch that gun. . . . Why does she have it? She's waving it around. . . . Stop, Mommy! Stop waving it! . . . Oh, now she's crying. Don't cry, Mommy, I'll be good. I promise, I'll be good. . . ." Suddenly a look of pure horror crossed

Helene's face. "No, Mommy! Don't do that! Don't ever point a gun at yourself! You said . . . oh!" The word, half bitten, fell from her mouth and Helene's gaze dropped to the floor. She stared downward, her chin working nervously back and forth. Several seconds passed then her voice resumed, quieter now, less terrorized. "Mommy? . . . Mommy, are you sleeping? . . . Are you sleeping, Mommy? . . . Wake up, Mommy! Wake up! . . ." Helene's hand touched the air in front of her and prodded it—first tentatively, then harder, then fiercely, pleadingly. Then abruptly she collapsed, curled into a ball, and sobbed.

"Yes," I soothed. "Yes . . ."

She cried for a long time, her head cradled in her arms, and then began to rock herself—slowly, almost imperceptibly—as if she were both mother and child.

"Helene?"

She stirred but didn't sit up.

"Helene, when you are ready, and you can take all the time you need, you can open your eyes and return to the present with me."

Helene groaned a little, then slowly raised herself to a sitting position.

"I didn't know. . . . I thought I found her. . . ." The words leaked from her slowly, flat and lifeless. "I let her down."

"Let her down? In what way?"

"I should have stopped it."

"You think you should have stopped it?"

She shook her head, chastising herself. "If I had been better . . ."

"But didn't you try every way you could to be better—and it still didn't make a difference?"

She stared sadly into my eyes.

"When you talk that way, Helene, it makes me think you forget that there were many other stresses in her life. Your father . . . perhaps her own parents. . . . Don't you think they might have had something to do with it?"

She looked at me for a second as if I had spoken a foreign language, then turned away.

"Don't you think it's possible that the forces that caused her to take her life were well in place before you were born?"

"Mm-m," she murmured. But her gaze remained even, focused out the window.

I thought about the "suicide note" Helene's mother had left—those four spoken words, "It's all your fault." The child would hear *I caused my mother's death; now I deserve to die!*

But that wasn't the only message Helene's mother had left. Through her relationship with Helene she'd conveyed another one, equally potent. She'd asked her daughter to share her bed; she'd claimed Helene was her only ray of sun; she'd organized Helene's life around meeting her own needs. Through those acts she'd exerted an iron-clad hold on her daughter—and left a profound unconscious message: *I need you, Helene; don't separate from me, Helene; don't leave me alone!*

Suddenly Helene's "script" was clear. No wonder she'd said it was "in the fiber of her body to die." It wasn't that her mother had fueled and modeled a suicidal depression. It wasn't even that Helene had witnessed the suicidal act. It was that her mother had planted those dual insidious messages: *I need you with me, Helene; you deserve to die.* Her mother had written that script for her until the day she died, and Helene had struggled with its inexorable finale ever since.

We were silent for several minutes while Helene sat staring at the floor. Her face gave no clues to the tumult inside—no hint of the monumental change that had just taken place. Thirty-six years before, a part of Helene had witnessed the suicide of her mother, and in that moment of unacceptable horror that part had cleaved off, banished from Helene's conscious mind. A split-second later a *different* part had surfaced to find her mother lying on the floor. "Wake up, Mommy," that part had cried, believing in all innocence that her mother might be asleep. For that part, freshly born, had truly not seen the mother's act.

Now suddenly the banished part had returned to awareness, and for the first time in thirty-six years Helene *knew*—knew and felt and sensed in every part of her—that she had been witness to her mother's death. And along with that knowledge came a pair of damning and distorted feelings: she felt responsible for the death because she hadn't stopped it; because she hadn't stopped it she deserved to die.

I observed her face, shroudlike in its barren stillness. "What are you thinking?"

She gave a profound sigh. "At least she stopped suffering." Her words were as much to herself as to me.

"Yes. And what does that make you feel?"

"I've been thinking about getting a gun . . ."

"So you could do what she did?"

"It's inside me. I can't resist it anymore."

"But you haven't gotten a gun?"

"No."

"Are you thinking of another way?"

Vaguely, as if her attention were really elsewhere, she nodded.

In the past Helene had toyed with various ways of killing herself but hadn't settled on one. A patient is deemed close to suicide when she has planned a method of killing herself *and* acquired the means. Divesting herself of meaningful possessions and attachments usually denotes the final stage of readiness.

"What is that?"

"Razor blades."

"Have you collected them?"

"Yes."

"Would you be willing to give your razor blades to me?" It seemed like a silly question. Even if Helene gave the blades to me she obviously could buy others. But once a person has determined her means of suicide, the instruments she plans to use become endowed with a kind of magical, emotional charge. When she relinquishes them to a therapist, she also relinquishes that charge—and the power to execute the act is at least temporarily deflated.

For the first time that session Helene looked me in the eye. "I couldn't do that."

"Helene . . ."

But she cut me off, rising suddenly from her chair. Her movement was brisk and precise; she seemed to rise like a phoenix from her lethargy. Her eyes were steely. "I appreciate all your help, David." Her voice was itself as flat and sharp as a razor. "But I don't think I'll be needing your services anymore." Then she turned and walked with stiff determination toward the door, her briefcase with its errant contents forgotten on the floor.

Something inside me grew cold. Depression, anger, misery—any strong emotion in a suicidal client is less frightening to me than cold detachment. A client once threatened to plunge a knife into her chest—after first putting my business card over her heart so that I would be implicated in her deed. Another held a gun to her head as she described to me over the phone her children, sleeping in the room next door. In those cases there was some investment—in me, in children, in life; something that could be worked with, cajoled, to lure those people into reconsideration. But when a client has let go, as Helene had, when her eyes grow cold, when a briefcase that has been carried like a talisman through months of sorrow is forgotten on the floor, when our relationship is so readily dismissed—then I am almost at a loss.

The only thing I could think to do was to appeal to the part of her that expected to take care of others the way she had taken care of her mother. "Yes, Helene," I measured my words, "you can leave. You can leave in a few minutes. But don't you think you owe it to me to have some closure here?"

Her eyes caught mine for a second, then flicked away.

I waited.

She didn't move.

"If you're going to fire me don't I deserve to have some sense of finishing with you? Or doesn't that matter?"

She stood, rigidly still, barely breathing.

"We've worked together for a long time now. Don't you think we should have a better ending?"

As if air were slowly escaping from a tiny hole, Helene began to sag.

"Helene." My voice was soft. "*You* want to die, but there are parts of you that don't. There are parts of you that still have hope . . . that believe there is a better way past all this. *They* need to be listened to as well."

Her head hung limply. She made no response.

"Do you know what my concern is, Helene? My concern is that if you die, those parts will get swept along too . . . the way you got swept along by your mother."

A soft moan escaped from inside her.

Almost a full minute passed before she raised her eyes. Her voice was a whisper. "She ended her pain."

The plea was unmistakable. Helene had stepped back from the edge, but barely.

"Helene, you're putting me in a position in which I'm obligated to take action. By law I have to try to put you in a safe place if you can't guarantee your own safety. Can you guarantee me that you won't harm yourself between now and the next time I see you?"

She closed her eyes, then opened them. "I can't."

"Then I think we have no choice. It seems it would be best for you to go to a hospital for a little while—until we can understand what's making you feel this way." I let my words sink in. "What do you think about that?"

Her eyes clouded. "What about Dulcy?"

Her dog. In her concern I found a note of hope.

"Can your cousin watch her?" Helene's cousin lived nearby and seemed to be her closest relative or friend.

"Hn-n." She nodded distractedly.

"Should I call her or would you like to?"

"You."

I looked up the cousin's number in my file and called; fortunately she was home. I explained the situation and asked her to pack a bag for Helene then pick her up at my office and take her to the hospital. While I talked I kept my eye on Helene but she made no move to leave. Instead she shuffled toward her chair and dropped, depleted, into it.

I then had to arrange Helene's admission to the hospital. As a nonphysician I have no admitting privileges so I called a colleague, a psychiatrist, who had helped me in this way before. His secretary promised to relay the message and a few minutes later he called back, agreeing to admit Helene to the psychiatric ward of a medical hospital.

All that was left then was to wait for the cousin to arrive. I sat in the chair next to Helene and studied her. I was concerned about her being in the hospital. Psychiatric wards in medical hospitals are not designed for doing in-depth emotional work. Their job is to stabilize patients—to make sure they eat and sleep and wash, to prevent them from committing suicide, to remove the stresses of daily life until a patient can cope again on her own. They lack the time to truly help a suicidal patient heal. My consultant would be Helene's attending psychiatrist, and would defer the work to me; I would rearrange my schedule so that I could see her every other day. Together we'd probe the feelings surrounding her mother's suicide. But I had no expectation that we'd make great progress; real healing would occur only after she got out. So my main hope was that Helene would cooperate with the staff and demonstrate a fundamental will to live so that within a week she'd be back home.

For her part, she seemed impervious to my presence. She sat hunched in the chair, head hanging over her lap, like a woman in a nursing home whose life has already ended.

Once in the hospital Helene became immensely difficult. My worst fears were confirmed. Her depression and suicidality were so profound that she became completely noncompliant. She resisted the staff's attempts to get her to dress herself. She refused her meals. She refused to go to daily group counseling sessions. I saw her every other day and we spent most of those hours discussing her latest refusal. Between visits I was besieged by phone calls from staff, all irritated and frustrated by Helene's latest "act of defiance." I saw them not as acts of defiance, but as signals that she no longer wanted to live.

The prospect that Helene would be released in a week soon grew dim. By the end of the first week it was clear she would be there at least one more. This made the hospital restive. By and large medical hospitals prefer psychiatric patients to come and go quickly. They are not in the business of long-term therapy, and Helene, in particular, was trying. So I found myself under increasing pressure to get Helene better and get her out.

One morning midway through her second week I received a phone call from the hospital. Helene had attempted suicide. She had used the telephone cord to try to hang herself.

After the day's last session I went to the hospital. If I had sensed impatience toward Helene before, it was now open hostility. The staff at the nursing station opposite the elevator rolled their eyes at me as I stepped out. *Now look what she's done,* they seemed to say, and I felt their gazes like a knife: *It's your fault,* they implied; *why isn't she getting better? When will you get her out?*

I desperately wished I had an answer. I hadn't given up hope: I still believed we could quell the suicidality. But our time was running out. The hospital was threatening to commit her to the state mental institution, an untenably depressing place too far from Seattle for me to see her regularly. Once there Helene would never improve. But what were the alternatives? Her insurance was running out. I had no colleagues at other hospitals who could be attending physicians. I certainly couldn't send her home. We'd come to the end of our options. Under the glares of the staff I felt a wave of desperation. Helene *had* to improve in the next few days—and I had no idea of how to make that happen.

Helene had been moved to a bare room stripped of all but a bed, a chair, and a dresser. Its single window, which looked out on a wall, was screened with wire mesh. Helene was sitting on the bed, curled in a ball, leaning against the headboard. Her back was to the door.

"Helene . . ."

At the sound of my voice she shook her head.

"Helene . . ."

She shook it harder, turning it vigorously from side to side as if to expel the sound of my voice.

"Helene, perhaps if you don't want to talk you could just listen to me?"

But she kept shaking and shaking, wedded to the movement even after I stopped trying to talk.

"Well, I can see you don't want to listen, so I'll just sit here quietly and we'll see what ways we might find to communicate."

I sat down in the chair, and a few moments later a social worker appeared in the open doorway: Helene was now on fifteen-minute suicide watch. I started to nod but the social worker had already turned her back, motioning me to follow. Dutifully I trailed behind, prepared for the latest barrage of complaints. But instead, out in the hallway, she pulled something out of her pocket and dropped it into my hand.

"She said to give you this."

I looked down. In my hand was a piece of paper that had been folded many times in an obvious attempt to conceal its contents. Inside was Helene's familiar school-teacher hand, its manicured lines now fiercely anguished. Smoothing out the paper's folds I read:

To David,

I am crying and crying and crying. They tell me it is good to cry, but they don't understand. For me there is no relief. I will never find relief. For I am mourning my own death. No one understands! There is so much rot in me. Rot and contamination. I am poison! A crazy bitter, ravaged, putrid, poisoned canker, deformed by years of crying crying crying silently while no one came. For years I have been living underground, far from the sun and human warmth, and I am chilled to the bone. There is no point now David.

You must let me go.

I caught my breath. The desolation in the words was so absolute that I felt I couldn't face the woman who had written them. But I read the note again, and the second time I heard another note behind the desolation: a note so sure, so desperate, that once noticed it had to be heard. Helene's letter was a plea, a hope against hope that for once someone might hear her pain. It was her last despairing scream from the darkness, hoping that this time someone would come.

I realized that the time had come for a different kind of move. All the attempts to talk about her mother's death, all the moves at stabilization, had only pushed her closer toward the edge. If Helene was going to improve before the hospital committed her to the state institution we had to try something radically different, a strategic strike right at the heart of her suicidality. But what?

I needed to get away—away from the staff, away from Helene, away to a place where I could clear my head and think. I followed the hall to the elevator and when the door opened I got in.

I knew from experience that in order to maneuver past the impasse I'd need to stop thinking consciously about it. If I could just let my mind drift, if I could release my current assumptions, my unconscious might suggest something useful. So under the pretext of having dinner, I went to the cafeteria, bought a sandwich and a cup of coffee, and parked at a corner table. There, amid the clatter of trays and conversation, I sat back and let my gaze wander. At a nearby table a mother and teenage son caught my eye. I watched them vaguely, only half seeing their interaction, and soon found myself thinking about my own mother. As I wandered in my thoughts in a natural state of trance, my mind drifted to her funeral several years before, and I remembered something the rabbi had quoted to me afterward:

Thou hast gone from me but the bond that unites our souls can never be severed; thine image lives within my heart.

At the time, I had heard his words as a figurative allusion to the spiritual bond between parent and child. *How true,* I'd thought, *even after death we don't let go!* But suddenly I heard the prayer differently—I heard it *literally.* We all carry parent parts within, and if we listen closely or go into trance we can communicate with those internal parents. Well, perhaps the bond itself—the force that unites us with our parents even after they have died—also exists within, in a form that can communicate. *Maybe the bond itself can be crystallized in a form that we can speak with.*

Two things were pulling Helene toward death: the feeling that she deserved to die, and the injunction to be with her mother. Both had been with her since childhood, had colored all her actions, and had formed a lens through which she viewed her life. They didn't exist inside her as a single locus the way the bad internal mother did, but urges as primal and life-shaping as those would infiltrate *every* part of her being. Would it be possible to "call up" this life-shaping force—to "gather" it from its sites throughout Helene's personality—and ask it to take on a voice that could speak to me? I had no idea; I'd never tried such a thing before. But if I tried—and if it worked—then I could talk directly with the force that was pulling Helene toward death. Suddenly my intervention was clear. I would hypnotize Helene and ask to speak to this "force." What I would say if it actually coalesced I didn't know. But at least—at last—I had a sense of what to do.

When I returned to Helene's room she was curled on the bed in the same position, an overgrown child in despair.

"I've read your note," I said.

To my surprise, she turned to face me. Her eyes were lidded and her movement slow, but once turned she held my gaze. I realized I was seeing two Helenes: the dark, despondent part of Helene that longed to die, but also the tiny, fragile parts that clung to life. Those fragile parts were the ones whose voices had called to me from her letter, and they were the ones that turned the heavy body toward me now, trusting me to help them defeat the pull toward death. I felt again the weight of my responsibility, the impatience of the hospital, Helene's steady, marked decline. And I saw how important it was for me to act decisively, for if I faltered those parts would feel abandoned. They would give up their will to fight and the intervention would certainly fail.

"I've done a lot of thinking," I said firmly. "I'd like to do some trance work with you."

For a long moment she remained still and closed, a funereal statue on the bed. Then very slowly she raised her head and opened her eyes. "Yes," she breathed.

I realized we were both relieved.

I arranged with the staff to leave us undisturbed, then I closed the door and pulled up the chair. Using a reinduction signal developed in the office when, on occasion, we'd done formal trance work, I helped Helene into a trance and then encouraged her to go deeper.

"With every breath you will find yourself becoming more and more receptive to ideas and ways of looking at things and listening to things that can help you get through the difficulties you have been having. . . ."

Helene had turned in the bed so that her back rested against the headboard and her legs, swathed in hospital blankets, lay straight in front of her. As I spoke her head grew heavy; now it slumped inertly to the side.

"And the more you seek to find a way to get through those difficulties, the easier it is for you to attend to your deepest thoughts, attitudes, and feelings . . . that's right. . . . Now, I'm wondering if it would be okay to speak with the force that has been pulling Helene so insistently toward death. . . . If that would be all right with the unconscious, then just let the head nod slightly."

Slowly Helene's head bowed and raised.

"Thank you . . . and now, as you drift deeper . . . I would like to summon, from all the aspects of Helene's personality, that pull toward suicide . . . all of that pull toward mother . . . and I wish for all of that pull to speak to me now with one voice."

I watched Helene's face closely. Her eyes were closed, her jaw slack against the collar of her gown. Her breath through her open mouth was brittle. She sat absolutely still.

"If that force is there can it please come toward this voice . . . please come toward this voice."

Helene stirred slightly.

"That's right . . . come closer . . . that's right . . . come into the room . . . this voice will carry you toward me . . . yes . . . ."

Helene stirred again, this time more strongly. Then suddenly her mouth flew open and an unfamiliar voice, frail and surprised, came out. "How did you know I was here?"

A chill went through me. *Who was talking?* I'd hoped to coalesce the force in trance, but I'd expected something far more vague—Helene's voice, trancelike and remote—not a distinct persona with a voice of its own. This voice had sounded the way I imagined the actual mother's voice to sound—young and desperate and scared. Was the force coalescing in the persona of the mother?

Whatever form the force was taking, it had answered. I felt a rush of elation. After months of wrestling with Helene's growing and formless suicidality I suddenly felt that I'd closed in on the core. Moments like these—when the client opens herself at the deepest level and lets me in—are the most intimate in therapy. And in them lies the greatest potential for change.

"I felt your presence," I said slowly. I wanted to respond in a way that wouldn't threaten what I sensed was a very tenuous alliance.

"What do you want?"

"I just want to talk."

"About what?"

"About Helene. She feels you pulling her toward death."

"I need her with me. I thought death would bring me peace. But without her there is no peace."

Again, the chill went through me: the voice was answering as if she *were* Helene's mother, still "alive" despite her death! For an eerie moment I felt her reaching from the grave. I had to remind myself that it wasn't really the mother speaking, but rather a construct of Helene's mind, a collection of feelings and attitudes that I had artificially coalesced.

And then it struck me: of course they would coalesce in the persona of Helene's mother—for the mother was the source from which they'd sprung. What better way to give them voice than as the being to whom they were so intimately attached? Unconsciously Helene must have felt those forces as emanating from the mother. For her they *were* the mother: the mother pulling her to the grave.

And that explained another reason for the force's strength. Helene had never separated from her mother. Denied the experiences that build autonomy, she had never developed an independent sense of self. When her mother died, it was as if a part of her self had vanished—and she'd been yearning to join it ever since. That's why the urge toward suicide was so undeniable. It was Helene's final attempt to cement that bond. If Helene were dead nothing could separate her from her mother. She would never have to face a life alone.

For a moment I felt gleeful: I knew what I had to do! Helene had laid it out for me as clear as a set of instructions. I had asked to speak with the "pull toward death" and Helene had presented me with this "mother." My job now was to negotiate with the mother, to somehow persuade her to release her grip. Would that be possible? I had no idea of what to say, of how to frame an argument that would convince her. But for several reasons I was hopeful. First, Helene had brought this "mother force" out to talk, which meant she was serious about making progress. Had she not been, she would have kept this "mother" under wraps. Second, by bringing the force out as she had, she'd brought her relationship with her mother into the room. As if both women were now before me, we could deal with the dynamic between them. And third, I believed that my work with Helene had truly strengthened her, that by resolving her issues with her father and with the bad internal mother, she had become strong enough to stand on her own. The only question was how to do it—and if I was up to the task.

Picking up on her last words, I tried another argument. "Is there *nothing* else that would bring you peace?"

"She's the only peace I'll ever know."

"But you're holding on to her now and you're still unhappy."

"She's not with me yet. I'm still alone."

There was such a haunting emptiness in her words. I pictured Helene's mother again. Despite the callousness of her actions, despite the narcissism with which she'd stolen her daughter's life, she hadn't meant to harm her. She was merely a frightened woman who had had a child while still a child herself. From the little that Helene had said, I could piece together her mother's life. She had been young, perhaps no more than twenty, when she had married Helene's father, a man nineteen years her senior. She was naive, insecure; the older man, prominent in town, held the promise of the life she'd dreamed of: wealth, security, and happiness. But her plan had backfired. Her husband was an alcoholic, and abusive to boot. Instead of sheltering her in love, he ordered her around, gave her no respect, threatened her with blows. Her dream withered before her eyes. Then she got pregnant—and in the baby saw the dream rekindled. Now she would have someone who would love her, someone who would respect her, someone who would be hers forever! But that dream, too, was ruined. Her husband took the dream-baby away—defiled her!—and, cowed by her husband, feeling no bigger than a child herself, she was powerless to fight. Worst of all, when her dream-baby needed her, when she called for her in pain, she was unable to respond because she was too afraid.

So she pushed the dream-baby away. She began to hate it, to blame it for the misfortunes that had befallen her, to believe that if not for the dream-baby she could get out of that hole and live the good life about which she still dreamed.

Still, though, there were moments when she could pretend the bad things hadn't happened; when she could pretend the dream-baby was still hers. Moments in bed at night, as she and the dream-baby curled against each other, when she could hold the dream-baby in her arms and tell her she loved her; tell her how much she meant to her, how she was the only ray of sun in a cruel and ugly world.

To reach the mother, I realized, I would have to appeal to that dream. I'd have to show her that despite the devastation of her life, part of the dream was still possible. She could still find honor and respect, could still make up for the harm she'd done her child. By giving her dream-baby a life, she could redeem her own.

That idea would be terrifying, however: she was so frightened of letting go, so invested in getting Helene to join her. I'd have to introduce it slowly, and only after letting her know I understood her needs.

"I can hear that you're very unhappy," I said to her gently. "You have no peace now, and had no peace in life. You must wish that you'd done things differently."

"It wasn't the life I was supposed to live." Her voice was sorrowful and resigned.

"It still can be. You can fix that."

"What do you mean?" Her response was quick enough that I knew I'd caught her interest.

"You feel like your life was a failure. You had a bad marriage. You think you were a bad parent. You think your life amounted to nothing. . . . But you can fix that. It's not too late."

"What do you mean?" she asked again, sharper this time, more interested.

"All the time she was a child, you put your hopes in her. You hoped she would rescue you. You hoped she would give your life meaning. You hoped she would make your life the way it was meant to be." I waited and watched her to see if I had read her motives correctly.

Her eyes were closed and her head down, but slowly, wearily, it nodded.

"She still can!" I whispered. "She still *can* redeem you . . . *if you let her.*"

Her head stopped nodding. Instead, it raised slightly and made a tight pained circle in the air as if behind the closed eyelids she were looking for the voice that had offered that idea.

"If you let her live, your life *will* have meaning. You will not have lived in vain."

"It's too late."

"It's not too late! You can still redeem your life."

"I am beyond redemption."

"Only if your daughter dies! Your life was hard; so much went wrong. But you gave the world a wonderful daughter. People love her." I paused. "Your life can be redeemed through this gift you gave the world."

She shook her head tiredly, as if my words had exhausted her.

"She still can bring you peace. A different kind of peace. The peace of knowing that you left the world this gift."

Slowly the shaking stopped and her head came to rest against her chest. Her shoulders sagged and she seemed folded in upon herself. From the hollow of her chest her voice came low and mournful. "But what would happen to me?"

It was so plaintive, the frightened question of a child. In that moment my heart went out to her, out to this unearthly woman who was drawing her daughter to the grave. "Then you could rest," I said to her quietly. "Finally you could rest."

She was silent for a long time. Nothing stirred behind her eyes; even her breathing seemed to have stopped. Finally she spoke, her voice a whimper. "I'm afraid to be alone."

Involuntarily I exhaled. I hadn't realized I was tense, but now, vertebrae by vertebrae, I felt my spine relax. She had agreed! Not yet in words, but in the resignation of her tone. The fear she was expressing was fear she had already taken on.

"Perhaps you don't have to be alone."

"I have no one else."

"Perhaps, in peace, you won't have to be alone."

"But who will be with me?"

"Perhaps you can see an image . . ."

"An image?"

"An image of something that can help you."

She was silent as if trying to interpret my meaning.

"Perhaps you can look. Perhaps there is something in the distance."

Behind her eyelids I could see a flicker.

"Do you see something?"

She was silent.

I waited. Her eyes remained intently focused, staring into the darkness behind her lids, perhaps willing something to be there.

"Do you see something?"

"Yes." Quietly.

"What do you see?"

"I see a light."

"A light?"

She nodded slightly, eyes still focused on their target.

"Is it coming closer?"

"Yes."

"Can you see what it is?"

"A being . . . a being of light."

"Is it close to you now?"

"Yes."

"How does it feel?"

"Warm, like the sun."

"Is it a good feeling?"

"Yes."

"I'll be quiet now while you take some time to be with that being. When you're ready to talk with me again just let your head nod."

A minute passed. She sat quietly, head bowed, eyes closed. Then very faintly she nodded.

"Can you tell me what that was like for you?"

"He brings me peace. He said he can show me the way to peace at last."

"How will that happen?"

"He says I can go with him."

"Is that something you want to do?"

She was silent for fifteen seconds. Then resolutely, "Yes. It is."

A moment later the fingers on her right hand twitched.

"Is he taking your hand?"

"Yes."

"Do you feel safe?"

"Yes."

"Do you feel alone?"

There was a pause of two heartbeats before she answered. "No." The word had a quiet grace, empty of fear.

"Do you think you're ready to go now?"

"Yes."

"Then in a moment you'll be able to do that. But first I'd like to tell you that I'm very pleased we've been able to have this talk. And I'm pleased you made the decision you did because I think it's the right one for you." I paused. "It's the most loving thing you could do for your daughter."

Her head raised slightly, as if leaning toward the words.

"And now, if you're ready, you can begin to go."

She sat quietly, eyes closed as they had been the entire time, and as I watched, the tension that had lined her face slipped away. Bit by bit, her face took on the easiness of sleep. Sixty, ninety seconds passed. Then, suddenly, as if she had received a blow to the solar plexis, she collapsed on the bed. Wails shuddered from her open mouth. Her back heaved and fell against the covers.

For three or four minutes the paroxysm continued until finally the wails subsided into sobs and the wracked convulsions of her body slowed. Her fingers began to knead the blanket. The hospital gown, pulled open at the back, revealed her white and freckled skin. Suddenly I felt embarrassed, as if, in the sight of her back, I had overstepped the bounds of intimacy.

A few moments later she drew herself up and, still crying,

pulled the bedsheet to her face. Suddenly I realized that the movements I was seeing were no longer those of a woman in trance. The woman I was watching seemed present, self-directing—awake.

"Helene?" I asked, surprised.

She nodded slightly through her sobs.

"That's right, that's right. You can finally cry."

As if my words had been permission, her crying intensified.

For the next five or ten minutes I soothed her, "held" her in my words, and gradually her sobs began to slacken. When they had largely subsided she used the bedsheet to wipe her eyes.

"Do you want to tell me about what happened?" I asked her gently.

She nodded tentatively as if unsure, and without thinking I put out my hand—whether to steady her, or reassure her, or to confirm that it was her, I didn't know. But to my surprise she took it in her own and touched it to her face. Her skin felt damp and soft beneath my fingers as she pressed it, first against one cheek and then the other.

She looked me in the eye and as we held each other's gaze I saw confusion and amazement cloud her eyes. "I had a dream." She peered into my eyes to see if it could possibly be true. "I dreamt she left. . . ." She closed her eyes and tightened them as if looking back inside. "She touched me here. . . ." Helene pressed my hand tighter against her cheek, "and then she whispered . . . just like she used to do . . . 'I love you, dream-baby' . . . and then she walked away." Tears flowed down Helene's cheeks. She put her hand over her mouth and began to cry again.

"It makes you sad."

She nodded.

After a few moments she sniffed and blew her nose. "I've never really felt sad about her death before. But now I feel . . ." She let out a tiny smile. "I feel lighter, like something has been released. And I feel terribly, terribly sad."

"It sounds like you're finally mourning your mother."

She nodded. Her mouth quivered with the competing desires to laugh and cry.

But Helene had not only lost her mother. She had gained her *self*. She had liberated the autonomous Helene who had formerly been denied. Her feeling of lightness, her urge to laugh: these were signs that Helene sensed that, too.

"You know, now that you've let go of your mother, I think you can see some things more clearly. You can see yourself, and all the needs you've had that your mother never filled." Helene had lived her life in service to her mother, her own needs pushed far out of sight.

Helene dabbed at her eyes.

"And I think now that you know you're separate from your mother, you can also see *her* more clearly—and see all the ways she didn't meet your needs."

Fresh tears slipped down Helene's cheeks and gathered at the corners of her mouth.

"And perhaps you can also see your mother as a woman who had a difficult life of her own, and you can know that it was aspects of her own life that made her behave the way she did. She didn't do what she did because of you."

At my words, Helene cradled her head in her hands and began to sob.

She would go through a period of mourning now, I knew—grieving the loss of her mother, both real and ideal; grieving the losses she now felt, as a person with needs of her own. But the depth of her mourning would be matched by the degree of exhilaration that would come in feeling, for the first time, free. Free of the shackles in which she'd been chained for most of her forty-five years; free to be the sole author of her life and to write her script as she chose.

We were silent for a few moments, letting the immensity of the experience settle over both of us. Then Helene leaned back against her pillows and closed her eyes.

I realized how tired we both were. My watch said 9:05 P.M.; we'd been working for over two hours. The night was hot, the hospital barely air-conditioned, and my body was wet with sweat.

"Looks like you need a rest." I spoke for both of us. "How about if I see you tomorrow?"

She nodded.

As I got up to leave she held out her hand. I squeezed it warmly, and then, without even thinking, touched it to my own cheek. Then I left, closing the door behind me.

On the way out I stopped by the nurses' station to recommend they take Helene off suicide watch.

Helene was released from the hospital three days later. After a week of rest at home she returned to work and finished the school year without incident. She continued in therapy for another year, during which we talked more about her mother and her childhood, as well as about present-day issues. She reported no more suicidal thoughts. Instead, she gradually came to feel a sense of "ownership" of her life, along with "glimmers of happiness" that she had never expected to feel.

The year after Helene left therapy I received a Christmas card from her. It was a card she had designed herself. On the cover was a glowing sun whose rays radiated out into a prism of color at the edges. Underneath, in Helene's perfect grade-school letters were the words, "Reaching out to you *with warmth* during this holiday season."

Inside she had written,

To David,
Thank you for unfreezing me.
                    Helene

Epilogue

The Workshop of the Self

I AM SOMETIMES JEALOUS OF MY CLIENTS. NOT OF THEIR LIFESTYLES OR their money, nor of any particular features of their lives, but of their capacity for trance. For many of my clients have an uncommon ability to use the phenomena of trance to achieve remarkable ends. I, for instance, could never anesthetize myself for five straight hours while a surgeon peeled and rearranged my face as Terry Yaekel did. Nor could I reinterpret my entire life in a matter of minutes as Carol, the bulimic teenager, did. Terry and Carol and many other clients have been particularly well endowed with hypnotic prowess—in part through personality, in part through the circumstances of their lives—and my own endowment is nowhere near as great. At times I envy them their gift.

Nonetheless, over years of practice I have become a capable hypnotic subject. I've learned to use hypnosis to manage stress, to solve problems, to explore my own psyche, and even, on occasion, to see deep truths about myself that my conscious mind could not admit. And twice self-hypnosis has arguably saved my life.

The first occasion was in the summer of 1985 when I was on vacation in northern Mexico. I was staying at a desert villa where, despite the 113-degree heat, I had gotten into the habit of doing a long afternoon run. On this particular afternoon I'd wrapped a wet T-shirt around my head, poured water over my neck and chest, and taken off, jogging slowly past the gate that defined the green oasis of the villa and out into the dusty desert hills. As I ran I picked up speed and the dry, dirt-dusted heat came up to meet me.

I had been running for about three-quarters of an hour when, coming up blind over a little rise, I stepped into a pothole. I heard the snap as I went down: a twig had broken underneath me. I bounded to my feet and instantly went down again, massive pain exploding in my ankle. I crawled to a sitting position and looked at my leg. Immediately I felt a wave of nausea. My left foot was canted sideways at 45 degrees, locked in that position by my broken ankle. It looked as if a foot from someone else's leg had been witlessly attached to mine, and the sight of that foot, so lopsided, so grossly twisted, horrified me. Without even thinking I reached down with both hands, grabbed the foot and twisted it back into position. I nearly passed out from the pain.

Panic, like an adrenaline shot, swept through me. I was at least three miles from the villa; there was no way I could make it back. But I couldn't stay where I was: the desert would broil me alive. The ground was already too hot to sit on and there was nothing in the way of shade. I was vacationing alone and had told no one at the villa where I was going. Days would pass before anyone would think to look for me.

Certitude settled like a poison gas: *You'll die! If you don't do something you'll die!*

The thought propelled me. Pushing myself up with my hands, injured leg in the air, I hoisted myself to a standing position. Tentatively I touched my foot to the ground. Flash! Pain drove up my leg and lodged in my throat like an urge to vomit. Immediately the panicked thoughts returned. The heat rose in my chest and head; I felt myself close to tears.

I tried to hop, but the pain from the jarring was as intense as the pain of putting the foot on the ground, and I knew there was no way I could hop three miles of loose dirt hills. I tried sitting and pulling myself along, but the heat of the ground seared my hands and butt, and the muscles in my leg quivered so badly that I couldn't keep my foot in the air. These short bursts of activity kept my panic at bay, but as each attempt turned futile the panic swept back in.

Get your wits about you, I warned. *You can do this if you keep your wits.*

I can't.

You can.

I can't!

*You can! Remember RICE . . . rest, ice, compression, eleva-
tion . . .*

A higher part of me was talking—a part that had experience
with injuries, a part that now, as the rest of me succumbed to panic,
surfaced, cool and steady, to formulate a plan.

You can't rest it, you have no ice, you can't elevate it, but you
can *compress it. Use your shirt, make a splint, tighten your shoe, use
hypnosis. Use hypnosis to contain the pain.*

I responded to the voice as if to a teacher. I stood up, left foot
elevated, and closed my eyes. Immediately I began to wobble. *I can't
do it,* I thought. *It's not going to work.*

Do it! the voice commanded. *Calm yourself down.*

I breathed in deeply, again and then again, and as I did I felt
my frightened heartbeat begin to slow. *One . . . inhale . . . two . . .
exhale . . . three . . .* As I breathed and counted, the panic began to
subside and I heard the voice talking to me as if I were a client: *Let the
heat of the sun melt your muscles . . . four . . . Nothing bad is going to
happen right now . . . Five . . . You've got the time to do this . . . six . . .*

By the time I reached the count of twenty I could feel myself
in trance. The panic was gone; I'd lost the sense that I would be
trapped out there to die.

*Now you're going to turn off that leg and walk out of here. Turn
off the nerves . . . just put them to sleep . . . because when the nerves are
asleep your leg will not hurt . . .* In my mind I visualized the network of
nerves inside my leg, a map of intersecting threads, turning from on to
off, red to blue.

I opened my eyes and looked out at the desert hills. They
stretched as far as the eye could see in every direction, ocher dirt stub-
bled with scrub and cactus. The hills in the distance shimmered in the
heat. I looked down at my ankle. It ballooned over the top of my shoe
as if made of turkish taffy, and I felt a flutter of panic, but I closed my
eyes and let it go. *The leg is turned off,* I repeated. *You can hardly feel it.*
My T-shirt was dripping with sweat, but I unwrapped it from my head
and tied it as tightly as I could around the ankle, forming a make-shift
splint. Then carefully I eased the foot to the ground and lowered my
weight onto it.

It hurt—but nowhere near as much as it had before. Quickly I
transferred my weight to the other foot. I'd taken a step! Cautiously I
lowered the injured foot again. Pain again, but endurable. I shifted
to the other foot; a second step. *Don't pay attention to it, you'll pay*

attention to it later. I took a third step and then a fourth. *One foot after the other. That's how you got out here and that's how you'll get back. One foot after the other; one foot after the other.* . . . The words became a lulling rhythm to which I walked.

In that pain-reducing trance I crept back toward the villa. It was surreal. I knew I was alone in the scorching desert with a broken ankle, miles from help. Yet I was also somewhere else: someplace cool and calm and disconnected. I tried hard not to think, for all thoughts quickly turned to panic. *I'll never run again . . . there are snakes out here . . . the sun is sinking* . . . I forced them from my mind. *You don't need to think about that . . . just let it go . . . one foot after the other . . . one foot after the other . . .*

At one point I saw in the far distance a rise that I knew was near the villa. As the path rose and fell with the hills, the rise would come and go in my view. Whenever I saw it I fixated on it with tunnel vision that took me out of myself.

Occasionally I lost my awareness of the pain altogether, and then I would get careless, stepping on the foot too hard, or leaving my weight there too long. Immediately my sense of the moment would come back and I'd have to banish it forcibly: *Your leg is turned off . . . just let it go . . . one foot after the other . . .*

Three hours after I'd broken the ankle I reached the rise that I'd been watching. From its top I could see the villa with its tile roof, its burbling fountain, its thick border of bougainvilleas, lying before me. Relief flooded me the way it had when I was five and my mother appeared in the middle of the department store in which I'd gotten lost. Involuntarily tears sprang to my eyes. At the same time I felt an enormous sense of pride. *I'd done it!*

Unfortunately, along with the pride came an intense awareness of the pain. As if now that I was safe I could shed the trance, the reality of the break came bursting in. I barely made it a thousand paces further, then stopped to lean on the villa's fence. Guests were lolling by the pool, ice clinking in their frosty glasses. I imagined the feel of their chilled drinks in my hand, imagined the coolness against my mouth, imagined it spreading, unblistering the sunburn I'd just begun to feel. As I limped into the courtyard under their mildly curious stares, I felt like a warrior returned.

In a perverse way my sense of victory was magnified a short time later when I inquired at the desk and found that there were no doctors in the immediate vicinity; I could see a veterinarian if I wished. *How fitting,* I thought. *I survived this ordeal solely by my wits, and now*

I get to finish it solo, too. The lack of a doctor—the laughable offer of a vet—only cemented my sense of accomplishment. So I packed the leg with ice, kept it elevated throughout the evening, and after a gruesomely painful stint of packing, hitched a ride the next day to San Diego. There, the emergency room doctor confirmed what I had suspected, that a ligament had torn away from the bone, pulling a piece of the bone with it. He put on a temporary cast and, addressing my worst fear, assured me I would run again. When he told me he had run the Boston Marathon I knew I could believe him and, still heady with my own fortitude, I boarded the next plane for Seattle.

It was only when I was on the plane that I fully realized what had happened—that thanks to my ability to use self-hypnosis to manage my panic and pain, I'd been able to walk three miles through a scorching desert on a broken ankle. What would have happened had I been unable to self-hypnotize? I know I would have made it back; I doubt death was as imminent as it seemed. But the trek would have taken longer; would have entailed a lot more pain; would probably have included dehydration and sunstroke. I had used self-hypnosis countless times in my life prior to that event, for pain relief, to speed physical healing, to summon resources to solve a problem. But this was the first time I felt that self-hypnosis had spared me from far greater physical harm. What I didn't know was that my experience in the desert was a dry run for a more frightening, and perhaps more life-threatening, experience exactly a year later.

I'd been home for about a week, wearing my cast like a war medal and still enjoying the challenge of cooking and dressing with one good leg, when my dear friend and running partner Nancy said, "Let's climb Mt. Rainier." I thought she was joking, goading me, since I'd suddenly made her a running widow.

"Right," I said. I'd just figured out how to go to the bathroom on crutches; why not climb Rainier? It's the third highest peak in North America, glaciated and crevassed from its "base camp" at 10,000 feet to its summit at 14,410, a training ground for Everest because of their similar terrains. "The mountain," as it is known, is also a totem of the Pacific Northwest, majestically visible in clear weather, but more often mystically shrouded in cloud. I'd looked at—or *for*—Rainier every day of my life since childhood.

"Not now. A year from now," she said. "We'll spend the year training." She turned her eye to my cast. "It'll be a good goal."

So we hugged on it and as soon as the cast was off we began a rigorous regime of running, stair climbing, and mountain hiking in preparation for our ascent. The following July, almost a year to the day after I'd broken my ankle, we drove to Paradise Lodge, the starting point for the climb.

Approximately 2,000 people climb Mt. Rainier each summer in professionally led groups of twenty or twenty-five, and for each a three-quarter-day training is required. So we spent our first day in the company of other Rainier novices learning mountain basics: how to use our ice axes and crampons to gain a toe hold in the ice; how to self-arrest in the event we found ourselves sliding down a glacier; how to handle the safety rope that would tie us in teams of four; how to brace ourselves against the mountain to take the weight of a team member who falls; and how to yell "falling" without inhibition should we feel ourselves start to slip. The instructors didn't need to remind us that two or three people die each year on Rainier; that was understood. They did, however, decrease the chance of it happening to any of us. Throughout the training they scouted for individuals who they felt were unable to make the climb, and by the time we'd finished training, our group was smaller by three.

The next morning we convened outside the lodge with our fellow climbers. For most of us it was a first ascent, and we traded nervousness and excitement as we stood at 6,600 feet, tightening our sixty-pound packs and tying on to them the crampons and helmets we would be needing the next day. At half past ten that first morning, we set off from the lodge, a straggly line of twenty-four climbers between two bookend guides, all grunting under the weight of our gear, trudging first on dirt trails and soon through fields of snow. We were lucky: the weather was good. The day before a group had returned from the summit on hands and knees, ducking sixty-mile-an-hour winds that reduced the temperature to below zero.

At five o'clock, we reached Camp Muir, a stone hut at 10,000 feet, and immediately began housekeeping: laying things out to dry, checking the equipment, cooking the dinner that no one wanted to eat because the air at that altitude dulls the appetite like a toothache. As the sun went down, a velvet-blanket blackness wrapped itself around us, penetrated by millions of brilliant, winking stars. In the distance, in a darker shade of velvet, the outline of Mt. St. Helens rose, forty miles away, backlit by the lights of Portland.

Disturbing the celestial tranquility of the setting, however, were the omnipresent sounds of the mountain. Rock slides and avalanches roared continually, like a train careening off its rails around and above us. Although I knew we were safe in the tiny stone hut, I found myself remembering a quote of Edmund Hillary's, the first man to climb Everest: "There are no conquerors of mountains, only survivors."

At one in the morning the guides woke us to prepare for our final ascent. (Leaving in the dark of night assured that we'd be off the glaciated parts of the mountain before the sun softened the ice, which would make descending treacherous.) The cold was extreme, and I layered on "expedition weight" polypropylene underwear, wool pants and a sweater, a down parka with a Goretex shell, and a pair of Goretex outer pants—and was still freezing. To this I added my safety helmet and crampons and the harness to which the safety rope would be threaded. By half past two we were roped together in teams of four and ready to begin the ascent.

My team was the last to go so as we stood, illuminated only by the small circles of light cast by the headlamps on our helmets, I was able to watch the first three teams start up the mountain in slow, silent lines. The sight was magnificent. Surrounded by darkness, invisible except for their headlamps, the climbers looked like pearls on a charm bracelet floating up into the stars. But as I watched them a realization overtook me: *You have to do that, too!* Suddenly panic struck. *This is crazy!* I thought. *You can't climb this mountain!* And with what felt like herculean restraint I resisted the urge to tear off my rope and dodge back into the hut. A moment later it was my team's turn to go. I saw my teammates stretch out before me into the blackness, felt the tug of the rope at my waist, and before I could do otherwise found myself moving along behind them, locked in my own small circle of light. *Focus on your feet,* I thought. *Focus on the rope. Forget everything else, just let it all go.* I closed my mind around those words and locked my eyes on the illuminated ground, which was rising steeply under my feet.

Although I had left half my gear at Muir, my pack, on my climbing-sore back, felt heavier than it had the day before, and with my crampons on it was almost impossible to get a grip on the loose gravel underfoot. Slipping and sliding, chilled to the bone, exhausted already, I was terrified; I didn't see how I could possibly make the climb.

The day before, they'd taught us pressure breathing, in which you expel the air noisily from your lungs with a loud *wshoo.* This forced expulsion creates a back pressure in the lungs that helps the thin air get absorbed. Now, panicked and committed by the rope that bound me, I forced myself to breathe. *Wshoo . . . wshoo . . . let the breathing carry you away . . .* I had the mildly conscious notion that I could use the breathing as a trance induction to find a way past my fear.

Get into it, I thought. *Take a step, take another . . .* With every step I wedged my ice axe into the crumbling rock to get my balance. *Step . . . step . . . axe . . . Step . . . step . . . axe . . .* The sequence made a numbing rhythm. To the rhythm I added my breaths. *Step . . . step . . . axe . . . wshoo . . . Step . . . step . . . axe . . . wshoo . . .*

As I climbed I remembered a feeling I'd had as a child. Each night as I lay in bed waiting for sleep, I would imagine myself at the bottom of a rowboat. Covered with blankets, snug against the night, I would let the gentle drifting of the boat lull me to sleep. The sense of safety and containment of that trance—for that's in essence what it was, a state of internal focus with the rest of the world screened out—was the most pleasurable thing I could imagine. It was precisely what I yearned for now, crawling up this fearsome mountain in the middle of the frozen night. So with that as a motivator, and my world reduced to what I could see in my two-foot circle of light, I focused on the regularity of my steps and breathing and shifted gently into trance.

For the next two hours we trudged slowly upward, the breathing of my teammates, thirty feet in front and behind, echoing my own. Suddenly a flurry of rocks hurtled through the spaces between us, pinged against the rope, and narrowly missed my head. I heard them ricochet off rocks farther down the mountain. I knew I should have been scared—I'd come that close to getting hit—but instead the incident seemed like a reminder of the mountain's living presence. "We climb the mountain only with the mountain's grace," I thought, and as I listened to the receding sounds it seemed as if the mountain itself were confirming that. I can flick you off like an insect, it seemed to say. And in that moment, so near the stars, that reminder of my smallness seemed almost holy.

An hour later we stopped to rest on a rocky shelf, four or five inches wide, along which we'd been climbing. All of our rest stops were brief, two or three minutes at the most, because the frozen predawn air induced a tooth-chattering chill in a matter of minutes. Now, hoping to relieve the pressure on my legs, I leaned back against the mountain, placing my back and heels squarely against its flank. As I did I glanced out in front of me, looking for the first time since we'd left Camp Muir, away from the mountain, out into space. Dawn was beginning to break, fading the darkness to gray, and as my eyes adjusted to the light I realized that I could see outside the circle of my headlamp. What I saw was my boots, pronged crampons spiking off their fronts, sticking a good two inches off the narrow ledge on which I was standing. Below them the mountain fell away in a sheer cascade to a limitless glacier 2,500 feet below. The surface of the glacier was pocked with crevasses whose bottoms were dark and invisible, hundreds of feet lower still. At just that moment a clump of dirt dislodged itself from my boot and spilled over the ledge into the nothingness below. I felt my body go with it.

Immediately I froze in terror. I knew I needed to turn my face away from the dizzying view, but I couldn't, for I knew the slightest movement would make me fall. I thought about turning my eyes, but knew the slightest movement of my eyes would make me lose my balance. I thought about calling for help, but I couldn't open my mouth, couldn't form a word, for the sound of my own voice would topple me. And I knew, with terrifying certainty, that in just a moment the rope would tug and I would have to move—but that first the pressure of the rope would send me head first into the abyss.

From there the scene unfolded before my eyes: my teammates, unable to brace because I hadn't shouted "falling!" would plunge over the ledge as well. I saw them falling through the sky above me, falling faster, head over heels, whirling through the air to the crevasses below. 120 feet per second, 2,500 feet: it would take us 20 seconds to reach the glacier. An eternity: time enough to think, to pray, to reminisce, to live a life. I was filled with shame. My teammates: dying because they were tethered to *me!* What could I do? Nothing. There was nothing left to do—but jump. I could jump and end it; I could soar . . . But I couldn't jump for I was tethered to my team, and in a moment the rope would tug and I would fall.

The circle snapped tightly on itself and as it closed I felt myself go mad. It was the end. I'd exhausted all solutions, used up any wit, or skill, or luck that could keep me alive. There was no use trying. Like a client who, realizing he can't open his eyes, accepts the fact that he's in trance, I resigned my conscious control and just let go.

Inside a tiny voice cried out: *Mommy!*

And in that second a small hole opened up in time. My mind fractured; I felt it go—felt it atomize into a dozen separate units, each with a task to do to save my life. One part held my body, maintained it safely on the ledge. Another planned for the tug of the rope; another tracked my fear; another calmed the frightened child. And above them all, a higher voice, calm and logical, reasoned with me, the way I try to reason with my clients.

You're scared, I heard it say; heard it not as me talking to myself, but as a foreign, reassuring presence.

Uh-huh. I could barely form an answer.

Well, listen, you had to have been at least as scared just a few minutes ago when you were climbing in the dark, only you just didn't know it, right?

Right.

Well, then, all you have to do is put all the fear back where you were keeping it before, right?

Before I could even answer I felt it happen. I felt the downshift out of terror and paralysis; felt a state of ease take over. A tremendous feeling of relief swept through me, the knowledge that something larger, more responsible than I had taken charge. And in that moment, as my muscles softened and the ledge solidified beneath my feet, I knew I would be fine.

Before me the red tip of the sun was just licking up over the horizon. As if it were truly generating heat, I felt suddenly warmer and wholly consumed by the image: colors so intense they might have seeped directly from the rising sun, the sky a vast and fluid prism. I was awed—by the sky, and by the realization that I and my teammates were high above the earth, witnessing a spectacle that no one else could see. A moment later the rope tugged, I pivoted my foot around to the ledge and continued climbing, all memory of the incident gone. I had a vague sense of having put something away, and checked for it as one would pat a pocket for missing keys. But not finding it, not *wanting* to find it, I settled back into the sheltering rhythm of the climb and let my crampons and ice axe carry me toward the summit.

The rest of the ascent was uneventful. At a point called Disappointment Cleaver, two hours shy of the summit, we were offered a last chance to quit the climb. Every muscle in my body cried out to stop, but I remained resolutely lashed to my team. At eight-thirty in the morning, with blinding headaches from the altitude and glare, we crested the summit. Impulsively, before I knew what I was doing, I reached down and touched the ground. Then Nancy and I hugged, tears streaming down our faces.

The celebration was short, however, since we had just twenty minutes at the top. I spent most of the time sitting, taking in the view, too happy and tired to move. As I sat I realized that I should make an entry in my journal, but my journal was in my pack and my pack was twelve feet away. I simply couldn't get up to get it.

You have to get up, I told myself.

I can't.

You have to.

I'll do it next time.

What do you mean, next time?

I'll do this again, I promise!

Apparently I convinced myself, for after a bit more sitting I joined my teammates in looking around the summit, journal forgotten. Then we strapped on our packs, hooked up the rope, and began our descent, one terrifying step at a time. With each step we kicked out into space, unable to see the ground below us, hoping to grab the ice behind our heels with our crampons. My legs trembled uncontrollably, and it seemed as if every organ would come loose from the relentless jarring of my free-fall steps. Four-and-a-half hours later Paradise Lodge, big as a matchbox, appeared below us.

As I kept the lodge in sight—imagining the smell of hot chocolate and the crackling of the fire—I gradually became aware of the fact that my feet were immensely painful. Every step felt as if I'd stepped into a bed of glowing charcoals. As I focused more and more on that sensation it became unbearable. I tried every configuration I could think of to minimize the pressure on my feet, but hiking downhill with a thirty-pound pack left me few alternatives. Finally we got to Muir where I picked up a pair of ski poles I'd left there the day before. By leaning on those I relieved a bit of the pressure.

By six o'clock Nancy and I were back in the car, stripping the boots from our feet. My socks were bloody from untreated blisters. It seemed clear that they had been that way for some time—longer than the two hours or so that I'd been aware of them. Yet in the process of focusing on the downward trek, in my exhilaration about the climb, in my eagerness to reach the bottom I had overlooked them.

As I stared at my bloody feet, suddenly another image swam into view: the view over the ledge as dawn revealed the glacier and crevasses below. Suddenly I felt the adrenaline in my stomach and the entire memory came flooding back: the terror and the panic, the sensation of falling, the image of my teammates sailing into the sky. It came back not as a memory but as the thing itself, each feeling and sensation fully formed. But this time, from the safety of my car, I could enjoy them. I could court them the way I'd courted terror as a child by daring myself to watch TV programs that I knew would scare me.

I had lost the entire episode! I realized then that I had gone into a trance; that my terror in the situation had selected that response in me. At the point when I had run out of options, when consciously there was nothing left to do, my inner mind had taken over. And had done so brilliantly! As I reviewed its words, I realized it had spoken to me precisely the way a gifted hypnotherapist would speak to a frightened client. It had *paced*, or ratified, my terror with the words "you're scared," creating a *yes set* that would prompt me to follow its next suggestion. It had followed that pace with *leads*, suggestions that enabled me to return the fear to its container. After each statement it had questioned, "Right?" creating another yes set and demanding that I respond, as if there were another person there, a sheltering father offering his embrace. And like a savvy therapist, it had asked no more of me than I could handle by speaking to me simply, as one would speak to a frightened child.

Once my fear was recompartmentalized and I was ready again for conscious control, this inner wise man had retreated. And now, if it weren't for the bloody, frightening sight of my socks, I might not have recalled him at all.

Nancy and I marveled about the human ability to split off pain and terror—she, too, had found the steady rhythm of her steps and breaths trance inducing—and I realized that this was the time to make that entry in my journal. I drew it out of my pack, opened it up and there, on the final page in handwriting obviously skewed from exhaustion and cold, was a single line: *Standing on the summit is like standing on the face of God.*

"Jeez, Nancy, when did I write this?" I cried.

But her team had been ahead of mine; we'd barely had time to hug at the top before they'd headed down, so she hadn't seen me open my pack. When had I written it? I racked my brain, going over and over my twenty minutes at the summit, but could find no memory of having drawn my journal from my pack much less opening it and penning that phrase. The best I could surmise was that as we were roping up, I did it quickly, then turned my attention to the team.

I marveled, yet again, about the human ability to dissociate. How many separate incidents of dissociation had occured in this thirty-one-hour ordeal! And not just to me. We'd all done it. We'd all dissociated: the knowledge that people die climbing Rainier, the discomfort of our bodies, our fear during the training and then at points along the climb. And now, as I sat in the comfort and safety of my car, I was encountering perhaps the greatest dissociation of them all: the realization that I wanted to do it again! The rationalization I'd offered to myself at the top I now meant sincerely: despite the pain, despite the fear, despite the blisters, I wanted to do it again. For while I held the knowledge of those factors cognitively in my head, the urgency, the sharpness, the *realness* of them was gone, subsumed under the exaltation of my triumph.

I also marveled at the human propensity for trance. Throughout the trek I had wandered in and out of trance through no conscious intervention of my own. The demands of the situation—my fear, my discomfort, my need to get through the ordeal—had been enough to induce the trances spontaneously. And again, not just for me. Nancy had noted a similar experience and, I imagined, so had almost everyone. Just as soldiers on a march find solace in the trance-inducing rhythm of their steps, amplified by the repetitive rhythm of their chants, I was sure our climbing partners had also relieved the stress of the ascent in trance. For the ability to segue naturally into trance is intrinsic to us all. In times of great discomfort we all find solace by going inside.

Often we don't even know we're doing it. Most of my trances on the mountain "chose me" rather than the other way around. Certainly in that moment on the ledge, when my conscious mind failed and I could imagine only death, I made no conscious choice to go into a trance. It was the demand of the situation that caused my mind to split and a higher self to emerge. Just as Jane's mind, facing the unbearable stress of chronic abuse, fractured into protective parts; just as Nancy's, facing the stress of impending cancer, found a way to repair her body; just as mine, facing the responsibility of a five-hour hypnoanesthesia, reduced my perceptive field to an essential circle, my mind responded to a most elemental drive: the drive to self-protect. In a way that was beyond my conscious ability to control, it found a way to save me.

Fortunately, the wisdom of the unconscious is also available on demand. One can self-hypnotize using a self-hypnosis tape, but there are also many less formal ways to access one's inner mind. My first hypnosis teacher taught me a way that I still use today, especially when I face a particularly thorny problem.

*   *   *

One . . . two . . . three . . . four . . . I count the steps as I descend: twenty narrow stone steps cut into the side of a mountain. At the bottom is the door to my mental workshop.

I built the workshop in my head, nail by nail, board by board, under the guiding hand of my teacher. In ten minutes that felt like weeks in trance, I raised the structure and laid in every accoutrement I could possibly need to solve the problems my future life might hold: a computerized archive of all my dreams, memories, and reflections; a bookcase housing every book I've ever read; an easy chair in which to read and ponder; a forge where I can wrestle with strong emotions and bend problems like molten metal until their answers are revealed in newly wrought forms; and, for more complex problems, an elevator that carries my questions to realms where long-term solutions can be found. On the floor below, unlimited "raw materials" are stored, resources for solving any problem.

I use the workshop in many ways: for unraveling dilemmas in my personal life, for examining stumbling blocks with clients, to see what I am not seeing in a situation. I type a question into the computer, or wrestle it on the forge, and after several minutes an answer— or, more often, a new perspective—emerges. Often the response surprises me, offering a viewpoint that seems independent of my own. I have come to treasure and trust these intuitions. Occasionally, however, not only the answer surprises me but also the *circumstances* of the answer, for on more than one occasion I've been presented with an answer to a question that I'd forgotten I'd asked. And at those moments the power of the unconscious has seemed shiveringly clear: while my conscious mind has been off at play—skipping, with its childlike short attention span, to other matters—my unconscious has been noting, mulling, synthesizing, working the assignment. Like a supercomputer simultaneously tackling a multitude of tasks, it has been able to govern my body; assimilate my experiences; fabricate the dreams and daydreams, anxieties, and symptoms that channel my interior realm; *and* plumb its database for an answer to a query that I, paddling my conscious little skiff across its surface, had almost forgotten that I'd asked.

Perhaps the most startling occasion of this resulted when I brought to the workshop a question about a family I was treating. The Rosencranzes were a staunch Germanic family concerned about their son who, at twenty-five, was having "crazy thoughts," was unable to get a job, and refused to leave home. However, after four months of treatment we were getting nowhere. So, stumped, I decided to bring the case to the workshop. I sat down at the keyboard and typed, "What about the Rosencranz case am I not seeing?" Several minutes later the monitor lit up and my face appeared on the screen. It fastened its eyes on mine and spoke. "What you are not recognizing is that Mrs. Rosencranz has a fragility that reminds you of your mother, and that you are behaving with her the way you behaved with your mother: you're protecting her; you're afraid you might hurt her; you're afraid you'll make her angry. As a result you don't comment on her intrusiveness in her son's life."

Immediately I had a flash of recognition: incidents in which I'd done precisely that sprang to mind. I turned off the computer and moved to the easy chair to contemplate what I'd learned. I wanted to mentally rehearse relating to Mrs. Rosencranz differently. I played out several scenarios until I felt I'd made headway against the pattern, and then I rose to leave. But suddenly something caught my eye. It was the light above the elevator door.

That's odd, I thought. I haven't put a question in the elevator recently. Why would the light be on? Perplexed, I walked to the elevator and pushed the button. Slowly the heavy door slid open, revealing the car inside. And there, wearing a curious half-smile like one she often wore in life, was my mother. I was instantly cheered to see her. Intuitively I knew, the way one knows things in dreams: *she's here to help me, she's here to answer my dream.*

"David," she intoned slowly. Her voice had a peaceful, otherworldly quality, like the voice of a returning angel. She then explained a dream that, puzzled, I had put into the elevator ten years before. It was a dream about a woman I had dated many years earlier, and as my mother spoke, I remembered my confusion about the dream—my sense of its significance, my inability to decipher its code. "David," my mother revealed, "this is a dream about me, and a dream about all women—about the way you behave with women, protectively, as if their needs supercede your own." As I listened to her explanation I knew that she was right: I had that same flash of recognition that I'd had about Mrs. Rosencranz.

When she had finished, she smiled at me slightly—a familiar smile as if to say, "You see? A mother knows these things." Then the elevator door closed and the car whirred away. Serene, profoundly satisfied, I closed and locked the workshop door behind me, retraced my steps up the stone staircase, and opened my eyes in my office.

As it often does, the session in the workshop made a noticeable difference in my practice. I saw the Rosencranz family for four more months, and with my new awareness was often able to stop myself when my personal "baggage" began to interfere. As a result I felt less need to protect Mrs. Rosencranz, and more willing to press her to examine difficult issues. By the time the family left therapy, the son had gotten a job and the family was making healthy changes.

The dream explanation, too, provided a deeper understanding about my feelings and behavior. As I looked back at past relationships I now saw a connecting thread between them, and I saw that I could rethink my "rules of relationship" going into the future.

But why, I wondered, had it taken ten years to arrive? My mother had died in the intervening years. Perhaps her absence gave me room to perceive our relationship differently, to see things that her proximity had obscured. And I had matured in the intervening time; perhaps I was now readier for truths that I had formerly dismissed. One can see the truth only when one is ready, regardless of its source.

But why that day? I'd been in the workshop numerous times in the preceding months. Why had the elevator picked that day to ferry this bit of wisdom? Because of its obvious relationship to Mrs. Rosencranz. The question and answer in both cases were the same, and triggered by that linkage, the elevator had summoned the answer to my dream. It was merely a conveyer, bringing my own wisdom to my attention—when I was ready to hear it.

What is it about the workshop that makes such discoveries possible? The workshop is no more than a device, really—a ruse, if you will—for accessing the parts of my mind that can help me in ways my conscious mind can't. The answers appear on the computer screen, in the elevator car, or on the forge, but of course they are really presentations of my own mind, supplied in a form that I find easier to read.

We all have the ability to create workshops in our minds. We've all had hunches we wish we'd followed. We've all had songs stuck in our minds whose words, once noted, bore an uncanny relationship to circumstances in our lives. We've all had slips of the tongue, when the word we uttered was far closer to the truth than the word we'd intended. And we've all had vividly improbable dreams that, on examination, clearly illuminate a heart-held truth. We all hear whispers from our inner wisdom. The workshop is merely a way of giving those whispers a more structured form, a way of bringing them within our deliberate reach.

Another way I access my inner wisdom is by looking in the mirror. Years ago I reread the novel *Kim* by Rudyard Kipling and was struck by how hypnotic it is. Among other devices, the young protagonist uses his name as a mantra, repeating it over and over to help himself fall asleep. At that time I was experimenting with ways of putting myself in a trance, so I decided to try Kim's device myself. I stood before a mirror prepared to say, "I am David, I am David, I am David . . ."

But as I stared into my eyes and opened my mouth a different phrase came out, a phrase closer to a Buddhist meditation I had been using: "Who am I? Who am I? Who am I?" That's odd, I thought, and tried again. But the second time the same thing happened. So I decided to go with it, and as I stared into my eyes, repeating the question over and over, I went into a trance. My vision narrowed until all I could see was the face in the mirror, which suddenly seemed separate: me, yet a thing apart from me.

Who am I? I heard a voice ask. This time the face was asking *me*.

"You must be my teacher," I ventured.

Yes, the face returned. And I realized that I was speaking to a quasi-autonomous self that I now think of as my inner core.

To this day I go to that core when I have a problem, when I feel confused, when I know I am not seeing myself or an issue clearly. The core has helped me understand when it's time to let go of damaging or unproductive situations, despite the fact that I've resisted that knowledge consciously. Consistently the voice is firm, honest, wise—a benevolent but demanding teacher who can say things to me that I cannot say to myself.

I don't always listen. Many times I avoid the mirror when I sense it holds a message I don't want to hear. I avoid looking into the mirror's eyes. I "tune out" while the mirror is talking. I avoid the mirror completely.

Sometimes the face in the mirror will challenge my avoidance. If I lose the thread, or tune out the mirror's words, the face may say, *So what just happened? Why did you stop listening?* Or another part of me, the therapist's voice, will question myself as if I were a client: *What does this mean to you? Why are you becoming anxious?* Sometimes when I have been avoidant, just making eye contact with the face in the mirror puts me more in touch with my feelings—closer to my inner core.

*   *   *

We all use a form of self-hypnosis to access our inner minds. The mechanic peering into an engine, lost to the world beyond the car as he probes for the source of breakdown; the negotiator, nervousness suddenly pushed aside as she argues fluently for her position; the basketball player, oblivious to the crowd as he intuitively senses the ball, the basket, and the other players; the teacher, who simultaneously uses multiple parts of her mind to track the time, the noise level, and the activities of thirty students: all have tuned out the extraneous, tuned in to an inner frequency through which knowledge, intuition, an inner sense can vibrate. We all have this voice within. Trance, invited or not, is merely the mechanism through which we let ourselves hear it.

Selected Bibliography

For more information on hypnosis, hypnotherapy, and other topics in this book, look for these classic books in print through your local bookstore or library system.

Bernheim, Hippolyte. *Bernheim's New Studies in Hypnotism.* 1888. Reprint edited by Richard S. Sandor. Independence, MO: International University Press, 1980.

> Reprint of Bernheim's classic *Suggestive Therapeutics,* in which he proposes hypnosis can occur in normal individuals—not just in hysterically diseased individuals, as was the common view in medicine at the time. Bernheim saw hypnosis as an exaggeration of normal suggestibility. At that time in France, there was considerable interest in the subject of suggestibility. Writers of the day described the role of suggestion in mob rule and in the social contagion of panic.

Chong, Dennis K. *Autohypnotic Pain Control: The Milton Model as Applied in a Case of Cholecystectomy for Cholelithiasis.* New York: Carlton Press, 1979.

> On February 17, 1978, Dr. Victor Rausch, a Canadian dentist, underwent surgery for the removal of his gall bladder using self-hypnotic hypnoanesthesia as his only anesthetic. There was no hypnotic operator present to assist him. He was given no presurgical sedative. His surgery and recovery were successful and uneventful. The author interviews Rausch and members of his medical surgical team about the patient's state of mind before, during, and after the operation. This amazing story shows the depth of human capacity for dissociation in the face of massive trauma.

Cohen, Barry M., and Esther Giller, eds. *Multiple Personality Disorder from the Inside Out.* Baltimore, MD: Sidran Press, 1991.

One hundred forty-six people diagnosed with multiple personality disorder speak out on issues of treatment, daily life, and relationships. Excellent glossary on dissociative disorders.

Ellenberger, H. F. *The Discovery of the Unconscious: The History and Evolution of Dynamic Psychiatry.* New York: Basic Books, 1970.

This highly readable triumph of scholarly research relates the history of hypnosis to the development of psychiatry over the last one hundred years.

Esdaile, James. *Numerous Cases of Surgical Operations.* Contributions to the History of Psychology Series, Volume 10. 1846. Reprint. Westport, CT: Greenwood Press, 1977.

———. *Mesmerism in India: And its Practical Applications in Surgery and Medicine.* Classics in Psychiatry Series. 1846. Reprint. Salem, NH: Ayer Co. Publications, 1976.

Reprints of the classical medical account of James Esdaile, a British army surgeon who performed a series of seventy-three major surgical operations in an eight-month period in a country charity hospital in India, all without benefit of medical anesthesia or analgesia. The author used "Mesmeric passes" alone to directly and indirectly induce anesthesia for assorted amputations, tumor extractions, cataract removal, sinus surgery, hemorrhoidectomy, teeth extraction, and so on.

Farrelly, Frank. *Provocative Therapy.* Fenton, MI: Meta Publications, 1974.

Explores the author's unique and masterful uses of humor, satire, confrontation, and challenge in psychotherapy.

Haley, Jay. *Uncommon Therapy: The Psychiatric Techniques of Milton H. Erickson, M.D.* New York: Norton and Co., 1973.

Highly absorbing presentation of the legendary psychiatrist Milton Erickson's use of *hypnoticlike* techniques in nonhypnotic therapy. Presents a range of fascinating cases across his life span.

Hilgard, J. R. *Personality and Hypnosis: A Study of Imaginative Involvement.* Chicago: University of Chicago Press, 1970.

A study of personality traits of adept hypnotic subjects.

Hull, Clark L. *Hypnosis and Suggestibility: An Experimental Approach.* Century Psychology Series. 1933. Reprint. New York: Irvington, 1988.

This 1933 book summarizes the first rigorous scientific investigation of hypnosis and dissociation. Led by famed psychologist Clark Hull at Yale in the 1920s and 1930s, this historic decade-long experimental study yielded thirty-two published scientific papers and this fascinating book. Among many topics, Hull presents a very convincing argument for the existence of traumatic dissociation and amnesia.

Lecron, Leslie M. *Self Hypnotism: The Technique and Its Use in Daily Living.* New York: Signet Books, 1970.

This twentieth-century classic remains an excellent primer and introduction to responsible self-analysis through self-hypnotism. Emphasizes the unconscious roots of personal problems.

Morris, Freda. *Self-Hypnosis in Two Days.* New York: NAL-Dutton, 1975.

This book describes a method for learning self-hypnosis that, if strictly followed, almost guarantees the reader will develop a "best personal approach" to learning and practice.

Napier, Augustus Y., and Carl Whitaker. *The Family Crucible: The Intense Experience of Family Therapy.* New York: HarperCollins, 1988.

Engaging and moving account of one family's struggle in therapy.

Ritterman, Michelle Klevers. *Using Hypnosis in Family Therapy.* San Francisco: Jossey-Bass, 1983. Reprinted by Ritterman, 1993. Available from author, 3908 Lakeshore Avenue, Oakland, CA 94610.

The first book to systematically integrate hypnosis and family therapy.

Schwartz, Richard C. *Internal Family Systems Therapy.* New York: Guilford Press, 1995.

For additional information on hypnotherapy or for referral to a qualified hypnotherapist contact:

American Psychotherapy & Medical Hypnosis Association
800-C Forest Oaks Lane
Hurst, TX 76053
800-687-0088 outside Texas
817-280-0101 within Texas

American Society of Clinical Hypnosis
2200 East Devon Avenue, Suite 291
Des Plaines, IL 60018-4534
847-297-3317

Milton H. Erickson Foundation
3606 North 24th Street
Phoenix, AZ 85016-6500
602-956-6196

National Board for Certified Hypnotherapists
8750 Georgia Avenue, Suite 125E
Silver Spring, MD 20910
301-608-0123
301-588-9535 (fax)

The Society for Clinical and Experimental Hypnosis
3905 Vincennes Road
Suite 304
Indianapolis, IN 46268
317-334-9470

About the Authors

DAVID L. CALOF is a family therapist and hypnotherapist in private practice in Seattle, and is a frequent lecturer at medical schools, colleges, and conferences throughout the world. He has published numerous articles and chapters in professional journals and textbooks, and his articles have also appeared in *Family Therapy Networker* and *Common Boundary*. He also edits the professional journal, *Treating Abuse Today*.

ROBIN SIMONS is the author of four previous books: *Doing Best by Doing Good: How to Use Public Purpose Partnerships to Boost Corporate Profits and Benefit Your Community; Filthy Rich and Other Nonprofit Fantasies: Changing the Way Nonprofits Do Business in the '90s; After the Tears: Parents Talk About Raising a Child with a Disability;* and *Recyclopedia: Games, Science Projects and Crafts from Recycled Materials.*